MY BLOODY EFFORTS

Life as a Rating in the modern Royal Navy

STEPHEN BRIDGMAN MBE

authorHOUSE®

AuthorHouse™
1663 Liberty Drive
Bloomington, IN 47403
www.authorhouse.com
Phone: 1-800-839-8640

© *2012 by Stephen Bridgman MBE. All rights reserved.*

No part of this book may be reproduced, stored in a retrieval system, or transmitted by any means without the written permission of the author.

Published by AuthorHouse   08/25/2012

ISBN: 978-1-4772-1801-3 (sc)
ISBN: 978-1-4772-1802-0 (e)

Any people depicted in stock imagery provided by Thinkstock are models, and such images are being used for illustrative purposes only.
Certain stock imagery © Thinkstock.

Because of the dynamic nature of the Internet, any web addresses or links contained in this book may have changed since publication and may no longer be valid. The views expressed in this work are solely those of the author and do not necessarily reflect the views of the publisher, and the publisher hereby disclaims any responsibility for them.

Chapter 1

The Happiest Days of Your Life

With perfect hindsight, it probably wasn't the best start to a sparkling naval career. Arriving at Plymouth train station on Tuesday 2nd November 1976, wide-eyed but making a brave effort to look as though I did this sort of thing all the time, I had approached a tough looking man dressed in the typical sailor's uniform, holding a clipboard and apparently crossing off names. "Excuse me Sergeant";—he had 3 stripes on his left arm with a badge depicting an anchor above it. On his right arm was a badge with what looked like 2 old-fashioned cannons crossed over each-other—"is this where I get the bus for the navy, I'm joining up today?"

To give him credit, he didn't just rip my head off there and then; after all, we were in the public gaze. He did go a very nice red colour in the face though. "What's your name Admiral?" he asked almost nicely, but with an unmistakeable gritting of the teeth. Of course I didn't notice any of this subtle stuff at the time; I was much too excited for that. It would come later though—oh yes.

After crossing off my name from his long list, "Bridgman—I'll remember that", he pointed me towards a large blue bus with 'ROYAL NAVY' emblazoned on the side, waiting outside the train station. "Go and wait in there". As I bounded like an over-excited puppy out of the train station and up the bus steps I came upon a sea of, well, mirror images of myself—half a bus full of petrified young blokes (we didn't start saying 'guys' until much later!), all wondering what the future, particularly the near future, held for them. I straightened my shoulders, stood upright and put my 'hard' face on to match theirs, but with me being 7 and a half stones and about 5'2" tall, they didn't seem all that intimidated. As I walked down the bus some of the boys nodded a greeting, others even gave a muted "alright?", and others were lost in their own thoughts and maybe fears, staring forlornly out of the big windows. I took a seat and quietly waited for the bus to fill up, watching the masks being fitted as each new recruit left the train station a happy-go-lucky young man, and entered the bus a stern, hard-faced but inwardly trembling kid. There was no talking, quite a lot of coughing and sniffing, and almost everybody smoked nervously.

Within a fairly short while the bus had filled up, and the sailor with the clipboard came striding out of the railway station. He stepped up into the bus and turned to face us. To me at 16 years old, he looked big, tough, very self-assured and worldly wise. I felt very young indeed.

"Right, listen in! If you are not here—raise your hand" he said, very loudly. The titters were few and far between. "I am Leading Seaman Graham. Just so there are no more stupid questions, I am not a bloody Sergeant! The Navy does not have bloody Sergeants!" He pointed to the anchor and stripes on his left arm. "This hook means I am a Leading Hand right? These stripes are called Good Conduct badges; you get them for being a good boy".

He pointed to the crossed cannon badge on his right arm. "This badge means I am a Seaman—best bloody branch in the Navy. Put these two together"—pointing alternately to anchor and crossed-cannons—"means I am a Leading bloody Seaman OK?" He seemed to be looking at me when saying this, but I got the impression that I wasn't the only one to make the same mistake. Without further ado he turned and had a brief chat with the civilian driver, stepped down off the bus and strode back into the railway station. The driver closed the door of the bus "Right lads, here we go then—welcome to Plymouth".

I had not been out of my home town of South Ascot in Berkshire too many times before, the last time being in the spring of 1976 on a day trip to Southampton for my pre-joining medical examination. I had certainly never been as far into the wilds as down here in Devon, and even the train journey had been an incredible 6 hours in these pre-Intercity 125 days—6 hours stewing in my own nervous energy, trying to remember the joining instructions and reading them over and over from the well worn page sent to my home as part of the joining package. The scenery from the train window had been spectacular on the way down, ending with a magnificent coastal ride where you could view lovely little villages and further out to sea than I knew existed. I saw none of it, nor I suspected did anyone else sitting on the bus that morning. Now as we drove through the city of Plymouth and on towards the Torpoint ferry, our eyes once again took in everything and nothing. It took all of my energy to pretend that all this was routine, and to give an outward appearance of self-assured calmness while inside my heart continued giving my ribs a right pounding, as it had been all day. From the look of some of the others around me I was very far from being alone.

HMS Raleigh in Torpoint was and remains the Royal Navy's New Entry establishment, as well as at that time being the training centre for members of the Seaman Branch of the Navy. To get to HMS Raleigh from Plymouth side of the River Plym you have to take the Torpoint ferry. The ferry even then looked old and worn, and was a hulking slab-sided boat with a large car deck area. The ferry pulled itself along chains fixed at both river banks and made a very distinctive "clanking" sound as it travelled from bank to bank. Those of us that stayed in the Navy got to know the Torpoint ferry very well, and spent a lot of time chugging backwards and forwards across the river on the damn things. It was remarkable that 26 years later, on finally leaving Plymouth for the last time after a long naval career, the very same ferries were still in operation—although looking a bit smarter these days. Driving onto the ferry also gave us our first glimpse of Devonport Dockyard, and a row of huge grey warships tied up alongside the piers as far as the eye could see. Looking towards the turn in the river leading out into Plymouth Sound, the whole horizon was blocked by the hulking shape of the pensioned off aircraft carrier HMS Eagle—tied to moored buoys on the turn in the river. At that time she had not been there very long and in the greyness of a dull November day still looked well maintained and menacing. It was daunting and exciting at the same time, and the experience of seeing the ships that later on we might be serving on had the effect of lightening the mood of the group and even eliciting some conversation. "I want to serve on the Ark", "I have a brother on the Bulwark", "Look at the size of the Tiger!", and "so, where are you from mate?" I got chatting to a Scots boy called Jimmy Carr. He was from Glasgow and to begin with I simply could not understand a single word he said "Alright Pal, I'm Jimma fae Glasgae—I'm Scowtush", or so it sounded to me. "No shit" was my immediate reaction. Anyway we attempted to decipher each-others words (he thought I spoke really posh

English—coming from Ascot and all "Tha's were they ha' the horse racin' no?"), and all in all we got along just fine, as people stuck together tend to. It was good to find a kindred spirit, even if he did speak a foreign language, and as it turned out we were destined to stay as mates only through basic training. After that we would go our separate ways and never set eyes upon each other again—an experience which was to become a common thread throughout my naval career.

The bus bounced its way off the ferry with 40-odd young men still straining to see the warships, and slowly drove through Torpoint and onwards. Signposts outlined in red pointing towards HMS Raleigh and giving the miles to go soon starting appearing along the roadside, and as the miles rolled down the mood in the bus once again became apprehensive. All talking ceased and everyone began once again staring out of the windows, seeking their first sight of the training establishment where many of our lives would change forever. Shortly a boundary fence started to appear beside the bus, high and with a bent over top of barbed wire, and with lamp posts sited at equal distances along its length. As HMS Raleigh came into view, the first impression, for me at any rate, was one of how modern the place looked, like a nicely built school or factory complex. All of the very square buildings I could see were new or nearly new, and looked very clean; and there was a very large flag pole (later, and forever after to be known as a 'mast') flying a very large and bright navy flag (soon to become known as a White Ensign, and forever after to be associated with the daily 'Colours' ceremony). After driving along a seemingly endless boundary fence the bus approached the entrance to the base. The entrance at that time consisted of 2 large inward opening gates, on the either side of which were "HMS RALEIGH" nameplates and crowned crests. As 2 sailors pulled open the gates a guardroom and wooden ships figure head on a concrete plinth came into view. Another sailor, who we now recognised as another Leading Seaman, waited clipboard in hand for the bus door to open. As the door opened, he climbed onboard, turned to face us and said. "Good Afternoon Gentlemen. Now then, is there anybody here who should not be here?" There was nervous laughter. "You may laugh, but its not the first time somebody has jumped on the bus thinking it was going somewhere else". "This is your final chance to get off here and now and walk away if you want to. After we're through the gates you will be in the Navy, and if you want to leave then, you'll have to go through the whole release programme. Final chance—is there anybody that wants to leave now?" He paused and slowly looked along both sides of the bus. Some just looked away, others shook their heads. There were no takers, and I wondered for a moment if there ever were—it would have taken some balls to stand up and walk away with all those people watching you. The 'you can leave if you want to' mantra was one that was to be repeated ad-nauseum throughout basic training, and in the case of the 'juniors' like myself, right up until my seventeenth and a half birthday, when in the eyes of the Navy I became an adult subject to more stringent leaving processes. "Right then" the Leading Seaman continued, "we will be going over to the New Entry block now, and settling everybody in. When we get there, grab your bags and follow the directions of the staff. OK driver, let's go". The bus started into the base, the sailors holding the gates open looking at us with as one would look at a spanked puppy—a mixture of superiority and sorrow on their faces. We exchanged worried glances. We had kind of expected to be screamed at from the word go, and yet so far it had all been a bit, well . . . civilised.

It was a short drive to the New Entry block, but it gave us enough time to quickly look at our new surroundings on the way. In the far distance, across the valley were rolling green hills and trees of south east Cornwall—not so spectacular for a country (ish) boy like me, used to trees and greenery, but to some of the inner city lads a whole new universe. Closer to us were more of the same new looking 2—storey square barrack blocks, most with more name plates on the entrance with names like 'Frobisher', 'Cornwall', 'Drake', which some of us recognised as names, but which did not mean anything to most at that stage. We would get to know them a lot better later. In the middle distance was a huge flat area of tarmac with the mast we had seen from the road at the far end of it, the Parade ground of course, and at this time of day we could see groups of recruits' either marching around or doing rifle drill. Thankfully we were too far away to hear them being shouted at by the Instructors—probably a good thing at this stage. As we were driven along nicely prepared driveways in the camp groups of recruits' marched along, sometimes with an Instructor bawling out "left, right, left, right", and sometimes not, and each time we passed a group we would be given the same look we had received at the camp gates—a mixture of pity and glee only managed by those who had been in the same position a few short weeks before. They were the 'old hands' now. Our turn would come of course, but for now we were a very long way down the food chain.

As we reached the New Entry block, the Leading Seaman at the front of the bus told us to get off, collect our gear, and to make our way inside. This we did, and as we started to enter the block we were met by a group of naval personnel, looking a little older and dressed differently to the Leading seamen we had encountered so far.

These people were much more stern looking as well, and had peaked caps that semi covered their eyes so that they had to tilt their heads back slightly to glare at the new recruits. The badge system on their arms had moved up a gear as well, and there were anchors crossed over, propellers, crowns, medal ribbons and sergeants' stripes all over the place. It was very confusing and quite frightening for a 16 year old lad. As each recruit approached the trio, he gave his name and the omni-present clipboard was consulted. He was then directed to a dormitory where he was then to await further instructions. As I got nearer to the front of the queue it struck me that the directions the man was giving to the recruits seemed to be in some sort of code—"2 Deck, 3 Mess", 1 Deck, 2 Mess" and so on. I was starting to panic. Everybody else seemed to understand what the hell they were talking about; at least, nobody was asking what the instructions meant. They all so far had just nodded, turned away and then disappeared either up the staircase or through some doors. Suddenly it was my turn:

"Name".

"Bridgman Sir".

"2 Deck 3 Mess. Pick a bed and wait for further instructions. Next!"

There was no way I was going to be the one to ask. OK, heads upstairs, tails downstairs. I turned away and started for the double doors.

"Where the fuck are you going? I said 2 Deck, 3 Mess. Now get upstairs". I felt 45 pairs of eyes burning into my back as I sheepishly turned and scrambled up the stairs. "Shit, shit, shit" I repeated to myself as I went. There was no way I wanted to get noticed by the staff. Be anonymous had been the advice of my elder brother John who had been in the Navy for about 5 years. "Don't make waves and just do as you are told and you will be fine". Good start so far then. The bastard could have given me a bit of training about the names of ranks and flags and bloody decks before I joined—he probably tried to, but I am not renowned for being a great listener.

As I reached the top of the stairs a large '2 Deck' sign appeared. I glanced back down the stairs and 'hey presto' there was a nice big '1 Deck' sign in the same place on the ground floor—as it would have been called anywhere else. Feeling even more stupid I moved towards a pair of double doors with a sign above reading '3 Mess' and pushed through into the room. It was a big room. Along each side of the room, and through the middle of it, were rows of single beds partitioned from each other by waist height boards, and with a locker next to each bed. On each bed was a mattress, and at the head of the bed were neatly piled blankets, sheets and pillow. A lot of people had already picked a bed and dumped their stuff on it, and were opening lockers and kicking around. I spotted Jimmy across the room and went over and grabbed a bed in the same row. After dumping my gear on the bed I went over to talk to him:

"Did you know what he meant about the 2 Deck 3 Mess stuff down there?" I asked him

"No, I didna ha' a clue" I think he said "I jus' took a guess and went upstairs"

"Shit, I started through the doors downstairs and had to be told to go upstairs"

"Aw, dinna worry aboot it—I bet the bastards' dey it on purpose for a laugh" Well, in my case it had worked a treat.

I wandered back to my bed and sat down on the end of it. It had been a long, stressful day. I had been up well early, and in truth hadn't had much sleep before that, and it was starting to catch up with me. I looked around the 'Mess' and at my new 'shipmates' milling around. Most were young, around my age or slightly older, but there were a few who were clearly older, maybe really old—20 or even 25. They looked relaxed and in control, while I felt slightly bewildered and a long long way from Ascot.

Well, I was going to have to just deal with it. In all reality I had left home that morning with what could only be described as a low-key send-off.

"I'm off then" I had said to my Mother as I grabbed my bags and made for the front door.

"OK, let me know how you get on" had been the less than emotional farewell, and I had shut the door and made for the train station. The rest of the clan had remained in bed—best not to get over-excited about these things after all. In fairness, I expect that there was no small margin of relief that there was one less mouth to feed there somewhere, and I know for sure my younger brother and room-mate Andrew was delighted to have me gone—he had struggled valiantly for a very short time not to show it!

It is fair to say that we were not a very closely knit family. Life had been fairly rough on us and we were from an almost stereotypical 'broken home'—arguing, then violent, then separated and finally divorced parents, bitter with each-other and life, and not slow to pass their angst on to the kids. My father had finally disappeared when I was 2 years old, but continued to pop around for a punch-up at irregular intervals for several years later. He was a scary Scottish man whose mood changed at the drop of a hat from mister perfect daddy—all smiles and playfulness, to aggression and violence. For years I could not understand the reason for this sudden change, and like all kids blamed something we had done for it, when in fact as I discovered later it was caused by drinking. After these incredibly stressful visits, where we sat waiting for the mood swings to turn into a screaming match followed by a good beating for Mum, he would slope off in drunken remorse, not to surface again for months. We eventually learned, even as three or four year olds not to miss the bastard, and to try to hide when he did show. In later years when he had settled down with another family he attempted to get in touch, and to try to make amends for our lost childhood. During and after the Falklands conflict he wrote me several long and rambling letters wittering on about religion, life and the universe, and daring to offer me the advice he couldn't be bothered to provide when I really needed it, like when I was buying my first car or my first house, or when my wife had a miscarriage. You simply can't treat people like that and then expect everything to be wonderful later on—doesn't work for me at any rate. I flatly refused to have anything to do with the man, and could find no sorrow in my heart when he died in the late 1990s.

My Mother came from good Berkshire stock, the Pratley family (thank goodness for small mercies—at least we got the name change!) from Windsor. My Grand-dad had been one of the Queen's gardeners in Windsor Great Park, and was a good no-nonsense bloke. He and my Grand-ma had been poor but happy and stable. He had fought in the First World War or 'Great War' as he called it, and been damaged by some kind of gas. We would ask him what it was like but he never spoke of the horrors he had witnessed and been through. My Grand-ma told me years later that he would still wake up sweating and shouting in the night, re-living some episode from that terrible experience. He died quite young, but before that he had ensured his only daughter had been brought up right. My Mother was well educated and well spoken, and should have had a good life ahead of her. As a child she had even played with the future Queen of England at functions attended by my Grand-parents, and later on named her first child after the Queen's sister Princess Margaret. After my Grand-father died my Grand-ma continued to receive invitations to the annual Royal Garden Party for many years, but could never bring herself to go. She was devastated by the loss of her husband and was never really the same person afterwards. She eventually came to live with us in South Ascot, and the addition of another person in the house caused my Mother many difficulties. Windsor in those days had been a fairly sleepy little place, and my Mother had told us that when she had first met her future husband he had seemed mysterious and exciting after such a low-key lifestyle, and she had fallen for the smooth-talking Scotsman straight away. A classic case of the small town girl being swept off her feet by the lure of excitement. Who knows, maybe it all started well, and they really were in love with each other, but in any case it was not to last.

Single mothers were not highly regarded in the mid 1960s and early 1970s it must be said, and there were plenty of snide remarks and stigma around after my Father had left for good. My Mother had no doubt struggled mightily to put food on the table (quite often beans on toast, or our other favourite, cheese on toast) and clothes on the back of 7 kids, 6 of them boisterous lads. Of course as children you don't notice that kind of thing until later on. We never went truly hungry, but I suspect she did. With perfect hindsight the job practically killed the woman, and as the years went by she started to rebel against the loss of her best years in looking after us. The good old demon drink raised its ugly head again and with it came bitterness and resentment. She started to go out at night and to leave us to our own devices, often returning late and drunk with some low-life she had met somewhere. We went through a phase of meeting new 'uncles' with depressing regularity—in fact we got good at guessing how long they would be sniffing around, and at fleecing them by doing the 'poor little Annie' act. Needs must after all, and our need for sweeties was great indeed! Generally though, a look at half a dozen little urchins had the desired effect and they would soon retreat to safer hunting grounds. Life continued that way for a while, until we were visited by a man in a suit. It turned out that some busy-body had reported our goings-on to the authorities and the council wanted to take us 'into care'. All hell broke loose and my Mother became a screaming banshee; setting about the poor bloke at full throttle, and running him off the premises in no uncertain terms. We didn't go that time, but the incident settled things down for a while, with the result that my Mother spent more time at home 'looking after' us, although the booze remained an important prop in her life. In my very early teens my brothers Neil, Andy and I ended up staying in some children's home for a short time, and although the people running the place were very nice in an officious kind of way, obviously it was not somewhere we particularly wanted to be.

All this was peripheral to the job of being a kid of course, and mostly we went about growing up in the same way, if somewhat poorer, as most other kids. We were fortunate to be living in a place like south Ascot, where at that time there were some great woods for us to play in—lucky really as most of the time we were not allowed indoors! "You bloody kids

Me (in the jacket) Andy, Karen, Sandra and Julie (Our Step Sister)

are always in here—get out and play!" would be the standard retort if we attempted to sneak in out of the cold. It was also pretty neat that there were quite a few of us in the early years, as we could form our own 'gang' and get up to plenty of mischief rushing around the woods as Cowboys and Indians, or beating back the imaginary Nazi hordes threatening the freedom of the proud British Tommy—or some such bollocks. Those were the good days before we knew the reality of our situation, when we were happy, dirty, smelly oiks, alive with the fun of just being kids and not being affected by the bad experiences yet. For me, the start of school pretty much put paid to these adventures. From that point onwards it slowly begun to sink in that we were 'different'. We where amongst the group at school who were given free milk and free school dinners, with the accompanying 'tut-tutting' of the supercilious milk-monitors and dinner ladies. Often I was so ashamed under their demeaning stares that I would not eat anything at school, and would tip the milk away so as not to have to take the hand outs. I always felt under the spotlight in the dining hall and the staff used to make it all worse. "Have a bit more Son—looks like you need it. How is your Mum treating you?" they would ask, and my mind would always flit back to the council man in the suit coming to take us into care. Our uniforms were 'hand-me-downs' and never quite achieved the smartness of the other children in the school—the 'normal' kids. Kids being kids meant that we were exposed to constant cruel taunts, and as a result we became a very self-reliant little group on our own, protecting each other as best we could. We got into some good scrapes and refused to step backwards from anybody—my best fight was an occasion where my little sister had been getting a bit of stick from a group of school bullies and I stepped in to protect her. Bad move! I got a right kicking, but did not regret it—actually I got the same treatment from my Mother who rather than being concerned at my cut and bruised face and black eyes, went off on one because of the ripped and torn school uniform! You can't win sometimes.

School for me, both primary and secondary was a living nightmare, a constant struggle to maintain dignity against the do-gooders and so called care-givers. I hated the fact that you had to appear truly thankful for their 'assistance', when all I could think of was that they were in reality just salving their own conscience. We were a proud bunch, from Mother downwards and hated having to take the hand-outs. My way of escaping this reality was to become an avid reader. I would read on the way to school, on the way back, in the evening and at weekends—I couldn't get enough. I perfected the art of reading and walking at the same time which became something of a family joke, and my brothers and sisters soon tired of ribbing me about it at every opportunity. The result was that at school, about the only subject I was any good at all was English. I really started to enjoy writing, and could easily lose myself for hours imagining some adventure that I could turn into an essay. Nothing came of it though—it was going to cost too much to pay for taking 'O' level exams so it wasn't going to happen.

Another reason that school took a backseat was the constant need to bring money into the house. What we received from the state was mostly used for the purchase of cigarettes and alcohol by my Mother, the remainder when there was any being used for such useless things as food, fuel and the like. We once heard that kids were given pocket money by their parents and we asked Mother if we could have some. "You want money? Do you think it grows on trees? You want money—go and bloody earn it then!" was the carefully measured response. We did not ask again.

Every Saturday from about the age of eleven or twelve me and my brother Andrew were sent to the local country animal food shop which doubled up as a coal-monger to buy a bag of coal. We were quite chatty with the owner of the place—Anthony was his name—and when I was thirteen or so I plucked up the courage to ask him if he needed a bit of help around the place. To my surprise he agreed straight away and offered me Saturday morning work. I was now a working man! It was great fun as well, with me mixing rabbit food and stacking the shelves with dog food and stuff, and it wasn't long before I was even trusted to operate the till—very intimidating to start with, remember we are not talking about electronic ones that do the adding up for you, this was an old brute of a thing. The customers would patiently wait (in most cases) for me to count my fingers to make a sum of their purchases, and then carefully check their change was correct. I soon got the hang of it though. Of course the money I earned in the early years went straight to my Mother to be used 'for the house'. If I tried to keep a little for myself I would be reprimanded as a selfish boy, so very quickly learned to tell her that I had earned a bit less that I actually had, keeping the extra stashed away—my plan was to buy myself a bike with my earnings—it was going to take a long time!

I went along like this for quite a long time, until eventually after I had been working Saturday's for about 6 months when Anthony asked me if I fancied working after school as well. Did I? I jumped at the chance and began going straight to work after school, and then working on to about 7 o'clock in the evening. With the Saturday work as well, I was starting to earn a bit of money. My Mother of course was quick to pick up on that fact and I had to give her a bit more of the earnings. Clearly she had worked out that I was earning more than I was telling her, and set about finding my nest egg. She is not a subtle woman and when she found my little stash, she cleared me out completely. When I got home from work and found the box empty, I knew what had happened, but said nothing. My Mother too said nothing, just sat there staring at me with watery drunk eyes—daring me to challenge her. Secretly I was absolutely gutted. I had been saving for a bike for a long time and had about thirty pounds saved. It was going to be a present to myself for Christmas. Human nature is a strange thing—my brothers heard about it all and took pity on me. At Christmas I had the surprise of my life when they called me outside and unveiled a bike they had secretly made for me from bits they had either found or nicked from somewhere. They had hand painted the thing to try to smarten it up and it was a mixture of all-sorts in the general shape resembling a push-bike. I remember being touched deeply by their thoughtfulness at the time, and it stands out for me as a high point of my childhood—even today. The bike was a god-send—I could now take on a paper round as well! I learn quickly from my mistakes and secretly opened a post office savings account—with a little paying in book as well. You needed your parents' signature in those days to open the account, but I had no qualms in forging them to get the account open—no point troubling my Mother with such trivia. Over the next couple of years I managed to build up a tidy little sum in that book, and became almost demonic in making sure it was always going in the upward direction. I got a bit of a complex about being poor and had by now realised that the only person who was going to prevent that was me, by my own hard work. It is something that has remained with me throughout my life. Forging my parents' signature had been a piece of cake, and would come in useful later for joining the Navy.

Even with all her many faults, my Mother had at least spent time ensuring that her kids grew up as polite and respectful people. She was congratulated on many occasions by neighbours and the like on how polite we all were. I was never sure why we wouldn't be, but people always seemed surprised that we were not some horrible bunch of hooligans. On one occasion my Brother Andrew and I were waiting in the Post Office queue for a couple of stamps, with the local ladies behind us. We got to the counter and I, as the elder brother said "2 3p stamps please" It must be said that we were probably not looking our smartest—we were very often a little whiffy, and the clothing was normally at best 'well-used'. Anyway, the ladies

My Bloody Efforts

were talking about us as though we were not there "That's the Bridgman kids—Phyllis does try to keep them well, aren't they polite little things?" We faced the front, trying to disappear, but wilting under the gazes of the waiting customers—the kind of gaze one might give to a couple of stray dogs. The ladies continued (whispering at about 90 decibels) "Yes, but they could do with a good bath though!" Andrew, not being the patient sort whipped around and exclaimed "Why don't you mind your own business you horrible women!" The Post Master hearing this shouted "Oi, you two, there's no need to be rude to people, get outside. I'll be telling your Mother on you!" So, out we went, accompanied by lots of shaking heads and 'tutting' ladies. When we got home without the stamps and complaining about the woman and the fact that we had not done anything, we were expecting a hammering. My Mother questioned us closely, making sure who had said what, and why we had said this or that, and after we had explained what had happened, to our huge surprise and relief my Mother, instead of having a go at us said "Right, nobody talks to my kids like that!", and promptly marched off in the direction of the Post Office. I have no idea what went on at the Post Office but we never heard any more comments about us in any queues!

I suspect that the money incident was probably the starting point for me to begin to realise that I didn't want to stay at home when I grew up. By now my older siblings were starting to drift away, and in some cases to flood away! The way it went was that they would start to spread their wings—go out, maybe have too much to drink, come home, have a huge argument with Mother and decide to leave. This would happen a few times and then they would actually go for good. Same pattern, different face. In the case of John, he decided to leave and join the Navy. I have no idea why it should be the Navy, as we certainly had no family history associated with it. My Father had done his National Service in the RAF apparently, although he certainly had not sat any of us on his knee and spoken about it—we only knew because my Mother often complained that going to Germany which had been a bit of a pain. My eldest Brother Michael had spent a little while in the Royal Marines—he had completed the basic training as far as I was aware, but had quit soon after. I remember him coming home on occasions while he was in the Marines, and coming out to the woods with us to show us how to rappel down from trees. He took it all very seriously and quite liked the barking out orders thing, making us line up and getting us to march around and stuff. He was a bit odd, and we were never quite sure if he was being serious or playing with us. At any rate he was the only in the Marines for a relatively short while. My sister Margaret too had a spell in the forces, and joined up as naval nurse. I had never had a great deal of contact with her, even from a young age. She had left home pretty much as soon as she was legally allowed to, and I never really knew her at all. I was to bump into her again during the Falklands Conflict, when she was based in the Gibraltar Naval Hospital. We found we had nothing in common, and made no great efforts to meet again.

John is 5 years older than me, and spent a lot of time away between visits back to South Ascot. Whenever he came home he was always jolly, smart and seemed to have a lot of money. He quite often brought back little souvenirs from some of the places he had visited, and seemed to be enjoying his naval life a lot. He sometimes took the time to tell a story or 2 about some of the places he had been to, but usually spent more time when he was home with my elder brothers Barry and Neil. They would go out drinking together, and although he was always friendly to us younger ones, he obviously related more to the older boys. During this time I was working as much as possible at the shop (Anthony's Dad, the owner of the place was called Robert, with a surname of Soul. Hence once I had realised this I started referring to working at 'R Souls' – arse holes – get it? shop—always got me a slap!"), and on the paper round to get the money in. Not surprisingly my school work suffered and by the time I came to leaving school, I only got to take CSE exams—in any case if I had wanted to take 'O' levels, as they were then, I would have had to pay some money. Money was in short enough supply as it was so really, although I was disappointed at not taking any, it was always going to be a non-starter.

We had a careers teacher or guide or whatever they call themselves at school, who started to get involved in the students lives at around 5th form level. He was more interested in the higher flying types at school, and so when I ended up in the seat in front of him I had the impression that we were kind of going through the motions. In any case I had absolutely no idea what I wanted 'to be', and told him so. He asked me if I was interested in cars, mechanical things and so on and since I had been taking 'Motor Vehicle Maintenance' in school it seemed like a fair enough assumption. Anyway he jacked up an interview for me with an electronics company in Bracknell which would be taking in mechanical engineering Apprentices in the following year. I pointed out that I would not be taking 'O' levels, but he didn't seem that bothered, arguing that the company would more interested in 'hands-on' people, and that they would give all the training needed to the people they selected. This seemed like a reasonable idea and so I agreed.

Arriving at the company on the day of the interview, I was struck by the smartness of the company building. I felt a bit shabby next to some of the other potential employees although I had made great efforts to look smart, but even my 'best' clothes had probably seen better days. That didn't bode well in the self-confidence stakes and I truly knew I had been stitched up when they others started talking. In today's terms they would have been known as 'geeks' or 'nerds', but at that time and on that day I just thought of them as bloody clever. They were talking about circuit boards and engine capacities and other deeply technical stuff, and I knew it was going to be a long day. I should have turned on my heels and walked away there and then, but being the polite fool I was, I waited patiently for the humiliation to begin. Soon enough, a young man walked through and joined us—think back to the 1970s arch-typical young professor and you will have him—frizzy hair, NHS spectacles, dull patterned tank-top and stay-press trousers. He warmly welcomed us to Radal, and took us through to a large class-room affair, tables and chairs arranged in neat lines, all ready for us 'boffins' to demonstrate our extensive knowledge of engineering and electronics—oh yes, the Careers Advisor had forgotten to mention that the company were a manufacturer of space travel quality electronic products too!

For the remainder of the morning we were invited to undertake written examinations in physics, mechanics, electronics and maths—all to a standard considerably higher that the ones I had done for CSE—I managed to get the date right on a few I think, but that was about it. At lunch time we were treated to a nice spread, and the others happily chatted about the easy exams, and how they had probably scored 100% in each "Is the speed of sound faster or slower than the speed of light?" "What did you make No.5—I made it 2.958328 nanoseconds"—I managed to keep a low profile. The torture continued after lunch, where we were individually invited to an interview and 'practical ability' session. The interview went quite well I thought, very friendly and not at all intimidating. The two interviewers asked me about my future plans (not considered), my interest in electronics (I couldn't even spell it!), and if I had any deeply interesting hobbies (I was too busy trying to earn a living!). They briefly went over my test scores from the morning period—very briefly. The icing on the cake was when as part of the practical ability test I was presented with a technical drawing and invited to construct the subject item using the drawing and a pile of cogs, wheels, springs and other assorted bits of metal and plastic lying on the table. It very quickly became apparent that I had absolutely no clue, and thankfully they took pity on me and allowed me to give up and scuttle away. They assured me that they would be in touch, and true to their word a few days later I received a standard "thanks, but no thanks" letter. This episode more or less sealed my fate in regard of joining the forces as it was clear I was not going to make a career in industry. There was also no way I was going to spend the rest of my life as a shop assistant. The Souls in all fairness had been good to me, but the work was monotonous and poorly paid, and quite frankly as a family business had no future prospects for somebody who was not family. Strangely enough, when I left to join the Navy (Anthony Soul gave me a leaving present of the Abba LP "Arrival"—I played it until it was wiped clean I think!), my Brother Andrew took over from me at the shop, and went on to stay there for about 10 years.

I seriously started thinking about a service career at this point. I took some time to try to get John to sit down and talk to me about being in the Navy, but pretty much in vein as he was not the 'fatherly advice' giving type. The Navy in his view was 'alright' and not much more or less. I also kind of liked the idea for some reason of being an Army tank driver. I have no idea where I got that from but for quite a while I looked at some detail into what joining the Army might be like, even going to the Army Careers office and the Aldershot Army display one year and getting leaflets and stuff. I dropped this idea like a hot potato though after talking to the Brother of a school friend who as in the Army, serving in Northern Ireland—remember this was at the height of the 'troubles' and he was being shot at with real bullets—voluntarily! The selection process after this became somewhat easier and went something like:

ARMY	NAVY
I might die	I shouldn't die unless I do something stupid
People will shoot at me	There are no navy personnel in Northern Ireland (I thought)
Might get bayoneted	Enemy should be well over the horizon!
Lots of shouting/foot stamping etc	A little bit of drill during Basic training and that's it
I will look like a tree	Nice Sailor's uniform = chicks!
Sleep in a hole in the ground (I had seen the films)	Comfortable hammock on ships
Eat slop cooked in a helmet	3 square well presented meals a day (films again!)
Lots of running around = tired	How far can you run around on a ship?
My friends' Brother looks well stressed	John is always jolly/drunk/rich/been somewhere nice

When comparing the pros and cons in this manner, and remembering that this process was at the age of 15 years, you can begin to understand that the Navy seemed quite a decent prospect when compared with life in the Army. The Army disappeared as a viable alternative.

My Bloody Efforts

I first entered a Navy recruiting office around the spring of 1976. It was all very friendly and inviting, with posters of young men doing exciting and technical things, like fighting fires, firing missiles at aeroplanes, and laughing jauntily at some shared joke in some exotic foreign looking place—just the sort of thing for me! I had an interview with a nice fatherly chap with lots of badges and medal ribbons on his spotless uniform, and he quickly put me in the picture of how wonderful the navy life was. He was going to ensure I had a great ship and wonderful shipmates, and visit well, pretty much all of the World! Of course there was some training to be done first, and we had to decide what job I would like to do in the Navy before we could go any further. Now, being a pretty sharp young man, I thought it would be better for me if I had a nice job maybe with aeroplanes, or missiles, or firing machine guns, or something like that—something really exciting but without too much work would be ideal thank you very much Captain!

The 'Chief' as he wanted to be called asked me if I would be taking 'O' levels in the summer, to which of course I replied that no, I'm afraid not. No matter he says, you can take our own internal test, and depending on the results we'll determine what naval career would be best for you. That sounded sensible and without further ado I was ushered into a little room with a couple of others doing the same thing, and sat the naval entrance test. At the time it seemed quite a reasonable test, and I was fairly confident that I had done well. This was confirmed by the 'Chief' who congratulated me on my score (although I never did learn what the score was!), and grandly announced that I had achieved a high enough score to allow me to join the Royal Navy as a "Marine Engineering Mechanic"!

Marine . . . what? The 'Chief' explained that Marine Engineering Mechanics, or 'MEMs' were the people responsible for making the ship float, move and fight. They were responsible for supplying everything from water to electricity, from air-conditioning to ship's propulsion, and that the work was going to be varied, interesting, and that promotion was quick in this new branch of the service. I would be learning engineering skills and achieving civilian qualifications second to none, AND while I was doing this I would be getting paid and visiting incredible places all over the World—what was there to lose? In my mind's eye I could picture myself in my smart overalls, fixing some vital piece of equipment, the Captain hovering nervously over me while I wiped sweat away from my strategically dirty forehead . . . "that's it Sir, you should be able to sail on the morning tide now". "Well done Bridgman, what would we do without you?" Yes, this was for me!

The Chief gave me some consent forms which had to be signed by my parents (yeah right!), after which we could start the process of becoming a Royal Navy Marine Engineering Mechanic. I couldn't wait.

I signed the forms on behalf of my parents—I couldn't be bothered to mess about trying to explain my career choices to my Mum, and even got a chance to talk to John before returning them to the Recruiting Office for the next phase of induction. "You're joining as a bloody MEM?—are you nuts? Why do you want to join as a bloody Stoker! They get all the shit jobs! Join up as a 'WAFU' or a Radio Operator or something easy" was his helpful advice. I had no idea what a 'WAFU' was, and of course he would say that—he was an MEM or "Stoker" himself, and just because he didn't like it did not mean I wouldn't, did it? Anyway the Chief at the recruiting office had told me that MEM was a vital position on the ship. John could get stuffed!

I returned to the recruiting office and filled in the papers and what-not, and a medical was arranged for me in the coming September, prior to joining up in November—the medical would be in Southampton for some reason, and the 'Chief' told be to expect more information through the post. We shook hands on the deal and went our separate ways. I still like to think the man was genuinely doing his level best for someone joining up, but who knows, maybe he was just filling quotas—the Navy certainly needed a lot of Stokers in those days of boiler rooms and manpower intensive machinery.

The months slid by, and I spent a lot of the time trying to find out how my new life was going to be. The recruiting office sent me a paper called "The Navy News" each month, which was an insight in itself. I remember being impressed that they would be so nice as to bother to send the paper to little old me—with hindsight of course it was just of case of keeping potential sailors interested, but it worked in my case! As well as that and through that Summer the television was running a 'fly-on-the-wall' documentary called "Sailor" about life onboard the aircraft carrier HMS Ark Royal, which of course for me was obligatory watching. As an added incentive my Brother John was serving on the 'Ark' at the time of the programme, so whenever it was on we would all gather round the TV set and see if we could spot him. In my case I was trying to look past the entertainment value bit of the programme and to glean some information on actual life in the Navy, but of course it was almost impossible given that the edited portion shown on the TV tended to be the most either exciting or dramatic events—obviously. Still, the programme certainly did nothing to dampen my enthusiasm for joining up, and with the 'jolly jack-tar' aspects being given prominence probably did much to strengthen it. I do not remember how many episodes of the programme there were at the time, but my Brother did not show up until the very last one (there were almost three thousand people on board after all!). On the very last episode there is a shot of a sailor walking off the ship down the gangway with a kitbag over his shoulder—that's John (I think. Looks like him anyway—from the back). The other thing the programme did was make me want to serve on the Ark Royal. Of course it would be nice to serve with John on the same ship, but more than that the Ark had an aura. She was the Flagship of the entire Navy, was big (no seasickness—wrong!), she clearly got around to some very nice places, and there were 100s of MEMs on the thing. I should be able to keep a low profile there then.

I had also finished school in the May of 1976, on something of a low unfortunately. Academically I had achieved effectively nothing, just some CSEs (one was a Grade 2 in English though, which I was assured was equivalent to a Grade C 'O' Level—get-in!!), and it had been frustrating having to hang around for a few weeks with the other dimwits at the end of term doing nothing but kicking around, while the swots waited to find out their scores before bursting into tears and doing the drama-queen act on receipt of their 15 grade A's. It had apparently been a kind of tradition at the school that the pupils leaving that year would symbolically rip up their school blazers and throw them around the place as they left for the last time—this was news to me, and in any case we (the Bridgman family) simply DID NOT rip up perfectly good clothing which could be passed down the clan. In my case the blazer I wore was the same one worn by the previous at least two brothers, and was good enough for the next one—no way was it going to be ripped up! The school headmaster shared this view apparently, and issued a notice decreeing that no school blazers were to be ripped up that year. Psychology clearly was not his strong point, as even to a thicky like me that was a red rag to a bull (try telling a 15 year old not to do something—what's the first thing they do?), and sure enough, as we were told to clear off the school premises for the final time, there was an orgy of ripping shirts and blazers. In all fairness I did bravely try to protect my own uniform, but was just overwhelmed in the melee. The headmaster and a few teachers eventually managed to regain control, and not surprisingly he threw his toys out of the pram. He called out a few names including mine to report to his office, and once there read the riot act to us. He was particularly disappointed in me he said, "knowing the circumstances of the family". I was and am a bit touchy on that subject and invited him to mind his own fucking business, at which point I was expelled. So ended my childhood education. Did somebody say something about your schooldays being the best days of your life? Oh yes, there was a PS to this story. When I got home sans school blazer, and with people's signatures all over my shirt (as was the other leaving tradition—signing each others shirts), my Mother hit the roof—and me! She was absolute livid and wondered why only I had managed to have my blazer trashed when the older brothers had protected it and so on. The upshot was that I was made to buy my younger brother a new blazer with my hard-earned cash. Did I learn a lesson? No, did I bollocks!

In about August of that year I received a request to visit the Recruiting Office once more. On turning up I was told that I now had a date for the pre-entry medical. I remember being given a train ticket and instructions for reaching Southampton, and then being given a meal ticket and even some spending money. While being worried about the journey—Reading was the furthest away from home I had ever been alone—at the same time I was very impressed at how well you were looked after, and me not even in the Navy yet! A meal ticket, spending money, a train ticket and clear instructions! I knew then I had made the right choice. The journey and the medical both went without a hitch (I was 15 years old and fit as a Butcher's dog from all the fetching and carrying at the shop and from hours on my bike on the paper round and to/from school), and all that now remained was the joining up date. This was set as the 2nd November 1976.

So, here I was, sitting on the end of 'my' bed, my battered old piece of crap suitcase packed with the list of gear supplied to me before joining, waiting to see what happened next.

Chapter 2

Do I look like your F*#king Mother?

My first day as a sailor closed fairly tamely. After waiting for the room to fill up—about 40 people in all, we all sat around nervously waiting for something to happen. Eventually one of the men from downstairs entered the room. We all fell silent.

"OK lads, listen-in!" This was to become a very common opening statement. "What's going to happen now is that we are going to go over the Mess Hall for some Scran, then after that we will come back here and sort our shit out. Fall-in in front of the block!"

Now, being about 6 o'clock in the evening by now, I managed to work out that 'Mess Hall' and 'Scran' were something to do with having a meal in the Dining Hall. 'Fall-in' I had heard before on 'It Ain't Half Hot Mum' on the TV. Apparently so had everybody else as there was a rush to get out the door. Outside we were being pushed and cajoled into forming nice straight lines in readiness for moving as a group to the Mess. While there was no attempt at this stage to get us marching properly, we were informed that from now on, we did not go anywhere singly except in the evening after 'Secure' had been ordered, and that once allocated our 'Divisions' we would march to and from anywhere we were going.

So, we shuffled in a group to the Mess Hall, looking and feeling quite ridiculous—all out of step, still in civilian clothing that really felt out of place in this smart base, and some with long flowing locks (I had taken the precaution of cutting my hair before joining), and very far from being a unit. At the Mess Hall our guide gave us a quick briefing before entry. We got the obligatory "Listen-in!" followed by "When you go in, go to the end of the serving area, grab a tray and then make your way down the line. Just so that you know, all of the others trainees are going to be waiting for you as you go in, and are going to rip the shit out of you. Ignore it, and just get on with your meal—they all had to endure it, so don't worry about it. Enjoy!" This should be interesting.

We gingerly headed towards the entrance, a few people coming and going to the Mess Hall giving us knowing little smiles and chuckles. I was towards the rear of the group, but as the front runners opened the door and went in a great shout went up in the hall. It was a half-cheer, half-boo affair from several hundred throats, and continued as we all made our way in. It was quite intimidating, especially to the really young ones like myself, and although there was of course no real threat, some of the 'old-hands' got quite carried away, sticking their faces a couple of inches in front of some of the new men and screaming stuff like "Great, fresh meat!", "Enjoy your last meal!", "Look at this wussy, he won't last long!", "Go back to your Mother while you still can!", and other such pleasantries. I for some reason was not really individually targeted, but others had one, two, or even three people ganging up on them—dependent really on their reaction to the offensive. Most of us gritted our teeth, put our heads down and made for the serving counter, but there were a couple of hot-heads who took exception to the abuse and either argued back or fronted up for a fight. This clearly was not unexpected and the staff stepped in whenever things got too heated—it normally ended with lots of finger pointing and threats of "I'll see you later you twat!", "Yeah? Your Mummy won't be there next time!" and so on. Suffice to say that our first meal in the Navy was somewhat tense, and the abuse continued heartily throughout. We were mightily relieved to get out of the Mess Hall and to then get back to the accommodation block. Once back in our Mess, the Guide got us all together and said "How did you enjoy that then?" There were a few mumbled moans and groans "Don't worry about it, don't take it personally, it's just a kind of initiation thing that happens to everybody—it won't be long before you will be doing exactly the same to the next new-entry class! You should count yourselves lucky. In the Marines the initiation is getting your face kicked in by the previous new class!" There were no more moans.

For the rest of that evening we were pretty much left to our own devices. We were told to put away, or 'stow' our personal belongings in the locker by the side of each bed "for now", and to just "settle in". Attached to each Mess or 'Bunk-space' was a lounge area, and as each person sorted themselves out they all migrated towards it. People slowly started to talk a bit more with each-other and introduce themselves, and before long there was a hubbub of conversation and even some laughter. Not surprisingly the older members of the group tended to be the ones a little more at ease with the surroundings, and they soon started to establish a pecking order. There were quite a few of us much younger boys in the group, many of us just turned sixteen (in my case only 2 months before), and we naturally tended to drift towards one-another. The conversation was light, of the

"Where are you from Mate?", "The train journey was a bastard eh?", "I've still got bloody indigestion from Dinner!" variety to begin with, but turning to wondering what the next few weeks was going to be like for us. At about 10:30 the guide came back in and announced that it was 'lights out' time, and told us all to get a shower, brush our teeth and to get to bed as "You're going to need all the sleep you can get!" The getting undressed and using the communal shower was a bit a 'football changing room' experience—lots of blushing and pretending not to be embarrassed, but there were lots of jokes and laughter too. It was very strange though lying in the steel framed single bed, others lined up either side of you, and feeling every body else lying awake in the darkness and staring at the ceiling just as I was. At the time there was a programme on TV called 'The Walton's', which always ended with each family member wishing the other goodnight—"Goodnight John", "Goodnight Mary-Ellen" and so on. Invariably this started to happen in the bunk-space—"Goodnight Dave", Goodnight Pete" and so on, which for no apparent reason everybody found hilarious. Before long shouts of "goodnight" were ringing out through the darkness. Suddenly the entrance door bashed open and in strode our guide "Right! Listen in! Keep the fucking noise down! After 'lights out' I don't want to hear a fucking squeak out of this bunk-space! Is that clear?"

Silence.

"I said, is that fucking CLEAR?"

"Yes Sir" A few voices shouted.

"Don't call me fucking Sir, I work for a living!"

Silence.

"Right! Go to sleep—or do you need a goodnight kiss from your Mother?"

Light laughter

"Well, do I look like your fucking Mother? You are in the "Andrew", and growing up starts right here. Go to sleep!" With that, he turned on his heels and walked out of the room.

Out of the dark silence came a whispered "Fucking hell!" That just about summed it up.

The following morning we were awoken at around 6 o'clock. Not a big deal to me but clearly some of my compatriots were far from used to opening their eyes before it was light outside. I quickly got up and had a wash and stuff, but by the time I returned the Leading Hand (as I found out his rank was called) was busy walking around the beds of those who were reluctant to rise, kicking the beds and gently encouraging the layers-in that maybe they should like to get up now please. At this stage there was no shouting or excitement, which surprised me somewhat, but of course that would change. "Just leave your beds tidy for now, we will sort them out properly later" said the Leading Hand.

We were once again drawn up outside the block and 'marched' over to the Dining Hall for breakfast. As we got nearer we started to feel a bit apprehensive about the impending ribbing we were about to receive once more, but to our enormous surprise there was relative silence as we entered the hall and joined the food queue. The animosity of the previous evening had disappeared and we were almost totally ignored. I later came to realise that most people had much more to worry about during the training than taking the piss out of new(er) recruits. They at their stage had done the initiation, which had been a small deviation from the daily stress, but that was over and there was their basic training to get on with now. We ate our breakfast in relative peace and returned much relieved to our barrack block.

This, our first full day in the Navy was going to be a busy one. We were informed that in the morning we were going to be officially welcomed into the Navy, and that we would be doing our 'joining routine'. In the afternoon we were going to get our uniforms (great excitement) and 'settle in' and get organised. The welcome was going to be starting at a half past nine, or "Oh nine thirty" as it was called in the Navy, where the 24 hour clock was always used, the Leading Hand explained. This could get confusing as one o'clock in the afternoon was now "thirteen hundred hours", seven o'clock in the evening was "nineteen hundred hours", whereas seven o'clock in the morning now became "oh seven hundred hours" and so on. I could feel the learning curve steepening already!

While we waited for the activities of the day to start, the Leading Hand took time to start to describe the training staff's expectations with regard to cleanliness in the block—both personal and 'housekeeping' wise. We started with bed making. "The first thing you do when you get us is to make up your pit. Get into the habit straight away and it will become routine" He approached the nearest bed and simply stripped all the bedding off onto the floor. "Don't bother trying to tart up the bed, just strip it all off and start from scratch every time—trust me—we will know when you are trying to cut corners. Then simply make it up like a hospital bed". He then reconstructed the bed linen, cleverly tucking in the corners of the sheets and blanket, and somehow pulling back the top so that a nice white turned sheet was exposed for about 8 inches. He then straightened out the pillow, took off the pillow case and replaced it with a new one "Keep one pillow case perfect just for show—change it before going to bed with the used one". He patted down the now perfectly made bed "Once the bed is made do not sit on it or put anything on it until lights out—now you give it a go!" The guy who owned the bed stopped looking so smug as the leading Hand stripped off the bedding once more.

I guess I was lucky. I managed to get the hang of bed making really quickly. I was able to fold the sheets and blankets around the corners of the bed easily and neatly, and could judge how far to turn back the top sheet without any difficulty. This natural affinity for neatness would stand me in good stead for later trials, but some others were not so lucky. Most got the hang of it fairly quickly, but one or two were simply hopeless and had to be assisted to make the bed. "Don't worry; you will get plenty of practise".

By now it was time for our welcome meeting, and we were once again marched along to a great hall for this. As we entered and were directed to rows of seats aligned to face a podium, our eyes fell upon a group of what seemed like very senior naval people. Several had the gold rings of officers on their sleeves, ranging from one very severe looking man wearing 3 rings on each sleeve, to several more sporting 2 rings. Others in the group were staring at us, clearly sizing us up, and most of these either had buttons on their sleeves or the crossed anchors we had seen previously. As we filed to our seats, one man, older and almost a caricature of a typical 'salty sea-dog'—craggy face and fierce beard, glared at us and shouted "Silence". It did the trick.

Once everybody was seated and settled in anticipation, the man with 3 gold rings approached the podium.

"Good morning gentlemen (it was all men in those days) I am Commander Crichton (so that's what 3 rings means), and I am the 1st lieutenant here at HMS Raleigh. Firstly, congratulations on successfully joining the Royal Navy. I want you to remember though that joining is the start, not the end of your journey. You have a great deal of training to get through yet before you may consider yourselves as complete naval ratings. I urge you to listen to your instructors, to do what they say, and to learn as much as you can from them. Try your hardest, and I am sure you will all pass out at the end of the 8 weeks. Good Luck!

In a few minutes time the Commodore of HMS Raleigh, Commodore Benson, will come and have a word with you. When he enters the hall, you will hear a shouted order 'Trainees . . . Ha!'. When you hear this, you are to sit upright with your knees together and your arms smartly crossed. You are not move from this position until you hear the order 'Trainees . . . sit at ease!', at which point you may relax. Is that clear?"

Silence

"Gentlemen, when I ask a question I expect a response. Is that clear!?"

"Yes Sir!"

"Good. While we are waiting I will introduce the training staff."

The Commander then proceeded to reel off a list of names, starting with the men wearing 2 rings on their arms—now named as lieutenants (but strangely pronounced 'Leftenant'). These were the 'Divisional Training Officers' and would be responsible for the standard of training provided. The gruff old sea-dog was introduced as the 'Fleet Master at Arms', or 'Fleet Joss' (what?), who along with the Commander was responsible for discipline. He was the rank of 'Fleet Chief Petty Officer', and we were advised not to get 'on the wrong side' of him. All officers were to be addressed as 'Sir' we were informed, and a Fleet Chief petty Officer was the only non-commissioned officer who was also to be addressed as 'Sir'—that's straightforward then. Next came the 'Chief Petty Officers (CPOs)' or 'Chiefs' who would be our Training Officers, and normally our highest point of direct contact, and finally the Petty Officers (POs) who would be our day to day Course Instructors. We were from now on to address the Petty Officers as 'Staff' for some reason, but the Chiefs were to be called 'Chief'. The assistant Instructors, the Leading Hands, were also to be called 'Staff'. Maybe they thought we would forget that these people were members of the training team. Still, it made life a bit easier not having to remember the different ranks for now I suppose. We were advised that if we had any problems, they should be brought to the notice of the Course Instructor, who would deal with it in the first instance. One brave soul asked what would happen if we were not happy with the response from the Instructor. He was informed that he would be!

All of a sudden a shout of "Commodore approaching Sir!" rang out across the hall. The Commander stiffened as the Fleet Chief Master at Arms came to attention and shouted "Trainees . . . Ha!". We all sat upright with arms crossed and knees together as we had been instructed.

"Sit easy please" said Commodore Benson as he approached the podium. The Fleet Joss then followed with a "Trainees—sit at . . . Ease!" and most of us relaxed a bit.

The first thing to strike me about the Commodore was the amount of gold braid strewn about his uniform. He had heaps of the stuff on the peak of his cap (later to become known as 'scrambled egg'), and on each sleeve of his jacket there was a single very wide ring of gold. On one shoulder there was also a gold epaulette, and emanating from that were a couple of gold tassels—looked like the sort of thing that held curtains back. To round off the impressive uniform the Commodore has a colourful row of medal ribbons over his left breast—obviously a man with plenty of naval experience.

He was quite an old man, but having said that, at 16 years old everybody was quite an old man, and now as he surveyed us below him, he appeared quite welcoming and friendly, in some opposition to the pervading sternness of the staff so far:

"Congratulations gentlemen for getting this far. The next 8 weeks are going to be tough for some of you, and not all of you will make it to the end of the course" This all said quietly and smilingly, his eyes slowly moving along each row of trainees, as though gauging who would, and who would not be there at the end. "If you are able to persevere through the first few weeks, it does get easier. Listen to your instructors (there it was again), do as you are told, do your best, and you WILL get through.

My Bloody Efforts

I wish you good luck, and look forward to seeing you again during your passing out parade. Thank you Commander—carry on please".

"Trainees . . . Ha!" screamed the Fleet Joss once more, as the Commodore took a salute from the Commander and wandered out of the hall, followed by his small entourage. The staff kept us sitting there at attention for a few minutes as they had a little chitchat, until finally one of the Chiefs ordered us to sit at ease.

The Commander approached the podium again "Right, this is what is going to happen for the rest of today. A lot of different departments will be coming over to introduce themselves, and there is a lot of joining paperwork and such to be completed, and there will be joining medicals. After that you will be assigned your divisions, and the Divisional staff will explain the plans for the rest of the day. This afternoon you will be visiting the barber (said with a knowing smile and nods to the staff) and you will be collecting some of your kit. Its going to be a busy day gentlemen, so stay awake and listen to what is being said to you". In the meantime another officer and a group of naval ratings had made their way into the hall. "OK, here we go then. This is Leiutenant-Commander James from the Pay Office, and he will take you through the joining paperwork".

The Leiutenant-Commander, or '2 and a half ringer' introduced himself and then launched into a description of some of the administration involved in joining, and being in the Navy. We were introduced to the Divisional System (around since the days of Nelson), how we would be split into divisions, then 'watches' and the kind of 'duty rosters' we might expect (1 in 3, or 1 in 4—meaning duty one day in three or one day in four). He explained how service documents, pay books and identity cards were issued and used ("Lose your ID card, and it will cost a day's pay!"), how leave was allocated ("You juniors will be allowed 'Cinderella Leave'—means you have to be back in your base by Midnight. You will be issued with 'Station cards' shortly"), and other myriad domestic issues. On completion, we were each provided with an absolute pile of paperwork to be filled in, and spent the next hour just filling in forms—a different staff member talking us through what each was, and what it was for. At the end of it our heads were spinning with the amount of information taken in, and each of us was in possession of a shiny new Service Number, ID card, Pay Book, Kit Book and Naval Ratings Handbook. My service number, which we all got to learn by heart, was D163242J—all the letters and numbers meant something, but I have forgotten what.

Next came the medical examinations. We were introduced to a naval medical officer, who explained how the medicals would work. He reminded us that we had already had a pre-joining medical, and that the current one was taking place just to ensure that nothing had changed since then. We would strip to our underwear, form a queue and file along a line of medics. In the meantime behind him the medics had set up a row of tables with forms and bits and pieces of medical equipment arranged along them, and at the end they had constructed a curtained area.

Many of us of course had noticed that many of the medical ratings were in this instance women (well it was tradition that nurses might be—right?). Now the only female I had ever undressed in front of was my Mother, and that was at an age where one didn't really give a toss. Clearly others were having the same thoughts, as there was a great deal of looking right and left at each other with some concern. Of course the medical staff had seen all this before, and they were quick to put our minds at ease—"Come of then—get your fucking kit off, the officer said, now move it!" came the caring and helpful advice, or "Come on, move it, these nurses aren't embarrassed at seeing your little tadger—why should you be?"

We self-consciously undressed in front of all the staff and lined up at the first desk. "Line up in alphabetical order here" came the order—a bit difficult as we didn't know each others names! This was quickly realised and so the order was changed to "Surnames starting 'A' here, 'B' here and so on", and we faced up to the coming ordeal. At the first desk we were asked our name and given another pile of paperwork, which would be completed as we moved down the line. As we progressed we were bombarded with questions about our state of health, any past illnesses, injuries, spells in hospital, family medical history "is your Dad alive? Your Grand-dad? Anybody in the family died of a heart attack?" and so on. At one desk we were asked in some detail about our 'bowl movements'—I for one did not know what a bowel movement was! Luckily it was swiftly explained in simpler terms by a friendly medical rating—"How often do you take a shit dickhead!" It was something I hadn't thought about that much, so I replied probably one a day? He seemed satisfied with that. As we progressed, as well as the barrage of questions, we were prodded, poked, inspected, and calibrated. Height, weight, distinguishing marks, scars "how did you get that then?", eyesight, hearing, head, chest and other body part measurement and lots of "breathe in, breathe out" going on all over the place. If the medical staff spotting something unusual they called over the medical officer, who then had a prod and poke before deciding all was well and no-one that I saw actually 'failed' the medical. Apprehension grew as we approached the curtailed area at the end of the line, as through the gaps in the curtain we could catch glimpses of the men getting their underpants off and being subjected to various bodily contortions for some reason. Finally it was my turn, and as I entered I got the now usual "Name!". I gave my name and handed over the paperwork to the fairly dis-interested medical person in front of me. "OK, take off your underpants and stand over there" I complied with huge embarrassment. The guy then approached me and basically took a good look at the old tackle, before telling me to cough a couple of times. He then instructed me to turn around and touch my toes. I thought I had misheard him and just stared at him. He repeated the instruction, and so that was that—a grown man staring up my arse. I could have died with embarrassment. It was alright for the medics to say that they had seen it all before, but I hadn't! and was mightily relieved when he said I could put my pants back on, go out and get dressed. I walked out of the enclosure and joined a few other guys putting their clothes back on in the hall—fair to say there was not a great deal of eye contact as we got dressed! The ice was broken though when one of the older guys came out of the enclosure and said dead-pan "Next time warm your hands up you bastard!"

We took a break for lunch after the medicals, but following that the time had arrived that I knew quite a few people had been concerned about—time for the extreme haircuts! We were taken over to the base NAAFI shopping area where the laughably called 'hair-dresser' was located, and formed into another nice military queue.

"Don't bother asking for any particular style—there is only one hair style on offer here, and that's what you are given!" the Leading Hand happily told us as we waited "first one, on you go then".

I personally couldn't see what the fuss some of the men were making was about—did they really think they were going to be allowed to keep long hair? I think a lot of it was show-boating, but I must admit the change on some of them from quite long hair to 'No.1' shaved was quite extreme, and very funny. We all made our way through at any rate, the 2 'barbers' expertly shaving each head in very short order, and enjoying themselves immensely doing it "Would you like some Brylcream on that Sir?, or Something for the Weekend Sir" were the usual repose, accompanied by great hilarity. All in all though it was quite painless for most of us, and not a small amount of fun was had with everybody taking the piss out of the (ex) hippies, and with the fact that we all looked more like badly plucked chickens than anything remotely resembling military personnel. If nothing else the whole hair cutting episode, along with the enforced familiarity of the medicals in the morning had the effect of getting us closer together as a unit, and after the shearing there was a lot of back-slapping and running of hands over newly shaven heads amongst the lads. Team building at a pretty basic level!

Following this hilarity it was time to make us feel even more part of the Navy as we set about collecting our 'kit' or uniforms and equipment. We were taken over to the stores area and once again formed into a long queue. This time we moved along a line of store men who handed out a seemingly endless pile of new equipment to each new recruit (and who took the Mickey out of our new haircuts!). The first things to be given to us were huge brown sausage shaped 'kit-bags' and a big green 'Pusser's' suitcase each. We were instructed to put all the gear we were being given in the kit-bag as we went on down the line. There was no measuring or being asked what this or that size was, the store men being so experienced they could seemingly tell our sizes just by looking at us. It was uncanny. As we passed along, first came parade boots, then working or 'steaming' boots, then shoes, plimsolls or 'pumps' for physical training (this being pre-'trainer' days of course), 2 working uniforms or 'No.8's' and a pullover known for some reason as a 'wholly-pulley', overalls, white-fronts, collars, 'silks', beret, sailor's cap, cap ribbon with 'HMS Raleigh' written in gold lettering on it, lots of badges for the different uniforms, and a whole load of other clothing and equipment. By the end of the line the kit-bag was bulging and incredibly heavy. We were informed that our best and second best uniforms (known as No.1's and No.2's respectively) would be ready in the following few days, and that we would be back to collect them—which was a relief as I was sure I couldn't carry another thing!

We were then formed up outside once more, and 'marched' back to our accommodation "Do NOT drag the kit-bags PICK THEM UP!" was the advice provided by the Staff, and the journey back to the block was a nightmare. The issue of our kit had taken all of the remaining afternoon, but we were far from finished for the day.

As we reached our block and struggled to drag and carry our bulging kit-bags up to the mess-deck, we found one of the Petty officers who had been at the introduction that morning, waiting for us:

"Put your kit on your beds and form up over there" he said pointing to the open area at the head of the room. When some of the men did not move quickly enough for him he shouted "Come on then—don't dawdle, MOVE IT!"

When we had formed up, he stood facing us, the 2 Leading Hands on either side of him:

"I am Petty Officer marine Engineering Mechanic James, and I am your Course Instructor for your Phase 1 training. That means I am your instructor for your entire time in HMS Raleigh. To my right is Leading Seaman Roberts, and to my left is Leading Seaman Jenkins, and they are my Assistant Course Instructors. They too will be with you throughout your time in Raleigh. If you have any reason to address any of us, you will call us 'Staff'. Is that clear?"

"Yes Staff" A few people answered.

"Right, lets get one thing straight from the start. The only way some of you people are going to make this course is for you to act as a team from day one. It is our job to ensure you do that. I get very upset when I notice that you are not acting as a team, like when some of you do not seem to be paying attention to what I am saying. NOW GET OUTSIDE—MOVE!"

We flinched from the volume and surprise.

"You heard the Petty Officer—MOVE IT!!" chirped in the Leading Hands. We moved.

"MOVE, MOVE" We all piled outside dressed in whatever we happened to be wearing, breath steaming in the cold November air, and the Leading Hands formed us up again amid much shouting and swearing. This sudden change had caught us off-guard, as it was supposed to, and we noticed that a similar thing was happening to some of the other recruits from some of the other messes too—they were being introduced to their course staff just like us.

The Petty Officer stood in front of us once more:

"On the deck! I want 10 press-ups—now!" Down we went, the staff snapping around us like demented dogs "Move, push them out!"

"Get up. Stand still!" We stood up, confused, surprised and getting cold.

"Listen in. My first impression of you people is not a good one. You all need to get serious, and pretty damn quick at that. When I or my staff gives you an order, it will be carried out instantly. Is that Clear?"

"Yes Sir!"

"Are you people fucking deaf, or just fucking stupid? How were you told to address me? On the deck—10 press-ups!!"

Down we go, lots of shouting from the staff.

"Stand up! Stand still! Are you getting the picture yet?"

"Yes Staff!"

"Better, get back indoors"

Inside we tumbled again, Leading Hand snapping at our heels.

Once inside and formed up again, the Petty Officer continued:

"We have just eight weeks to turn you from civilians to sailors. We do not mess about, and there is a lot of stuff you people have to learn in a very short time. If you do not understand something you are being told, you ask. Is that clear?"

"Yes Staff!"

"Now then, you may or may not have realised that you are all Stokers in this Mess. That is not by accident—you are the Stoker Division for this intake. The other divisions are Seamen, or Greenies, or Pinkies or whatever—it doesn't matter. What does matter is that the Stoker division passes out at the end of this course as the top division—clear?"

"Yes Staff!" (No idea what the hell he is on about, but looking attentive)

"OK, we'll worry about that later. This evening you will be sorting out your kit under the direction of the Assistant Course Instructors. They will show you how to stow it all, and what to concentrate on looking after first. Listen carefully to them, and it will save you time later. They will also be showing you how to iron clothes. Again pay close attention—they will only show you once, and after that you are on your own."

So, if anybody thought that the evenings would be free was in for a nasty surprise. That evening, and pretty much every evening thereafter during basic training we would be doing 'domestics'. This meant preparing the clothing you would need for the next day, as well as maintaining the remainder of the kit in pristine condition for the regular 'kit-musters'. This involved of course polishing shoes and boots, whitening 'pumps', washing clothes in the communal wash rooms and then hanging them to dry in the always too crowded drying rooms, desperately hoping they would dry in time for their next outing (or ironing them dry if they did not!), trying to iron straight creases in trousers and shirts sleeves, and then folding everything to the regulation size. In addition to this there was the living areas to clean, including the Mess, washrooms, bathrooms, toilets, storage rooms, and other communal areas, and when I say clean, I mean 'eat your dinner off the floor' clean. Needless to say that the close confines and the constant search for a spare sink or iron, as well as other cleaning duties was a massive cause of friction almost from day one, and would turn out to be the biggest causes of conflict (verbal and physical) during the phase 1 training course as the race to try to achieve perfection went on.

One of the first things we had to do was to mark all of our kit with our names. Leading Seaman Jenkins soon explained the reason for this to us:

"In a ship you do not have a lot of space, so it's vital everyone knows who belongs to what. Just so you know from day one, we in the Navy hate thieves. There is nothing worse that a thief onboard a ship, because it means you can't trust your shipmates—and ships work on trust. If someone at sea is caught stealing something from one of his mess-mates, he can expect swift justice—he will have his fingers shut in a hatch! I have seen it done and it is not pleasant, so don't be tempted". Can't argue with that!

To mark our kit we had been given a wooden block thing with our names cut out on the bottom of it. The idea was to dip this into paint, and then stamp each item of clothing and equipment with it, leaving a nice neat painted name behind. This went fairly well, and without too much mess, but then, the paint has to be allowed to dry, and before long the whole Mess area, every bathroom and washroom, and every other free space was festooned with people's clothing and equipment hanging out to dry. Remember this was November, and even with central heating on it was going to take some time. The Leading Hands were clearly scowling at the untidiness in their nice clean Mess, and made it quite clear that the clothing was to be down by morning—dry or not!

The leading Hands had told us not to mark up one set of working clothes or 'No.8s', as we would need them for the morning. The next surprise was that we had to do some sewing! As part of the preparation for wearing the No.8s tomorrow, we needed to sew on some badges—a nameplate above the left breast pocket, and a propeller badge, indicating our chosen branch on to the right arm of the shirt. Leading Seaman Jenkins got us all together and demonstrated where and how the badges were to be attached, and used the kit-book as the measurement for positioning the badge on the shirt. He started sewing away saying "Nice small stitches like this—see? I don't want to see any homeward bounders alright? We looked at each other confused. "Homeward bounders—bloody great stitches—trying to finish the job too quick. You need a bit of patience for this." So, we went away to our beds and set-to. After plenty of stabbed fingers, swearing, starting and stopping my badges were attached, as were most others, but they were not good. The staff came around as we were sewing, offering advice and guidance "That's shit! Take it off and start again" was the most frequent comment, and the whole process took hours. The thought that we had to repeat that process for all the other uniforms was a nightmare. It was already past 8pm and we were nowhere near finished yet!

Next came the beret. Easy you might think, but oh no! The next lesson was in how to wear the beret 'properly' "You are not some ponsy onion eating Frenchman, and I don't want to see any Frank Spencer lookalikes. The beret (pronounced 'berry') is worn with the badge above your left eye and with the right hand side pulled down over the right ear—Try it". We spent the next half hour fitting the beret badge and trying the thing on. Because they were brand new we were advised that "The best way to soften them up is to wet them and then put them under your mattress". At this stage though they simply refused to bend over the ear, leaving us all looking like lunatic Frank Spencers', and despite the order of the Leading Hand, a few people could not help themselves doing a fine "Ooh Betty!" and mincing around. For the rest of the evening we had the pleasure of wearing a soaking wet beret around, trying to get it to sit properly and more importantly to look hard!

Footwear came next. This in time would become our greatest bugbear through the entire basic training. For this evening we just had to give the boots and shoes a general polish. The leading Hand gave us a quick demonstration on how to spit shine the boots and shoes, and promised us that by the end of the New Entry week we would become experts. After giving it a go that evening, it seemed very unlikely.

The final job for the evening was a bit of ironing. I had had a go before, but again there were quite a few men present who had never even seen an iron close up. The Leading Hand quickly went through ironing a No.8 shirt and trousers (or 'trollies'), and then left us to get on with it. By the time we were all done or done as well as it was going to be, we were all knackered and quite happy to turn in. Tomorrow would be our first day in uniform!

The remainder of this introduction week was very much dedicated to easing us new boys into the idea of being in the forces, and with preparation of uniforms so that they would be of an acceptable standard prior to us starting our training proper. To most of us the uniforms, even the working ones seemed perfectly smart, but the instructors insisted that they be washed and ironed continuously, and using liberal amounts of spray on starch (I still remember the smell!), until they were stiff as boards. We were introduced to the intricacies of the White Front (worn under the sailors uniform), which needed a perfectly ironed crease at the front (no 'tramlines' allowed), the Collar, the complicated blue affair which flows out over the shoulders of the uniform, and which required one perfect crease on the inside and two outside of the damn thing, and the dreaded sailors blue bell-bottom trousers which needed to be ironed with either 5 or 7 horizontal creases, exactly spaced apart at pay book distance, to represent (we were told) either the 5 oceans or 7 seas—not surprisingly the 5 oceans were much more popular! Once cleaned and ironed, all of our uniform clothing then had to be folded in such a way that it would fit into the lockers we would be using onboard the ships. That meant that every single piece of kit had a particular system of being folded, which we were required to perfect. To that end we were each given a photo of a perfect 'kit-muster' laid out on a bed, which we would have to perfect over the coming weeks. We would be subject to weekly 'Kit Musters' where we would have to match our kit with the picture to exact proportions or suffer the consequences.

We were instructed on how to tie the cap ribbon on our new sailor's caps, ensuring that the bow on the side of the cap was perfectly square and neatly trimmed. I had a nightmare with this thing, and eventually had to be given another cap ribbon which was then tied by one of the smart-arses who happened to be able to do it with no trouble. I would continue to have trouble with cap ribbons throughout my time as a junior rating, and was much relieved to be rid of the things when I became a Petty Officer.

In the meantime though we spent every evening of the days remaining prior to starting training in the tedious process of polishing (or 'bulling') our shoes and boots. Polishing boots and shoes to a high gloss finish is something of a fine art, which some people just never seem to manage. I was quite lucky in that I am a fairly patient sort and am able to concentrate for a while at a time. It really is about taking the time to add the polish to the boot, spit on it and the rub it in, using small circles. You build up layers of polish and then just buff them up. It seemed quite straightforward, and most guys soon realised that there is not a short cut to the process. In my case the boots and shoes were decently shiny in a relatively short time, after which I would just need to keep on top of them. Shoes and boots would become quite a source of contention over the coming weeks as time got shorter, inspections got more intense, and people literally stepped on each-others shiny boot toes. When this happened it tended to result in a flare-up, because the owner of the now damaged polish area would know that he now needed to start again on that boot!

The remaining few days passed in a flash of washing, ironing, neatly folding clothes and endlessly polishing shoes and boots. Before we knew it, we were ready to start basic training week one.

The next morning came around in a flash, and it seemed that I was awake before my head had even hit the pillow the night before. Leading seamen Jenkins and Roberts were in fine form, and set about dressing us as sailors with gusto. On went our new No.8 uniforms, with 'wholley pulley' over the top. Out came our berets from under mattresses—mine still seemed as stiff as a board, and 30 men tried to get to the full length mirror next to the door all at once, tugging down berets, and adjusting strange shirts and trousers before all mustering outside in the freezing morning to be inspected by the Course Instructor.

This inspection, our first of at least one a day for the duration of basic training, did not go well of course. After forming us up into something approaching a military formation, the Petty Officer started the inspection by slowly approaching each man in turn, looking them up and down, and then pointing out the (many) faults in the man's appearance. We would become very familiar with and would learn to dread, this format over the coming weeks, but this first one was a terrible shock.

"Did you shave this morning?" to the first man in line

"No Staff"

"Why not?"

"Er . . . I've never shaved"

"Your face is covered with fucking bum-fluff—are you blind? In the Navy you will shave EVERY morning. Right! Now get inside and shave. You will be back here in 5 minutes—GO!" The boy went.

He turned to the rest of us, and raised his voice to a controlled snarl:

"LISTEN IN. If there is anyone else who has not shaved this morning, go and shave NOW! If you have not shaved before, watch the person next to you! Every one of you is to shave EVERY morning. Is that CLEAR!"

"Yes Staff!" About 10 of us disappeared inside at the rush, and very quickly had a rough shave. It was lucky I had been pre-warned and had brought a razor with me, although I had hardly ever used it! A couple of the others had to borrow a razor between a few of them. That would hurt later! As we ran the blades over our stubble (or bum-fluff in most cases) one of the Leading Hands snapped around us, swearing, shouting at us to hurry up, and not to be the last man out. Finally we rushed out, the last man being awarded with 20 press-ups as he tumbled out of the building.

There had been no time for after-shave, and my face felt red-raw and sore as the inspection continued.

"Gentlemen, today is the only day where you are advised of your faults. From tomorrow's inspection, you will be punished for any faults to your dress".

He moved down the line, a comment here, an adjustment to some item of clothing there, and I started to get an uncomfortable feeling as he approached. I mentally reviewed myself to ensure I had dressed properly, and as the Petty Officer stopped in front of me, the apprehension was terrible. He looked directly at me, his eyes then moving to the top of my head and then down the whole uniform—cold and dispassionate:

"Stand upright—you will have to get used to standing still for a long time. Move your toes around in your shoes, you won't get cramp then. The beret badge goes over your left eye—check yourself in the mirror before you come out." He moved the beret on my head slightly. "Pull the collars of your shirt over the neck of the wholley-pulley". He did so. ""You need to take your trousers up an inch ok?"

"Yes Staff!"

All this said at conversation level, as though it was just me and him there. I would find this over the course, an inspection being an impersonal but at the same time personal event. As the Staff got to know you more, the way they inspected you became much more targeted as they learned what motivated an individual. Some had to be screamed at, others (particularly the younger ones like me) needed to be encouraged and praised. All that would come later though. For now he moved on to the next man, and I breathed a sigh of relief.

The inspection dragged on for what seemed an age, but finally the Petty Officer was satisfied and we went off to breakfast.

The basic (or Phase 1) training in the Royal Navy at that time lasted for a period of 8 weeks. We were starting day one of week one, and it was going to be a long training day! We were introduced to the Royal navy 'Divisional System', a kind of welfare organisation within the navy where the next rank up from you was supposed to help you out with any problems, as well being the source of advice and encouragement. The way it was supposed to, and did work, was that if you were unsatisfied with the response of the next rank up, you could take your complaint up again—in theory right up to the First Sea Lord. In reality of course you would be sorted out well before that, but the system had been around for a very long time and was well proven. After that we were given basic instruction about the major areas and names of parts of a ship (Port.—left, Starboard—right, Numbers to port—even, numbers to starboard—odd, bow—front, stern—back, decks going down from the 'weather deck' 1, 2, 3 etc, and going up from the weather deck, i.e. the superstructure, numbered 01, 02, 03 etc). We were each helpfully given a copy of these details for later study, and informed that we would need that information later.

In the afternoon we were given a nice surprise. We were to be taken on a boat trip around the Devonport dockyard to have a look at some of the ships alongside! So, we were bussed to a place called Jupiter Point, where we boarded, 8 to 10 to a boat, some sturdy looking 'Whalers'—wooden open boats about 20 feet long. We couldn't help but notice that the engine in these things looked rather small, and that there were huge great oars piled neatly in each boat. Before we boarded and sat down on the bench seats, we were each given a life-jacket and 'oil-skin' coat to wear (it was November and pretty nippy). Another Leading Hand climbed in, and announced himself as the 'Coxswain' of the boat. He warned us to remain seated at all times in the boat ("don't fucking move unless I say so" where the actual words used), and to keep our hands inside the boat ("don't want to see anyone trailing their hands through the water like a fucking pansy—this isn't a pleasure cruise!"), started the engine and off we went.

Our little flotilla chugged our way down the river Ply towards the dockyard. This was more like it! It was a beautiful bright winter's day. The Coxswain looked the very caricature of a naval rating, standing in front of us with his cap on and collar of his oil-skin turned up against the cold, looking steely eyed into the distance as he steered the boat. "What you fucking staring at—do you fucking fancy me or something?" Spell broken.

My Bloody Efforts

For the next hour and a half we chugged around the dockyard area, passing close to the ships tied up alongside. As we went, the Coxswain named and described each of the vessels we passed "That big bastard over there is the 'Hermes'. It started out as a small carrier, but is used as a Marines support ship. Don't ask for a draft to it—the Booties are a pain in the arse" would come the advice, or "That's a Leander Class frigate—the 'Dido'. Good sea boats they are" We would all nod sagely, as though we were completely aware of what a 'good sea boat' was. Along with the ships, the Coxswain also pointed out some of the areas of interest on land too. HMS Drake, the main accommodation base in Plymouth was pointed out, as was HMS Defiance, a floating maintenance base "Most of you young Stokers will probably end up there". He showed us the 'married patch' or married quarters area called St Budeaux (or 'Budo' as he termed it) across the water from the dockyard. Finally was we made our way back up river he gave us a lengthy insight into the joys of downtown Plymouth of an evening, and some of the interesting hostelries we might like to frequent after finishing training.

By this time we had been in the boat for some time, engine chugging away, Coxswain wittering on, and the cold creeping through our clothing. We were heading up river with the tide against the boat, which was slowing perceptibly in the tide. At this point the Coxswain said "OK boys, you are looking a bit chilly sitting there, so lets have a bit of exercise to warm you up a bit". We were instructed to fit the oars and to start rowing. Not surprisingly this took a bit of coordination, and the Coxswain expended a lot of energy instructing and cajoling us into some semblance of seaworthiness. Eventually though we got a nice rhythm going and starting pulling on the oars with gusto, the Coxswain yelling "In, Out" to keep the pace going. It was hard work though, and somewhat disappointing to notice that even with all our effort, we were not actually gaining any headway against the tide. A glance across at the rest of the flotilla confirmed that they too were more or less stationary while rowing like buggery too. Quite quickly the rowing went from a nice afternoon novel experience into something approaching torture. The oars were heavy wooden things with large blades dipping into the water, and with the life-jacket and oil-skin on, it very quickly became very hard and hot work. The air became thick with laboured breathing, and we implored the Coxswain with our eyes to re-start the engine and allow us to stop rowing, but he mercilessly continued the steady "In, Out!" chant, interspaced with the occasional "Come on—pull!" or "put your backs into it!" After what seemed an age the rhythm started to falter as people became exhausted, and eventually totally disintegrated, oars smacking together out of time, and the Whaler loosing headway against the tide. The Coxswain started the engine and we gathered the oars in the boat, chests heaving and sweat soaking our shirts under the oil-skins.

As the boats pulled alongside the jetty back at Jupiter Point and we disembarked, we were gathered together and told "Remember that the water is very dangerous and unpredictable—if you ever had to abandon ship, you might have to row for hours or even days—this was just to give you a taster of how difficult that would be". We all agreed later that that was a lot of bollocks—they just wanted to see us puffing and sweating. Whatever.

The remainder of the day and evening was spent with preparing and cleaning our kit. Boots and shoes were now starting to look quite clean.

The next day dawned with another long clothing inspection—lots more press-ups and warnings of dire consequences if improvements failed to materialise. Today we were informed, was going to be heavily biased towards fitness and sports.

Certainly the fitness aspect was very heavily introduced! Part of the kit we had been issued consisted of 'sports gear'—a pair of what appeared to be WWII plimsolls or 'pumps', a couple of pairs of heavy white shorts and a couple of white t-shirts. I along with most of my classmates had shoved these items into the bottom of the kitbag, and not really thought about it since. The previous evening one of the instructors had reminded us that physical training or 'fiz' was scheduled for the following day, and warned us that our sports gear needed to be "spotless", as the Physical Training Instructors (PTIs) were renowned as being very tough on those who's gear was dirty. We had spent the evening whitening the pumps and ironing the shorts and t-shirts to perfection, and were confident that the PTIs would find no fault with us.

So here we were, lined up at ease in the Gym being introduced to the Chief PTI—a huge well-built and very fit looking bloke—surrounded by the lesser PTIs or 'Club Swingers' as they were known—a nickname referring to a pair of crossed over batons on their branch badge, all miniature versions of the Chief. They were a tough looking bunch that's for sure, and I for one, although I considered myself fairly fit from all the work before joining up, did not like the prospect of this lot setting about us. Sure enough, we were in for a rough ride:

"You lot look like a bunch of shit!" the Chief kindly informed us "Leading PTI Smith front and centre—GO!" A perfect physical specimen leapt forward and sprang to attention in front of us. "This gentlemen, is the standard of kit turn-out I expect from my trainees at the start of every physical training session"

He walked to the statue-like Leading PTI "You will notice that his pumps are spotless, his socks are neatly folded to the same level on both legs, his shorts and t-shirt are perfectly clean and pressed—the creases are sharp and single. "This is how you will be every time you come to this Gym—is that clear?"

"Yes Staff!"

"Today you get the benefit of the doubt—because you are new, and your instructors probably did not emphasize what we expect from you" Smiles all round between the PTIs "Tomorrow though, you are not new anymore, and there will be no excuse for sub-standard clothing—Leading PTIs carry on"

Three PTIs stepped out of line and came towards us—one taking each row of trainees. They then commenced walking down the line very loudly pointing out the faults with each man's clothing. They were very intimidating and looked ready to punch us all for daring to even breathe. When the guy got to me I got the same treatment as everybody else—my pumps were 'filthy', my shorts and t-shirts looked as though I had "fucking slept upside down in the bastards!" Apparently I needed to "get with the fucking programme". Although I did not quite understand which programme I had to get with, the message was pretty clear to all of us, and if it was not, it soon would be!

Having got through the introduction, we were then 'invited' to carry out a fitness test. This of course is before the days of 'beep' tests and other scientific means of assessing a person's level of fitness, and basically consisted of a cross-country run of an indeterminate distance, followed by violent circuit training until the trainee vomits. The fitness test completes when the trainee displays the 'bottle' to continue circuit training after having thrown up. It soon became apparent that all the PTIs wanted to see then and in the future, was a person's determination to 'front-up'—that is to fight through the pain barrier and show some spirit. The PTIs hated people who in their eyes were 'wimps' and who 'wimped-out' of pushing themselves a bit. Most of us realised early on that this was the case, and always saved a bit for the last display of the fighting spirit the PTIs seemed to thrive on, but as always there was some easy meat—people who had never got a sweat on in their lives. I am sorry to say that we were glad there were some people who were easy targets for the PTIs, because that took the pressure off the rest of us, and made our lives a little easier. To begin with though, the physical training was very tough—even though I was naturally fairly fit, I had never done any kind of circuit training before, and the exercises initially felt uncomfortable and awkward. Throughout basic training the 'fiz' would be torture, both physically and mentally, as the standard of kit turn-out was never to a high enough standard for the PTIs, and I recall that just about every session ended with the whole course throwing up. We did get fit, that's for sure, but I understand that these days the process is a little more scientific—there were a large number of injuries from fiz in those days, which caused quite a few people to be back classed as a result.

The incident that summed up the whole attitude towards physical training in those days was the 'milling' session we had to take part in. Milling was the name given to basically a short boxing tournament that we were required to be part of during the basic training. The idea was that this gave the PTIs an idea of our 'toughness', 'bravery', 'fighting spirit', who knows, but I thought at the time and still do that actually it was entertainment for the bastards. The way it worked was that we were lined up in two ranks, supposedly alongside someone the same height and build as you, and that person would be your 'partner'. In two's, we were then put into a square of gym benches representing a boxing ring, given some boxing gloves, and then told to batter the crap out of each other for one 3 minute round—gum shields and head guards were not part of the kit! Luckily this was quite early in the training so most of us ran out of puff pretty quickly. I don't remember much about my opponent except that he made my nose bleed and I split his lip, but the thing I recall most is that the PTIs were all there—even the physical training officer—baying like a bunch of savages as the fights progressed. Was it valid training or entertainment? Whatever, that was the way it was then.

There was actually one area of physical training where I was one of the 'wimps' and that was swimming. Not unnaturally being that it was the Navy we were joining, we were all required to pass the naval swimming test. This was brought on quite early in the training, to allow for swimming lessons should any numpty fail the test. I could swim—but not very strongly (I could only do an untidy version of the breast stroke), and not very far. The swimming test consisted of swimming 2 lengths of the swimming pool, and then treading water for a certain amount of time—in overalls! There were two problems with the thing for me—first you had to jump in at the deep end and then start swimming, and then there was the treading water part. Previously at the local swimming baths I had always kind of gently waded into the water, and I had never willingly let go of the side when floating around the pool. To be fair they did ask us before we started if there was anybody that could not swim, but hey, I COULD swim, just not too well.

The whole exercise was under the control of the club swingers, and as usual they were pretty unsympathetic to anybody getting into difficulties, and doing something pathetic like drowning! As the first group jumped in and started swimming strongly, my trepidation began to grow. The stronger guys had gone first of course, with us less confident swimmers hanging back hoping some miracle would come and save us. Of course none came and before long we were lining up along the end of the pool, massive soaking wet overalls on, waiting for the off from the PTI. On the signal in we jumped, and that was where it all started to go wrong for me. I had not figured on the amount of splashing about all those around me would do, and I felt like I could not free my face from water to take a breath. As I thrashed around like a demented duck, my antics came to the attention of the club swingers along the side of the pool.

"Are you drowning Sonny?" the first shouted "Fucking calm down and swim properly or I will fish you out!"

I was not the first to be struggling, and we had been hearing similar shouts at other swimmers previously, but once a weak swimmer is identified, the pack of PTIs gather and life becomes quite unpleasant.

I managed to grab a breath as the group of swimmers moved away down the pool, and was I able to start to very slowly follow then, the huge overalls acting like a drag-anchor behind me. I had previously decided to stay by the side of the pool as I swam, just in case I did need to grab it, but was forced out into the middle of the pool by everybody else having the same idea. It soon became apparent that I was making painfully slow progress, and the ever attentive PTIs were starting to make a lot of noise around me—"You need to speed up Bridgman!", "get away from the side of the pool!", "keep going—catch up with the rest Bridgman!". It was an uncomfortable feeling being the focus of attention, and rather than spurring me on, it made me tense up and swim even more awkwardly. This barrage kept up the whole time I swam along, and by the time I had struggled like a wounded turtle for two lengths, the rest of my group had done the treading water bit and had left the pool. I got to the deep end, and was instructed to tread water. As soon as I stopped swimming I went under, and didn't really know what 'treading water' was. I struggled to the surface again, to be met with what seemed like about 10 club swingers shouting 'advice' to me "just kick your legs", "lay back and fucking float", "stop swimming, take a deep breath, and just lay back—you will not sink!" All this hit me as a wave of sound, but the dedicated attention on me had completely overwhelmed me, and all I could feel were the huge overalls dragging me under. I bobbed under a couple of more times, and started taking mouthfuls of water and then coughing it out. It became clear to me that I was drowning so I started to swim for the side of the pool. At my 'giving up' there arose a great chorus of derision from the club swingers—"You fucking wimp", "where the fuck are you going?", "who told you to stop swimming?", "my fucking three year old daughter can swim better than that", and other such niceties. I was dragged over the side of the pool, and uncermoniously instructed to go and stand with the other "non-swimmers" in a miserable little bunch in the corner. Being one of the 'losers' was not a pleasant feeling, and the scorn of the club swingers made the whole thing even more painful. When the remainder of the trainees had been marched out of the area, we were addressed by the senior club swinger:

"When we started this morning I asked you twats if there were any non-swimmers here. Not one of you said you could not swim! I do not like fucking liars! Change into your sports gear and report back to me in the Gym—GO!"

Off we scampered and got changed. We knew we were in for a 'beasting' for 'lying' about not being able swimmers, and even though it was totally unfair we had accepted our fate. We returned to the gym to be put through a bunch of even more circuit training—accompanied by lots of verbal abuse to boot! Over the period of the initial training though, we were given extra swimming lessons and eventually we all managed to pass the swimming test before leaving HMS Raleigh.

The highlight of our first week was our watching the weekly "Passing Out Parade". This was where the senior class officially completed their basic training, and in so doing got the privilege of turning out in their finest uniforms in front of friends and family, and then doing a bit of drill and stuff to impress them. I must say that the look of pride on the faces of the families was something to see, but for me it just emphasized how much I was on my own in this little venture—I did not expect my family to be there when it was our turn. All in all though, the smartness of the Royal Marines band, the precision of some of the gun drill of the guard, and the shouting and stamping around of the Gunnery Instructors was very impressive, and we were enthused with the idea that in 7 weeks that would be us passing out.

The following weeks of training were a strange mixture of stress, weariness, excitement and fun. The pressure on us to continually improve the standard of our uniforms and general presentation was intense, and each week there was an ever more stringent 'Kit Muster', culminating in a set of formal kit inspections in the later weeks. We must have spent hours washing, ironing and polishing over those weeks, and certainly in the first weeks it was not uncommon for us to have our entire kit thrown out of a window by one of the instructors, as an indication that some improvements were needed! We all eventually passed the final kit inspection in week 5, and the relief was incredible—we could at last be trusted to keep ourselves smart. The exception to this of course was with sports gear, which throughout training never reached the standard required by the club swingers—we got used to doing a lot of press-ups!

Fitness training or 'fiz' became an almost daily occurrence, and after the initial shock of hard physical exercise, we got used to the circuit training and quickly achieved a good level of fitness—although we always left the fiz session wobbly legged with exhaustion. As the course progressed with outdoor assault courses and countryside treks as well as the fiz, the wear and tear on bodies began to take its toll, and it was not too long before strained ankles, dodgy knees and the occasional broken limbs started removing people from the training. These unfortunates were put in the colloquially named 'cripples' class, to be either 'back-classed', or if the injury was serious enough, perhaps even taken out of training. There was always a flash of sympathy for people suffering injury, but I am sorry to say that we were gladder that it was them and not us—The idea of doing all this again was not one we were keen to contemplate.

My Bloody Efforts

In between the kit inspections and fitness training some highlights of the training stick in the memory. Weapons training of course created huge excitement among the class, and we were not disappointed when we got our hands on the Self-Loading Rifle or 'SLR'—the weapon in use in those days. The Gunnery Staff were correctly very strict in explaining the weapon and how to use it, and by the time we actually got on to the firing range I didn't know whether to be more afraid of firing the damn thing, or of catching a boot from one of the Staff if I dared ask any questions! Firing the SLR was a shock to the system—it was a brute of a rifle and kicked like a Mule—suffice to say that it was lucky they did not need snipers in the Navy—I was a rubbish marksman. The noise the weapon made on firing was tremendous—they did not supply ear defenders in those days, and I am sure that I was concentrating more on the noise than where the bullet was going. In any case we all passed the gunnery test, and in my case I don't think I held another weapon for a good number of years after this initiation—after all, I was a Stoker not a Sailor, what did I need to learn about guns for?

Another part of the training that stays with you forever was the Military Drill part. This was where we learned to look a bit more military, to march, stand to attention, to do gun drill and so on. The Gunnery Instructors or 'GIs' were incredible people in many ways—they only spoke in clipped English, usually at very great volume, they were very upright in their posture, and they were always abrasive in their nature. 'Drill' became one of those subjects we enjoyed and hated in equal measure and we knew how the session would go on seeing which instructor we had got that day. There were a couple of them who had razor sharp tongues that could cut through you like a knife, and continually had you quaking in your boots. Others used a very clever mixture of force and humour to get the message across, roughly ribbing individuals who made mistakes, and making the whole experience serious but entertaining. When we had one of those the drill was an excellent experience, when we did not, it was torture. A common punishment for cocking up during drill was to run around the parade ground with the SLR raised above your head, until the instructor told you to stop. The thing weighed about 10lbs and it tended to focus the mind very effectively! To start with, drill was very confusing to a lot of people, and it was quite amusing to watch the poor buggers turn the wrong way, or to 'tick-tock' (swing the same arm and leg together—try it, its actually quite hard to do!) when trying to march, but over the weeks of training we became more and more proficient. It's sad for an ex-stoker to say, but there is something satisfying in being part of a squad of men doing drill all together in perfect unison, and to get a "good—well done" at any time from a GI is worth all the effort!

As the training progressed, it became apparent that some people more than others really wanted to be in the forces. In the first week there had been a fairly large number of people leaving, having realised their mistake in joining in the first place for whatever reason. After this initial exodus, the rate slowed down pretty much each new week, until finally the only ones leaving the class were those who were forced to go through injury. The most noticeable thing as the weeks progressed was how the individuals that had joined a few short weeks before had become a team. When we first started, it was very much a case of 'everybody for themselves', but the pace of training meant that we had to co-operate with each other, or suffer the consequences. We very quickly learned that we could achieve more as a team, and this of course was emphasized by the staff that would mercilessly punish the whole class for the misdemeanours of a single person—we thought this was very unfair at the time, but of course it was part of the plan to get us in team mode.

This all came together during 'Fire Fighting and Damage Control' training. This was a phase of training where we were taught basic shipboard fire fighting and how to patch up a ship that had been attached, and which had sustained damage. This was all totally new to all of us, and the fire fighting was hard going. Part of the training was to have a fire ball roll right over our heads in a compartment in the fire training area, and the way they did this was to remotely tip a bucket of water into an oil fire. The sight through the breathing apparatus visor of that roaring flame coming towards us was terrifying, and the first instinct was to run away as quickly as possible. Standing up at that point though would have been disastrous, and even then in training the discipline was sufficiently imbedded to make us stay put as we had been told. For the damage control part, we were put into a mock-up of the inside of a ship which had suffered damage, and instructed to stop flood water coming into the ship using wooden wedges, mattresses, clothing and anything else that came to hand. Teamwork in this instance was vital and we had to work together to stop ourselves drowning! The set-up was not very high tech, but with the outer doors and curtains closed, lighting turned off to leave just red 'action lighting' illuminated, and the public address system or 'broadcast' alternating between "Action Stations" and the background sounds of bombs exploding, ships weapons firing and the like, you got the feeling that although you knew it wasn't real, it was serious! All of a sudden there was an extra loud bang, and water started to spurt into the 'ship' through numerous 'shrapnel' holes. Some of the lads were instructed to pretend to be wounded, and lots of fake blood started being chucked around—the 'casualties' screaming like banshees and glad to be out of the hard work. The water was coming into the 'ship' pretty fast and we set about filling the holes—smacking soft wood wedges into the smaller ones, and rigging mattresses over the larger ones. The Staff were instructing us where to attack first, to leave the wounded and get on with saving the 'ship' and on jury rigging structures to push the mattresses against the larger holes. The water kept on rising, and the noise was incredible. Remember this was December, and the water was being taken from the River Plym—it was absolutely freezing, and as it reached waist level and above our work rate slowed as our bodies froze. The water kept pouring in despite our efforts, eventually rising to chest level (or in my case neck level!) before the exercise was halted. We came out of the 'ship' frozen and exhausted, but it gave us a very good idea of how difficult doing any kind of damage control would be if it happened for real. In my day this training was done in a stationary structure mocked-up to look like the inside of a ship, but these days trainees carry out much more realistic damage control training in computer controlled and hydraulically operated training environments which actually move around to simulate being at sea. It must be quite something.

We were rapidly approaching the end of basic training, and it felt good to be the senior class. In the last week of so, with the final kit musters, the final fitness test, the parade drill test and other major milestones completed, the staff begin to lay off us a bit, and we really started to believe we had been 'accepted' as sailors. As senior class we were given a pair of 'puttees' to wear to indicate our high status, and we could, if we wanted (and we wanted), discipline other new entrants—just to ensure they were marching correctly, not talking in the ranks and that kind of thing you understand. During the last week we still had to do a thing called a 'squad run' where as the name suggests we completed a long run (I think it was 5 miles, but could be mistaken) formed up into a squad. That meant we were running 'in step' together, and by this time in the training it was a breeze, and really quite enjoyable—the staff relaxed, and lots of banter and encouragement for each-other. As well as the run there was the 'long assault course' to complete as well, and this was a bit more serious. The run was done in teams, and of course was timed. Being young, foolish, full of ourselves from having nearly finished training, and probably stupid, we all attacked this course with a vengeance, and with visions of glory on achieving a new track record (the record at the time had been set by the PT staff—in Summer!). What we failed to factor in was the time of year—late December, and the fact that wet and icy overalls and thick mud are not conducive to fast times. Nonetheless all of our teams attacked the course with vigour, and we threw ourselves about like lunatics—not a good idea really as people were being battered silly falling off logs and missing rope nets and so on. I recall there were a lot of injuries resulting from the assault course, and even the ones who escaped unscathed had bruises for weeks afterwards. Needless to say, the record time for the course was never really under any threat from us!

Passing Out day came upon us very quickly, and after all the kit preparations in the days prior, the actual day seemed to drag like crazy with nothing more to do. Before the families arrived around lunchtime we had a bunch of lectures and presentations by staff and officers. They were all along the same lines of course—'well done', 'this is the start and not the end', 'good luck', and that kind of thing, The Commodore popped in again for a few minutes and congratulated us all on passing out, and we were told to make our families proud of us during the Passing Out Parade.

I had left home to join the Navy a couple of months before, and had not really contacted my family much during the training course. I had not invited them down to Plymouth for the Passing Out Parade, basically because I thought they would not be able to afford the train fair, and in any case I didn't think anybody was interested. Imagine my surprise then when on marching out for the final parade, I spot my Mother, her new 'boyfriend' (actually he looked far from being a 'boy'—he was a large middle aged man, with a gut which gave an indication of the rich lifestyle he enjoyed), and a couple of brothers sitting in the stands. It turned out that the Navy automatically invites relatives to these things (I found out later), and they had decided to come and have a look. After the parade we got together of course, and I must say that the look of pride from my Mother made me glad I had stuck in there. My brothers were totally excited around all the uniforms and guns, and chattered away like little chipmunks. I was introduced to Mum's new boyfriend Mick, who turned out to be a very nice jolly man who clearly loved my Mother, and more importantly made her life a bit happier. They later married, and he looked after her until his untimely death in 1996—a genuinely good man. My Mother kept repeating that she could not believe the change in me over just 2 months, and of course how smart I looked in uniform—well, a Mother would!

So, that was it then—basic naval training completed. It had been hard to start with, and quite a struggle a lot of the time, but I never really thought I would not make it. I wanted to be in the Navy, and was enjoying being part of something. On leaving HMS Raleigh I, and the other remaining Stokers were given orders to join HMS Sultan in Gosport Hampshire after leave at home to enjoy Christmas 1976, where we would be undergoing a 12 week engineering mechanic training course, known as Part II training.

Chapter 3

Suck, Squeeze, Bang, Blow!

Christmas leave came and went, and to be honest I was glad to be going back to work. Home was still a stressful place for me, and after all I had only been away for 2 months, even if it had seemed much longer at the time, so not much had changed. Mum had found a new 'fella' and was acting like a love-struck teenager, but the house was still full of shouting, fighting and general mayhem, which I just didn't need right then.

HMS Sultan was and is the Navy's Marine Engineering training school, and is a sprawling shore establishment located down in Gosport Hampshire—the other side of the river from Portsmouth Harbour. The place at one time had been some kind of airfield, as witnessed by a series of Hangars which now housed the various practical set-ups at the school. At Sultan they train naval mechanics and engineers ranging from new-entry stokers, right through to nuclear submarine engineering officers. Not surprisingly we, as the most junior class undertaking basic engineering training, were considered to be lower than a snake's arse, and were to be treated accordingly.

On gathering late Sunday night and reporting to the Regulating Office we were unceremoniously directed to collect bedding and report to the accommodation block we would be using during training. The Christmas leave stories or 'dits' came thick and fast, and everybody was excited to be at the start of our 'proper' training.

The first morning for us at our new establishment was something of a whirlwind of introductions, visits, instructions and orders. It very quickly became apparent that far from being 'old-hands', having successfully completed the basic training, at Sultan we were going to be treated very much the same as we were in Raleigh. We were required to march everywhere as a group; saluting any officers we bumped into on the way, and generally being abused by anybody above the rank of Junior Stoker as we trooped along. The basic Stoker course was the only Mechanic course required at that time to do that, and the more senior courses took great delight in ripping us up for any real or imagined misdemeanour as we marched to and from classes around the establishment "Class Leader take charge of that class!", "No talking in the ranks!", "March properly young man!" and so on were the usual cat-calls, but occasionally an officer or Senior Rate would really go to town and report us to the Gunnery Staff, resulting in extra drill instead of lunch!

We quickly noticed that a couple of other classes were required to march around like us. These were the Artificer Apprentice courses, who were strange to us in that they dressed like Senior Rates, with peaked cap and jacket etc, but who were not yet of any rate at all—just like us! The big differences of course though were that they were educated (you had to have a certain number of 'O' levels to be a "Tiff"), and if they passed all of their exams, they were more or less guaranteed a defined promotion route, ending with their reaching the rate of Chief Petty Officer at age of just 25. We instantly hated them! Our promotion was by 'Promotion Board' and in the 1970's the waiting time for selection to even Leading Stoker was really long—up to about 4 or 5 years as I recall. That potentially meant that some of us might not make Chief Stoker until our mid 30's—a lifetime away for a 16 year old! Throughout our mechanic training we were continuously reminded by our instructors that Stokers were not supposed to like 'Tiffs' (or more usually expressed as 'Fucking Tiffs!'—and followed with a theatrical spitting on to the ground!). I must say that I really never warmed to the idea of disliking people I had never even met, and throughout my naval career tended to get on just fine with pretty much everybody. Of course there were some arseholes who happened to be Tiffs, but there were plenty more who were not! In addition, there were plenty of Stokers around with pretty large chips on their shoulders, who resented the fact that Tiffs got automatic promotion—a free ride in the view of some of the Stokers—but my feelings were that the Stokers had just as much chance of bettering themselves as anyone else. There was a couple of ways Stokers could make Tiff and hence automatic promotion, which I will describe later.

That problem was too far distant to worry about as a VERY junior Stoker, and the aim right then was to get through this batch of training and to get out into the fleet.

The basic Marine Engineering Mechanics training course in those days was split into 2 groups—those with a mechanical leaning, and those more electrically minded. The way a trainee was selected for either stream was decided by the results of an engineering aptitude test consisting of written and practical elements. There was also a bit of "Hands up if you want to be mechanical", and "hands up if you want to be electrical" from the instructors who went for the 'one volunteer is worth 10 pressed men' approach. So, volunteers went first, and if the class numbers were too lopsided a few people were transferred either way—so long as there were no major disagreements, the instructors were content. As it transpired, people were moved around during training in any case, as it became apparent that some were more mechanically or electrically adept than others (the electrical training was more difficult in reality). I did not like the look of electricity and opted to be mechanically trained—to become a 'Clanky', or 'Grease-monkey', or 'Spanner-wanker', or 'Shit-shifter', or 'Steam-queen' or the many other names given to us. The guys who opted to become electricians would henceforth be universally known as 'Greenies'—the only nickname they were ever called. The name 'Greeny' came from the fact that electrical engineering officers in the old days used to have green coloured stripes between the gold ones of their rank badges—I think the mechanical officers used to have purple stripes between their gold ones—thank goodness we were not called 'Purplies!' I was now given the grand title of Junior Marine Engineering Mechanic (Mechanical) or shortened to JMEM(M). I would remain at this rate until the age of 17½, at which time I would magically lose the 'Junior' bit, and become an MEM(M) Second Class or 'MEM(M)2'. That promotion was still over a year away though!

At that time in the Royal Navy, the work horses of the fleet were the steam frigates. For the 1970s these ships were quite impressive to look at—streamlined and businesslike. They has a large central funnel and helicopter hangar and landing pad taking up most of the after end, and were equipped with a wide range of weapons, depending on their assigned role. Anti-ship frigates had a double 4.5 inch gun turret at the front;

anti-submarine frigates an IKARA torpedo launching rocket system and so on. The new class of gas turbine powered 'Type 21' and 'Type 22' frigates were just starting to make an appearance, but the 'Rothesay' and 'Leander' frigates were the mainstay of the fleet. There were even a couple of 'Tribal' class boats doing the rounds I think, but they were pretty much obsolete by the time I had completed training. With this in mind, our training revolved around what would be our first job out in the Real World, that of 'Boiler Room Stoker'. We learned about the construction and operation of the centre piece of the Boiler Room, the Y100 boiler, fuel burner gear, fuel pumps, water level control, steam pipes, connections, maintenance, and all of the associated bits and pieces that came with it. The course was quite intense, as the most mechanical thing that most of us had done previously was to tinker with cars or motorbikes. This was serious engineering, and the instructors never missed an opportunity to remind us that the Boiler Room on a frigate was potentially an incredibly dangerous place—it was hot, noisy, smelly, moved under the influence of the sea, the steam could scold you to death, a lot of the machinery could snag your clothing and kill you, the fuel could ignite and burn you to death, you could fall off a ladder, and many other ways in which you could be 'terminally challenged'. As mostly kids though, we didn't pay too much mind to that kind of nonsense, and were excited by the heavy and loud machines we could now be working on. As the training progressed we moved more from the theoretical to practical training, and were let loose on small pumps, complete motors and auxiliary machinery, and even stripping and rebuilding a diesel fire pump, which we then had to restart and get running on completion. It really gave you a sense of achievement to hear the thing start-up properly—it felt like we were starting to know about this engineering stuff!

Of course our training at Sultan was not just engineering. We were still new boys, and the naval general training as they called it continued alongside the engineering. We were required to have parade training every few days, and once a week there was the passing out parade for whichever class or classes completed that week, be they an Artificer course or Submarine Nuclear Operators Course (you could always tell when it was a submarine course—they always looked like sacks tied in the middle!). The 'fiz' continued as well, although it was much more enjoyable at Sultan, where as well as the pure circuit training we were used to from Raleigh, they started to introduced real sports—football, rugby, squash at lots of other stuff like that. I took a liking to rugby and started to play a bit, an interest that stayed for a few years—until the opponents seemed to be getting bigger, and the cuts and bruises took too long to heal between matches!

Some of the other naval general training revolved around general naval knowledge—ship construction, the different branches and ranks in the navy, leadership exercises, weapons training, and something we had been introduced to at Raleigh—'NBCD', or Nuclear, Biological and Chemical Defence. This was a system of protection against biological or chemical attack by an enemy, and for the individual consisted of a chemical protection suit (or 'Grow-bag' due to its colour and texture) which one had to wear, along with a 'Respirator' as the modern gas-mask was called. Now, in order to ensure that the Respirator worked properly, it needed to be tested, and that was done in a little stone-built room in Sultan—rather attractive known as the 'Gas-Chamber'. We had never done this before and were very concerned about it. They used tear-gas as the testing agent, and we had been given horror stories of what this stuff did to people if their mask failed to work properly. Before going in to the chamber, the instructor briefed us on what would happen, and on what to do if your respirator failed. He continued that even with a good respirator we would smell the gas, but its effects would be neutralised by the filter in the mask! On the way out of the chamber we would all be given a sniff of the gas (yeah, right!), just to convince us that our respirators were good kit, and that it was really tear gas the man was using.

So, in we trooped, gas-masks very carefully and tightly fitted. We lined the inside of the gas chamber facing inwards, the only sound being a Darth-Vader like sucking of air through hopefully good filters. The instructor ignited a tear-gas charge in the middle of the room, and a fizzing heavy mist soon formed. "Breathe normally—don't try to hold your breath!" muffled the instructor as the mist rose to head level. I took a tentative breath and instantly a metallic smell assailed me—"Oh God, the respirator is not working!", but I can still breathe, there is no burning in my eyes and throat, Phew! Around me I can hear but not see people breathing heavily, the relief apparent just by the sound, then suddenly, coughing and spluttering a shadow passes by, heading for the door "Stay calm!, get in the fresh air—do not rub your eyes!" shouts the instructor as the body crashes through the door. The instructor closes it afterwards. We stand and wait content that our masks are working. We are instructed to count from one to ten and back, just to make sure we are breathing (like we could hold our breath for 5 minutes!). Finally the instructor says "OK that's it—as you walk past me and out, I want you to take off your respirator, and tell me the name of your favourite football team". Panic! I don't have a favourite football team! Quick, I know, what's a short name for a team—should stop me breathing too much gas! As the lads start passing the instructor I hear "Portsmouth United!"—cough, splutter. "West Ham United!"—cough splutter. My turn "Leeds" I scream—the gas instantly smacks me in the face—eyes streaming, throat on fire, even my ears seem to be burning! "Wait" says the instructor grabbing my shirt, "Full name of the team!" He has obviously had this trick tried before. I take a deep breath ready to shout the name—big mistake! My lungs seem to explode with pain as the tear gas fills them. I cough, splutter, retch and try to pull away from the Petty Officer, desperate to escape the gas "Give me the full fucking name of the team!" he snarls at me, and I manage to croak "Leeds United" back to him. "That's not the full name" he says, holding me in the tear gas. Clearly I have pissed him off, and I try to concentrate on answering as the effects of the gas get worse "Leeds United Football Club!" I manage to get out and he releases me—I fly out of the gas chamber and gasp in lung-full's of fresh air. My whole face and even my hands are alive with a stinging red-raw sensation, any my eyes, nose and throat are just leaking water at an incredible rate. The instructor walks around us, directing us to pour water over our hands and faces, but not to rub our eyes, and assures us that the effects will soon pass. He is right, and within a few minutes we begin to feel better. I had taken a great lung full of the gas and was still coughing and retching over in one corner when he came over to me. "You would have been better off not to try to pull a fast one Skin ('Skin' was the nickname given to anybody under the age of about 18)—it wouldn't hurt so much then would it?" "No Staff" I coughed out "I couldn't think of a football team". "Then you are a fucking Plank aren't you!" He got no argument from me on that one.

Another delight introduced to us at Sultan was that of the 'Duty'. Clearly the armed forces are a 24—hour organisations which means that personnel are required around the clock to guard establishments, to man ships overnight when they are in harbour, and so on. HMS Sultan was no exception, and although pretty much all of the training took place during normal working hours (except simulator training and some of the weapons night exercises), the place was a huge establishment which was guarded in those days by naval personnel—i.e. us! 'Duties' are a fact of life in the Navy, and from joining HMS Sultan as a 16 year old to leaving the Navy at 42, there was not a period where I was not subject to having to do them. Duty rosters varied from 1 in 4, to about 1 in 6 or more if you were lucky, and that meant that for instance in the case of 1 in 4 you would be 'duty' one day out of every four. By being 'duty', it meant that you were required to remain at work for the entire 24 hour period of the day in question, and in the case of HMS Sultan as a Junior Stoker, it meant that you would be actually working more or less for the entire period. The duty period commenced at about 7.30 AM when those who would be duty for that day would gather (or 'Muster') in the Guard Room, to be allocated their duty station. The junior class members never got any of the cushy duties like Chief's Runner or Regulating Office Sweeper or whatever, and were always given the job of Main Gate Sentry, or in my case (probably due to my small stature which would hardly scare off a determined Cornish Pasty delivery man on the gate, let alone a Terrorist!) Security Rounds man. This entailed donning a WWII vintage infantry helmet, being given a pick-axe handle and a whistle, and then being sent out into the depths of the establishment on set 'security' rounds routes at all hours of the day or night. We despised it with a vengeance.

Following the morning muster, we would be despatched to our classes for the day. Then at about 5 pm we would all muster again at the Guard Room, which would then be our base for the night. The Guard Room had a dormitory on the top floor which we could use between rounds, but of course with all the coming and going sleep was always impossible. At our allotted time we would present ourselves to the Guard Petty Officer, be briefed, 'kitted-up' and sent on our merry way with strict orders to report back at a set time (normally up to a couple of hours later), and the warning ringing in our ears that we were 'being watched'.

Imagine the scene. I was almost 16½ years old by then, I weighed at most 8 stones dripping wet, I was wearing a red painted Second World War vintage kind of paratrooper shaped helmet—oversized and worn out by continuous abuse so that the straps did not work, resulting that every time I turned my head the bloody thing stayed still! It hurt like hell to wear it after about 5 minutes as it dug into my head, but I dare not remove it. I was carrying a pick-axe handle which made me feel a bit tougher, but I was sure that being so far away in the depths of the establishment, the whistle would not be heard—even if I got the chance to use it. It was little wonder we were known as 'Swan Vestas' as we wandered around—the red helmet nicely topping off the match sticks below!

At 'stupid-o'clock' on freezing January mornings wandering around a dark imposing former airfield, alone, small and frankly very frightened, your mind tends to play tricks with you. If you recall, the 1970s was a very active decade for the IRA, and even though they had not specifically targeted the Royal Navy we were still very wary that they might. To be honest, they missed a good opportunity, as entry to HMS Sultan in those days would have been comparatively easy—they would have had little resistance from the Swan Vestas who certainly in my case, were more worried about freezing to death than confronting an armed terrorist. Hopefully the bastards would blow up the sodding Guard Room! I wandered around in constant fear, seeing shadows moving under every tree or bush, and around every corner. The worst part was when I reported back to the Guard Room. They would all be sitting inside warm and cosy—steaming mugs of tea resting on the arms of chairs in front of the blaring TV. They would reluctantly slide open a side window a fraction—"Finished Skin? Alright, take route number 4 next—see you at 0330 then—off you go". Bastards! It was extremely exhausting as well, and usually the next day it was heavy eyelids throughout the day. Couldn't have done much for studying, but we were young and got over it pretty quickly.

HMS Sultan was the first real chance we had had as a class to get to know one-another. At HMS Raleigh life had been too hectic to take anything but a passing interest in my class-mates, but at Sultan, sitting for long hours in classrooms or working on machinery together, people's real identities started to come through. It's too long ago to remember people in detail, and as I mentioned you tended to stay with a certain group only for the period of a standard 2-year posting, but what has remained with me through the years was the diversity of the people in the class. We had come from all corners of the UK and yet managed to knit together as a team in such a relatively short time. The language difficulties could sometimes be quite intense—I could more or less understand the Scotsmen or 'Sweaty Socks' or 'Jocks', or 'PJs' (Poxy Jocks) or at least those from the Edinburgh side. We had one lad from Glasgow who was just totally unintelligible apart from the swearing, which always came through loud and clear! The Welsh contingent was not too bad, and I quite liked the accent. In addition, the Welsh were always the funniest for me—always jolly and smiling. They of course were always nicknamed 'Taff' or 'Taffy' or 'Blodwin'. The Irish were quite nice people as well, but quick to 'flash-up' and pretty much always ready for an argument or ideally, a fight. The southern Irish accent I could understand with no difficulty, but the Northern Irish one might as well of been Chinese to me—sounded very harsh. I always got on with the Irish lads, particularly since their accent and manner always seemed to attract the girls out on the town. Again it should be little surprise to learn that any Irish person normally ended up being known as 'Paddy'. We had a lot of guys from the Newcastle area in the class as well. Again their accents sounded weird to my untrained ears at the time, all elongated 'L's. As well as being 'Geordies', they were also collectively known as 'Monkey Hangers' in the Navy, and it took me years to find out the reason (which could well be a load of crap anyway!). Apparently the name came from a period when England was at War with France, and the people of Newcastle hung some monkeys they had captured, believing them to be French spies. I will believe anything so you will have to excuse me if that is nonsense! As well as the collective nicknames used for groups of people, there was a very complicated personal nickname system for individuals as well. 'Whacker' Pane, "Stirling" Moss, 'Soapy' Watson, 'Buster' Brown, 'Dinger' Bell were common, but sometimes you came across unusual and unexpected nicknames too. One of my favourites concerned a Petty Officer I came across later in life. To his face his name was 'Stu', short for Stewart, but when he was discussed in the Mess (as everybody was!) I noticed that he was being referred to as 'Pid'. I didn't click at first, but when it struck me I cried with laughter—'Stu-Pid'—brilliant! I loved that kind of inventiveness, and came across it all over the place in the Navy. People from the South West of England were always 'Jan', from Liverpool 'Scouse', and so on.

For those people without the sort of common name ripe for a usual nickname, the name you ended up with depended entirely on you really. When I was on submarines we had a junior officer that joined us who said to us "Hello Chaps, I am Lieutenant Jacobs, but you can call me Dicky in the Mess"—henceforth, and for the remainder of his 2½ years on the boat, he was called "Dicky in the Mess" by everybody from Captain to junior seaman—fatal! On another occasion, a new Chief Petty Officer with the surname Temple had a couple of cans of beer, and happened to mention that on his previous boat he had been referred to as 'Shirley'—a nickname he hated. Silly mistake from one so experienced really—guess what he was known as thereafter? In my case, for the first couple of years in the Navy and along with most of the younger guys, I was generally referred to as 'Skin'. I got my first name back on joining the Ark Royal, and thereafter was generally known as Steve, with the exception of one particular Commander who I will come to later, who insisted in calling me 'Bridgers'

The names of people were not the only abbreviations and nicknames we at this stage were trying to get a handle on and almost everything we came into contact with in the navy seemed to have a shortened name. This was even the case of the names of ranks and ratings. Several hundred years of tradition had resulted in every level of rank seeming to have about half a dozen different names—a Leading Hand could be a 'Killick', a 'Leader', or a 'Hookey', a Petty Officer might be a 'PO', a 'SPO' if he were a Stoker, and a Chief Petty Officer could be a 'Chief', a 'Mech', a 'Chief Tiff', a 'Jossman' or a 'Sparks'. It got no clearer with officers either. A Midshipman was a 'Middy', while a Sub-Lieutenant would be a 'Subby' or 'Snotty' (Yes, even the older ones that had come through the ranks!). A Lieutenant was a 'Two-Ringer' while a Lieutenant-Commander was a 'Two and a Half'. Everything above that was very much 'Sir' I might add. We had lots to learn yet, and barely a day passed without us being baffled by another new abbreviation. It didn't take too long for us to get into the naval lingo though, and we quick to be talking to each-other in what we took to be normal naval-speak—"Casting off for the NAAFI at Stand-Easy for big-eats and a bar of nutty" might mean that at our 10 am break we might visit the canteen and buy something to eat and a bar of chocolate. Oh yes, we were getting there alright!

Another first for HMS Sultan was the opportunity for us to get shore leave. In HMS Raleigh, we had had only one 'Run Ashore', and that had been a heavily chaperoned affair where we were required to wear uniform, and had to be back at camp by 10 pm or something. For me, although the uniform requirement has disappeared, and because I was below the age of 17½, I was required to be back at camp by Midnight each day. This was unsurprisingly known as 'Cinderella' leave, and to ensure compliance, the juniors were all issued with a card that had to be left with the Guard House when we left the camp, and collected on return. Although it was tempting on occasion to stay out later, the guards were very thorough on checking ID cards of people entering the camp—especially if a card had not been collected, so it was not worth the risk.

For me at that time there was little point in going out into town much. Being, and more importantly looking, below the legal drinking age meant that the joys and pitfalls of excessive alcohol consumption were still a couple of years away—in theory at least. That just left shops and cinemas as the major form of entertainment for me and the other 'Sprogs', and when we did bother to venture out, it was to catch the latest movie doing the rounds. Another factor was pay, and in those days I was earning a massive 15 pounds or so a week with which I was required to pay for my shiny new smoking habit, all the cleaning gear necessary to keep my kit spotless, all the sweeties and soft drinks necessary for a 16 year old, and spending money when I got the chance to go home for the weekend—lets face it, I had to splash the cash a bit when I was home to maintain the image of being a free-wheeling Matelot!

My Bloody Efforts

The engineering training progressed nicely against this background, and thoughts started to turn towards where we would all like to be drafted on completion of the course. We were introduced to the Drafting Preference Form for the first time, and given very intense instructions on how to complete it. We were regaled with horror stories of people that had requested a posting to say, a Mine-sweeper based in Portsmouth, and ending up in a Rosyth based Destroyer because they had failed to tick this or that box on the form. In truth, it was a very confusing form to fill-in. It asked you for preferences of ship type, ship name, shore base name and location, which was preferred other the other and so forth. We were specifically warned not to tick a small inconspicuous box entitled "Volunteer for Submarines" unless that was what we wanted, as people had been whipped away as quick as you like for ticking that particular box! I had asked specifically for a draft to the aircraft carrier HMS Ark Royal, while others opted for frigates, destroyers and even a couple for submarines. We would just have to wait and see now—the drafts would be announced at the end of the course.

By now, as we were coming to the end of our engineering training, we were fairly comfortable with naval life. To complete our engineering training, we were required to spend a weekend manning the machinery on the Harbour Training Ships. These were 2 old ships tied up in Portsmouth Harbour, both with operating machinery that was started up and used to train us and more senior classes in 'hand-on' practical work. One of the ships was a 'Daring' class destroyer of World War II vintage, with scary open-front boilers and really old and worn machinery, while the other was a relatively newer 'Tribal' class frigate, on which was fitted the kind of machinery we were more like to come into contact with. The idea was that for the weekend in question we would be the boiler and engine room crews, and would carry out the 'watches' as if we were at sea. Good idea in theory, but mechanical breakdowns on the ships meant that they could not be started—we suspected that the more senior guys didn't fancy hanging around on these hulks for the weekend and planned the failure. In any case we were released for the weekend instead of working, which is always a nice bonus!

The final week of training soon came around, and with it the usual passing-out parade. This was a much quieter affair than the HMS Raleigh one, and very few family and friends attended. Course marks were handed out, and the top couple of people became 'Specially Selected MEMs' or 'SSMEMs', who would receive accelerated advancement for their efforts. My marks were average it must be said, but at that time my main aim was to be very much anonymous, and to just ease my way through. More important was the news of our postings. There had been a few surprises, and a couple of lads had ended up on either different ships to what they had asked for, or at different home bases. In my case I had ended up in Plymouth as requested, but not on HMS Ark Royal. I was being sent to the maintenance base ship HMS Defiance, where I would be part of the Fleet Support organisation. My instructor in HMS Sultan assured me that from there I would probably be sent to a ship of some kind, as Defiance was used as a personnel reservoir. We would see.

Our basic and engineering training was now complete, and it was time to say farewell to being a trainee. In the case of HMS Sultan it was only a temporary parting however, as I would in total spend over 3 years of my naval career undertaking various levels of marine engineering training in the place. For now though, I was proud to be starting my naval career proper, as a newly qualified Junior Marine Engineering Mechanic (Mechanical) 1st Class no less.

Chapter 4

Finding the Golden Rivet and Feeding the Seacat!

Back in Guzz (Plymouth), but this time as a fully fledged, fleet-ready, qualified mechanic, I joined HMS Drake in readiness for presenting myself onboard HMS Defiance the next morning. Joining Drake had been what was to become the usual pain in the ass whenever I went to a new place—that is finding someone to log you in, finding bedding, finding the transit mess, lugging your kit around and generally being somewhere totally new. At that stage I had never even been in the Dockyard, and so did not even know where I was supposed to go, at what time, who to report to or anything.

The following morning I decided to wander into the dockyard and find HMS Defiance. As it turned-out, that was not too difficult, as when I asked somebody where the gate to the dockyard was, the reply was that I should follow everybody else, and sure enough it seemed that a whole crowd of naval ratings was heading in a single direction. I quickly tagged along, pretending for the entire world to see that this was a regular walk for me—new? No, no, not me.

As I walked into Plymouth Dockyard for the very first time, it was striking that there seemed to be thousands of dockyard workers walking through the main gate, and off to their work areas. Into this throng the navy contingent mixed, and then split away towards the Fleet Maintenance Base area—the navy manned and operated part of the dockyard. There was quite a lot of gentle rivalry and Mickey taking as the groups mingled and merged—"Alright Jack—managed to wake up this morning in time then?" "Hey Jan, don't eat too many of those oggies, or you'll end up an even fatter lazy twat!", and other such pleasantries. I was to discover that to the dockyard workers every sailor was 'Jack', while to the sailors every dockyard worker was a 'Jan Dockey'. Cornish pasties, sold at canteens throughout the dockyard were 'oggies', while the gorgeous but artery furring, heart-attack in a bun breakfast rolls containing egg, bacon and sausages which I was to become addicted to were locally known as 'train-crashes'.

All that would come later though. For now, I was wide eyed and somewhat overwhelmed at the size of the dockyard, the ships alongside the wall as I walked along with the other guys, and the great workshops, stores and massive cranes. I wondered how anybody ever knew where they were, or where anything else was in the 'yard, and how long it would take me to get used to the place. After walking for 15 minutes or so I started to see what was obviously HMS Defiance in the distance. I was pretty disappointed. She looked old, dirty and rusty, and was hardly the cutting edge of naval efficiency I had been hoping to serve on. She was a big ship, and looked something like a large civilian cargo steamer that had been painted grey—all large cranes, big funnel, square superstructure and so on. In a previous existence she had been a submarine supply ship, and was now the base for the shore naval engineers and mechanics that helped ships to complete their maintenance programmes more quickly when they were in harbour.

I followed the crowd up the gangway and on to the quarterdeck of the ship—unlike the American navy, we in those days did not salute the flag on entering or leaving a ship—we just flashed out ID cards at the Quartermaster. The other people disappeared into the bowels of the ship, but of course I had no idea of where I should be going next. Eventually the Quartermaster took pity on me:

"You a new joiner Skin?"

"Yes, Leading Hand"

"OK, report to the Regulating Office, 4-Charlie starboard"

I looked behind him. There were 2 sets of double ladders (as stairs are called in the Navy) descending into the depths of the ship. I had already noticed that the right hand set was for going down, while the left hand set was for going up—again, another navy convention. The Quartermaster had already moved on to other things, so I did not fancy disturbing him for more instructions. Right, 4 Charlie starboard—4 deck, 'C' or Charlie section, starboard or right hand side. I started off down the ladder from 1 deck. That meant I had to go down 3 ladders to hit deck 4, then go forward towards the bow of the ship until I got to Charlie section, and the office should be on the right hand side somewhere. It was easy to find—there was a long queue of people outside it also waiting to join the ship, or base, or whatever it was.

As was to become usual, the joining routine was a pain in the butt. To join HMS Defiance, I along with the other new faces, ranging from junior stokers to chief Tiffs were presented with a joining card. This card had on it written a list of places we were to visit to be issued with tools, equipment, kit, bedding, pay details, instructions and the myriad other domestic details of our new posting. In order to collect all the stamps a new boy had to wander around the dockyard and HMS Drake the accommodation centre—both places we had never been to before, visiting offices and depots tucked away here and there. The grief of it was that many of the places to be visited had defined 'new joiners' opening hours, which of course a person would not know until he got there! As it was I was able to follow a couple of the more experienced guys around, and got most of the boxes stamped in quite short order. This 'joining routine' was something that had to be completed whenever a person was posted from a ship to a shore establishment (and on a ship of course, but there was no distance involved there), and as technology improved over the years it never failed to amaze me that we still had to traipse around from pillar to post getting the damned card stamped.

Having officially joined the Fleet Maintenance Base (or 'FMB') I was assigned to join one of the 'Units'. Their base of operations was one of the workshops on the old ship, and I was instructed to wait in the workshop until the team returned from wherever they were currently working.

I got bored waiting after half an hour or so, and decided to take the opportunity to have a look around the old girl that was HMS Defiance. The ship by this time had been tied up alongside for a good number of years, and was something of a stop-gap while a brand new maintenance base was being constructed on shore. She was a big old ship, and as I began wandering along wide passageways, and into and out of large workshops I became confused about where I was. The structure and fittings in the ship were as old as the hills, with massive lathes, pillar drills and bending machines which seemed to hearken from a long distant past. That didn't stop the machinery being used though, and everywhere I visited there were mechanics and technicians bending, bashing, drilling and welding away, making or fixing some piece of equipment. After an hour or so I decided that I had better get back to the unit workshop—which by now was easier said than done! I was somewhere deep inside the bowels of the ship, and had absolutely no idea how to return to where I came from. The way it was supposed to work was that every location had an alpha-numerical code to identify it, but on this ship there seemed to be none. I figured that upwards was always a good bet, and so leapt up every stairway (or ladder as they were known) that I saw, intending to emerge on the upper deck t some point. It was a good theory I thought, but I had omitted to factor in the superstructure, and before long I was standing about 5 decks above the upper deck, looking down at the water of the river Plym about 80 feet below. I could see the quarterdeck far off in the distance, and started making my way down again towards it. By the time the Quartermaster had re-directed me to the workshop ("That way—Dickhead!"), I had been away for well over an hour, and as I walked in to what was now a well populated unit workshop, a large, bearded angry looking man wearing heavy and very dirty overalls turned his head towards me over his steaming cup of (presumably) tea.

"You Bridgman Skin?" He asked—quite nicely I thought

"Yes Sir" I replied

"Two things, one, don't call me Sir—I work for a living, its Charge Chief to you" he said, "and two, WHERE THE FUCK HAVE YOU BEEN!?" Conversation stopped and what felt to the back of my neck like 100 pairs of eyes turned towards the source of this outburst.

"I—I was having a look around the ship Sir" I mumbled and stumbled.

"Don't call me Sir again" sniggers from the audience "when you are told to wait somewhere, you bloody well wait, understood?"

"Yes Chief"

"Charge Chief! Are you simple or what?" More sniggers from behind. Suddenly he softened slightly.

"We need to know where you are at all times—if you just go wandering off whenever you fancy it how are we supposed to know where you are if there is a fire or something? Go and see LMEM Standish, and he will sort you out. Welcome to the unit".

"Yes Charge Chief". I turned towards the laughing faces behind me. I must have been an impressive shade of bright red in the face, and wished that the deck would open up and swallow me. A group of 5 or 6 in the corner were gesticulating to me to join them, and sheepishly I wandered over.

"Come on Kid, grab a cup of tea from the fanny" said the one I took to be LMEM Standish—he had a hook on his arm in any case, as I was handed a plastic mug. I poured the tea and gingerly sat on the edge of the group, the audience attention had by now moved on to other entertainment.

"While you're at it!" said another of the group and thrust his empty mug towards me—quickly followed by 5 others! "No sugar for me", "Cheers Skin", "Good move!" I collected the mugs and poured away, handing them back to their owners.

"Welcome to the unit" The LMEM said "That was Charge Chief Wallace who just bollocked you—don't piss him off again. What's your name?"

"JMEM Bridgman, LMEM"—Howls of laughter from the gang "Did you hear that—LMEM!" I was embarrassed again, and was starting to get a serious inferiority complex.

"No, what's your first name, or nickname. What do you want to be called? Relax, you're not in training now ok?" he said wiping away laughter tears.

"Its Steve" I said, expecting another tirade.

"Right, that's better. Welcome Steve. I'm Stanny, when there is no brass around, LMEM Standish when we need to be formal—just listen to the lads. Around me here there's Dave (a nod from the corner), Knocker ("Alright Skin?"), Charlie (another nod), Pete and Eric. We form the technical support section, and what that means is that we are basically tool bag carriers for the Tiffs. We go on jobs with them and carry their gear around because they are too bloody idle to lift a bloody finger! (Nods and groans from the support). When we are on a job we are also their 'Gophers'—go for this, go for that ok?"

"Yes . . . Stanny" It was hard to get that one out—I had never addressed a senior person (well, senior to me anyway) by first name before.

"Good, just stick with the group for now, and once we are back at the job I will tell you what to do".

The men turned back to their conversations, tea and cigarettes, leaving me to stare around and to try to get a grip on proceedings. No-one was unfriendly, but equally, no-one was too matey either. This again would be a pattern throughout my career—it took a long time to fit into an established group, and generally everybody took a 'wait and see' attitude to new boys. The way to fit in was to shut up, pay attention, and not speak until and unless spoken to. The first impressions were very important, and an established group generally started to accept a new boy after a few days, so long a he was not 'gobby' (talkative), opinionated, stupid (although that could be handled so long as it was 'good' stupid—i.e. somebody to take the piss out of!), a 'know-it-all' or a 'wannabe' (somebody volunteering for everything in order to advance). Thankfully I think I was none of those things, and was pretty well accepted in every new team I joined—the notable exception being when I worked for a short while in the Galley of HMS Seahawk, a naval air station which used to be in Portland. I hated the work, the Chefs (as the Cooks insisted on being called), the drudgery of preparing food, and all that went with it, and so rebelled. Luckily I was only there for a few weeks, but it was a taste of how a group of people can make another person's life a complete misery. Of course being 19 and calling the Cooks "Slop artists" and "School meal preparation specialists" didn't really win me too many friends I suppose.

After a fairly short while, the group started to stand up and get ready to move. I followed suit, and we all started moving off the ship and into the dockyard, heading for our place of work. It seemed a bit odd to me that we would have to leave the ship we would be working on to get a cup of tea during our break (or 'stand-easy' as the break was known), and then again for lunch, and again for the afternoon break. Seemed like a waste of time to me, but being young and new and enthusiastic, I had yet to realise that the idea was that the normal practise at that time, for both naval and civilian dockyard workers, was to avoid work at all costs! Time spent trudging through the yard, or collecting spares from workshops on the other side of the yard, or on visiting the dentist even, was better than getting your hands dirty. I came to understand the reason for that in pretty short order. For the Tiffs it was a different matter—they had real jobs to do, like overhauling engines, or fixing steam valves, or assembling new equipment, but for the Stokers life was tedious. Our job description was one of assisting the Tiffs in their work, but in reality we were used onboard ships as extra 'harbour crew', and often ended up cleaning or painting or generally being dog's bodies. This was particularly the case for us Junior Stokers of course, as the better (for 'better' read cushier) jobs would invariably be nicked by the more experienced and older men. In the first year of my naval life I became expert in the sacred art of 'wetting the tea'—not too weak, let it stew for 10 minutes, plenty of sugar—don't forget to serve the Chief first! In addition, I became very good at disappearing for a couple of hours looking for a spare part or tool for somebody—wandering around the dockyard looking at the ships was much more interesting than cleaning out the inside of a boiler on a frigate somewhere.

That was all in the distance as in the meantime, on this my first morning as a real Stoker in the fleet, life was getting pretty interesting. We were working on one of the Leander Class frigates tied up along the wall, and this would be my first visit to one of these work horses. They looked pretty sleek close up, with wide flared bows, a squat middle section and square stern. They were at that time fairly well known as the aggressors of the Cod War of the early 1970s, and that was really where I remembered their shape from. Once onboard the ship I was allocated to one of the Petty officer Tiffs and off we went down the Boiler Room. He about 15 stones carrying nothing but his beret, while I, all of 8 stones had to carry/drag his bloody great tool box down the ladder!

The Boiler Room on a Leander Class frigate is not a huge space (although probably the largest open space on the ship). It is of course packed with machinery, not just boilers, of which there were 2 Y100 types fitted, but also the 'auxiliary' machinery supporting the boilers, producing electricity, and all sorts of peripheral things. In addition there are endless lengths of pipe work of various sizes carrying steam, water, oil, fuel and pressurised air, as well as electrical cabling running in all directions. This was not the clean and ordered space I remembered from the harbour training ships, but now, during the middle of a maintenance period the place was almost unrecognisable as a Boiler Room. Pipes were gaping open, machinery covers removed, cabling hanging down in bunches, and missing deck plates made the place dangerous and confusing, and I was glad to be following the PO. We would be working behind one of the boilers on some leaking pipe work, and my job was to pass in the tools as the man crammed himself into a ridiculously small space to fix the leaking joint. It was a bit like being a nurse in an Operating Theatre—"5/16 open ended", slap as the spanner hits the hand, "flat screwdriver" slap! Easy but boring for me.

For the next couple of months my daily routine followed much the same pattern—turn up at Defiance in the morning, make tea, wander off to the ship of the day, take a stand-easy at 10 AM, make tea, back to the ship, lunch—make tea after lunch, back to work, afternoon break, make tea, end work. Even though I spent a lot of time making tea, I was also learning more about the machinery and tools of my trade. The Tiffs liked it when one of the Stokers asked them to explain how a machinery or equipment worked, and for me it was free instruction. I was getting a reputation of not being a whinger, and therefore tended to end of with the more likeable Tiffs—it made my life easier, but also gave me a bit of 'protection' against being hammered for the crap jobs all the time. In the evenings, still being well below the age of being legally able to drink alcohol, I spent most of my time flopped in front of the TV in one of the communal TV rooms in the barrack block—another pain in the butt, as the system was that there was one TV room for (in those days) each major TV station (basically BBC and ITV), so you had to more from one room to another to catch your favourite programmes! Every 4 weeks or so we would have to attend "Divisions" on the parade ground, and go through the rigmoral of being inspected, marching, saluting and all the other pleasant drill stuff. All in all though, so long as we kept a low profile, and turned up for work on time in clean uniform, we were pretty much left to our own devices.

Of course being new, I was always being targeted for pranks. I had to go to the store for a 'long weight' (long wait get it?), a "2lb percussion instrument", and an "adjustable screwdriver", and once during a discussion (contrived for my benefit) concerning ships companies having pets onboard (banned in the 1970s I understand), I was told that the ship we were working on at the time secretly had a cat onboard as their pet, which they could only allow out once the ship was at sea, so that it would not be confiscated in harbour. I was all ears and took in every word, wondering at the daring-do of the whiley sailors! The Chief was in on the scam and had got one of the ships own Petty Officers involved too. He sat with us during the discussion, and on the spur of the moment (yeah right!) asked me if I wanted to feed the Seacat, as it was called. Would I? Up I jump, and ask where the thing is. Follow me says the Petty Officer—we'll grab the food on the way. So, up ladders and down passages and up more ladders we go, and finally end up on top of the Hangar. What are we doing here I ask, and the Petty Officer points to the missile launcher a few feet away—the name of the missile system—yes you guessed it—it was called SeaCat!! The long journey up to the Hangar had allowed the rest of the group to be waiting to spring out and take great delight in my confusion—bastards!!

The only other prank I fell hook, line and sinker for was the one involving the 'Golden Rivet'. Once again I had been set up nicely, and during a tea break one of the Chiefs innocently asked me if I had seen the golden rivet on the old ship we were working on. Everybody managed very well to keep straight faces as I replied that no; I had not seen a golden rivet—what was that then? The Chief explained that when a ship was built, the first rivet that was put into it was always made of pure gold—it was a superstition thing he went on. It seemed a bit odd to me (duh!) that gold would be used to join 2 plates together—surely it would not be strong enough? Oh no, the Chief said, one rivet amongst all those others would not make a difference. Rather sensibly I thought, I pointed out that ships these days were all welded anyway. Yes, lamented the Chief, it was a shame that the old traditions were dying, and that's why it was important for me to see the golden rivet while there was a chance to. Where is it I asked, Oh, you'll normally find it on the hull in the Boiler Room of the ship, of course you'll have to scrape a bit of paint off the heads of the rivets to find the right one—they paint the golden rivet the same as the others so no-one will be tempted to drill it out for the gold see? Yeah, makes sense.

Off I trot to the boiler room, and in no time at all I am deep in the bilge with a screwdriver, scraping paint off one and then another, looking for the tell-tail gold colour. The Boiler Room is a noisy place at the best of times and I do not notice as a crowd slowly gathers around me, until I glance up and see the smiling faces staring down. Oh shit!!

Thankfully I reacted well to these jokes and pranks, and was soon accepted as one of the boys in the unit. Life for me at that time was pretty good—plenty of laughing and joking, and a fairly easy job to do. I spent the next couple of months in the unit, learning probably more in that time than I had throughout the whole of the training at Sultan. All in all it was a happy time for me, but I was very keen to get onboard a ship and be part of a ship's company. The chance at last came when the Ark Royal got back from her latest trip.

CHAPTER 5

The 'Ark Royal'—Boiler Front Stoker in 'Lazy-Y'

I was called to the Regulating Office on the Defiance during April 1977, and informed that I would be joining the Ark Royal when she returned to port in May. I was as pleased as punch and asked whether I could serve in the same unit as my brother John. I was told that it was unlikely that I would be allowed to do that, as navy policy was supposedly that 2 brothers should not even be on the same ship, let alone the same working place onboard the ship. I waited impatiently for the next couple of weeks to pass, and on the day of the ship arriving in port, begged my boss to allow me to watch the ship coming alongside. He knew how keen I was and let me go early, so I could be on the jetty near the ship as she came in. There were literally hundreds of people waiting on the jetty—families of the ships' company, and I managed to find a place behind this throng from where I could see down to the turn in the river from where the great ship would come.

The quiet hum of the crowd suddenly grew in volume as word was spread that the Ark was on its way. Looking down the river Plym, the arrival of the ship was announced by a flotilla of small craft turning up the river towards us, seemingly being chased by some huge monolithic slab of steel moving serenely forward. Emerging from the shelter of the turn in the river, the Ark Royal, flag ship of the entire British Royal Navy, seemed to grow and grow and grow before our eyes. First emerged the huge overhanging bow, several stories high and with massive anchors rust streaked and weather beaten. This was followed by the unending flat flight deck, empty of aircraft which had flown off prior to the ship entering harbour, but now lined at even intervals with sailors in their No.1 uniforms, looking at this distance like tiny toy figures against the massiveness of the ship. In the centre of the flight deck the 5 storey high island superstructure came into view, topped with a great turning radar structure, and with brightly coloured signal flags cracking briskly in the strong wind. At this point the ship was sideways on to us, and looked truly awesome. At the front and rear of the long flight deck flag poles had been raised, and from the front pole was flying a Union Jack, whilst the naval ensign was raised at the rear pole. These flags must have been about the size of a tennis court each, as even from where we were standing they appeared truly massive. As the ship was pulled around the turn in the river and started to make headway towards her berth, she came head-on towards us. Not only was she very long, but head-on we could see the breadth of the ship—she seemed to be almost too wide for the river, and with the overhang of the flight deck she towered above every other vessel in the harbour. This was the first time I had seen the ship close up, and I must have stood there open mouthed in wonder that I would soon be joining her. I stayed long enough to watch the ship tying up alongside—even more impressive in size and complexity as she got closer and closer to me, until I was starting to get looks from passing officers and senior rates probably wondering what I was doing there, and decided to make an exit—I would join the Ark tomorrow!!

I was at the gangway bright and early next morning, gazing up at my new home and workplace combined. My brother was unaware at that stage that I would be joining the ship, and I had not been able to contact him to give him the news either—I was very much on my own for now, as the bulk of the ship's company had disappeared on leave.

Making my way up the steep gangway, I alighted onto the part the weather deck where the officer of the day and the quartermaster were stationed. On smaller ships this area would normally only be manned by one Able Seaman and a runner, but of course on this major warship the entrance was manned by an officer, a Chief and several other ratings. Joining instructions in hand, I approached one of the seamen and asked where the Regulating Office was, and was pointed along the way, I think heading towards the bows of the ship. Luckily the Regulating Office was on the same level as the deck I was currently on, so getting lost would not be an option this time.

I had a couple of routes available in getting to the Reg. Office I was informed. I could either walk through the lower hangar, or follow the exposed deck around until I came to the right place. The second seemed the best option as it should avoid me getting lost in the labyrinth of the ship, and in any case I wouldn't know how to find my way out of an aircraft hangar at this stage, so off I went into the ship.

The path I was following was one of the main passageways around the ship I was to discover in the coming weeks and months, off which a person could find spurs into different areas of the ship. In my case I followed the passageway all the way along one side of the ship, then into a cross-passage and out again on the opposite side, and hence onto the mirror image passageway along the other side of the ship, with entrances to offices and workshops and such dotted at intervals along the passage. I wandered along checking the nameplates on the doors as I passed and alternately looking down a long way to the water below and up at the great overhang of the flight deck blocking the view of the sky way above my head. Eventually I came to a door signposted as the Regulating Office, checked that I was properly dressed—a pre-requisite to any visit to the Reg. Office, knocked and went in. There was already a queue of new joiners formed, awaiting the attentions of the duty Regulator (or "Crusher")—never a pleasant experience.

Crushers were (and probably still are) strange people. They are effectively military policemen, there to uphold the rules and regulations of the service, and that's fine. The problem with them was that they very often took a bit too much pleasure for my liking in instilling discipline in us poor buggers, and they usually took every opportunity to pick us up for something, anything, whenever we were unfortunate enough to be around them. Case in point was when joining or leaving a vessel, when we were fair game for a lot of abuse. Strangely enough, I never saw any of them checking our dress or length of hair in a boiler room at 3am!

This visit was no different, and following a bollocking for long hair and dirty shoes (what-ever!) I was handed the obligatory joining card, and ordered to report back at the end of the week with the thing fully stamped. I was further ordered to report to the Chief Stoker of "Y Unit"—no name, no location but I didn't mind. I was just glad to get out of the Regulating Office as quickly as possible.

I wandered around again for a short while, trying to look as though I knew where I was going, but soon realised that I was completely lost in the depths of the beast. Spotting a few men in overalls I asked for directions to the Chief Stoker of Y Unit's office, and thankfully, rather than just telling me, one of them led me down through more passageways, workshops, machinery spaces and offices until eventually, with me having absolutely no idea where I was, we reached a small workshop/office space—the Chief Stoker's office. The Chief Stoker clearly was not that interested in small talk with new Junior Stokers, told me unceremoniously that I would be working on the boiler front, and in short order phoned somewhere else in the ship. Pretty soon a Stoker appeared and motioned for me to follow him. We followed another totally confusing path through the bowels of the ship, heading the Stoker told me for the Y Unit mess deck. Up and down ladders, along passageways and cross-passages, passing myriad compartments, workshops, messes with brightly painted doors, we finally reached a door sporting a large painted Stokers badge with the words "Lazy Y" emblazoned across the bottom of the painted propeller—this was my new home, "Y" Unit mess deck. In we went, and with many of the ship's company away on leave, the mess was pretty quiet.

The mess deck was in this case aptly named. In front of me on entering the mess was a space taking up almost the entire width of the ship, and of an equal length, making the space more or less square. This space was in turn split into 4 distinct areas surrounded in each case by stacks of 3 bunks, one on top of another, leaving a space in the middle of each square of bunks, known rather obviously as the "Mess Square", where there were sited tables and chairs. In between each square of bunk beds (or "racks") were corridors, again lined on each side by yet more bunks. Alongside each stack of bunks were located personal lockers, each about the size of a single kitchen cupboard, where a person was expected to stow all of his service and personal gear while at sea. Leading off one end of the mess were the toilets and showers for use by the mess members, commonly known as the "Heads". The mess, as with every other mess onboard was run by the "Leading Hand of the Mess", normally a senior Killick, and his job was to ensure order in the mess, and to make sure it was cleaned regularly and so on by allocating various jobs to the people in the mess (known as "Mess Cooks"). Of course, as with all aspects of naval life there was a pecking order in the mess, and once again me being a Junior Stoker meant that in this particular food chain I would be going pretty hungry! The best bunks were taken by the leading hands and more senior Stokers, who tended to close certain areas of the mess off using curtains to form "Gulches", thereby effectively banning us lesser mortals from entering (except for cleaning of course). The worst bunks were those surrounding the "Mess Square", simply because the mess square was where mess members socialised, usually drinking beer and playing cards or "Uckers" (a form of draughts) until all hours of the day or night rendering sleep impossible for the poor unfortunates located there—guess where I would be sleeping (or rather not sleeping) then! At that time there were no TVs in the messes, but in later years the blaring TV would become the bane of the lives of the people unlucky enough to end up with a rack there—not all innovations made people's lives better. As people joined and left the ship, the junior mess members could progress up the food chain, slowly acquiring a better bunk, or locker, or cleaning station, maybe even making it into a gulch—I never did!

Having been given my bearings I was sent away for the rest of the day so that I could move my gear from HMS Drake to the ship. It is incredible the amount of "stuff" a person accumulates, and in no time my kit bag and suitcase were crammed full. I had to repack on a couple of occasions, mindful of my tiny locker in the mess, and busily weeding through everything I owned in a mad effort to go as light as possible. It took me 2 journeys to the dockyard to get my gear onboard, but eventually everything was in my new mess, ready to be stowed away. There was no way that one suitcase and one kit bag full of uniforms, civilian clothes and everything else I owned was going to fit in my new locker, but that was not a problem as I found out that the unit had a little store room they used to keep excess luggage—thank goodness for that! Deciding what to keep handy and what to store away took some doing though, and it would take the next few weeks for me to finally end up with the things I needed close to hand. As the day drew to a close I found myself trying to make my bed in the middle of the mess square, surrounded by noisy, drinking and boisterous men, ribbing the new boy and keeping him awake long into the morning—this would become routine.

Reporting back to the Chief Stoker's office the next day, I was given the next couple of days to get my joining routine completed and returned to the Reg. Office. It was a good move really as I couldn't do much until that was out of the way, and it also gave me the ideal opportunity to have a good look around the ship, as the stamps I needed were spread all over the place. I was advised to go to a place called "HQ1" first, as there would be detailed deck by deck maps of the ship there, which would be very useful to me in getting around. It was good advice—HQ1 was the damage control headquarters of the ship (in fact HQ1 was the title given to the damage control headquarters of every warship), way down in the bowels and well protected from enemy action, it was where damage control parties would get their instructions in time of conflict. Finding the place was an adventure in itself, but once there it was worth it. On the walls (bulkheads) were huge plan diagrams of each of the 11 decks, and 5 superstructure decks of the entire ship, compartments neatly labelled and accesses clearly marked—this was ideal. Unfortunately in those days photocopiers did not exist, but there were some miniature diagrams that I could use to help me find my way around. I got talking to a couple of the guys manning HQ1, and they advised that for now I concentrate on my work and living areas—again very good advice. They made good sense in telling me not to bother with the island, as this was generally "officer country" and best avoided. Also many of the aviation areas were "out of bounds" to the non-aviation community onboard, and I was to avoid anywhere with "OOB" stencilled on the entrance (of which there were many). So armed, I set off on a self-guided tour of the ship, using my miniature diagrams for guidance. This little trip merely served to remind me of how massive this thing was, but after a couple of hours I felt I was starting to get a glimmer of understanding of how the decks, passageways, compartments etc were at least identified and marked, and was starting to identify some of the main travel ways used by the ship's company. I had noticed that many of the broadcasts over the ship's PA system called either individuals or groups to muster at a place called the "canteen flat"—clearly one of the main meeting points on board, and so I set about finding the place. Eventually my search led me to an area near the front of the ship—quite near to the Reg. Office I had visited yesterday, where I discovered a large open plan area leading off one of the passageways. This was the Canteen Flat, so named after the large NAAFI canteen/shop located there. It was a big space, and as well as the canteen, in this same area could be found the entrance to the Sickbay (including dentist), access to both external passages, heads, and access to the forecastle area of the ship. I would spend quite a lot of time here in the coming months, either mustering as part of the ship's duty watch of the day, or waiting for the start of a particular training operation for instance.

Having got an idea of the overall layout of the ship, I decided that the next phase of my search should be in the area of where I would be working, and so I set off to explore some machinery spaces. On the way back towards the rear of the ship I came across one of the armoured entrances to the aircraft hangars onboard. The doors were very heavy, but were not marked with "OOB" so I took a chance and entered the upper hangar. There were no aircraft onboard at this time with the result that with the hangar empty I could get an impression of the size of the place—it was huge, and there was another hangar underneath this one! With aircraft lifts located at both ends of the hangar, the space was simply stunning to my inexperienced eyes, making me wonder once again how this incredible machine even floated! I was looking forward to seeing all of the aircraft onboard later.

Returning towards the machinery spaces, I managed to find my way back to the office of the Chief Stoker. I had noticed that as I descended deeper into the ship, that the doorways and hatches were becoming thicker and heavier. I was now in the "armoured belt" area of the ship, where the ships hull was thickly armour plated and double-bottomed to protect against torpedo strikes, and where all of the deck opening (hatches and doors) were heavy duty watertight fittings, in many cases eight inches or more thick, and operated by hydraulics or with winches. These doors and hatches were often left closed, and access through them was normally by the use of small "kidney hatches" about 18" in diameter—no problem for a skinny runt like me, but interesting for some of the beer bellies around. I spent the rest of the day finding the entrances to the machinery spaces that I would be working—namely the "Y" unit boiler room and engine room.

My Bloody Efforts

HMS Ark Royal had a displaced weight of around 58,000 tons with aircraft and weapons onboard. That was quite a bit of weight to push through the water at a top speed of about 27 knots (I don't know if she ever achieved that though). In order to move the ship she was fitted with 4 huge propellers, and attached to the propeller shaft turning each propeller was a gearbox the size of a house, in turn attached to very large High Pressure and Low Pressure steam turbines, driven by superheated steam produced in fuel fire boilers, known as "Admiralty Three-Drum" boilers. The steam having passed through turbines was then cooled in seawater condensers beneath the turbines, converting once again to water which was then pumped back into the boilers once more—known as a "closed loop" system. In addition of course there were masses of supporting or "auxiliary" machinery—steam turbine electrical generators, steam and electrically driven pumps for water, fuel, oil and so on, as well as miles of pipe work and electrical cabling to carry steam, water, pressurised air, electricity and the myriad other fluids from one place to another between the machinery spaces and throughout the ship.

Each of these combinations of machinery from boiler to propeller was known as a "unit". As was traditional naval nonclamenture, those parts of a ship grouped together forward were numbered "A" onwards, while those aft went from "Y" backwards (got it?). So in the case of the machinery units, they were known as 'A' Unit, 'B' Unit, 'X' Unit and 'Y' Unit. 'A' Unit was the overall control one, where the on-watch Engineering officer was stationed, and where the Commander (E) positioned himself for action stations and the like. 'A' Unit would dispense instructions to the others constantly, and was where all engineering reports were directed. In addition, the steam for the aircraft catapults came from 'A' boiler room, so all in all the 'A' Unit guys considered themselves to be a bit of a cut above.

In reality most people were thankful not to be in 'A' Unit. For us minions that would have been a nightmare, as that unit was the one that had to be constantly tip top clean for visits by dignitaries and the high and mighty. We lesser units had a slightly easier life in that respect, but for me it would be hard to start with to notice any difference.

My first look around 'Y' boiler room was quite a muted affair. A lot of the ship's company were away on leave at the time, and in the boiler room were just a few workers tweaking this or that, but no real heavy engineering going on. Entry to the boiler room was through a large square armoured hatch, and then down a set of steep steps to reach the 'plates' in front of the massive boilers. There were 2 boilers in each boiler room standing side by side, with an operating position between the two, from where the Boiler Room Stoker Petty Officer managed the rate of steam production using a whole series of valve hand wheels leading off variously via extended spindles to fuel pumps and airflow regulators. On the front of each of the enormous boilers were 6 'sprayers'—6 foot long fuel injectors with nozzles on the end, connected by flexible hoses to the fuel supply rail, and used to spray the heavy furnace fuel oil into the boilers in a pattern designed to make it burn fully and efficiently. The sprayers could be slid in and out of the furnace and turned on and off as determined by the steam requirement from the engine room. This was a manual job known as 'punching sprayers' and was the job of the 'Boiler Front Stoker'—i.e. me!

For now the boiler room was cold and quiet, but even like that it was an awe inspiring machinery space, and I could imagine the noise, smell, leaking steam pipes, the heat and the fear already. Looking around at all the gauges, hand wheels, valves, machines, pipes and equipment made me wonder if I would ever be able to master it, as though I had a choice in the matter. It would be a case of listen, look and learn, and then hope I was good enough to do the job.

As it was, I would have little opportunity to get to grips with any machinery for a while. For the next couple of weeks my main task in life seemed to be to clean just about every single piece of brass work I could find in the boiler room. Believe me, in the boiler room of a 1950s built warship there is a lot of brass work, and I got pretty familiar with all of it! This was to be a feature of my time in the boiler and engine rooms of the Ark Royal, but I didn't mind really—there was something satisfying in getting the stuff shiny. The 'Brasso' was always nearby whether we were at sea or in harbour, and literally every spare minute was spent polishing some bit of pipe work or machinery.

Training in earnest for me started on the guys returning from their leave. I was attached to one of the boiler front stokers as his 'dog'. He became my 'Sea-Daddy' and would be responsible for teaching me the ropes on the job. All I had to do was basically follow him everywhere, and do whatever he told me to! Easier said than done—the guy was like a whippet and got around the ship with such speed and unflinching accuracy that it left me dizzy. He had a confidence and sureness that I only dreamed of at that stage, and particularly in the boiler room, seemed to know more than I ever would on and around the boiler front. He carefully explained to me how the sprayers worked, how the fuel was pre-heated by steam before entering the boiler, the hand signals we would get from the Boiler Room Stoker Petty Officer to instruct us to put a sprayer in or take one out (it would be too noisy for verbal instructions), and a whole plethora of other instructions, processes and procedures. He warned me not to piss the Stoker PO off, as they were not a very forgiving breed.

I was to find this out for myself shortly afterwards. My 'Sea-Daddy' told me to take a piece of equipment called a Lucas Torch Ignitor down to the boiler room from the workshop. The ignitor was a piece of equipment used to light boilers, and was a kind of flame thrower thing consisting of a tank of fuel connected by hose to a nozzle affair, which was connected to a fitting on the front of the boiler. When a handle on the tank was wound, a spark was produced at the nozzle which was used to light an emerging jet of fuel, hence starting up the first sprayer when lighting a boiler. The ignitor weighed about 40 lbs, which for me was quite a lot of weight. In order to get it to the boiler front I had to clamber down two ladders, one hand holding the ignitor, the other gripping the ladder hand rail. As I was coming down the second ladder the ignitor slipped from my grasp and crashed to the deck plates below, narrowly missing 2 Stoker Petty Officers standing there. I jumped after the ignitor and stood ready to apologise to the POs. Without a single word, the first walked up to me and punched me straight in the mouth, turned back to his companion and continued his conversation as though he had just swatted a fly. I lay on the deck plates head spinning until I was helped up and taken away to the workshop where my bloody nose and mouth could be seen to. The incident was not questioned or mentioned again, and was considered a fair response to my mistake by all. I was advised that in future anything heavy should be lowered down ladders on a rope—lesson learned!

Boiler Front Stoker in 'Lazy Y' – HMS Ark Royal 1977

Over the next days and weeks, as the ship prepared for her next deployment, I was to learn that the life of a lowly Junior Stoker was pretty rough. We were of course everybody's work horse, and were routinely treated like dirt. That to me though was pretty much expected. What I was not expecting was the physical violence around at that time. Correction usually consisted of a slap around the head or a punch on the arm—mine after a couple of weeks were black and blue! I suppose it had the effect of concentrating the mind, and certainly one tended to pay more attention to the speaker when there was the inherent threat of a smack around the head if you missed something!

When I had reached what was considered a decent level of knowledge to attempt to become a boiler front Stoker, I was put through a trial run with the boilers shut down. A Leading Hand stood where the Petty Officer would in reality, and shouted different instructions to which I had to react—"One in" (and accompanying hand signal), "One out" (hand movement) and so on. It was hard work even without the boiler operating, but at least I understood the orders, and knew where the different parts of the machinery were located—I was ready!

While I had been busy living in my little world down in the machinery spaces, the rest of the ship was starting to shake herself loose from the dockside. The build-up was palpable in the ship herself—small vibrations through the deck as some piece of long silent machinery was started up, huge containers of food and stores being brought up the gangways and stowed away, groups of ratings being ordered here and there to prepare for departure and so on. It was a strange time for me—part of the ship's company but feeling as though I was watching the whole thing as a spectator. In reality of course I did not really have a clue as to what was happening and just rode along with the flow.

It was at this time that I had the chance to get together with my brother John onboard. By this time he was a Leading Stoker, working in the aircraft fuelling department up in the dizzy heights of the flight deck somewhere. He lived up in the flight deck stokers or "Badgers" mess, located at 2EZ1 (2 deck, E section, starboard outboard), otherwise known as "Two Easy One" mess. The flight deck stokers were known as Badgers due to the colour of the surcoats they wore on the flight deck. On the flight deck each specialisation wore different coloured surcoats so that they could easily be identified—aircraft handlers wore yellow, weapons guys wore red, aircraft engineers brown and so on. The flight deck stokers wore a white surcoat with a large black vertical stripe down the front and back—hence the "Badger" title. I managed to find the mess easy enough—and that's where the trouble started!

My Bloody Efforts

There was a tradition (unknown to me at the time) that should you be invited to another mess, then each member of that mess was honour bound to buy you a drink. You were then honour bound to drink that drink! In Two Easy One mess there were about 35 people, but of course some would be on-watch or otherwise working, so that in my case there were maybe 15 people there. Before I could say "Hi John, long time no see" I had 15 cans of beer in front of me. I of course thanked everybody but pointed out that I was under age—no problem, if you don't tell anybody I won't—he he.

I had never really talked to John before. He had always kind of just been there—the brother away in the Navy, pops home for the odd week here and there, but that's about it. Now as I sat next to him in his mess, he seemed very grown up, assured and the experienced older brother. He asked me how I was getting on down in the units, which mess I was in and other domestic stuff. At the time I still had a bit of bruising from the punch in the nose from the Stoker Petty Officer, which of course John noticed, but I told him it had been an accident. He probably didn't believe me, and told me to tell him if I was being bullied. I assured him I was not, and that I would be sure to tell him if anything like that happened.

As we sat there chatting, it became apparent to me how much John was respected in the mess. Lots of his mess mates came over and introduced themselves, having a laugh and joke with John (or "JB" as he was known to everyone). They also had a few good words for me, and it was nice to be able to have a giggle outside my normal circle. The beer was doing the job after only a couple of cans, and I asked John to help me drink them. He assured me that if I failed to drink them I would not be welcome to come back! Thankfully he relented and put the ones I could not drink away somewhere "for next time"—sometime soon as far as I was concerned.

I had only drunk a couple of cans of beer but felt pretty pissed. This was my first venture into alcohol, and with it being about 2pm and a normal working day, I was worried about leaving the mess and then being caught by a Crusher for being drunk onboard. In the end, sad as it was, John escorted me back to my own mess, probably irritated at having such a wuss as a brother! Two Easy One would become my second home while I was working in the machinery units, and eventually I would become one of the flight deck stokers. John would become my confessor and protector, and then my Boss, but before that I would spend long months in the heavy machinery spaces of the Navy's flagship.

My first trip to sea in 1977 was incredible in so many ways. Whenever the Ark sailed from or entered a harbour there was of course the fanfare attached. When the ship sailed from Devonport the decks were lined with sailors dressed in their finest uniforms, a band was playing on the dockside, and families were waving goodbye to their loved ones, as had become the usual practice for the great ship. I saw none of this. Prior to sailing I had been up all night watching for the first time the lighting of the boilers, the raising of steam pressure, and then the one by one starting of all of the massive machinery in the boiler and engine room of "Y" unit, culminating in the testing of the main engines about an hour before sailing. The same thing had been happening in the other three machinery units, so that by the time "Hands to Harbour Stations" closely followed in the machinery spaces by "Obey Telegraphs" had been ordered, the entire ship had been transformed from a cold piece of floating steel into almost a live thing—decks quietly trembling, smells, noise and movement everywhere. It was scary and tremendously exciting all at one time.

I stood in the background of the boiler room as the first telegraph orders jingled onto the repeater in front of the Boiler Room Petty Officer. Immediately he signalled for another fuel sprayer to be inserted into each boiler in anticipation of the drop in steam pressure caused by the steam being admitted to the engines next door. Both boiler front stokers smoothly and efficiently punched the sprayers in, and then opened the fuel valves, peering through the tiny viewing window in each boiler to ensure the extra fuel had ignited. As each valve was opened a scary "whuff" emanated from the boiler as the extra fuel ignited, and each boiler jumped against its mountings with the force of the ignition. As the telegraph orders jangled from "Slow Ahead" to "Slow Astern", then "Half Ahead", and as the Revolution Orders changed, the Boiler Front Stoker Petty Officer and the stokers got into a frenzied rhythm—smoothly increasing or decreasing air and fuel flows using the hand wheels, or punching sprayers in and out of the boilers, all in an effort to maintain a steady steam pressure for the engines and electrical turbine generators. In the meantime the Leading Stoker on the level above carefully monitored the water level in the boilers, adjusting as necessary to maintained "half a glass" throughout the manoeuvres—no one wanted to have a dry boiler—there were horror stories of boilers running out of water and melting! It was impressive to watch, until suddenly the telegraph and revolution orders stabilised, indicating that the ship was out of harbour and on a steady course. Over the broadcast came "Fall out from Harbour Stations" and the Petty Officer turned to me and made the sign for tea—back to normal then.

So, that was it. There I was at sea in the largest ship of the proudest Navy in the World. As my watch finished I had my first chance to have a look at the sea from the upper works of the ship. I made my way to the flight deck for a better view—as we were allowed to do until the aircraft joined us the next day—and instantly regretted the decision. It was bitterly cold standing 100 feet or more above sea level, and the wind was absolutely wicked, cutting through my thin overalls like a knife. I stayed for a few brief minutes though just to enjoy the sensation of being underway for the first time. It was incredible to me still that we could push this thing through the water, but the smoke and steam coming from the massive funnel high above my head was proof that we could. Not surprisingly there was very little movement of the ship under the influence of the swell, merely a slow laborious roll, hardly noticeable really.

Now that we were at sea my life became subject to a strict routine of work, study, cleaning, eating and sleeping. The Stokers in the units worked a shift or "watch" system known as "1 in 3 West Country". It was a system that rotated over a 3 day period, and meant that a person on that system only actually got a full night's sleep once every 3 days. It went like this for one cycle:

Over 3 days the watches would go: day one—Forenoon Watch (0800-1200), then the 2nd Dog Watch (1800-2000), then the Morning Watch (0400-0800). Day two—1st Dog Watch (1600-1800), then the Middle Watch (0001-0400). Day three—Afternoon Watch (1200-1600), then the First Watch (2000-0001), and then back to the Forenoon Watch on the fourth day. These were the periods actually spent in the Boiler Room, but in between these there were other working periods:

Following the Forenoon, we would be required to work during the 1st Dog Watch (1600-1800) on cleaning duties (either machinery or in the mess). After the Morning watch we had to do Mess Cooks, that is cleaning the mess until 1000. After the 1st Dog we had engineering training—we were required to pass a certain number of auxiliary machinery examinations for certain pay increments and promotion, so in actuality it was quite a lot of time awake. In addition to these hours, we were of course at the bottom of the heap in the mess, and would always be called on to do some extra bathrooms and heads cleaning, or making tea for the Killicks and "Three-Badgemen"—the experienced old hands. In between all of this was to be added the "whole ship" exercises and evolutions including fire-fighting drills, damage control and so on, which although they did not always involve us directly required us to be up and about.

I found this watch keeping system totally exhausting. While we were on watch we were constantly on the move, and each watch had its own particular form of torture waiting for us. The worst for me was the middle watch, when we were required to "blow soot". This involved climbing up between the boilers and then opening a series of steam valves to blast steam on to the inside of the boiler uptakes and funnel, to remove the build up of soot deposits accumulating there throughout the day. The temperature in the boiler room was excessive at the best of times, but up between the boilers it was even hotter. The steam valves were large, heavy and invariably very stiff to operate, as the grease always melted off them, and added to that the stench of sulphur from the soot being blasted off was enough to make me gag. Soot blowing always wiped me out, and I would come down from between the boilers soaked in sweat and shaking from the physical effort. Not a few times did I vomit (hidden away from the Stoker PO) from the shear strain of the exercise, and I learned to loathe the whole process. During other watches we had to clean the sprayer nozzles, involving taking the 6 foot oil sprayers to bits and cleaning the nozzles at the end. For such large bits of equipment, the nozzles themselves were quite fiddly, and oily hands made them hard to control. We dared not drop one though, as quick as a flash the Petty Officer would have you up to your knees in bilge water looking for the damn thing. Most of the other watch routines revolved around cleaning various bits of machinery, polishing brass pipes and gauges or scrubbing deck plates, of which there were lots. All in all life at sea for me at the beginning was just good old plain hard work.

My first few days at sea then were a real eye-opener. Perhaps I had previously had some idealised vision of looking steely jawed into the distance, singing jaunty sea-shanties and catching the eye of the pretty girls in my sailors uniform. The reality was very far removed from that! I was constantly tired, used as a cleaner, tea-maker, greaser and oiler and not much else, constantly verbally and even physically abused, hot, sweaty and dirty, and working in a noisy, highly dangerous and utterly confusing world of the boiler room, where patience with new boys who didn't learn fast enough was thin. Time and familiarity though tended to blunt the initial trauma, and once I had a few cycles of watch keeping under my belt, and my body had gotten a bit more used to the strange sleeping pattern, the work started to feel a bit easier.

This, my first experience at sea was actually quite an important one. With the ship completing a mini refit, we sailed from Plymouth to carry out some post refit sea-trials. On completion of this, our next operation was to be acting as flag ship for the Queen's Silver Jubilee Fleet Review. The date was 28th June 1977, and I had been in the Royal Navy a total of just 8 months.

The Royal Fleet Review was a pretty grand affair—well, to anybody above the rank of Petty Officer anyway. For us junior ranks it was a complete ball-ache! The cleaning work load on the ship for us was pretty high at the best of times, but in preparation for the Queen's visit the standards went sky-high. We spend hours and days scrubbing, painting and polishing everything that didn't move, and saluting everything that did! We were pretty sure that the Queen was unlikely to be paying us a visit in Y Boiler Room, but they still had us painting the lagging white just in case. On a visit to one of the Hangars I saw the aircraft mechanics buffing the steel Hangar floor to a lovely shine—and they were not too happy with greasy stokers walking all over it either!

On the day of the Fleet Review my biggest job was to keep as low a profile as possible. That was not difficult as everywhere above about 5 deck was crawling with Crushers stopping us lower deck scum from getting anywhere near the important people. That was fine with me; it meant we would be left alone down below! I was not involved with the lining of the flight deck and the cheering bit as the Royal Yacht sailed past, so could just keep out of the way. My abiding memory of the day though was coming off the morning watch at 8 am, climbing up from the boiler room and looking out of one of the scuttles to see more or less the entire British Royal Navy fleet spread in 2 long lines in front of me, with the Ark at the head of the first line. Ships like the Hermes, Tiger, Blake, and the Commando landing ships looked large and aggressive in the early morning light, and one could not but feel proud to be part of this imposing presence.

The remainder of the Fleet Review for me was pretty much a non-event. I spent the entire day either in the mess or on-watch, and mostly listened to the progress of the day through the public address announcements coming over the "tannoy". "Ark Royal Ha!", "Stand at Ease", "Three cheers for Her Majesty Queen Elizabeth the Second—Hip, Hip Hip Hooray!" and so on. We were obviously not permitted on the upper deck or on the flight deck, and ended up watching some of the thing on the TV. I was hoping to get to see the Queen in real life but unfortunately it was not to be. She did come onboard in the evening for some dinner party, but strangely I was not invited.

The following day we did a sail past involving 62 ships as a farewell gesture to the retiring Admiral of the Fleet (I think it was). Again I was able to witness some of this from the vantage point of a scuttle nearby to the Boiler Room, and was again impressed by this show of maritime force. On completion of the sail past we set off towards Plymouth to carry out some deck landing training and exercises—up to now there had been no aircraft onboard, but that was about to change.

Over the next couple of days we steamed around just outside Plymouth carrying out flight deck landing practices with a couple of each of the type of aircraft we would be carrying. Down below in the Boiler Room I was becoming more familiar with the machinery and routines, but to add to my workload I had by now been enrolled in the "On Job Training or OJT" programme. For me this was a programme of completing 8 Auxiliary Machinery Certificates (or AMCs), which involved learning about 8 separate pieces or systems of support machinery including Main Steering Gear, Turbo Generators, Diesel Generators, Motor Boats and such like. In theory this was a good thing, because in order to be promoted a Stoker had to have passed all of the AMCs. For me though at 16¾, I couldn't even be promoted to Stoker 1st Class until I was 18, so the extra work seemed unnecessary and unwelcome. The OJT Stoker Petty Officer in charge was a horrible jock bastard, who appeared to take great pleasure in waking me up after a night watch so that I could go and look at a bloody diesel engine being started or something equally "interesting". With perfect hindsight I should have just got stuck in and finished the AMCs as quickly as possible, but because I resented it, the training dragged on and on—for about the next 6 or 8 months in all, so no wonder the Jock got a bit miffed with me.

I didn't get to see the aircraft trials, as we were all so busy doing our own drills onboard. We practised fire fighting, damage control and machinery breakdown drills almost continuously in preparation for the work-up that would be coming after summer leave, before we sailed off for the autumn deployment to the Mediterranean. The couple of days between Portsmouth and Plymouth soon flew by, and as we entered Plymouth Sound, this time it was me standing up on the flight deck in my best uniform. The view from the deck was a different one from where I was watching last time—it was bloody cold standing up that high in a sea breeze!

In no time we were back alongside the wall in Plymouth, and off on Summer Leave for a couple of weeks. When we returned off leave this time, it was a return to preparations for a work-up followed by exercises and deployment to the Med—my first foreign trip (although Portsmouth counted as far as I was concerned).

Following the success of the programme "Sailor" on the TV, the Rod steward record "Sailing" had become somewhat popular. In ay case, it was announced that the BBC wanted to make the record as a single, using the ship's company for vocals! It was said that Rod steward himself would be coming onboard for the recording—remember in those days he was a top flight artist. It was all very exciting, and on the day in question we were all mustered in the Hangar, where a band had been set up, along with a bunch of microphones surrounding us. The BBC producer got up and told us what they wanted to happen, and great hilarity was had with taking the piss out of the poor chap, who happened to be somewhat effeminate. Eventually though we settled down (the arrival of the Fleet Joss on the scene had something to do with that I suspect), and rattled out a shaky version of the record. Afterwards it was announced to us that Rod Steward could not make it, but had sent us a load of singles as presents. Quick as a flash people were signing the record covers in the name of Rod Steward with the intention of giving them away later on. It was a good fun morning. We later heard that the record got to something like number 60 in the charts of something.

After a week of taking on stores and final checks of machinery, we were off again, sailing out into Plymouth Sound and then turning right and making for Scotland. The intention was to do a week of work-up before setting off for sunnier climes. All the way up the western coast of the UK we did more machinery and whole ship drills, and soon fell into a routine of watch keeping, drills, cleaning, sleeping and eating. It was hard work but interesting to see the whole ship coming together as a team. In all honesty, my action station was down in some grotty little flat in the bowels of the ship, where I was supposed to react to any emergency by telling whoever was on the end of my telephone line the problem. Where I was though was pretty far from the beaten track so usually I wasn't bothered by anybody, and so could pretty much just relax and read a good book! I was very careful to keep a good eye on the ladder, and to never fall asleep—that would be asking for trouble.

The next highlight on the agenda for me was witnessing the fixed and rotary wing (helicopters to you and me) aircraft returning to the ship. The helicopters came first. The Ark carried a number of Sea King helicopters operated by 824 Squadron onboard, some used for Search and Rescue, and I think some used for hunting submarines. Up on the flight deck island was a viewing platform where we were able to watch flight deck operations, and I got the opportunity of watching it all from there. The helicopters approached the ship in line astern, flew alongside the flight deck, and then simply travelled sideways to land on the deck. Having landed, and in no time at all, the rotor blades on all but one of the helicopters were folded back over the body of the machines, the tail rotor stocks were swung around to wards the front of the aircraft, they were rolled to one of the aircraft lifts and taken down to the Hangar to leave the flight deck clear.

The helicopters had been impressive—large, noisy and full of movement, but what came next was incredible. After the arrival of the helicopters, and following their transfer to the Hangars, the flight deck once again became a sea of movement as people wearing different coloured surcoats moved around, tending to flight deck tractors, or fuel hoses or trolleys carrying this or that around. The flight deck broadcasts was blaring instructions and teams of men walked along the whole width of the deck, looking for loose equipment or debris (later I would come to know this activity as a FOD—Foreign Object Damage hunt) that might get sucked into an engine of one of the aircraft and damage it.

As the time of the arrival of the aircraft came nearer, the flight deck slowly cleared of people until the only ones left were the Yellow surcoats (aircraft handlers). One by one they pulled out, inspected for damage and then reset the 5 heavy arrestor cables—2 inch thick steel hawser used to snag the aircraft arrestor hook when plane landed on deck. Finally they raised the massive aircraft arrestor net on its booms. This was a net stretching for the whole width of the flight deck, and was used as a last resort to snag a plane that for some reason could not use its hook. It looked pretty flimsy to me, and I hoped it would not be required any time soon.

It was announced that the aircraft would be arriving soon, and that before landing they would be carrying out some "touch and go" practice landings. Small dots started appearing in the distant sky, and within what seemed like seconds the scream of jet engines got louder and louder. The Buccaneers of 809 Squadron had arrived. They streaked past the ship at very low altitude, disappearing upwards in a straight climb, they peeling off to form a line astern formation in preparation for landing. The remaining helicopter took off from the flight deck and took up station alongside the ship, hovering there with a swimmer at the open door, ready to leap to the rescue of the crew of any aircraft involved in a landing accident. I noticed also that one of the ship's escorting frigates took up station directly behind us, again to offer immediate assistance in the event of an aircraft having difficulties and ending up in the sea.

By now the first of the Buccaneers was making its approach. With landing lights blazing, nose high and engines constantly adjusting power to achieve the correct glide-slope angle, it was an impressive sight. To my inexperienced eyes the aircraft looked much too big to land on this (relatively) tiny deck, but it came on regardless, and within seconds smacked hard onto the end of the flight deck. The engines went straight to full power, and the aircraft rolled past the viewing platform, already with nose rising towards the sky once more on take-off. The whole process had taken just seconds, but I was left with ringing ears and a sense of wonder at the violence with which the aircraft had struck the deck. It seemed incredible to me that the aircraft had not been damaged by the impact, but I later found out that they had all been fitted with strengthened undercarriage because of the increased stress expected when landing on aircraft carriers. One by one the aircraft lined up and smacked onto the deck for a practice landing—some clearly more confident than others, hitting hard and then blasting away again, or floating down and hitting further along the runway before racing away again.

After this practice, the time had come for the real landings. This time on approach, the arrestor hook fitted to the rear of each aircraft was lowered in preparation for being snagged by the arrestor wires stretched across the rear of the flight deck. The first aircraft again lined up, and rushed down onto the middle of the 5 arrestor wires. On landing the pilot would push the engines to full power in preparation for a "go-around", of course not knowing if the hook had snagged until he felt the aircraft being dragged to a stop. In this case the hook snagged correctly and the massive arrestor wires and gear pulled the heavy aircraft from maybe a hundred knots to a full stop in the space of about 120 feet. As the engines spooled down, the aircraft gently rolled backwards. The arrestor wire was released from the hook and was rewound into its housing, whipping dangerously across the deck as it went, until it was lined up once more alongside the remaining wires. At the same time an aircraft Marshaller jumped out in front of the landed Buccaneer and started giving the pilot taxiing instructions, directing him to a parking area at the front of the flight deck. The engines revved up again and the aircraft moved off to the parking area, wings cleverly folding in on themselves as it went! From hitting the deck to being clear of the runway had taken about 2 minutes—it was very slick. The remainder of the squadron followed their leader in, and safely landed on deck, some catching the first arrestor wire and other the last. The episode gave me a lot of respect for the pilots—they had to be either seriously brave or seriously nuts to land on the Ark!

Some time later the F4 Phantoms of 892 Squadron arrived over the ship. These were the fast fighters carried onboard the Ark, and were the thoroughbreds of their day. It was fair to say that by the late 1970s they were probably reaching the end of their effective operational life, but were still very impressive machines! They looked sleek and menacing, and the noise as they screamed past on afterburner was phenomenal. Having flown past the ship they in turn lined up and landed without any fuss, pilots leaping out of the aircraft and striding confidently away into the island. The final aircraft to arrive and land onboard were the 4 strange looking Gannet aircraft of 849 Squadron. These were radar carrying propeller driven planes, and were strange in that they actually had 2 propellers in line at the front of the aircraft, and compared to the jet-engine Buccaneers and Phantoms looked very old fashioned and slow. Unfortunately I was unable to see them landing on this occasion but would have lots of chances to later.

The week at sea flew by, and soon enough it was time for my first foreign "run-ashore" (Scotland—pretty much a different planet let alone country!). We anchored off a place called Leigh in Scotland, which in itself was a quiet little place, but which for us was a gateway to the delights of Edinburgh. We were there for about 5 days and all had a chance to get a look around the old city. Edinburgh castle remains in my memory as a highlight of the visit. All in all, with me still being under age for drinking the run-ashore was a pretty quiet one and we were soon raising the anchor and setting off again, this time to my first real foreign run-ashore—Hamburg in (what was then) West Germany.

As always between visits, the time at sea was spent exercising the ship. For the stokers this was carried out at varying levels of participation, from very basic machinery breakdown drills, right up to whole ship "Action Stations" or "Emergency Stations". It became fairly routine in most cases, and was considered by all as a large pain in the ass! This was due mostly to the fact that all of the exercises encroached into valuable sleeping time, a resource always in very short supply—particularly for the junior stokers!

Prior to entering harbour in Hamburg, the older guys had promised to take out the juniors to show them the "Reeperbaun", a renowned sex industry area of the city. This they did, and boy was it an eye-opener for us! Some of the lads went with some of the prostitutes (some for their first sexual experience), but I was much too shy for that kind of thing. I must say I was faintly repulsed by the whole "sex on a plate" thing going on there—some of the "ladies" looked as though they were train crash survivors, and even the younger (and fitter!) ones looked hard as nails, as I am sure they had to be. No, this was way too commercial for me. I had a chance to have a look around the city a bit more later, but of course with the language barrier it was difficult to travel around there.

The remainder of my first deployment went along in much the same vein. On this trip after Hamburg, we visited Gibraltar, Malta and Naples, with a couple of large exercises with foreign navies in between. In those days it was always good to visit Gibraltar (I was to go there about 40 times through my career), as in order to get an extra allowance called "Local

Overseas Allowance" or "LOA", the ship first had to go there. Once "Gib" had been visited, the ship's company received LOA for the remainder of the deployment. We were always happy to see the Rock!

Life onboard for me was becoming ever more difficult. It was fair to say that I was not a big lad, and I was finding the rate of work too heavy in the Boiler Room. The constant heavy workload was making me a physical wreck, and I was just constantly knackered—never seeming to have enough sleep to recuperate did not help matters. In the mess, the three-badgemen were making mine, and the other junior's lives a misery—constantly on our backs to clean this or that, or to wet the tea for them at all hours of the day. For me the crunch came when I was awoken one afternoon having just had a couple of hour's sleep, to make tea for the old men. Enough was enough, and basically I told the guy ordering me (he was the same rank as me—just an old bastard who could not be arsed to seek advancement) to fuck off and make his own tea. I made the mistake of doing this from my bunk bed or "rack", and within seconds I had been thrown out of the bed and was on the deck having my face punched. The guy was pretty irate and had to be pulled off me by some of the others, but in the few seconds he had managed to blacken one eye and split my lip for me. I made the tea.

On my next visit to my Brother's mess, he of course asked me what happened to my face. I lamely tried to tell him that I had walked into a post or some such bollocks, but then broke down and admitted to him what had happened. He calmly asked me the name of the person who had attacked me, but then said no more on the subject. I had become friendly with quite a few of the guys in the Badger's Mess and many of them expressed their outrage at the state of my face. Life went on as normal for the next few days until coming off watch early one morning I bumped into the 3-badgeman who had attacked me. As he walked past me I was shocked to see that his face now bore the signs of being punched—black eyes, bruises and thick lips. I thought no more of it—thinking that he had obviously gotten into another fight with somebody his own size, but on visiting the Badger's Mess I was solemnly told that the guy would not be bothering me again. I was glad that the bastard had gotten his just deserts, but not happy to have "big Brother" protecting me, and told John as much. He just nodded. Secretly I was delighted to have a friend in need, and it was nice to know help was there if I needed it.

The fact that I was struggling had not gone unnoticed in other places either. The Chief Stoker called me into his office and asked how I was getting on. I of course replied that everything was fine, but he was not to be persuaded and was adamant that I tell him who had punched me. I refused, and thought I was going to get another smack in the face for that too! Eventually he calmed down and told me that I was being moved to the Engine Room—his thinking being that I was fighting with somebody from the Boiler Room. Either way, it did me a favour as life in the Engine Room was much more tolerable.

Moving from the Boiler Room to the Engine Room on the Ark Royal introduced me to a whole new set of machinery. As with everything on the Ark, the engines and gearboxes were massive. The engines consisted of separate HP and LP turbines sets, with huge steam condensers slung beneath. To drive the ship forward and backwards steam from the Boiler room was admitted into the turbines through great big throttle valves, with hand wheels as big a wild-west wagon wheels. When the ship was manoeuvring, the engine-room chief, and the engine room petty officer would each man one of the throttle wheels, and there would follow a demented dance as they whirled the great valves open and closed in response to the tinkling telegraph orders from the bridge. Life for me in the Engine Room of 'Y' Unit was massively different to being in the Boiler Room. For one thing it was much cooler in the engine room, so I didn't feel like I was sweating to death during every watch. Also, the engine rooms were run by Artificers and Mechanicians rather than Stokers. I seemed to have a lot more affinity with them than with the "rougher" Stokers. The "Tiffs" and "Mechs" were much less aggressive (in most cases) than the Stokers, and critically, were always happy to explain how a piece of machinery or system worked—I was much happier learning rather than just doing. I felt that I flourished in my new role, and before long I had been given what was considered the privilege of becoming a "Main Gearbox Watch keeper". This involved looking after the house-sized gearbox attached to the main engines, and was the only engineering position solely manned by a lowly Stoker—normally single watch keeping positions were the territory of Leading Stokers. I was much chuffed with this, and was incredibly diligent in making sure the logs were filled in, grease points greased, oil wiped up and so on. I must have spent hours polishing the gauge lines, so that the pipe work was sparkling in that gear room.

It was at about this time that I was taught a very good lesson regarding trust and alcohol. This one evening I was waiting to start the Middle (Midnight—4am) watch, when my Brother called me up to visit his Mess. So up I went, and as usual cans of beer appeared like magic. I tried to refuse, telling them that no, I couldn't because I had the middle tonight. Nonsense, a couple of cans won't hurt. So we chatted for a while, me sipping one, then two, then three then four cans of strong beer. I was pissed. I went dizzily back to my Mess and changed clumsily into my overalls, and off I went to the engine room. On arrival, the Chief looked at me and knew right away that I was drunk—I could see it in his face. He was a good man and said nothing to me, just told me to get on with something. For the remainder of the watch he kept me very busy, but always in his sight, making sure I could not damage myself or anything. By 2 am I was feeling pretty unwell and wanted to go to bed. By 3 am I was desperately watching the clock and willing the minute hand to spin faster. At five minutes to 4am my replacement turned up and I hastily handed over and set off up the ladder out of the engine room. "Steve, wait there" called the Chief as I reached the top of the ladder and stepped out into the deck passageway above the engine room. Eventually the Chief came up the ladder.

"Steve. I know you were drinking last evening, and that you came on watch pissed. You have now got 2 options—I can "troop" you and you will be in the hands of the Crushers for punishment, or you can take my punishment. It's up to you".

"But Chief—I wasn't drinking"

"I am trying to do you a favour here sunshine—you do not come on watch pissed—ever!! You have 2 seconds to decide. The Crushers or me?"

"Sorry Chief. It won't happen again—I'll take your punishment".

"Right. Go below and grab a paint brush and a tin of white paint. You will stay here and paint the engine room hatch. You are not to leave until the Chief on watch is satisfied with the paint job—got it?"

"Yes Chief"

"OK. Good night. Take it as a lesson. You have spoiled your copybook tonight young man. DO NOT let it happen again" With that he turned on his heels and walked off.

I turned and looked at the hatch behind me. When I said I had come up the ladder, what I meant was that "ladder" was the collective name for any set of stairs or steps on a ship. The ladder to the engine room was actually a set of double width stairs, up to a hatch the size of a small barn door. The hatch was armoured, meaning that it was about 8 inches thick, and lowered by the use of hydraulics. Groaning I returned to the engine room, to be armed with a 2-inch paintbrush, can of white paint, brush, cloth and bucket of water. I had to brush the hatch to remove any dust, then wash it (making the tea for the engine room crew while waiting for it to dry), and then paint the bloody thing. By 6am I had painted about a quarter of the hatch, and was feeling very rough indeed. The hangover was hitting me really hard, and by 8am, and having just finished the job, I was ready for bed. Although at the time it did not feel like the Chief had done me any favours at all, his disappointment and punishment stayed with me for the remainder of my naval career. In all that time (and with plenty of opportunity) I never once went on watch drunk again.

The next few months went by fairly routinely. I was enjoying the responsibility of having 'my own' watch keeping space, and I was becoming more used to both the high workloads, and the banter in the Mess. I was getting into the training as well and finally feeling I was moving onwards and upwards. Life onboard the Ark Royal getting much more pleasant, and I was even starting to take an interest in the places the ship was visiting. The highlight of this period was a visit to the ship by the Queen Mother at which the oldest and youngest members of the Ship's departments would be

My Bloody Efforts

presented to her. It so happened that I was the youngest in the propulsion department around at the time, and was chosen to meet the Lady. I got dressed in my best uniform, and wandered up to the upper hangar as instructed. Once there I was met by a whole bunch of Crushers, who of course never missed an opportunity to rip us up for something—'dirty shoes', or long hair or whatever. In due course we were lined up oldest to youngest by departments, and then called to attention. The Queen Mother was then led along the lines, stopping here and there to chat to somebody or other. As she progressed along the line, there walked behind the line of sailors, opposite the Lady as she walked, the Fleet Master at Arms—big, menacing, ominous. As the Queen Mother got nearer the apprehension increased—I could physically feel the presence of the Fleet Joss behind me now, his laser-like eyes cutting through me and everyone else in the line. The Queen Mother approached, and then Oh no, she's stopping in front of me! Panic starts to grip me as she beams at me and extends her hand. Suddenly I feel a breath on the back of my neck—"Squeeze her hand too hard young man, and I will squeeze your fucking head!" whispers the Fleet Joss in my ear. Camera flashes blind me as I VERY gently take the Queen Mother's outstretched hand. I am conscious of the hawk-eyed stares of officers with more brass on their arms than I had ever seen in my life. The Queen Mother asks me how long I have been in the Navy and onboard the ship, and where I am from. I am not sure if I actually replied or not, and in an instant she and the entourage has moved on to the next victim. I take a deep breath to steady the shakes that seem to have gripped me. In a short while the presentation has finished and we are dismissed—as usual we are only needed for the publicity photos and stuff, while the finger food and drinkies are reserved for the important people. Later on I was called to the photographic section and given a photo of the occasion as a souvenir. The picture shows the Queen Mother beaming at the chap next to me in the line taken from just beside me—and very clearly shows my nose and one eye. I can tell it's me though.

The Ark Royal was an old ship by any stretch of the imagination. Because of that, and also I think because of cost implications of operating the thing, it was decreed somewhere that she was to be scrapped. Her last voyage would be a cracking one though, and would last for three quarters of 1978. During the Ark's last trip we would be visiting a lot of Europe, and be nipping over to the United States as well—very much another first for me. Another improvement as I saw it at the time as well was that I was notified that I would be getting transferred to another job within the ship—working on the flight deck fuelling system with my Brother John. This was a total shock to me, but a pleasant one. I still do not know to this day how John managed to wangle that move, but it was one I was very grateful for. In no time I had moved up into 2EZ1 mess just under the flight deck and was getting ready to take on my new role.

We sailed from Devonport on the Ark Royal's last voyage in early April of 1978—band playing, flags waving and the full bells and whistles this time. My new job was very different from being in the Boiler and Engine Rooms. As part of the flight deck stokers department, or "Badgers" my role was twofold. During each 4 hour shift (or "watch"), I would spend 2 hours checking on the many remote aircraft air conditioning machines spread around the ship. These machines were used to cool the aircraft electronic machinery when it was being tested in the Hangars—they blew cool air through trunking to plug-in socket outlets in each Hangar. The actual checks on the machines took just a few minutes, but they were spread far and wide around the ship, and most of my time was spent walking from one to the next. It was good to be moving about the ship though. For the

My Bloody Efforts

second 2 hours of the watch I was required to operate and monitor the aircraft fuel (known as "Avcat") pumps and distribution system, from the huge storage tanks in the bowels of the ship, to the refuelling points spread around the flight deck. Two hours was the maximum staying time in the Avcat pump room due to the fumes given off by the fuel, which tended to make you feel sick after a while. It was a good job and I enjoyed it a lot, even though the fuel fumes tended to give me a screaming headache. Also of course there was no smoking while on watch which was a pain. I soon settled into the new job, and enjoyed having John as my Boss, even though in reality I didn't see him much as I was either out on 'rounds' or in the pump room.

Life in my new Mess was a major improvement too. The lads for one thing were as a group quite a bit older than down in Y-Unit, and as a result were more mature. Here I was not expected to make the tea all the time and the cleaning duties were fairly spread between everybody. Of course the Killick of the Mess was still the top man, but he did not need to keep telling everybody their duties—they just got on with it. The Mess was a happier place too, with lots of laughing and joking—and plenty of piss-taking into the bargain. I still remember this period as one of the happiest in my naval career.

On the career front, I was now 17½ years old and therefore no longer a "junior". This happy event resulted in my first promotion in the Navy—from Junior Marine Engineering Mechanic 1st Class (more commonly known as Junior Stoker 1st Class), to Marine Engineering Mechanic 2nd Class (or Stoker 2nd Class). There was no pay rise involved, but a greater benefit to me was that I no longer had to be back onboard the ship by midnight (Cinderella leave), and could stay out all night if

I fancied—just in time for the whole crop of ship visits coming up on the Ark's final deployment! My bubble was burst though then the lads took great pleasure in telling me that in America the drinking age varied between states from 21 to 25 years!

With my promotion safely in the bag, I now wanted more! As we sailed away into the Atlantic I decided to get serious in studying for the exams I needed to pass to be promoted to Stoker 1st Class (and the associated pay rise). My new job was a great opportunity for studying due to the fact that when I was in the Avcat pump room all I had to do was watch some gauges and report certain parameters, leaving plenty of room for reading on watch. Luckily for me the bosses were happy for people to study on watch, so long as they did their job properly. It was not long before I had cracked the four basic exams I needed, and having got the studying bug I soon managed to finish another 4 or 5 other tests that would come in useful later on. Before embarking on this path I should have checked the conditions needed for the next promotion though, as I discovered that I could go no further until I reached the age of 18½—another year away! Nonetheless, it was now just awaiting game for me, which meant nobody bothered me about exams for the whole of the last trip,

The last farewell of the Ark Royal was a long one, lasting from April until December 1978. For me personally it was an incredible experience. I felt much more settled both in the Navy and onboard the ship and this was going to be my opportunity to see the World, experience the differences, and to truly embrace the naval life.

Our first port of call on that trip, following a short 2-week passage across the Atlantic, was a place called Roosevelt Roads in Puerto Rico. It was a huge naval base with every available facility you could think of—in fact I don't think I even left the base! It made Devonport look like a small fishing village by comparison and the NAAFI store look like the village shop. We were amazed at the whole set-up, but were to find this to be the norm for anything American in the coming weeks. Puerto Rico was my first taste of a tropical environment, but to my undying shame and at the age I was, I was much more interested in partying than in doing anything remotely educational. With perfect hindsight of course it would have been an ideal opportunity to "see the World" and experience all that these destinations had to offer, but common sense was in very short supply with me at that time. Alcohol was available (and cheap!) and the people serving it were not too fussed about age—I don't recall a great deal about Costa Rico except that I think we had some cracking beach parties!

It was very quickly back to work after sailing from Costa Rica. We spent the next 2 weeks in an area known as the Atlantic Fleet Weapon Ranges so that the flyboys could play with their toys. There was a lot of live firing by the aircraft, which in turn meant that we spent a lot of time at Action Stations. The air-conditioning on the Ark was effectively non-existent, and I was soon earmarked as the ice carrier for the flight deck fuelling section. I started spending almost my entire watch going back and forth to the fridge spaces collecting great big chunks of ice in buckets, to be added to the drinks which had to be constantly available to the flight deck crews to prevent dehydration. Being young and fit it was not too much of a burden, although drinking the awful orange or lime flavoured drinks was! The stuff came in a powder form and was universally known as "Limers"—whatever the flavour was supposed to be. Invariably there would be disagreements about how much powder was supposed to be added to the water, and for some reason the older guys used to prefer it strong enough to melt plastic! I hated the damn stuff, and was convinced that it was in fact pure citric acid—designed to rot your guts and ensure your early death! (Which in turn would save the government a pension?—the most common conspiracy theory for many of the dangers we faced at that time).

It was a very busy two weeks for the whole ship, not made any easier by a visit to the ship of the Flag Admiral in charge of carrier operations. As usual in preparation for the visit of anybody above the rank of Captain we were required to clean every nook any cranny of the ship, a very onerous task considering her age, and in this case it had to be even cleaner as he was to carry out a set of rounds of the ship—as if he could realistically gauge the state of the place by wandering around it! As it was, he did his rounds, but it was his entourage of Captains and Commanders and so on that gave us all the grief—poking into every little corner of the ship and producing huge long lists of more cleaning to do. To cap it all off we had a set of Divisions on the flight deck (we looked *GOOD* in our white tropical rig!) so that the Admiral could wander around asking us daft questions:

"How are you enjoying the last cruise?"

"Have you been with the ship for long?"

Bit of a waste of time and effort in my view—getting dressed in your best rig and lining up on deck in the middle of the Caribbean Sea seemed a waste. At least get some Public Relations advantage out of it—still, that was the military way in those days I guess.

The next port of call was St Thomas in the US Virgin Isles. Now this was the place! When you look at postcards from what is the generally accepted definition of paradise—long sand beaches, palm trees, lazy hot days and so on, you could well have been looking at the Virgin Isles. The image was only spoiled by two and a half thousand British sailors romping around the place getting drunk and "boisterous" around the place. In my case, because we were using the ship's boats to get people ashore, I spent a lot of time as boats crew and missed some of the fun. For the remainder of the crew, after the first day of frenzied alcohol consumption (it was fairly normal to blow off a bit of steam the first day) they settled down to a very nice routine of half day working followed by a serious beach session, followed by an evening barbecue helped down with a beer or six.

Soon enough we were back out on exercises, this time doing a "work-up" during the passage to our next port of call, and what was to be my first trip to the USA. This passage was a bit special too—we were travelling through the infamous Bermuda triangle. Of course all of the stories of missing ships and aircraft came bubbling through, and for us young gullible ones, caused a bit of worry. Amazingly though, we managed to survive the experience, and the WAFUs spent a few days playing war games. Throughout all this I was becoming more familiar with the machinery and equipment I was looking after, and was now quite comfortably getting around the ship checking this temperature, or that oil level. One of the highlights of this period for me was a mini air display that was put on purely for the ship's company, to demonstrate the power of the aircraft we operated. The Buccaneers dropped bombs and the Phantoms fired rockets and cannons, while the Seakings whizzed around doing aerobatics I didn't think helicopters were capable of! All very impressive. Those pilots were bloody good. There was a rumour going around that one of the Phantom pilots had scared himself so much doing one of the routines that every hair on his body had fallen out! He supposedly tried to fly between the masts of the Ark, and when he landed, he took off his helmet and all the hair on his head came with it. It was true enough that there was one pilot that I knew of who was completely bald (and maybe completely hairless, but I didn't ask)—who knows, but a good tale nonetheless.

As the period on passage started to draw to a close, our thoughts turned to what was, in my case, my first visit to America, to a place called Fort Lauderdale in Florida. As we manned the flight deck in our No.1 tropical uniforms for entry into port, we caught our first glimpse of the place—long sandy beaches backed off by huge square skyscrapers. The weather was warm and sunny, and it all looked very inviting. Soon enough the American tugs (and they were typically American—low, squat brutes) were heaving us alongside, watched by an incredible amount of private boats and yachts which suddenly surrounded the ship, no doubt curious about us.

As we fell out from manning the flight deck, pay parade was piped for all hands. This was a routine fortnightly process whereby the crew collected their pay. This was always a pain in the arse due to the fact that the Regulators used the opportunity of the ratings standing in a nice orderly queue to dish out bollockings and orders, normally along the lines of "Get your bleedin' hair cut", and "Report to the Regulating Office in 1 hour with clean shoes", but in this instance, turned out to be a nice surprise. As I stepped in front of the pay desk, cap and pay book in hand, and calling out my serial number, I was totally stunned to hear the paymaster say "Pay 15th to 30th May Seventeen hundred dollars". I stuttered my thanks, turned away and looked again at the pile of money in my cap. I knew that when we were abroad we received an extra payment known as "Overseas Allowance", but this much? As it turned out, this was thanks to an advantageous exchange rate between dollar/pound. I was rich! Seventeen hundred dollars—a fortune. America here I come! This windfall would be a feature of our entire visit to America, and for the entire time money was not an issue to this 17 (and a ½!) year old globe trekker.

Fort Lauderdale was a strange kind of place—modern and lively at night, yet packed with old retired Americans during the day! We of course preferred the modern and lively bit, and although I was still much too young to get into the clubs and bars, I was plenty old enough to enjoy the incredible beaches and more importantly, the nubile young ladies almost wearing bikinis lying around on them. Regrettably they were mostly accompanied by loud and large boyfriends, so opportunities were few and far. It took most of us a while to get used to the armed policemen and women in the states, and also to their no-nonsense approach to policing! When they said don't do something, boy did they mean it—we had an early example of that when we were asked, initially quite nicely, to move ourselves off a part of the beach which was for some reason not open to us. We obviously did not move fast enough, because as quick as you like the policeman hand his hand on the gun handle and was snarling at us "Move your goddamn asses NOW!". We moved.

Along the same lines, one of the highlights for me on this visit was a spell of Shore Patrol with the Fort Lauderdale police force. Shore patrol was something I occasionally got stung for as part of the boat's crew—obviously it was not fair for us to have no duties when the boats were not required (yeah, right!). There were a couple of us pinged for the patrol, and our understanding was that we would accompany a policeman, with a view to preventing drunken sailors getting into deeper trouble by upsetting the locals—see a friendly sailors face so to speak. As it was, I did not see a British sailor all night, but rather had the privilege of driving around with an American policeman on his usual beat—it was great! The copper showed me his "shooter", and I sat in the co-driver's seat with a pump-action shotgun resting against my leg. I got to see "domestics"—bust ups between husband and wife, a man in a hotel who has slipped a disc (he was leaning for support on to a food trolley at some function, and we got to scoff all of the food while we waiting for an ambulance), and got to use the car mounted searchlight to check for "perps" in some neighbourhood. I used to smoke in those days but quickly learned not to ask my new cop buddy if he wanted a "fag". He assured me that should be get into a fight that he "had my back", and that I could use his night-stick to beat the shit out of someone. Best of all was when we attended a road traffic accident, and he asked me to direct the traffic around the pile-up in the road. The look on the faces of the drivers going past was classic "What the hell kind of cop is THAT?"—Wonderful. I recall being mightily impressed when we went back to the police station for a break, and I found that I could buy self-heating cans of food—you were lucky to find an out of date Mars bar in the NAAFI back home. When we had finished the shift the police presented us with sew-on Fort Lauderdale police badges, and we gave them Ark Royal cap tallies. What an experience. The remainder of the visit was taken up with sun-bathing and chick-watching, both very enjoyable. We managed to get a bit of sport in there too, between ourselves, the local expat community and even against the locals. Football, or Soccer as the Yanks preferred to call it was just starting out there at that time, and we did what we could to encourage it. We on the other hand were not impressed with American football, which in our view took too long and was very confusing—rugby with armour plating!

We sailed from Fort Lauderdale around the middle of June, and for most of us it was for a week's passage to our next port of call, Mayport Naval Base in Florida. During the week at sea it was pretty quiet for everybody except the flyboys, who were as usual taking part in some exercise or other. They all flew off to any American airbase a couple of days prior to our entry into Mayport, which gave the rest of us a chance to use the flight deck for a bit of sport and exercise.

We entered the naval base at Mayport towards the end of June 1976, and the intention was to stay there for six whole weeks while the ship underwent a shortened maintenance period. Mayport Naval Base is absolutely immense—somebody said that there were more ships in that one base than was in the entire British navy—and this was in the days when the British still had a navy! As far as the eye could see in every direction were ships of all shapes and sizes, berthed, in dry dock, or in various states of repair. The base itself was gigantic, and stretched for miles. Inside the boundaries of the base was every facility you might wish for, including a number of MacDonald's, Burger King and other well known food outlets, along with the famous "PX" military shops, which we found with our newly found wealth absolute Aladdin's Caves of cheap and good quality "stuff". One of the best things I remember buying from the PX was a fantastic model of a working V8 engine—you had to put it together like an "Airfix" kit, then you could watch the internal workings of the thing operating under battery power. It only cost me a few dollars, and I spent hours putting the thing together over the next few weeks at sea. It was an amazing model and I have never seen anything like it since. Goodness knows where it ended up—probably binned in preparation for Captain's Rounds one day!

The plan for Mayport was for us to carry out a bit of a maintenance period. For us on the flight deck fuelling party, this meant changing all of the big aircraft fuel filters lining the flight deck. This initially seemed a pretty good number—out in the pleasant sunshine, nice straightforward engineering, off ashore, get pissed! In reality of course it was nothing of the sort. The filters in question were each about the size of a dustbin, and had a ring of large bolts holding a domed cap in position. Over the couple of years since these filters had last been changed, they had been exposed to the elements including sea-salt spray, and had seized solid. We had to smack the hell out of them with large hammers to get them to undo, and in the heat of a Florida Summer the job soon turned into a nightmare. As we got each filter open, we were faced with emptying the jet fuel out of each and then replacing scores of individual paper filters elements, all soaked through with fuel. By the end of each day we were exhausted, and stinking of aircraft fuel, which seemed to soak into our very skin. It was hard exhausting work, and in the end took us a good 3 weeks of the 6 weeks in port to complete.

In between the work there was plenty of time to enjoy ourselves though. I along with a group of others managed to get to Walt Disney World (or Land or whatever it's called), but only for a day. Although it was not really long enough to get a proper look at the place, we got a pretty good introduction! The remainder of our entertainment consisted of . . . well, drinking mostly. The booze was cheap and plentiful on the base, and they did not seem too concerned about age.

It was during a night at the "Enlisted Men's Club" that we witnessed the strangest thing. The bar was of course pretty large, and in the seventies style consisted of a long bar, surrounded by lots of smallish round tables and chairs, leading on to a dance floor. We had by then got into the habit of occupying a number of tables in a group at one corner of the bar, and were generally well settled there. We got on very well with our American hosts and would have a laugh and joke with them. The bar was always busy and noisy, but on this particular night it became apparent that one of the barmaids was having a problem with what we guessed to be an old flame or something. He had walked into the bar and started a slanging match with the girl, which quickly turned pretty ugly. In the end a couple of our guys had pulled the bloke away and escorted him out, apparently in fairly good humour—we thought nothing more of it. A couple of hours later everybody was well greased up, the noise level was high too, when we suddenly heard the pop, popping noise followed by shouts and screams. The yanks had all hit the floor straight away on recognising gunfire, but we Brits were all standing up, looking around and trying to figure out what was going on. It turned out that the ex-boyfriend of the barmaid had decided to return to the bar with a handgun, had walked up to the bar and had shot the girl dead! Within no time the bar had filled up with US shore patrol people and the civilian police, and we were all ushered out into the street and sent on our way back to the ship. The bar was open for business believe it or not the very next night, and the story went that the bloke refused to give himself up to the police, and was shot dead in the bar as well. Nobody seemed surprised by the whole thing—weird!

I seem to recall that during our stay in Mayport there were a couple of deaths amongst our own crew as well. One occurred at the naval air station when one of the aircraft ground staff was driving an American aircraft tractor. As I recall they were much taller than the British ones that the man was used to driving, and as he drove under the wing of one of the aircraft he was crushed between the wing and the tractor. He was very badly injured and died some weeks later. In the other case, one of the lads was walking back towards the ship and stepped out in front of a car which he thought was stopping to give him a lift—died instantly. I recall that we were all very shocked by the deaths, particularly so in the case of the airman because he seemed to be recovering before he died.

The remainder of our time at Mayport was spent pretty much in the same way—work hard, play hard seemed to be the motto, and on 8th August 1978 we sailed away into the sunset, on our way to Norfolk Naval Base in Virginia USA.

After only a few short days at sea to recover from Mayport, we arrived at Norfolk—another incredibly large US naval base. Although we were by now getting used to the concept of everything in America being enormous, this base once again managed to make our jaws drop. We berthed in the base in an area known as "Aircraft Carrier Alley" for the simple reason that next to our jetty, and for several jetties along, were berthed either nuclear Nimitz class super carriers or huge battle ships.

The super carrier berthed next to us was in fact USS Nimitz herself, at that time a very famous ship in her own right, both for being so massive, and for being nuclear powered. As we pulled in alongside her, we looked like one of her seaboats returning to base! She displaced something like 95,000 tons, and had an air wing approaching 100 aircraft compared to our measly 20 or so. The thing that fascinated me was that there were almost 5500 people onboard the thing!

After a couple of days in Norfolk, which in terms of facilities and so forth was much the same as the other US bases we had been to, some of us were lucky enough to be offered a walk-around the Nimitz. I jumped at the chance to get onboard the beast! We were met at one of her gangways and taken onboard, alighting in the hangar of the ship. It was standard on the Ark that the air wing flew off the ship before entering harbour, but on the Nimitz the hangar was filled with aircraft. The hangar itself stretched far away in both directions, and the width of the thing was incredible. After a wander around the hangar looking at the different aircraft types we were taken out onto one of the aircraft lifts attached to the side of the ship—each capable of lifting 2 fully fuelled and bombed up aircraft up at a time (compared to our one at a time), and taken out onto the flight deck itself—well, airfield would be a better description! We looked across and down on to the Ark's tiny flat top from this huge acreage, and our esteem for the British pilots landing on that tiny thing knew new heights. On the Nimitz everything that we had on the Ark was in place, only on a much larger scale—our fire trolleys became a full sized fire engine, our small wheeled crane a full sized one and so on. Finally, we had a look around the island on the flight deck—of course 10 storey tower block might be a more accurate description! Following our tour we were taken down to a mess deck somewhere in the bowels of the ship for a cup of coffee and donut. We were disgusted to find out that American ships were "dry"—no alcohol carried onboard, and the Americans were in turn impressed that we had booze. We asked what it was like living on a ship of 5500 people, and were told that there were actually ghettos onboard the ship, and that if you were a certain race, colour, or from the wrong crowd it was actually unsafe to visit particular areas of the ship—even the ship's own police force were afraid to go to some areas. We eventually left the Nimitz promising a return visit and swopping cap-tallies with the baseball caps the American sailors wore as working rig. I still have my Nimitz baseball cap at home, although it is looking a bit careworn these days.

We were only in Norfolk for a week, and the opportunity was taken to prepare ourselves for the upcoming seven weeks at sea—the longest period at sea of the whole deployment. We spent a lot of time taking on provisions for the coming trip, and on preparing for a couple of big exercises that were going to take place during the trip—lots of fire fighting and damage control practise and so forth.

On the second to last night in Norfolk I managed to get into a bit of unprovoked trouble. As was becoming normal for these visits, a lot of us from the flight deck stokers department had kind of set ourselves up in one of the many bars just outside the naval base. In this instance we were in the bar playing pool, having a drink, chatting to the locals and generally just enjoying the evening, when we were joined by some of the blokes from one of the boiler units onboard. I particularly knew one of the guys, a man called Hampton, who was slightly older than me but had joined up in the same entry as me. We had not really been mates, but knew of each other. Anyway we got chatting, drinking and playing pool, and by late evening we were both pretty plastered I suppose. For some reason, and to this day I do not know why, it all suddenly turned pretty nasty and we started arguing and wrestling. We were pulled apart with no real harm done, but as the guy shook off his restrainers, he grabbed a pool cue and managed to connect it with my head once before being jumped on, and slung out of the bar. I sat dazed on the floor of the place, blood dripping down my face from a deep nick in my scalp, as everybody around me shrugged at each other and wondered what that was all about. Eventually I was helped to the bathroom where I could clear my head and wash off some of the blood, check the severity of the wound and wonder along with everybody else what the hell I had said to piss the guy off so much. It was quite a nasty little cut on my head, and continued to bleed for quite a while before eventually stopping. I had another drink to calm down a bit and then decided to go back to the ship to sleep it off—I was going to have a sore head in the morning that was for sure. Some of the people in the bar were quite keen for me to be taken to the sickbay for a check-up, but I insisted I was fine and just wanted to get my head down.

It was not too far to walk back to the ship through the naval base, and on the way I set about cleaning and straightening myself up for the ordeal of getting up the gangway and past the Quartermaster. My clothing was a bit scuffed and ruffled up, and there was some blood down my front which I could cover up with my jacket, which luckily had been off during the scuffle. Nonetheless I probably looked like a sack of crap walking up the gangway. Keeping myself as straight as possible in my drunken condition, I flashed my ID card at the Quartermaster as I crested the gangway and stepped out onto the deck. To my horror I then noticed that not only was there a Quartermaster tonight, but also the Duty CPO and the bloody Officer of the Day there too—I must have just caught them on their rounds of the ship! My heart leapt into my throat as they both turned their heads in my direction both at once, took in my bedraggled state and turned towards me, no doubt to totally ruin what was already a pretty rough night.

They didn't get a chance to intercept me. As I waited for the inevitable hard time form the approaching authority, out of the corner of my eye there was an incredibly quick movement followed by a body crashing into me and knocking me flat on my arse right in front of the Officer of the Day (OOD) and duty CPO. A fist connected with the side of my head, sending stars and fireworks flashing in front of my eyes for a second time this evening! It was Hampton, who must have been waiting for me in the shadows. The OOD and Duty CPO must have grabbed him at this point—I was once again dazed and pretty much unable to defend myself in any case, while the Quartermaster must have rung somewhere for assistance, as within no time the place was flooded with people. Before I knew it I was being assisted to the Sickbay nearby, and was put onto a gurney while the duty Doctor was summoned. It felt as if my left ear had been ripped off, and the cut on my head had started to bleed again. I had a tremendous headache too, and could not seem to shake the stars in front of my eyes this time. The Doctor turned up pretty quickly and spent a lot of time asking me what day it was, to recite the alphabet and to count fingers. He shone a torch into my eyes and ears and wanted to know how much I had drunk—giving me a stiff bollocking into the bargain for drinking underage. By this stage I couldn't really give a toss—I was feeling decidedly rough by now, dizzy and nauseous and asked if I could just lie down somewhere to sleep it off. A Regulating Petty Officer turned up as well, and surprisingly nicely asked me what had happened. I explained and asked him about Girling, who he said was at that moment in the ship's cells trying to break his way out! The guy had totally lost it apparently and was in deep shit. It seemed that my story was being believed, which was a relief, and I was soon getting the sympathy I deserved! A nurse (male unfortunately) cleaned up my battered head, and I was allowed to go to sleep at last. I was suffering from mild concussion and had a headache for a couple of days—along with 5 stitches in the wound on my head.

The following day I had to go and make a formal statement to the Regulators, and that was about it for me. I had another good bollocking from them about drinking under age, but it was not dished out with any venom—remember these were the days of a strong drinking culture in the Navy, so there was tacit acceptance. As for Mr Hampton, I have no idea of what happened to him. I never saw him again onboard the Ark, and indeed in the rest of my naval career, although I understand that he did stay in. He just disappeared from the scene really; maybe he was taken away in a straightjacket or something.

Straight away after this incident we sailed away from Norfolk and indeed America, after what had been a cracking first trip for me (notwithstanding the kicking of course). We were now off to sea for seven whole weeks of intensive exercises. This might have been the longest period I had been at sea so far as I remember, but the routine soon set in, and we just got on with it.

After sailing we were right into exercises with American and other area forces, or rather the aeroplanes were. As a generalisation, we on the lower decks did not get too involved in the exercises undertaken by the air wing, but every now and then we had to close up for Action stations, sit around for a couple of hours in fire fighting suits, and then fall out. In those (pre-Falklands war) days we did not use pressurised hoses and get all of the gear out to do damage control exercises, so it was relatively easy. As I recall, we didn't even crash stop the ventilation for fires, so it didn't even get too hot in the fire fighting gear (known as "wholley Bear" suits). We had in those days 2 bottle sets of breathing apparatus known as Internal Compressed Air Breathing Apparatus or ICABA, which you had to switch over from one bottle to the other in use, by means of a small valve located between the bottles on your back. This was a tricky task wearing the thick fire fighting gloves, and led to endless hilarity as people in the stress of the moment forgot to switch over and begun to suffocate in their masks, until some kind soul switched over for them. Luckily we never had to use them in anger against a real fire (in my case anyway)—I imagine there would be enough to worry about without the added burden of having to remember to change air bottles whilst spraying water around!

About 2 weeks out into the Atlantic myself and my Brother had a bit of a cock-up with taking on aircraft fuel (or "AVCAT" as it was known) one day during a Replenishment at Sea or "RAS". The way that the onboard fuel system worked was that the jet fuel was stored in large storage tanks in the bowels of the ship. It was allowed to settle here (so that any water in the fuel separated to the bottom of the tanks) for a couple of days before being pumped to "Ready-Use" tanks closer to the flight deck. Under no circumstances was any fuel moved anywhere without it first being tested for the presence of water, which of course could not be in the fuel (it tended to cause the jet engines to stop—not a good thing in an aeroplane apparently). The fuel was supposed to have been separated in the tanker before being pumped to us, again as a precaution against water being present in the fuel, but whether that happened in practise—who knows.

We needed to bring on a lot of fuel from the tanker alongside us, and for this I was stationed on the valve chest that controlled the flow of fuel into the storage tanks. I had never done a fuel RAS before, and the plan was that John, my Brother and also my Leading Hand, was going to give me some on-job training. As we waited for the deck-apes to connect up the fuelling lines from the tanker, he took me through the filling process, which valves to open and close, in which order and so on. He went on to show me how to "dip" the tanks to determine their level, and how to smear water detecting paste on to the "dip-tape" when checking the level. He made it clear that a change in colour of the paste meant that water was present in the fuel, and that if the colour changed we must stop filling the tanks immediately. At that point the bugger disappeared—maybe to the toilet, but more likely for a fag somewhere, maybe thinking that the connecting of the hoses was going to take longer, who knows, but leaving me to fend for myself in any case.

Surprise surprise while he was away the sound powered telephone trilled, and somebody on deck asked if we were ready to receive fuel! I asked him to "wait one" and desperately looked up the long ladder hoping that John would be on his way back down. He wasn't. I remembered that he had told me we were in the correct line up to start filling the tanks, so I crossed my fingers and reported that we were ready to receive fuel. Much to my surprise the pipes started thumping and banging around, and my dip-tape indicated we were receiving fuel, but at an alarming rate! The tank was filling so quickly that I did not have time to put any water detecting paste on the dip-tape, indeed I was struggling just to take a measurement because the fuel was coming in so quickly. I needed to get them to slow down the pumping rate and snatched up the sound-powered phone. I turned the handle frantically, but no-one answered. As the first tank filled, I tried to remind myself the valve positions for switching over to the second tank—if I messed it up and shut off the fuel flow completely I could cause a back-pressure in the hose which could rupture it—not a good career move at this point. I manipulated the valves and took to crossing my fingers again as the fuel flow seemed to stop, and then restart into the second fuel tank, which in turn started filling at a ridiculous rate. I dipped and checked, checked and dipped and wondered at what point I was supposed to tell the people on deck when to "stop pumping". I had to be careful not to stop too early or late, as I could either leave room in the tank or make it overflow. I decided that overflowing was worse in the scheme of things than under filling, and was just getting ready to talk to the deck when John reappeared.

"How's it going Skin?"

"What's if fucking look like—where the hell have you been. Both tanks are nearly full already"

"Shit! Why didn't you tell them to slow the pumping down! Having you tested for water?"

"No, I haven't had a chance to. Nobody is answering the bloody phone!"

He quickly and expertly dipped the second tank and then the first. He picked up the telephone and wound the handle like a lunatic—somebody answered this time. "Turn down the pumping rate you fucking idiot—we are going to have a fuel flood down here—you know the flow rate should be much lower than this!"

Instantly the noise in the pipes from the flowing jet fuel lessened dramatically.

"That flow rate is much too high—you should have told them to slow it down. How can you do your water checks if the fuel is coming in too fast?"

"I couldn't get an answer on the phone—what was I supposed to do?"

"In future if that happens, throttle the flow on this valve here. That will increase the pressure in the hose and make them reduce the flow at their end to protect the hoses—Got it?"

"Why didn't you tell me that before you left? It's a bit fucking late now isn't it!"

"Listen. If anybody asks, I was here all the time right?"

". . . Right".

While we spoke John was moving valve handles, dipping the tanks, and finally smearing some of the green water finding paste along the dip tape. He dropped the weighted end of the tape into the first tank, reeled it out and back in, and as it came out of the dip tube we could clearly see that the colour of the paste had changed from green to a light pink—indicating that there was water in the fuel. He repeated the process with the still filling second tank, and with the same result.

"Get the Shell detector kit—quick!"

This was a second way of checking whether the fuel had any water in it. In this instance some fuel in pulled into a syringe through a chemical embedded in a filter. If the colour of the filter went from a neutral to a green colour, it indicated the presence of water in the fuel. We tested both tanks again using the Shell kit, with different batches of filter, then again with paste. There was no doubt that all the fuel we had taken had a lot of water in it.

"I don't fucking believe it!" John dashed to the phone and ordered "Stop Pumping"

The flow ceased immediately, and as we reset the valves to their normal position, the phone range. We looked at each other and John grabbed the phone. I could only get one side of the story:

"AVCAT pump room—LMEM Bridgman speaking"

"No Sir, we are not full, I stopped pumping due to water in the fuel"

"No Sir, we just detected it"

"No, we have been testing with paste and Shell detectors every 5 minutes Sir"

"Well, I don't know how either Sir"

"Roger Sir, we will be there in 15 minutes".

John replaced the phone, looked at me and said "You and me are in deep shit sunshine. Square off down here, take the final tank readings, then we have to go up and explain ourselves to the Boss".

We took a final dip of the tanks, and calculated that we had taken on about 100 tons of fuel. We checked them again both with the paste and Shell detectors—water was still there—there was simply no way around it.

We made our way slowly up to the flight deck fuelling office in the island, were ushered in and told to wait. Within minutes Lieutenant Graveney, our Boss slammed his way in, told everybody but us to "clear out!", and then sat down in front of us. John passed him the piece of paper with the tank levels and water test results. He was a fierce looking man at the best of times, and I as a worthless drone, had not really had much to do with him. In reality I had made it a point to keep a very low profile whenever possible with anybody wearing officer's white overalls. He was not a happy bunny.

"Thanks to you two Scrotes (a very popular word in those days), I have just had to explain to the Commander why we now need to let the AVCAT storage tanks settle for TWO DAYS! What the fuck were you doing down there—chatting about family history or something?"

"No Sir" from John, "There was no indication right up until I ordered Stop Pumping"

The Lieutenant looked at John "I suggest you zip it Leader. Do I look like a fucking moron? Do you expect me to believe that there was no water in 100 tons of fuel—except for the last bit? Think carefully before you speak again".

We didn't speak again.

He pointed at my Stokers propeller badge on the right arm of my overalls "You are coming up for MEM 1st class soon. So far young man, and on this performance, its not looking too bright is it?"

I wanted to cry my innocence, to explain how it wasn't my fault; a big boy did it and ran away, whatever. Instead I replied "No Sir".

"In future, if you do not understand something being said to you, or how a system works, you are to tell your superiors—is that clear?"

I wanted to tell him that hey, the Leading Hand wasn't there—who could I ask (never mind this brotherly love shit, this was business!). Instead I said "Yes Sir".

"Right—get out!" I got out.

John returned to the mess about 15 minutes later. He had received a good bollocking from the Boss, and was suitably chastened. Luckily the fuel we had taken on was in addition to that already in the ready-use tanks, so flying operations would not be affected, but it was a wake-up call for all of us. We were lucky to get away with not being brought up in front of the Captain for Defaulters on this occasion, but could be sure that if we cocked up again we would have the book thrown at us. The cobwebs from all of the recent "Jollies" had now been firmly swept away, and we needed to get back into professional sailor mode.

About half way through the period at sea it happened to be my 18th birthday—a big deal to me (I could now legally enter a drinking establishment, in the UK at least!), but not too much of a big thing for anyone else. My brother and Boss John had apparently not taken heed of any of my subtle hints ("Hey John—it's my birthday next week/in a couple of days/tomorrow!"), and there seemed little chance of any celebration taking place. My birthday had almost passed without anything being mentioned at all, and as I trudged up from the fuel pump room to the Island office, I was getting a bit down about the whole thing—maybe I could get a can of beer in the Mess when I went off watch. I was now of an age when I could apply for my "Beer Card", the authorisation that everybody over 18 carried to allow them to draw their 3 tins of beer daily (should they want to—and believe me everybody wanted to, as beer was an excellent bargaining tool).

As I entered the office, John nodded and said "Alright Steve? Oh, yes forgot to say Happy Birthday—I'll let you buy me a tinny later to celebrate"

"Yeah thanks. Want a coffee—I suppose it's my turn to make it as usual"

"Before you do that pop out to the flight deck, Leading Airman Hall wants to see you"

"Who? What have I done now—I haven't even been on the flight deck today!"

"I don't know what he wants. Just pop out and get it sorted out"

I huffed and puffed and reluctantly went out on to the dark flight deck. Surprisingly (duh!) the guy was waiting for me directly outside the office:

"You Steve? Come with me"

"Listen Leader, what is it I have done?"

"Just follow me"

We walked along the flight deck to the line of parked F4 Phantom aircraft towards the rear of the ship, all pointing menacingly inwards with their rear ends hanging over the sides of the flight deck. My mind was frantically searching for the reason I might be here, but confusion reined as no incident that I could think of might lead to me being here.

As we approached one of the aircraft, we came across a small group of air engineers, preparing to do something with the plane. They were purposefully tweaking this or that on or around the aircraft, and as we got nearer, the two glass cockpit covers hissed upwards and open, giving the Phantom that familiar and impressive pure-bred fighter silhouette. I hadn't spent that much time close to aircraft, and close-up the Phantom was pretty large.

The Leading Airman stopped, turned and faced me:

"Right, Happy Birthday Steve. We've got a little birthday treat for you—how do you fancy sitting in the back of this Phantom while we test the engines?"

"Er… Yeah, great, thanks a lot. I'd love to". I was so surprised I nearly walked off the side of the ship! A ground run in an F4 Phantom—brilliant!

Somebody slapped a pair of ear defenders over my ears, and pointed me towards the steps on the side of the aircraft leading into the rear cockpit. At the same time what I assumed to be an air engineer clambered up into the forward cockpit and strapped himself in. Somebody else leant into my cockpit and started pulling straps around and over me, all joining together at a central ring affair:

"If the shit hits the fan, turn the toggle this way and then slap it to release the clips OK?—the ejector seat is not armed so you won't be going anywhere fast!" He was gone.

"Alright Steve, I am closing the canopy—keep your fingers clear" This from the front cockpit. The canopy hissed down and clicked into place. Instantly there was almost total silence in the aircraft. This was getting surreal! I was sitting in the rear seat of a Phantom—I was still struggling to get my head around it!

I drew a deep breath and looked around the cockpit. At the moment all was dark and quiet, and as I looked through the armoured glass I could see preparations continuing to start the engines. The cockpit glass (or Perspex or whatever it was made of) was thick and gave the shadowy ground staff strange reflections as they toiled away. In no time a pair of bright wands appeared in front of the aircraft, making strange and unfamiliar shapes as signals were passed to the guy driving.

"Steve, ground power is coming on. Stuff will start to light up in front of you. Keep your hands in your lap and don't touch anything ok?"

A switch was flicked and a low electrical hum could be heard and felt through my backside. On the panel in front of me lights started to blink on—some staying bright and other flashing steadily. I tried to read the names stencilled on the lights as they came on and off, desperately trying to take in everything that was happening, but the abbreviations meant nothing to me.

"OK Steve, about to start No.1 engine—you'll love this!"

The electrical hum deepened as more switches were flicked in the front. A low whine started deep inside the aircraft and a light vibration started in my seat. Dials and gauges in the panel started to flick and count upwards as the turbine started running up. The whine got louder and the vibration stronger, until levelling out at a steady rumble, presumably with the engine at idle.

"No.1 engine running, about to start No.2" the engineer in front shouted above the noise now apparent in the cockpit.

Switches clicked, dials and counters started registering, and the second engine was run up, adding to the noise and vibration in the aircraft. As I looked around the panel, the Phantom seemed a totally different animal to the dark menacing machine of just a few minutes before. With the 2 turbine engines running at minimum speed the aircraft sat on its landing gear shuddering and vibrating against its tie-down chains, like a live thing keen to get moving.

Above the noise of the engines, the engineer shouted to me that they would be carrying out some engine testing and that the engines would be throttled up and down as necessary—I was to sit back and just enjoy the ride!

And what a ride! The engineers started through their testing programme, throttling each turbine up and down in turn to increasing higher powers. With each increase, the Phantom leapt around against its chains like a wild thing from the engine thrust, and the roar from the engine under power grew louder and loader, until eventually I could feel the power of the thing through my chest. The power of the engines was at once awesome and frightening, and my mind's eye fleetingly pictured the scene should one of the engines burst into flames—I didn't dwell there though.

After what seemed an age the engines returned to idle.

"OK Steve, there's one last test. We are going to throttle straight up to full power and then test the afterburners for a couple of seconds each. This should be good. Sit tight".

Without further ado, the whine and roar of the turbines increased and the Phantom bounced hard against its restraints. As the engines reached maximum power the aircraft lashed around, vibrating so hard that it was hard for me to see the panel ahead. At the next instant the dark of the night was lit up almost to daylight as the afterburners were lit up. At the lighting of the burners the Phantom reached new heights of thrashing around on the chains, and for a brief moment I honestly thought she would break free and go careering along the flight deck and into the aircraft parked opposite. An instance later darkness returned and the movement of the aircraft decreased with the slowing of the engines. The noise and vibration decreased to nothing as the engines were shut down. I was glad and disappointed at the same time that the test was finished—this was exciting and scary. I could understand why the fly boys got addicted to this—pity I was not more educated. A lot more!

As the cockpit canopy hissed open and I was help out of the harness and down from the cockpit, the grin on my face must have been from ear to ear! "Enjoy that Skin? Happy Birthday from the Flight Deck"

I made my way back to our office to see John lying back in his seat, smug look on his face:

"You thought I had forgotten didn't you? How did it go?"

"Cheers John that was brilliant. Tell you what, I'll even make you a coffee for that".

I was chuffed with that. There were not too many 18 year olds (and about 5 minutes) who had sat in the back of a Phantom with its engines running. I went to bed happy with life. Not only had I done a ground run, but I could also now have a beer to celebrate—tomorrow though, this fighter pilot stuff was hard work!

We had been at sea for a few weeks now, and during that time had moved steadily north away from America and towards colder climes. We had taken part in a number of large exercises, or rather our aircraft had, and all the while the weather had been getting steadily worse. It was fair to say that the Ark didn't really move too much at sea normally, and I had never until then suffered from sea-sickness. With our mess deck high up and near to the bow of the ship, what we normally experienced was a slow and ponderous rise and fall of the ship, which if anything was quite relaxing.

On this occasion though the weather really did turn nasty. The flight and weather decks were put out of bounds due to strong winds and flying spray—for the first time since I had been onboard. The ship moved around more like a frigate than 58,000 tons of steel, and getting to the mess deck was becoming quite an adventure. The slow ponderous up and down movement of the bow had become a heavy plunging action which meant that as the ship ploughed into a wave and the bow was lifted upwards, you felt the whole weight of the thing pressing you into the deck, and then when the bow dropped into the next trough you quite literally became weightless as the deck fell away beneath you! This was amusing to begin with, but quickly got very unfunny when the up and down movement was coupled with a cork-screwing action as the ship went beam-on to the sea. The rear end of the ship would be lifting up, and then as the wave passed along the length of the ship would drop again at an angle, twisting the ship over one way and then the other as the wave passed—it was a movement I would get to hate later onboard frigates and survey ships, and felt very uncomfortable indeed on a carrier. I started to feel decidedly rough, but luckily because there of course was no flying, I could turn-in and stay in bed in this weather.

This particular bad weather, which I recall was the tail end of a hurricane, lasted for a couple of days, and caused a load of damage to the quarterdeck of the ship. There was a big fuss made about the damage since by now we had reached Scotland and were getting ready for a last visit to the ship by the Queen Mother. In any case she was flown out by helicopter while we were in the Moray Firth, and spent a day wandering round and meeting the troops. Always got the Officers excited, but just meant as always extra work for us.

Back out to sea we went, heading for Gibraltar. This time there were no exercises on the way and life was fairly relaxed—except for the Shipwright's who were busy fixing the storm damage. I recall that there was a "Sod's Opera", a kind of self-produced talent show, the first I had ever seen which I thought was excellent. One particular guy stood out for me. I think he was a Leading Seaman, and he sang the song "Salome". It was hilarious and the guy should have been on stage. The BBC was back onboard as well, and made a recording of a couple of songs although I can't remember what they were (or if they sold any).

We berthed in Gibraltar soon after and stayed for a week—for most of us our first touch of land for 7 weeks. For some weird reason whenever we visited there (and this was throughout my naval career, on whatever vessel I happened to be serving on at the time) some people felt the need to run up to the top of the rock in the quickest time possible. This was something that never appealed to me, but on this occasion I gave it a go. All that happened was that I ran out of puff about half way up the damn thing, and from there took a nice stroll up the rest of the way. Nice view though—from then on I would see the view from the top of the Rock a good number of times in the future, having been brought to the top by the nice cable car!

At this time, Gibraltar remained something of a sticking point between the British and Spanish governments, and as a result the border to Spain was still closed. Gibraltar is not a huge place, and is even smaller when being frequented by 2000 sailors! The novelty of the place wore thin pretty quickly and most of us were glad when we sailed after a week.

For the next 2 weeks the Ark participated in another set of war games, this time with a number of European navies and the Med American fleet, including another nuclear powered American carrier USS J F Kennedy. For my part, in between dressing in fire fighting equipment occasionally for Action Stations or cleaning up somewhere for the visit of another set of VIPs (couldn't be many now who hadn't visited!), I sank back into the routine of AVCAT pump room and radar cooling machinery watch keeping, interspaced with visits to the Island office for chats with John or other Badgers. I was pretty much well into a comfort zone with this stuff by now, and was enjoying the role. Whenever I could I would also visit the engine and boilers rooms, or some of the other machinery spaces to try to learn a bit more about the machinery, but there was little pressure for me to do that then. Anyway, it was more fun to sit up in the Island Office and listen to the stories (or "Dits") from some of the older guys. One particular man fascinated me. He was an older Lieutenant-Commander and had the title of Flight Deck Officer (I think). In any case he would appear in the Office late most evenings, always sizzled. He was a nice old chap, always friendly and chatty (which was not usually the case—at my level anyway!) and absolute full of tails of flying incidents and such like. I assumed (with the arrogance of youth!) he was just an old wino and took it all with a large pinch of salt. John however, cautioned me not to take the guy so lightly, saying that one day my opinion of him would change.

I didn't know what he meant until one evening when the man turned up even more pissed than usual. He had a habit of either playing music or Monty Python sketches over the hangar and flight deck broadcast systems late at night ("Keeps the morale of the Chaps up!"), and we knew when he was well oiled, because he would put the volume up to maximum. We would surreptitiously turn it down behind his back as he rattled on about some escapade or other. On this occasion he became really Maudling (as he tended to) and starting chatting about a particular incident. It turned out that he had been a Gannet Observer back a few years. On being catapulted off the ship once, the catapult had failed half way along and instead of taking off, the aircraft had just kind of rolled off the end, falling into the water at the bow of the ship, which was steaming along at 25 knots or something. The 3-man flight crew, as part of their training had been told that should this happen, they should stay in the aircraft as the ship rolled over them, wait for the ship to pass over, and then clamber out, float neatly to the surface and be rescued by the SAR helicopter. Nice theory.

In reality fear overrode the training, and on tipping over the front of the ship and landing in the water, this officer's two colleagues bolted out of the aircraft only to be run down by the ship, and more particularly the ship's propellers, and were killed. He stayed with the aircraft and waited for the ship to pass over him. It had all been a sad story up until this point, but he then brought out a set of photographs showing the Gannet falling off the front of catapult and disappearing from view in front of the bow of the ship, and of him stepping out of the SAR helicopter after the accident. Clearly it had affected him badly—hence his behaviour each night I suppose. As a result of the accident the catapult system on the ship had been fitted with steam pressure reservoirs which ensured that once the "Launch" button had been pressed, there could not be catapult failure during that cycle. Too late for this aircraft, but I suppose it is from accidents that improvements come.

Our next port of call was to Naples once more. I had not really enjoyed the place the previous year, and was not particularly interested in the place this time. I did take the opportunity though of joining a trip to Rome and the Vatican. It was a remarkable trip, too short by half to really see all that was on offer. I was totally blown away by the Sistine Chapel and the Roman Coliseum (both of which in those days before serious terrorism were totally accessible), and could have spent a week looking around them, but the day disappeared in no time at all. I promised myself to get back to see them again—some thing I eventually managed to do in

2007—but on that visit the Sistine Chapel was closed for refurbishment or something, and the queue for the Coliseum was about 3 miles long! Sometimes it's better to just have nice memories and not to try to re-live the moment I guess.

The passage from Naples to Athens was for us non-aviators a relatively routine one, the only real highlight being the final live ammunition air display put on by the Phantoms and Buccaneers for a large group of visiting VIPs. As always the noise and violence of the attacks against towed targets was excellent.

Athens was a new destination for most of us on the ship. We had to anchor in the Bay of Athens (probably has another name), and unfortunately for me that meant I was going to spending a lot of time as part of the Boat's Crews. Actually I never really minded that duty—I used to like zipping back and forward on the big Whalers, and sometimes I would be allowed to be the Coxswain for a couple of legs. It was all good fun—apart from climbing out on to the boats from the ship, which involved walking along a spar projecting from the side of the ship to which the boats were tied, and then climbing down a rope ladder to get onto the boat. The spar was about 20 feet from the surface of the water, and when you looked upward, there was the massive overhang of the flight deck above you. It was quite intimidating, and on one occasion I managed to knock my cap off and into the water as I climbed down the boarding ladder onto the boat. One of the crewmen managed to fish it out using a boat hoot, but for the rest of the day I had to wear a soggy misshaped sailor's cap around. I tried to claim a new one, but was simply told to be more careful climbing down boarding ladders. I was not happy having to spend a few quid for a new cap and cap tally!

When not manning the boats, I did get a chance to see the Acropolis (again in those days very close-up), and again enjoyed the historical aspects of the country. It wasn't all history though, as I soon returned to type upon being introduced to the local hooch—ouzo! Very dangerous stuff. It was cheap and too plentiful, and managed to trash me on a couple of occasions during the visit.

Prior to the visit to Athens, and indeed all of the destinations we went to, there would be a briefing over the main broadcast system, describing the place we were going to, its history, customs and so forth. In the case of Athens there had been a particular warning concerning the local police force, who were apparently not the friendly "local bobby" type, and who should be approached with extreme caution. Another warning had concerned the fact that the Greeks particularly disliked anybody messing with their national flag, and that the flags on any buildings were to be left alone at all costs. While the warning was of course given in good grace it was a bit daft really—it was like telling children not to touch anything in a sweet shop. Guess what happened when some of the lads had imbibed a bit of ouzo. Greek flags became the targets of opportunity, and not only were they being stolen, but were being worn around people and so on. It all ended pretty nastily when there was a large punch up between a bunch of Matelots and the Greek police. Not altogether surprisingly, the police with their big sticks won. A number of the lads were arrested, and had the shit knocked out of them in the police cells before being returned to the ship. Top tip—don't mess with the Greek flag!

Following a short passage, it was back to Malta for a couple of weeks. I had been there the previous year and had enjoyed the visit, so was looking forward to this one also, even though the period was to include quite a bit of maintenance that we had to catch up on.

As it turned out this trip to Malta was a special one, as although I did not know it at the time, this was to be where my future wife and I first met! It was something of an adventure going ashore in Malta, as rather than using the ship's boats, we used the local small boat taxi fleet, known as "Die-so's" (actually in Maltese called "Dhaghxa")—excellent little boats with absolute character drivers. On this occasion myself and a few buddies had gone ashore and ended up in a little disco (they were discos in those days alright?) in Valletta. Anyway I got chatting to this lovely little thing—beautiful dark eyes. She was called Anna and mentioned that the next day was her birthday. Check this out for corny—I went out the next day and brought her (of all things!) a smart writing pad thing so that—get this—she could write to me when the ship left!! Mr Romantic is my middle name I think you will agree. Anyway, must have struck a chord because she did. We wrote to each other and visited regularly for the next five years, and she has been by friend, confidant soul mate, and eventually wife since that day. Strange how life goes full circle—the Ark was berthed in a place called Kalkara Creek during the visit, and now 26 years later myself and Anna live in . . . Kalkara.

Apart from meeting the future Mrs Bridgman in Malta this time, we had a chance for a good few nights out and even a "Banyan" (Barbecue/beach party) at Golden Bay, as well as some serious maintenance. One of the jobs I was involved in was the cleaning and then painting of the funnel. I don't know how the flight deck stokers got stung for the job, apart from the fact I suppose that it was where we worked, but nonetheless we won it. There was a bit of grumbling about what a waste of paint the job would be—we were scrapping the bloody thing in a couple of months, but by now we were all pretty used for aimless cleaning and painting! It is fair to say that the Health and Safety arrangements in this case were somewhat basic, and on turning up for the job I found that the Sailors had strung a great big climbing net up and around the funnel, up which we were required to climb clasping buckets, scrubbing brushes, cloths, paint and brushes, and goodness knows what else. Not such a bad thing until you recall that on the flight deck side of the funnel the drop was about 50 feet (onto effectively concrete), while on the outboard side of the funnel the drop must have been about 150 feet straight into the Grand Harbour! It was best not to look down! Anyway we got on with it, and soon became used to climbing around like chimps—its amazing how quickly one gets used to strange situations, and we took great pleasure calling to the girls in the passing pleasure boats, and chucking stuff at the people going ashore in the Dhaghxas.

Anna and I in Malta 1981

All too soon the visit came to a close. I and Anna said a fond farewell—promise you'll write. We sailed from Malta for the final time at Procedure Alpha—all dressed up and lining the flight deck. There were thousands of people lining the huge battlements surrounding the Grand Harbour waving us off. Blaring car horns being answered by the ship's whistle. Saluting cannons firing from HMS St Angelo and other ships in the harbour. The Ark was flying her "Paying-Off" pennant which was so long that it had to be supported by a couple of weather balloons, and it stretched all the way along the flight deck and over the stern of the ship, regularly threatening to topple sailors over the side as it was so heavy. It was an amazing scene to be part of, and now that I had a "pen-pal" in Malta I was sure to be going back.

The Ark was the last ship that I was on which visited Malta. The British were due to leave for the last time in 1979 anyway, and Mr Mintoff, the Prime Minister at the time made it pretty clear that Brits were not very welcome after that time. I visited pretty regularly after that during my leave and so forth, and it was a shame that the Maltese were unable to make (at that time) good use of many of the ex-British bases on the island. Unfortunately many were just left to rot, and it is only now that they are starting to be put to good use.

We were on the last leg of the journey now, and after sailing from Malta had only a single visit left. On the passage to Mallorca we did the usual flying operations and had an even higher number of VIP visitors than usual, including the First Sea Lord, another film crew and the famous artist David Shepherd (no disrespect, but I hadn't ever heard of him). There was a big fuss about the Wardroom firing their old piano off one of the catapults (good TV I guess), and one of the Gannets was the last aircraft to carry out a fixed wing recovery on the ship. All "golly good stuff chaps" for the "hooray Henries", but the lives of us minions continued much as normal—watch keeping, maintenance, cleaning, eating, and sleeping.

The trip to Mallorca was an interesting trip for me. A very neat and tidy place, we were able to take a good look around the place as we were working a half-day routine known as "make and mend routine". The highlight was a medieval night where everybody dressed up as knights and watched a bunch of people knocking the crap out of each other during a "joust", while being filled up with plentiful food and booze. Top stuff. The other memory of that trip for me was the welcome that the crew got in Mallorca, both from the locals and visiting British tourists. There were plenty of "grippos" going on—people adopting a sailor and then proceeding to pay for pretty much anything, not least because of the fact that us junior ratings were required to wear uniform ashore. That doesn't happen anymore in these days of random terrorism, which is a shame.

On sailing from Mallorca I received a bit of a shock on being informed that I was being removed from the Flight Deck Stokers section and being re-employed elsewhere. This was due to the fact that the air wing was leaving the ship for the final time over the next couple of days, and subsequently the aircraft fuelling section was being disbanded. I quickly found that I was going to end up down below again, although I would be staying in the Badgers Mess, my new job would again be down in "Y" unit, my old hunting ground, but this time I would be a "Shaft Passage Yo-Yo!" This was the title of a particularly arduous job which would involve me visiting and taking temperature readings of all the supports and bearings along the length of the propeller shaft from the "Y" unit gearbox to where the shaft exited the ship—all of the Plummer blocks, bulkhead glands and the stern seal. Again that doesn't sound too bad until you realise that to visit each one, I would have to climb down a ladder about 5 decks (or 55 feet or so), take a couple of temperature readings, climb back up and then move on to the next one and so on, and I had to do it once each hour! To make sure I had done it, I would have to return to the "Y" unit engine room each hour, and transfer the readings taken to another log. This was going to be fun.

For the first few days it was agony! Up and down ladders, the rungs digging into my feet, knees and ankles aching, and getting back to the engine room just in time to start again. Soon enough though routine set in, and the process became easier, and I was certainly getting fitter. One of the problems with the rounds route was the danger involved in climbing down a straight ladder, and on a couple of occasions my feet slipped off the rungs while climbing. I always managed to catch myself, but one guy was not so lucky. Early during one set of rounds in another unit, the guy was climbing down a long ladder but slipped off and fell a couple of decks down, only to be snagged by a projecting ladder support on the way down. The projection caught the back of his overalls and slammed him into the ladder, breaking his right arm and leg as I recall, but also, with the sudden and violent stop, the crutch of his overalls basically managed to dig right into him between his arse and bollocks, splitting the area there quite badly. He wasn't due to return to the engine room for another 45 minutes or something so the poor sod swung there for an hour before the search party was sent out. After that we were required to phone the engine room each time we visiting a compartment. It got pretty tedious for us and the engine room crew, and soon petered out.

The fixed wing aircraft departed for the last time a few days after leaving Mallorca. All of the flight deck stokers were now effectively unemployed, and there was a huge influx of people into the units, who really didn't want them (at last there was no great amount of cleaning to do!). I stayed as shaft passage yoyo for a couple of weeks, but was then moved on to a new job. A couple of parties of guys were formed up to become "ditching" squads—our job would be to ditch over the side stuff that it had been decided would not be worth returning to stores on our return to the UK.

We assumed that we would be throwing away a few old bits of stores/tools and that kind of thing. Oh no, we spent the remainder of our time at sea on the way back to the UK throwing over the side all sorts of stuff—spare parts, machinery (including lathes, drilling machines etc), tools still in their wrappers and goodness knows what else—there must be a trail leading from Mallorca to Plymouth about 10 feet high! I swear the ship must have risen about 5 feet in the water with the weight of all the gear we ditched removed!

As we neared Plymouth after having been away for almost 8 months the helicopters started to shuttle the ground crews, WAFU's and Airy Faireys off of the ship, until they too had all gone home. It was very strange around the ship at that stage, the hangars all empty of aircraft, personnel and all of the paraphernalia that normally went with it, but we were now more concerned with getting alongside for the last time.

The Ark Royal entered Plymouth for the final time on 4th December 1978. We manned the flight deck in our No.1 uniforms (it was bloody freezing!) and took in the crowds manning the shore, the ships companies manning the side and the ever growing flotilla following us in. Once again the "paying-Off" pennant threatened to brush us off the flight deck, but we shrugged it off as we came alongside to the cheers and massed bands welcoming us in. Many of the guys of course had family waiting for them on the jetty and there were many teary faces around. We were (unusually) told to wave back to the crowds, a first as far as I was aware for a ship at Procedure Alpha, but were glad to get off the deck once we were stood down.

Leave was granted to those apart from the ones required for duty on the ship, and off we went for a couple of weeks. On return to the ship I found that many of my colleagues had already received draft orders and had either left already, or were in the process of going. One of those was John, who had received orders to join the Maintenance Base before going eventually to the new (at that time) Type 21 frigate HMS Avenger. I wondered where I would be going, but by the end of December no draft order had arrived for me.

Chapter 6

From Badger to Ship's Cat!

On rejoining the now very quiet Ark Royal in the new year of 1979 I still had not received any drafting notice, and was starting to wonder if they had forgotten about me. Of course now that the ship was going for scrap I had no real job in engineering onboard, and to my disgust I was seconded to the Writer's office in the ship. Here we go again I thought, back to being the bloody Gofer! To my surprise I was welcomed into the office and straight away put to work not ditching rubbish, but handling all sorts of personnel paperwork (under the supervision of the Leading Writer of course). I found that I really enjoyed the work (it was so different from anything I had done up until then) and took quite an interest in it. Along with my new office job I was required to be duty (i.e. a full 24 hours onboard) every 4 days, where I would be required to sleep onboard and carry out regular rounds of the machinery spaces, making sure there were no fires or floods going on in the depths of the ship.

As the days stretched into weeks, the once mighty ship was systematically stripped of all useful equipment and machinery, slowly losing her personality to become more of a hulk than a famous warship. Along with the equipment, personnel continued to disappear, until there were just a small group of staff including me left. On the positive side, with so few naval personnel onboard I had pretty much free access to the entire ship. During the operational period I had never for instance visited the Bridge, or the Admiral's Bridge, but now I could. Also, some other Mess deck areas were now open for a good wandering around, and it was only now that I could appreciate the incredible size of the ship.

The duties were now becoming a bit scary. As I wandered around the ship in the dead of night, some of the spaces were by now losing their lighting, or the strip lights were not being replaced, making them gloomy and ominous. There were a few occasions where the hair on the back of my neck stood up as the ghosts of 40 years of service made their presence felt in the ship. On one particular night I was down in the bowels of the ship, in one of the stern gland spaces when I swear I saw a ghost.

In order to get down into the stern gland compartment, one had to climb down about 5 decks, pass under a hatch, and then walk along a grating into the space. On this night, I passed under the hatch and started walking along the grating to have a look at the stern gland seal to make sure it wasn't leaking. As I walked along I glanced over the shaft, and noticed that there was a dockyard worker or "Docky" sitting on the other side of the shaft reading a newspaper (not unusual). As I passed by the guy lowered the paper, nodded at me, and then raised the paper again.

You often saw dockies sitting around reading papers, but not usually at 3 am in the morning! Still, whatever. I didn't think anything more of it. I finished the set of rounds and returned to the Damage Control Headquarters, which at that time was being used as the rounds control room, and asked the Petty officer in charge what the docky was doing down in the stern gland compartment:

"What Docky?"

"The one down in "X" stern gland compartment"

"What the fuck are you on about?"

"There's a dockyard worker down in "X" stern gland compartment"

"Well there shouldn't be—we haven't been told that there will be work tonight"

With that he rang the gangway—still manned by naval personnel at that stage:

"Why haven't you notified me that there are dockyard workers onboard?"

He listened to the response—eyes swivelling to me as the Quartermaster spoke. He put the phone down.

"The last docky left the ship at 2300. The QM says there are no dockies onboard"

"But I saw him there—he was reading a paper"

"Better go back and check then—off you go"

This was weird. I had seen the bloke sitting there. I made my way back to the stern gland compartment and started down the ladder. That was when it hit me that this was a very scary situation, and that the guy might have been a ghost. I stopped halfway down the ladder as goose-bumps erupted on my body. I was suddenly very spooked and leapt back up the ladder to the safety of the semi-lit compartment above. I sheepishly made my way back to the control room and reported that I must have been mistaken. After this incident I became pretty jittery for the remainder of my time doing rounds of the ship. Thankfully rounds became the responsibility of the dockyard some time after that so I was spared too many repeat performances.

My day job now consisted entirely of helping in the Ship's Office, and with the continued slow depletion of the crew, including the Writers; I was becoming ever more involved in the office processes—even so far as (one-finger) typing of some letters. Most of my work though involved checking correct, and then sending by post the documents of the people who had either left, or were leaving the ship, on to their new vessels. I enjoyed it a lot, and when the Petty Officer Writer asked if I was interested in becoming something called a "Marine Engineer Officer's Writer", I jumped at the chance of applying—possibly with hindsight a bit hastily.

Marine Engineer Officer's Writers (MEOW) were Stokers who undertook all of the administrative functions involved in the running of a ship's engineering department, thereby relieving the Marine Engineer Officer of the burden, and allowing him (and latterly Her) to concentrate on more important things. In order to become one, a Stoker had to be recommended (I was) and to attend the 5 week training course on the subject at HMS Sultan. 5 weeks seemed a bit extreme to learn how to file and type, but hey, I was willing to give it a try, and so without further ado I applied and was accepted for the next course, running a few months later.

Finally I had a draft order to leave the Ark. I would be literally one of the last to go, and would first be going to a place called HMS Gannet in Portland for a couple of months "marking time" until my MEOW course started in Portsmouth. My last job on the Ark Royal was in fact to send out 2800 "HMS Ark Royal 1976-1978—The Last Commission" books to all those people who had been onboard during the period. This got pretty tedious I can tell you—address the envelope by hand, insert book and "with compliments" chit, stick down envelope (cheap MoD crap—always had to use selotape), collect a batch together; take to HMS Drake for postage. The whole process took me several weeks. For anybody who got one, hope you enjoyed it!

I had been living in HMS Drake for the final couple of months onboard the Ark, as all of the living and Galley areas onboard had now been stripped out. My final day onboard came along, and to be honest, I was glad to go by then. The crew was literally down to single figures now, and after a few goodbyes I walked way from the old girl without a second glance. I never saw the ship again, as by the time I next returned to Plymouth she had been towed away for break-up in Scotland somewhere. For me, the last few months on the ship had made me realise that it was the people onboard that gave it life and "personality", and once the majority of the crew had initially left she became just a cold lump of metal. The crews really did give a ship its character, as I would find out through the years—it only needed the change of a few of the key ships company members to alter the entire "feeling" of the ship, in some cases for the better and in others for the worse.

My Bloody Efforts

I had a bit of leave to take before joining my new shore base HMS Gannet. In truth I had never even heard of the name, although I was reliably informed that the place was "something to do with" helicopter operations. Likewise I wasn't quite sure where Portland was either! I had a travel warrant to get me from Plymouth to Portland, and when I enquired about the route was given an incredibly roundabout railway journey. In any case I arrived at the dates to the base late one Sunday night, was shown to the "Transit Mess" and told to report to the obligatory Regulating Office in the morning.

I had been wondering why a Stoker was being sent to a Naval Air Station, and evidently so had the Regulating Staff at the place. When I turned up at the Regulating Office the next day, it was pretty clear that I was about as welcome here as a banana in a pie-eating contest. It soon became clear that the Navy was struggling to find places for the 2800 people that a couple of short months ago had been manning the Ark Royal, and as a result people were being sent to some pretty unusual places. In my case, I just needed to be employed until the start of my MEOW course. The "Buffer's Party", the usual placement at any shore base for temporary draftees was already full, so I was sent away to lend what assistance I could to the Galley!

For Stokers, the galley was synonymous with being under punishment. It was where one ended up working if you happened to be placed under "No.9" (extra work) punishment. The Cooks (they preferred to be called Chefs for some reason) usually took an inordinate amount of pleasure in ordering the men under punishment around, and for this reason I was very much less than happy with my new situation—I might as well have been sentenced to 2 months punishment!

As it was, the two months passed pretty quickly and not too unpleasantly. Although it would not be correct to say that I was welcomed to the Galley, I was not mistreated either. I fairly quickly got into a routine of peeling vegetables in the morning, doing the servery bit for lunch, helping with the washing up and then being allowed to disappear in the afternoon. Downtown Portland was not much to write home about in those days, and so most of the off time was spent in the pretty well appointed Junior Ratings club. My only memory of that particularly place was that having treated myself to a nice new wrist watch, I had somehow managed (probably being slightly pissed) to smash the damned thing against a fire extinguisher, braking the glass and destroying the watch face. I was gutted—it had cost 35 quid! Still, lesson learned—I don't think I have ever bought a watch worth more than about a tenner since!

I joined HMS Sultan for Marine Engineer Officers Writer's course towards the end of 1979. This was the first time I had been back to Sultan since basic training. It had not changed much in the 2 years or so (the Regulators were still a pain in the arse), but this time the major difference was that as MEM1's we no longer had to march around in squads to and from our classes. It made us feel slightly superior to the poor basic trainees, and of course no opportunity of taking the piss out of them was ever wasted!

The course itself was excellent—I enjoyed every minute of it. Our main instructor was an old Chief Stoker who took great interest in teaching us the ropes properly. From day one he made the point of instilling in us the knowledge that when we were the MEOW onboard a ship, we would be on our own. We would be responsible for all of the "engineering returns" each month, of making sure that there were all of the engineering administration stores available (machinery record sheets for instance were used onboard a frigate at the rate of about 25 a day—they didn't appear by magic), and for the running of the engineering office. When it was run well, nobody noticed, but when there was the slightest problem it all came to the MEOW. As he so rightly put it: "Always remember, shit rolls downhill!"

During the next five weeks we learned all about filing systems, letter formats, how to write signals and the correct way of addressing correspondence. We learned about books of reference, Defence Council Instructions and all kinds of stuff that I had never even heard of before. On the engineering side we learned about engineering returns, a monthly set of ship operating figures that were sent back to the Admiralty each month, stability graphs, machinery trend monitoring, and a whole load of other stuff that we were going to be responsible for. I took to it pretty easily, despite my relative lack of schooling. The only place I struggled a bit was when we were required to take notes from a supposed meeting, and then turn them into meeting minutes—the spelling was a bit suspect I have to admit.

The aspect of the course I enjoyed the most was learning to touch-type. The process started almost from day one with an introduction to the typewriter. It was all a bit girly for us macho men, with the "secretary" connotations, and it took a while for us to get serious about typing. When we were then told that by the end of the 5 weeks we were expected to have a typing speed of at least 60 words per minute, and that without even being able to look at the keyboard, we were aghast! There was no way that could happen—we couldn't even find the bloody letters on the keyboard, let alone hit them with any speed. The first week of training just gently got us familiar with the keyboard, and where to place the fingers, but after that the pace increased steadily. We would all be sat in a room full of typewriters, all with headsets on. Slowly at first, the instructions through the headset would be "A—now, B—now, Q—now" would come, and we would all hit the appropriate typewriter key with the correct finger. It reminded me of something out of George Orwell's "1984", rows of people plugged into some brain washing machine, all acting in unison—"A—now" CLICK, "B—now" CLICK, except that in our case it was "A—now" CLICK, "Bollocks!", "B—now" CLICK, "Shit!" and so on.

As the weeks passed the speed of the instructions increased, so that by the third week it sounded like some demented sewing machine factory in the typing training room, fingers flying across keyboards and the steady smacking of letters against the return carriages, but still interspersed with the more than occasional oath as keys were missed. So far we had trained with our eyes very much on the keyboard as we went, but for the final 2 weeks we were entering the touch typing phase.

For the final two weeks, and culminating in the final typing exam, we were put into a new training room. Here we had individual cubicles, headphones, and on the front wall of the room a huge representation of a typewriter keyboard. What we had to do now was to listen to the headphones while watching the keyboard on the wall, where every time a letter was heard through the headphones, the corresponding letter on the wall would light up, and we would hit the letter on our real keyboards. It felt strange at first doing everything by touch, but it was remarkable how quickly we adapted, as evidenced by the slow reduction in both the volume and frequency of the swearing as letters were missed. All in all the typing training though monotonous was incredibly effective, and I passed the final exam with a typing speed of about 60 words per minute.

My Bloody Efforts

As the course drew to a close and people started to receive their new draft orders, the Chief gave us a couple of bits of information to bear in mind. Firstly he said, people doing the MEOW job onboard ships were entitled to be promoted to the "Local Acting" (i.e. only for the length of the draft) rate of Leading Stoker. This was excellent news! I was some way off from being in a position to take the exam for promotion, but now there was no rush! Secondly he advised us to "keep our hands in" with practical engineering while we were onboard as our promotion structure was no different from any other Stoker—we still had to do all of the standard engineering exams to get promoted, and of course if we were not getting involved in the practical stuff it would be harder for us to pass all of the exams.

Soon after this I received orders to join the frigate HMS Ajax in Portsmouth as their new MEOW. The Ajax was a "Leander" class frigate, configured as "Anti-Submarine" type, fitted with an "IKARA" missile system and 10" anti-submarine mortars. She was getting on a bit by then, and her machinery, consisting of a couple of Y100 boilers and associated steam engines, although well maintained, was getting a bit tired. She was due for refit in Gibraltar the following year.

I joined the ship, which after the Ark Royal seemed like a small sea boat. The guys in the mess seemed ok, asking if I was the new ship's cat (MEOW—get it?), and in no time I was introduced to the Marine Engineer Officer Lt Cdr Bull. He wasn't the friendliest person in the world, and made it clear from the off that I would not be promoted any time soon to Local Acting Stoker. He told me that I needed to "prove" myself first, and then he would review the situation. In the meantime I was to get stuck into the Technical Office, find my feet and make him trust me. Deflated, I made my way to what was "my" office, had a look around, and introduced myself to the Fleet Chief Artificer who would be sharing the office with me. The Fleet Chief was equally unwelcoming, told me to keep out of his way, and turned back to his colleagues. Good start then.

Soon after I joined the ship we were deployed. We would be taking part in some exercise up near Iceland, then working our way down into the Atlantic and onwards to the Med. I very quickly discovered that frigates move around a lot more than aircraft carriers! Luckily, being the MEOW I was working effectively a normal day at sea (although in reality I actually normally worked 10-12 hours a day, even though I was supposedly "Day work"), which meant that when the sea-sickness got too bad I could cry off and lay down for a while.

After being at sea for a while and starting to find my feet around the office, the MEO and Fleet Chief started to get slightly friendlier with me. While we were very far from being on first name terms, they could see, I think that I was trying hard, and they started to give some input into directing me properly. The first few letters I typed for the boss were appalling badly typed and with "Tippex" (which only came in bottles with little brushes in those days) splashed all over them. As I typed in the office, the Fleet Chief would grumble from the corner "My fucking daughter could type faster than that—and she's only 3! How the fuck did you pass the course?" and other such pleasantries. Oh yes, things were going well.

One thing they had forgotten to mention on the course was that I in fact had another aspect to my new job, that of Damage Control Headquarters or "HQ1" "Incident Board Operator". In this role, whenever there was a shipboard emergency or when we were at Action Stations, I was responsible for communicating from HQ1 to the 2 damage control stations (one forward and one aft), and for making the appropriate markings on a large 2D plan diagram of the ship, showing each deck and compartment onboard. This was an entirely new thing for me, and I soon found out that during simulated damage to the ship, my position was a key one. I had a whole new damage control vocabulary to learn (shoring, free-flooding, attack party leader, semi-submersible pumps and god knows what else), as well as coming to grips with the sound-powered telephone switchboard that was now my responsibility too. The bloody thing had inputs from about 20 locations around the ship, and of course when a whizz-bang went off somewhere to start an exercise, everybody tried to ring me at once! As well as taking and passing messages and instructions, I was expected to draw in details of any incidents on the Incident Board using wax pencils of different colours, drawing coded symbols to indicate the type and seriousness of an incident. An example would be that a fire in a compartment would be a red circle with a capital "F" surrounded to the extremity of the compartment by red cross-hatching. The start, "under control" and "fire out" times would be noted too, along with any other notes that might be useful.

To start with I was all over the place with this system. As always there was little sympathy for my lack of knowledge, and no consideration or extra training time allocated to ensure I was competent in the position. The reports continued mercilessly to pour in a seemingly endless stream while I tried to keep up on the board and with the passing of information. The first couple of Action Stations were a disaster, and I was roundly bollocked after each. I put a lot of work though into learning how things should be, and eventually got my head around the job—to everybody's relief I suspect.

After struggling hard to gain a bit of respect onboard, things went horribly wrong when we got to Spain. We berthed in Malaga, but some of the lads had organised a trip to Torremallenos, just up the coast. It was a bit of a trip there, and the ship would be sailing fairly early the next morning, so it was best not to get too wasted. Nonetheless I was still very much the new boy at that stage, so was keen to be seen as "one of the lads".

The evening started off well enough, plenty of drinking, joking and messing around. Sometime during the later evening though I got separated, and decided to make my way back onboard . . . after one last nightcap. I rather stupidly went into a bar alone and ordered a drink. Looking around, I saw a very attractive young lady sitting alone at the bar and with drunken bravado decided to go and chat her up. I had made my introductions and was (I like to think) getting some response when "Whallop!"—I was punched in the side of the head. I dropped like a sack of potatoes to the floor, and started being assaulted there by somebody. The guy was shouting in Spanish, and the girl was adding to the noise level too. I don't remember it, but the Barman apparently jumped over the bar and pulled the bloke away—throwing him out of the bar. Anyway the Barman sat me on a stool and gave me a drink and a towel or something to stop the blood that was emanating from around my starboard ear. He and the girl fussed around me asking if I was ok. I asked who the guy was, and he turned out to be the ex-boyfriend of the girl. I guess he still had some feelings for her then!

I was quite enjoying the sympathy, and when the girl asked me if I wanted to go to her place and clean up I agreed at once. We got to her little flat somewhere, and to cut a long story short I ended up spending the night there. As I awoke in the next morning and glanced at the clock in the bedside unit, I saw that it being 6.30am I had plenty of time to get back to the ship.

I stretched and put a hand up to my right ear—bad move—touching it sent a wave of pain through my head. I didn't touch it again! It seemed odd that now, mid-autumn that it should be this light for half six in the morning, and so I looked at the clock again.

Oh Shit! The clock was actually lying on its side! It's not 6.30am it's fucking 8.45pm! Oh no! What time was sailing? I couldn't remember in my panic. I leapt out of bed and into my clothes, screaming at the girl to tell me where I could get a taxi—quick!

I left the flat without a goodbye, a wash or even a look in the mirror. I had scrambled into the same clothes from the night before—jeans with spots of blood on them, and a tee-shirt with blood stains from the right shoulder downwards. I must have looked a mess—I certainly felt like shit!

I found a taxi quickly enough, and to be fair the driver didn't even turn a hair at my appearance as I jumped in, threw all of the money I had in my pocket at him asked him in sign language to take me to Malaga harbour "as fucking pronto as you like". It was already way past 9.00am by now so I was not too hopeful of getting back in time.

Sure enough, as we got closer to the berth it was becoming clear that the ship had already sailed—I should have been able to see the masts from quite a long way away. We reached he berth to see dockies coiling up their ropes and stowing gear, so I couldn't have missed her by much. Man, I was in very deep poo!

The driver shrugged and drove away, leaving me to my fate. I was quite literally at a loss of what to do next. I was in a foreign country, I looked like I had been pulled backwards through a thorn bush, I was dirty and unshaved, hung-over, and I had no money because I had just given it all away to the bloody taxi driver. I plonked myself down on a bollard and tried to clear my head.

I had been there some time when I had a brainwave. There must be a British Embassy in the city right? I would make my way there and tell them my sob story. They would sort me out and get me home—no problem—it must happen all the time. With renewed enthusiasm I set off in the general direction of Malaga central to find the Embassy. It was a bloody nightmare! After wandering around looking for what might look like something approaching an Embassy for a couple of hours I had got nowhere, so I started asking passersby for directions. Unsurprisingly considering my appearance, I did not get a lot of response—I guess most of the people thought I was begging. Eventually though I asked (by pure accident) an English lady who lived in Malaga for directions. It became clear to me then that one of the reasons I could get no directions previously was that there was no Embassy there! In Malaga they had a Consulate! Anyway I was kindly pointed in the right direction and found the place about 4 hours after the ship had sailed.

As I entered the British Consulate and prepared to say my piece, to my utter astonishment the man behind the counter said:

"Ah, you must be Stephen Bridgman right? We've been expecting you".

"Er, yes that's right"

"What happened to you then? You look like you've had a rough night".

"I got mugged last night. They took all my money and gave me a kicking. Its taken me this long to find my way back" I lied easily.

The man looked at me for a moment

"Ok, whatever. The main thing is you are safe. We can signal your ship now to tell them we have found you"

They had found me? That was a bit rich. I didn't make an issue of it though—not really in any position to comment on anything.

The Consulate signalled the ship, who apparently replied that they were very much looking forward to meeting up with me again back in Portsmouth! In the meantime the Consulate had to arrange a temporary passport to get me back to the UK, which would take 3 days to organise. They gave me some money (which I would pay back in fines later!) and arranged for me to be put up in a local Student's accommodation block until the flight back to the UK was arranged.

3 days later I found myself at Malaga airport boarding a plane for Heathrow. I had been briefed that I would be met at Heathrow by a couple of Naval Policemen who would then drive me as a prisoner down to Portsmouth, where I would wait under open arrest in the barracks for the Ajax to return. This was going to be bad.

I arrived at Heathrow and gave my temporary passport to immigration, passing out of the Arrivals lounge and expecting to see two strapping

Crushers waiting for me. Nobody approached me, and there were certainly no people dressed in sailors uniforms anywhere around. I thought for a moment that perhaps they had decided to wear civilian clothes to come and get me, and so I walked around for a bit, still in the expectation that at any minute I would be apprehended. Eventually though it sank in that there was no-one there—here we go again I thought; now I am stranded at Heathrow airport, not a penny to my name.

Another brainwave followed. I knew there was a police station at the airport, so I decided to go there and ask them for a travel warrant to get me back to Portsmouth—my understanding (for some reason) was that the police would assist a serviceman like that. I managed to find the place on a map and eventually got there, presenting myself to the nice Sergeant on the desk:

"Good morning Sergeant, my name is MEM Steve Bridgman from HMS Ajax (show him ID card). I have just flown back from Malaga where I was left behind when the ship sailed, and need to get back to Portsmouth. Could I have a travel warrant please? Oh yes, can you make it to Portsmouth with a stop-off in Ascot—I need to just visit home for a couple of hours to get some clothes".

The Sergeant looked at me, most probably noting my grotty appearance and bruised and battered ear. He took my ID card and asked me to wait. I sat on one of the plastic benches.

After some time the Sergeant returned, with a couple of policemen by his side:

"Mr Bridgman, would you come through please?"

He lifted the stable door affair into the inner office and ushered me through. As I stepped through, the policemen on each side of me grabbed an arm each, and "assisted" me along a corridor and into a cell. The Sergeant followed us in:

"Ok Steve, I have phoned the Navy, and they are sending someone up to collect you. You are not in any police trouble; we are just holding you here until they arrive for you. Do you want a cup of tea?"

I was a bit surprised by the sudden frog-marching, but in a way relieved that events had taken this turn. I agreed to a cup of tea, and to their amusement asked if they had anything to eat as well. A PC brought in the tea and a sandwich, and I told him the full story. He thought it was hilarious, and word soon got round the place. At least they could have a good laugh about it, but for me the reality of what I had done was starting to sink in.

The light mood abruptly changed with the arrival of the naval patrol. The police handed me over to the two stony faced Regulators, and they without further ado put me in the back of the meat wagon—barred windows and all. As we left Heathrow one of the Crushers spoke to me for the first time:

"Why didn't you stay in Arrivals—you knew there was someone coming for you!"

"It seemed to be the right thing to do when there was no-one there" I replied.

"You are not on fucking holiday now Sunshine. You will address me as Leading Regulator, got it? You made us look like cunts back there, turning yourself in and asking for a fucking travel warrant!"

"Yes Leading Regulator". There was no further discussion.

By now it was early evening, and the rain was falling steadily as I sat on the wooden bench in the darkness at the back of the van. The windows were covered in a mesh affair which made looking out difficult, and I felt very alone there as the two guys in front chatted away about trivia. In fairly short order I began to recognise that we were driving through Portsmouth, and then in through the gate of HMS Nelson, the accommodation base. To my surprise though we didn't stop at the Regulating office, but drive past and onward towards the "Recess" building—the place where they took serious prisoners before they were transferred onwards to Colchester and proper, long military prison sentences. I began to get scared then.

The van stopped and the rear door crashed open:

"Out! Stand over there. Say nothing" I got out and walked into the entrance of the dreaded "Recess", Crusher each side of me. I couldn't help noticing the floors—they were like glass!

I stopped in front of a reception type table, behind which sat a Regulating Petty Officer.

"Name!"

"MEM Bridgman Regulating Petty Officer" I nervously replied

"You will address all staff in this building as "Sir". Is that clear?"

"Yes Sir" I wasn't arguing.

"Give me your Identity Card. Empty your pockets. Take your watch off" I did as instructed. Everything (which wasn't much) went into a small plastic bag.

"MEM Bridgman you stand charged with failing to rejoin your ship under sailing orders, and with being absent from place of duty, namely HMS Ajax. Do you have anything to say?"

"I didn't miss the ship on purpose Sir, it was . . ."

"Shut it Sunshine, you can explain it all to your Captain when the ship gets back. Until then you will be staying here. Now, get to the bathroom, shower, shit and shave, put the No.8s provided for you on, and report back. Got it?"

"Yes Sir".

I was escorted to the shower block by one of the Crushers, who then proceeded to stand by and watch me get cleaned up and changed into the uniform, which included gym shoes without laces "so you can't top yourself" as he charmingly explained. Afterwards I was escorted back to the Petty Officer.

"Right, because you haven't been formally charged yet, we are going to treat you a bit more lightly than some of the others that come in here.

Tomorrow morning you will help with serving breakfast rather than scrubbing out alright? Leading Reg, take him to cell No.8"

Again I was escorted like some hardened criminal to the entrance of a cell, and invited to enter. The cell was about 8 feet long by 6 feet wide, with a barred window high up on the wall. There was a bench at the end of the room with a mattress and blankets stacked on top. There was nothing else.

"Count yourself lucky—normally its just blankets"

The thick metal door clanged shut. A few minutes later the lights went out. I think I cried.

Somehow I managed to sleep in the cell. The lights came on and the door clanged open sometime later. I had no idea what time it was, but it was still dark outside.

"Get up! Shit, shower and shave" I was passed a plastic razor, toothbrush, some soap and a postage stamp sized towel. Again I was escorted to the bathroom, and the guy waited while I had a birdbath and shaved. I was escorted back to the cell and ordered to dress. I asked the Crusher what the time was:

"You got a fucking appointment somewhere then have you?"

"No Sir"

"Then you don't need to know what time it is do you?"

"No Sir" I didn't ask again.

Once dressed I was escorted to the galley of the Recess building. There were already 2 people there, and they didn't look like cooks either. They were busily preparing food and paid little attention to my arrival.

"Johnstone, Bridgman here is going to help you this morning—show him what he has to do"

"Yes Sir!" shouted the first guy without even looking in our direction.

"You will be cooking breakfast for the prisoners waiting to be transferred to Colchester" said the Crusher to me "top tip—do not spoil it or I guarantee you will not be popular!" With that gem, he turned and left me to it.

I don't think I have ever been as desolate as I was at that moment. It was "stupid o'clock" in the morning, I was in the kitchen of a naval cell block cooking breakfast for a bunch of fucking hardened criminals, my future uncertain. All I had done was miss the ship sailing, not murdered somebody, and I just could not comprehend why I was being so badly treated.

In any case I had no time to worry about that now—my full attention was needed for the next piece of trauma. "Johnstone" obviously did not want to get personal or to enquire about my well-being:

"Can you cook Skin? What branch are you?"

"I'm a Stoker" I replied, "but I did work in the galley at Osprey for a couple of months".

"That's close enough. Grab a frying pan and start on the snorkers (sausages)—we'll see how we go. This fucking dickhead" waving at the second guy "burns soddin' cornflakes!" It was not said with humour. The guy in question neither acknowledged nor responded to the insult.

It was odd that there were no dedicated cooks there, but then again that would really be a choice draft for some poor sod I suppose. In any case I grabbed a large frying pan, turned in the big galley range and started cooking:

"How many people are we cooking for" I asked

"Just keep cooking the stuff until I tell you, alright"

I cooked a large packet of sausages and then moved on to bacon, and the rest of what would be a full English breakfast for what seemed to be a very large group of people. We did not cook any eggs, and I was told that they were cooked on demand—not bad I thought for a cell block breakfast!

After about half an hour we were laying out the food on the serving counter—plastic utensils and paper plates being the only difference from a "normal" dining room, when "Johnstone" said:

"Right Skin, they will be coming through in a minute. You take the egg orders, and be quick about it—they will try to make you take your time—gives them longer out of the cell see? Don't take any shit from them.

I was grateful for the advice.

A couple of moments later there was a concerted clanging of cell doors, shouted orders and sounds of people moving around. Within 5 minutes people started appearing outside the dining room door, forming an orderly queue under the direction of a Crusher. When they had arranged themselves to the satisfaction of the Crusher he allowed them into the room and up to the food counter.

"Johnstone" and the silent one were manning the servery and started shovelling food onto plastic plates:

"Alright Pete—2 snorkers today? What eggs you want?"

"'Morning Jonno—I'll have scrambled"

"You know we don't do scrambled—how about a couple of fried?"

"Oh well, worth a try. Go on then"

I started cooking fried eggs, concentrating on the frying pan as though my life depended on it. I surreptitiously glanced every now and then at the "proper" prisoners, but desperate to avoid eye contact. There were about a dozen people in all—more than I would have expected to be waiting to go to the military prison. They didn't look like I kind of expected prisoners to look—they were just ordinary blokes. A couple of them were obviously Marines (the moustaches were a dead give-away), and a few had some serious tattoos, but by and large they didn't look too dangerous!

"Hey Jonno, who's the new Sprog then?" I froze.

"Dunno. Just turned up this morning"

"Oi Skin. What you in for then?" This from a large man waiting for his eggs at the counter.

"I missed my ship when it sailed from Spain" I replied, eyes fixed on the frying pan.

"Shit man, that's desertion—you can still be hanged for that under the Articles of War!" Laughter

"Bbbbut I didn't do it on purpose—I was pissed!" I blurted out. More laughter

"Just cook the eggs Skin. Leave him alone Mike alright?" This from Jonno.

"Just make sure you don't burn the buggers, or I'll be over the counter!" Said the big man. His mouth said he was smiling but the eyes gave him away.

I was pretty spooked by now, but managed to make it through the rest of the breakfast unscathed. The Crushers came in eventually and ushered everybody back to their cells while we cleaned up after the meal. I found out that breakfast was the only meal cooked for the prisoners, who received "meals-on-wheels" lunch and dinner from the main galley of HMS Nelson. By the time that stuff reached Recess it was pretty grotty, and the prisoners looked forward to breakfast with a vengeance as a result.

For the next 3 days my routine consisted of working in the galley/dining room for all the meals, sweeping and cleaning floors, toilets and offices in between that, and then, being a "Trustee" being allowed to watch 2 hours of TV in the evening before being "banged-up" for the night. For the entire period I had not been formally charged with anything, and when I plucked up the courage to ask if the intention was to keep me there for the remaining week before the Ajax returned, I was simply informed that I would be kept wherever they decided to keep me. For the entire period the Crushers were unfailingly bastards.

I woke up the fourth day to a different routine. Instead of being escorted to the galley, I was taken back to the "Reception" where another Regulating Petty Officer was waiting.

"Right Bridgman, here's your gear—check it and sign here"

I was confused, but tipped out the small bag, checked it was all I owned and signed the bit of paper.

"Go with the Leading Regulator"

Still wearing my prison garb—ill fitting No.8s and plimsolls without laces, I followed the Leading Regulator out into the dark of the morning. My watch told me it was 6.30am.

The Leading Regulator walked in front of me, barely acknowledging my presence.

"Excuse me Sir—where are we going?"

"We are outside Recess now—its Leading Regulator"

"Where are we going Leading Regulator?"

"You'll know when we get there" Bastard! I wondered if it were part of their training.

We wandered across the parade ground heading towards the Main gate of HMS Nelson, and it crossed my mind that I was simply going to be chucked out of the gate and told to "piss off—we don't want you anymore". But surely there had to be some kind of trial or something didn't there?

We passed the main gate and now headed towards the base Regulating Office. By now it was about 10 minutes to 7.00am and there was only a single person inside the office—another Leading Regulator. We went in:

"Sit there" I sat there.

My escort went off to talk to the other Crusher. They had a long discussion, heads occasionally turning in my direction before the escort finished, walked past me without a glance and disappeared.

My new nemesis approached me, stood hands on hips in front of me and said:

"Well, you look like you've had a shit couple day's mate".

"Yes Leading Regulator".

"Look, we have to wait for the Fleet Joss to get in, to see what to do with you. Why don't you go over to the JRs dining room and get some breakfast".

I looked up at his face. This chap was a bit older than the bastards I had come across to date, and I think I saw a bit of genuine sympathy in his eyes.

"I'm not hungry Leading Regulator. In any case—look at me"

"Ok point taken. You wait there then—I should be able to manage a cup of tea at least"

True enough he brought out a cup tea, and even gave me a smoke. I was still very wary and even though he was trying to be kind I simply could not relax. He tried to chat but I think got fed up with my "Yes Leading Regulator, No Leading Regulator" routine, and so finally gave up.

From about 7.30am onwards people started to come into work at the office. All were of course Regulator's of varying rank, and as they entered and walked past, they were of course curious about the ragamuffin sat on the bench. There was a lot of whispered conversation and staring, which was incredibly unsettling. Finally at about 8.30am the Fleet Master at Arms entered the office, took one look at me and said:

"Leading Reg—take this man to my office"

I was taken to an inner office, and within a few minutes the Fleet Joss came in. He was an intimidating bloke—physically big, with sharp piercing eyes and a permanently angry face:

"Sit. MEM Bridgman, you have been released from Recess this morning, but you will remain at open arrest pending the return of your ship next week, understand?"

"Yes Sir"

"You will report to the Regulating Office each morning at 08:00. In between you will work as part of the accommodation party in HMS Nelson. When you leave here now you are to report to the accommodation Petty Officer, Understood?"

"Yes Sir"

"Listen. You were incorrectly placed in Recess—you should not have ended up there, but that will be taken into account in any punishment you are subsequently awarded. Understood?"

"Er . . . yes Sir"

"Think of your time in Recess as a learning experience—if you have any sense you will make sure that you never put yourself in that position again. You can go"

I as was taken out of his office and pointed towards the accommodation office. I felt a complete prat walking along the base main road in my unlaced plimsolls and crap No.8s, and was relieved to reach the office and hopefully normality. A Petty Officer and Leading Hand were in the accommodation office. They looked me up and down, looked at each other and burst out laughing:

"You Bridgman?" I nodded, heart sinking even further—here we go again.

"Take a seat—you look like shit—you want a cup of tea?" A cup of tea appeared in my hand

"Couldn't the bastards at least have given you some fucking decent clothes?"

"You must have really pissed off somebody to end up in Recess!"

"You look fucked mate—I think for today we will sort you out some clothes, and a bed. You can tell us the full story tomorrow". I was home.

Good as their word, that morning we went to the clothing store (slops) and an emergency issue of uniform was made, so that at least I could get dressed again. We then went to the bank and I managed to draw some money just on my ID card, so at least I was solvent again. Lastly I drew some bedding and was given a single cabin (a luxury normally reserved for Leading Hands). I was then left alone for the first time in what seemed like months, crashed out, and did not wake up again until the alarm clock woke me the next morning. The effect that the small kindness of these people had on me was amazing. I felt ready to face the World again.

After reporting to the Regulating Office as ordered, I returned to the accommodation office the next day to be similarly welcomed with a cup of tea and endless banter:

"Looking a bit better today Skin, how you doing? Take a seat—we want to hear the full story"

For the rest of the morning I was plied with tea and sympathy as I related the whole sorry tale to my rapt audience. The story was interspersed with "oohs" and "ahs" and "no shit!" or the occasional "bastards!" as it unfolded, and come the end of the tale I can pretty well assume that their esteem of me had risen by a few notches.

HMS Ajax was due to return to Portsmouth in 4 days time, at which point I would rejoin her and face my punishment. In the meantime it was agreed that I would simply man the accommodation office as messenger/receptionist. This I did for a very pleasant and stress-free four days—I could have stayed there for an entire draft!

Time moves on though and before I knew it I was standing on the quayside of Portsmouth harbour watching HMS Ajax preparing to come alongside. I had been away from the ship for almost 2 weeks by now, and wondered what the charges against me would be—probably "absent from place of duty" for 2 weeks—nightmare! As the ship drew nearer I saw the Engineer Officer looking at me from the Bridge. The Captain joined him at one point and they both stared in my direction for a moment. I cringed.

Finally the ship was tied up alongside and the gangway lowered. As I walked up the gangway and on to the flight deck I was greeted with:

"The wanderer returns!"

"Good to see you back Skin—enjoy your vacation?"

"Thought you were dead in some gutter in Spain Skin!"

The Master at Arms was waiting for me, and ushered me down to his office onboard:

"Ok Steve, I understand you have had a bit of a rough ride since you got back. What happened?"

I explained the sequence of events from missing the ship, to spending time in recess and finally being under open arrest in HMS Nelson. He was not happy. Because I had at no time been charged with any offence, I should apparently have been made an "offender at large" when I returned to the UK, rather than being shoved in cells and then being restricted to the base. He told me that this was good news for me, as I had already been punished, and that if I wanted, that I could make an official complaint about my treatment. He advised me not to though. He went on to tell me that I would be facing the Captain this very afternoon.

Following release by the Master at Arms I went to see the Engineer and Warrant Officer. They took me into the Technical Office and closed the door. They were not interested in my story, why it happened or its twists and turns, but rather concentrated on the shame that I had apparently brought to myself, the department and the ship. They assured me that the trust that had started to find in me was now wiped out, and that there was absolutely no chance while they were onboard that I would ever be promoted to Leading Stoker. It was a quality bollocking, but frankly after what I had endured recently I was getting good at looking apologetic and in taking flak.

That afternoon I was dressed in my No.1 uniform and facing the Captain's Defaulter's Table (or Captain's Table). This was the first time I had been

"Trooped", and it was an uncomfortable experience. I was marched in, had to "off-caps" and stand at attention under the withering gaze of the Captain. The charges were read out:

"Did absent himself without leave for a period of 14 days"

"Failed to rejoin the ship under Sailing Orders"

"Was absent from Place of Duty for a period of 14 days".

The Captain, still giving me the Paddington Hard Stare, asked if there were any mitigating circumstances. There were none.

He then asked the Engineer Officer for a character reference. To my surprise the Engineer gave me a very good write-up, describing me as hard-working and keen to learn, and generally starting before this incident to fit in well with the department.

The Captain listened to all of this, and then asked if there was anything else before he passed sentence. This was clearly a rehearsed move as the Master at Arms stepped forward and gave a full description of what had happened to me on my return to the UK.

Finally the Captain looked me directly in the face, and then commenced to give me the biggest wake-up call of my life. I don't recall the actual words, but he basically told me it was time to grow-up, that I had potential but needed to focus, that if I continued along my present route I would end up being discharged from the navy and lots of other stuff. It was sensible, good advice, coupled with a complete bollocking, and it had the desired effect. Now for sentencing:

"MEM1 Bridgman, taking into account the punishment so far received in HMS Nelson, you are hereby ordered to lose 14 days pay, be fined a sum of 180 pounds and to carry out 2 days No.9 punishment. Do you wish to contest this punishment?"

"No Sir"

"Dismissed".

So, I was losing the pay for the days I was away, being fined 180 pounds for the flights and passport, and was getting 2 days extra work—result! It meant that I would finish the punishment just in time for Christmas Leave. I was slightly miffed about be chucked into Recess, but it was done and dusted now. Anyway if I had not been such a prat in the first place it would not have happened.

In reality the episode cost me a great deal more that the 14 days pay and the price of the flights. In did have the effect of straightening me out, and in fact I was never trooped again during my remaining 24 years of naval service, but on the debit side it stopped me being rated Local Acting Leading Stoker for almost eighteen months—the length of time it took for me to rebuild the trust that was lost. In the end Lt Cdr Bull never forgave me, and it wasn't until a new Engineer took over that I was eventually promoted.

I did my two days of extra duty—most of it spent telling my story to the rest of the ship! Most of the junior ratings and a lot of the senior ones saw the funny side of the whole thing—even the Warrant Officer had a bit of a chuckle eventually. Off I went then to Christmas leave, after which the novelty wore off enough for me to get on with my job, and back to normality.

The remainder of my time on the Ajax was thankfully a lot less active than my first couple of months, and by the Summer of 1980 we were in Gibraltar, getting ready to transfer lock stock and barrel to the newly refitted HMS Ariadne, another Leander frigate, but much newer than the Ajax.

The Ariadne was in fact the last of the Leanders to be put into service, and by the time we clambered onboard she was still relatively young at only 10 years old. She was classed as a "GP" or General Purpose frigate and was fitted with a main armament of two 4.5" guns in a single turret at the front of the ship, as well as the usual machine guns, torpedoes and helicopter. On the machinery front she was a massive step up, being fitted with more powerful Y160 boilers, and having an air-operated machinery control system which remotely operated things like the throttles, boiler sprayers and other important stuff so that the machinery could be operated from closed in control rooms, particularly in the Engine Room.

On the MEOW front, I was by now pretty settled in the role, and was comfortable with all of the aspects of the job. I was going to be put to the test on this ship though, because as well as having an Engineer and Artificer Warrant Officer, the Ariadne was the Squadron Leader of the 8th Frigate Squadron and so carried the Squadron Engineer Officer, a Commander called Parry. My workload instantly doubled, but I was to find that both the Commander and the new Engineer (Bull left the ship in Gibraltar) were going to have a huge impact on my future.

My Bloody Efforts

Commander Parry was a big man in size and character. He had a large craggy head and a nose that had been broken at some point. In his younger years he had been something of an explorer, and had the rangy looks and tough body type of an explorer still. As soon as he gripped my hand in a vice-like handshake and boomed "Nice to meet you young man—sure we'll get on just fine" while staring hard into my eyes, I knew he was going to have an effect on my life. Without further ado the letters to be typed from that moment on came thick and fast, a never ending stream of long complicated communications to the Engineers in the Squadron, to the maintenance base, to the Fleet Engineering Captain, and to just about anybody else you might think of.

To begin with I struggled to match his expectations of speed and quality. I was not a particularly fast typist, which would have been ok if I had been accurate to make up for it!

"Bloody hell Bridgers—you're going to have to do better than that lad" he would tell me—Bridgers was what he called me from day one, whether we were just talking, at Action Stations or in front of the Captain.

"Tell you what, let's get the old typewriter out and have a practise—see if we can't get you up to a decent speed" Now that was encouragement, and it worked. Within a couple of months I was producing good stuff, my fingers flying over the keyboard and rarely hitting the wrong key. It felt good to be efficient at last.

Likewise Lt Cdr Smith, a less "in your face" man from Birmingham with a broad, very un-officer like Brummy accent was equally patient and helpful with me. He always addressed me as "mem" Bridgman" (you have to say it in a broad Brummy accent), and later as "L—mem" Bridgman. I almost fell off my perch one day when he said "Thanks Steve" after I had taken something up to his cabin for signature.

Another aspect of my job which used to be a laugh was my "Special-Sea-Dutymen" post, which I was required to man for entering or leaving harbour. On the Ariadne this meant that I was positioned in the Engine Room, making notes of every engine and shaft revolution order, and at the same time relaying and taking messages over a headset from the Commander who was manning the bridge. The Boss was located in a nice quiet bridge, while I was surrounded by noisy machinery. The headphones were sound powered, and were very faint, meaning that often I either misheard or did not hear at all what he was saying—used to drive him nuts!

"Bridgers! I said, tell the Boiler Room to stop making smoke! Pay attention man!"

"Sorry Sir, can you repeat that—I can't hear you"

"Bloody hell Bridgers—wake up man! Make sure the headset is tight for God's sake! I said tell the Boiler room to stop making smoke!"

"Tell the Boiler Room to make smoke—Roger Sir"

"No, you blithering idiot! Tell them to stop making smoke!!"

"Ah, this thing is crap! I can't bloody hear a thing. I'll ring you Sir"

I would have to ring him then on one of the Bridge phones. He would pick up instantly:

"Bridgers—you have to clamp the bloody thing tight on your head"

"Sir, if it gets any tighter my fucking head will explode. You have to speak up Sir, its noisy down here!"

"Righto—but I can't shout too loud up here—pisses the Captain off!"

So for a while he would make an effort to speak nice and loudly into the microphone, and all would be well. After a while though the whole process would be repeated, much to the amusement of the engine room staff. This went on for the whole time I was on the ship, although I eventually got to know the sort of information he wanted, so that it got much easier. Often on a long harbour entrance he would witter away:

"Bloody hell Bridgers, just saw a Cormorant. Bloody lovely bird"

"Nice Sir—unfortunately there are no windows down here!"

"Tell the chaps that we should not be too much longer—so long as the bloody deck apes can sort themselves out! Honestly, these fucking sailors are as thick as shit!"

"Tell the Boiler Room to check the sprayers on the port boiler—bit of smoke coming out, they must be dirty"

I would pass the message to the Chief Tiff in the Engine Room, who would phone the boiler room and just tell them to make sure no smoke was being made. He would then say to me "Tell the silly twat that we are not making smoke and to mind his own fucking business"

"Hello Sir? The Chief Tiff sends his regards and has ensured that the Boiler Room is not making smoke"

"Jolly good Bridgers"

I was still suffering the effects of my Spanish expedition on the promotion front, and it seemed pretty clear that I would not be getting promoted to the Acting Local LMEM position I was entitled to just yet. After a few months on the Ariadne the MEO called me to his cabin, and we had a chat about the situation. This was probably about a year after the event, and by now the MEO and the Commander had had an opportunity to form their own opinions about me. Basically they were not averse to promoting me in the position, but did not think it was fair for me to be promoted while I had not completed the "Auxiliary Machinery Certificate" or "AMC". They wanted to prove to themselves I think that I could handle the extra training workload, and that I still had a mechanical aptitude. I thought this was a fair deal and set about completing the 4 or 5 subjects required for the qualification. In honesty it was good to get back into the overalls, and despite the ribbing from the other guys, I managed to spend a lot of time down in the machinery spaces in between my normal duties. After taking over the ship in Gibraltar the next phase of bringing it back into service was sea trials. This was an ideal opportunity for me to get around the machinery onboard, and to get the outstanding exams cracked. Over the next 6 months or so I did get a lot of studying done, and helped the boys out a bit by effectively being an extra watch keeper in the shift system, giving some of the guys an extra "all night in" now and again as I gained the engineering experience in each position. This carried on when the ship finally left Gibraltar and embarked on becoming the Caribbean guard ship for the next few months. I must admit it was a bit tough maintaining concentration on studying while visiting places like the Bahamas, Barbados, Antiqua and so on, but I kept my head down and got it all cracked. I was now what was known as a "Scale B" Stoker. To qualify as an Acting Leading Hand I would now have to pass the "Fleetboard" for LMEM or Leading Stoker, which consisted of a written followed by an Oral examination. I was still some way away from that though. The best I could hope for now was a Local Acting promotion.

Antigua—Caribbean Guard Ship—HMS Ariadne 1981

I knew I had finally "made it" when one evening at sea I was walking along "2 deck passageway"—the main thoroughfare through the ship on my way to the Diesel Generator Room to check out some systems there, and on passing in front of the Wardroom door, it was flung open:

"Bridgers! What the bloody hell are you doing man?" boomed the Commander, a little worse for a couple of "G and T's" by the looks of it

"I'm off down the diesel room Sir. Just checking out a few systems down there".

"Good show! Bloody good news about you getting your hook—well done"

"Er . . . that's news to me Sir"

"Is it? Oh bollocks! I thought the MEO had told you. Oh well, wait there a minute" he disappeared back into the Wardroom. A couple of minutes later the door opened again, and out pops the Commander and the MEO, pint of beer held in his hand.

"There you go Bridgers, drink that! Congratulations—well deserved. All you need to do is qualify for the bloody thing now, what?"

"You were supposed to find out tomorrow mem-Bridgman" said the MEO with a sidelong glance at the Commander, "but since you now know, congratulations, I have recommended to the Captain that you be promoted to the rate of Local Acting LMEM while you are the MEOW onboard, ok?"

"Yes Sir of course its ok—thanks very much" I replied, sinking the pint sharpish.

"You would have got it quicker under different circumstances, but you deserve it. Anyway we'll sort it all out tomorrow. Well done."

The very next day I was brought to the Captain and promoted. He made a point of ensuring that I understood that I would lose the rank on leaving the ship, unless I took and passed the exams for "normal" promotion. The onus was on me therefore to ensure that I studied and took the exams as soon as possible. I agreed of course. On leaving the Captains table I was presented with my single anchor Killick badges, and told to sew them on straight away, or I would be trooped for being "out of the rig of the day"! The badge felt strange and heavy on my left arm—my first proper promotion, but very nice indeed.

My leadership style, if I had such a thing, was normally pretty relaxed. At the end of the day, one had to live with you guys you were supervising, so there was little point in being a complete twat all the time. I never had any real problems getting what I wanted done, and found that it was much more effective being reasonable, but then throwing your toys out of the pram every now and then to make the point, rather than screaming and shouting as some others tended to do.

The next year or so for me was some of the best time I spent in the Navy. On the Ariadne at that time everything just clicked nicely into place for me. I was loving the job in the Technical Office, and finding that I was being increasing trusted as a source of engineering knowledge (on the procedures and paperwork side at any rate) by the entire department, had the damage control and special sea duties roles totally under control, and was spending plenty of time down in the machinery spaces, which I was also totally enjoying, learning the intricacies of the machinery systems. On the social side, the ship was spending a lot of time around the Mediterranean and even more in the Caribbean, and while I still enjoyed a good run-ashore, I now had a "Stop" button and no longer allowed myself to get so pissed that I didn't know what I was doing. I was now engaged to Anna, and looking forward to, as well as saving for, a 1982 wedding.

CHAPTER 7

The Falklands?—I Was (Almost) There!

THE SPRING OF 1982 found me and HMS Ariadne in Gibraltar, taking part in the annual "Spring Train" naval exercises. I had done this a few times now, and the visit to Gibraltar was by now getting a bit "samey". In the Technical (or Tech) Office, I was in the middle of making sure I had all of the documentation, forms, stationary and stuff that I would need for the next few weeks at sea during the upcoming exercise, while the remainder of the department were busy checking over the machinery, making last minute repairs and so forth before we all headed out into the Atlantic once more.

I first became aware of the "Falklands Crises" whilst out for a run-ashore one afternoon. In those days there were little shops all the way along the "Main Drag" in Gib, all of which had UK newspapers for sale outside on little carousels. Somebody had bought "The Sun" or some such paper, and as he sat opposite with the paper open (probably checking out Page 3), the headlines read something like "MARINES HUMILIATED ON SOUTH GEORGIA!" In any case conversation started, wondering where South Georgia was, what all the fuss was about, if we would be affected, and just general sitting in the warm sunshine sipping a beer chit-chat. When we found out that the Falklands was a little group of islands 7000 miles away a) we were incredulous that it was British owned, and b) that anybody would want to live on the god-forsaken little rock in the first place. Let the Argentine's have it! It was a joke—the politician's would sort it out.

That changed a couple of days later with the invasion of the Falklands. Pictures in the papers of Marines being laid on the ground at gun-point by Argentine Special Forces hit a nerve—not surprisingly our own small on-board Marine detachment were getting themselves all over-excited, puffing themselves up and swearing bloody murder at anybody stupid enough to listen. It soon became apparent that there was going to be a British response—Margaret Thatcher made it clear that the country was not going to stand-by and let the invasion happen, and it also soon became clear that the nearest available British force was those ships taking part in the impending Spring Train exercise—i.e. US!

We were up for it. We were ready! That's what all the training was for, now it's for real! It WAS real, but in a very kind of "it's not really going to happen" way. We were all thumping our chests and whooping it up, but deep down we kind of expected that the politician's would sort it all out long before we even got close to the place—after all, it was going to take something like 3 weeks of hard steaming to even get there! We took on stores, including lots of live ammunition the same day and sailed out of Gibraltar the very next morning, along with HMS Sheffield, a number of other destroyers, frigates and Royal Fleet Auxiliaries. A much larger Task Force would be following, but we were going to be the spearhead. At that stage we (by "we" I meant us on the lower deck) still had no idea of exactly where the Falklands was, or what kind of forces the Argentines had at their disposal.

We turned right out of Gibraltar and headed for the Atlantic. Not surprisingly we started exercising action stations, emergency stations, and weapons firing drills and machinery breakdown drills almost as soon as we sailed, and continued night and day from there on. I had never seen such dedication during the drills before, and now that we were heading for a real fighting war, we suddenly didn't mind spending hours cooped up in our little compartments, ant-flash gear on and surrounded by emergency and survival equipment. The drills became more and more dedicated and complicated as we steamed along at maximum speed towards Ascension Island, which would be our gathering point before moving onward towards the Falklands, and an exclusion zone that had already been set up around the islands by our submarines.

About 10 days out of Gibraltar, disaster struck for the Ariadne. We had been steaming hard for the entire period since leaving Gibraltar, and finally the wear and tear told on our main machinery. One of our main engines lost oil supply to its main bearings, resulting that the bearings "wiped", requiring us to stop the main engine. The engine would need replacement bearings in order to get back to full service, and since we were now down to a single engine, we could no longer keep up with the rest of the fleet. With perfect hindsight I guess we were lucky not to be involved when the bullets started flying, but for now we were gutted. Our last participation in the Falklands war was transferring our live ammunition to some of the other ships in the Fleet, one of which happened to be the Type 42 destroyer HMS Sheffield. Finally we turned away from the fleet, whistles blowing, battle ensigns flying and signalling "Good luck, Good hunting!"

to the fleet as they disappeared into the distance. We headed at "lame duck" speed back towards Gibraltar, and the mood onboard was sombre. The engineers were getting a lot of grief from the sailors, who presumably imagined that we could just swop one engine for another, but in truth we shared their disappointment.

It was a slow return journey to Gibraltar. The days were long and slow now that we were not frantically exercising every 5 minutes, and the disappointment of not going to the Falklands with the rest of the fleet hung heavy over us all. We were keeping up with the news about the war by listening to the BBC World Service bulletins, but for quite some time there seemed to be little happening. That all changed of course with the news that the Argentine Cruiser "Belgrano" had been sunk by one of our submarines. At first there was jubilation and an "I told you so" mentality around the ship—this "war" would be over in no time, we would soon sort out this bunch of clowns! After a while though, we as fellow sailors started to imagine what those poor guys must have gone through—a torpedo strike out of the blue, the shock, fires, flooding, and if you survived that, jumping into the South Atlantic Ocean. It was a sobering thought, more so for us Stokers stuck down in the machinery spaces with little chance of escape in those circumstances than perhaps the gun crews or flight people. We knew by then that a lot of the servicemen in the Argentine navy were conscripted, and somehow that made the whole thing worse for us—at least we had chosen to be here, and while of course none of us had any wish to be injured or even killed, the general feeling was that it was what we were paid to do. We considered ourselves, even at our young age and limited experience to be professionals, and at this stage of the conflict felt a kind of sympathy for the poor fools who had rather stupidly dared to take on the Royal Navy. With the tragedy of the sinking of this outdated World War 2 vintage cruiser we imagined that the Argentine's would finally see sense, declare a cease-fire and get around the negotiating table. How we were proved wrong!

A few short days after the sinking of the Belgrano we received the news that HMS Sheffield had been destroyed by a missile attack from the air. As I recall about 20 guys were killed and a whole bunch more wounded, and following a massive fire onboard, the ship could not be salvaged and was scuttled. I remember standing in the mess on the Ariadne, the radio speaker surrounded by absolutely dumbstruck sailors. The Sheffield sunk? How could that be? We were waving and shouting at them a couple of weeks previously, passing over our spare ammunition and war stores, and now we were hearing that some of those same guys were dead? We simply could not believe it. This was the first British warship sunk in action since the Second World War—it was unbelievable.

It is safe to say that we took the news badly. Initially the entire ship was in complete shock, from Captain to Junior Cook. It had all seemed so unreal, so *distant*. With this news though, reality had come crashing in. The Argentine's (or "Argies" as they had by now been christened) were not some tin-pot little flotilla, and half-arsed air force, but were in fact as professional and proud as we were, and were bloody dangerous. Shortly after the Sheffield had been sunk, there was another blow with the sinking of the "Atlantic Conveyor", and we were finally realising that we had a proper war to deal with, one in which there was a real chance that we really could be wounded or killed, and that the Royal Navy might for the first time in a very long time, have its arse well and truly kicked!

By the time we limped back into Gibraltar the war was well and truly under way. We were keen to get back out there and help out, but it became apparent that the repairs to the main engines were not going to be quick. Initial investigations indicated that the bearings on one of the engines were completely knackered and would require replacement, which in turn required half of the engine room to be de-lagged—a not inconsiderable job in itself. A time of war, whether declared or not, was not ideal to be taking apart one of your warships, so it was decided that the work would wait for now.

The lead up to the Falklands war had been a bit of a lean time for the Royal Navy. During the period 1979 to 1982 the size of the fleet had decreased very rapidly, and ships were being taken out of service all over the shop. Following the decommissioning of the Ark Royal, the government had decided not to replace her with another "proper" aircraft carrier, but had instead commissioned a number of "Through-Deck Cruisers" as they were initially called. These were mini aircraft carriers, and were able to carry the Sea Harrier aircraft, again at that time not really considered to be "true" fighter aircraft, and more likely to be used in a ground attack role in support of amphibious landings. Quite possibly the Argentine's had been watching this re-organisation in progress and had taken a punt at occupying the Falklands in the expectation that the British would not be able to support an operation to recapture it. They were nearly right. Just about everything and anything that would float and could carry the ensign was pressed into service to either go to the Falklands, or to support it in some way. In our case, and although we only had one "good" engine, our new task for the duration of the conflict was to act as Gibraltar Guardship. We were not happy.

At the time of the Falklands War, British relations with Spain with regard to the ownership of the rock of Gibraltar were still "tense". There had been a vote or referendum or something by the inhabitants in the recent past as to whether they wished to remain British or to become Spanish. The result was that they overwhelmingly wanted to stay part of the UK, and the British government had promised them that that would be the case. The Spanish did not like that answer, and the border crossing remained a choke point for anybody wanting to cross from or to the mainland. The Spanish were not slow of course to realise that a very large percentage of the British navy were down in the South Atlantic, and there were rumours that they might take advantage of the situation and make a bid for the Rock—they would have to get past a partly crippled Leander Class frigate first! We sailed (slowly) up and down the Gibraltar/Spain coastline looking out for any military activity for the next couple of months, but thankfully apart from a few moments of excitement when we saw some practice beach landings being carried out by Spanish Marines, the only activity we recorded was that of holidaymakers enjoying the Sun, Sea and Sangria. It was pretty strange being closed up at action stations, fully spammed up with anti-flash gear, respirators, and survival suits and with the guns manned, while a few hundred yards away people were sunbathing, surfing and setting out to sea in their pedaloes!

So, my Falklands conflict was over before it had begun, and like the great percentage of the UK, we watched the story unfold on the TV. Other ships came and went, either on their way to, or returning from the conflict, and of course we got some fairly hair-raising stories from some of the participants. There were stories of casualties, bombs hitting ships but failing to explode, frigates acting as decoys for Exocet missiles so that the carriers were protected and so forth. We were all at once jealous of the action and glad that we were spared.

Of course I was worried about my Brother too. He was serving on HMS Avenger during the conflict. The Avenger was a Type 21 frigate, relatively new and considered to be first rate. The Type 21 though were not fairing too well so far in the conflict, with HMS Ardent sunk by bombing, and HMS Antelope destroyed after an unexploded bomb detonated while being de-fused. He later told me that the Avenger spent most of her time in the "Gun Line"—a picket of ships fitted with the 4.5" gun turret, whose job was to respond to calls from the ground forces for supporting gunfire. As a consequence of their positioning though, these ships tended to be on the flight path of both incoming and outgoing Argentine attack aircraft, and were regularly "strafed" with cannon and machine gun fire. They spent a great deal of time at action station, and his station was down below in one of the diesel generator compartment onboard. He said he was happy there because he could take cover between the 2 big diesel engines, and so had a substantial amount of metal between him and any incoming bullets. The Avenger was strafed and damaged by aircraft during the conflict, but as far as I am aware, nobody was killed or injured. John subsequently returned to the UK on the Avenger, and left the Navy the same year, as had been the plan prior to the Falklands conflict starting.

As it became clear that Britain were going to win back the Falklands, our world started to settle down a bit. We were returned to the dockyard in Gibraltar, and eventually had the long broken engine repaired by having the main bearings replaced. Gibraltar was always the kind of place where a person had a number of choices—spending the entire time in a drunken haze, the choice of many it must be said, by getting seriously fit, or by having a hobby or project to concentrate on. Although I wasn't a complete swot—I had a few good nights out, and even ran around the rock a few times, I had been using my time fairly effectively and had finally reached the point where I was in a position to take the examination for promotion to Leading Stoker. I took the exam in Gibraltar on 27th May 1982. The written exam was no problem, but this was my first example of a formal oral exam. In this case I sat in my No.1 uniform before my own Engineering Officer, Deputy Engineer, and another Engineering Officer from the Gibraltar naval base. I was very nervous, but managed to answer the questions satisfactorily I guess, because I passed. I was now a "Scale A" stoker, meaning that I had passed for promotion, but now had to wait in a roster system to be actually rated as a leading hand—at that time, the wait was in the region of 18 months—in actuality it took over 2 years for me to get the rate. The date of the last people to be given promotion was always posted in the Navy News, and for the next 2 years I was, along with everybody else waiting for promotion an avid reader of the paper! Some months the date of seniority for promotion never seemed to shift, and the months dragged on endlessly. It was very frustrating waiting to be promoted having done all of the hard work to get there, but there was no other alternative than to wait my turn. At least in my case I was already a Local Acting Killick, but that would not be case any more when I left the ship on completion of my draft. I was naively hoping that I would be promoted before I left, but unfortunately that did not turn out to be the case.

I left the Ariadne in around May or June of 1982, when the ship finally returned to Devonport. She was a good ship for me and I was sorry in many ways to leave her—not least of all because it now meant that I was dis-rated from the Acting Local Leading Stoker rate, and hence was now a

MEM1 again. It hurt actually, both to my ego and of course in the pocket since the pay drop was pretty noticeable too. I rejoined HMS Defiance—by now a large modern building in place of the old rusting ship—and became part of one of the mobile repair teams doing the rounds at that time. It was quite sobering to watch and then work on the ships returning from the Falklands—they were all well worn from the journey and experience, and some of the stories from the crews were hair-raising. I particularly remember working on HMS Plymouth. She had been stuck by a total of five 500lb bombs—all of which had mercifully failed to explode. She still bore the scars when she returned to Plymouth, showing hastily welded patches over the bomb entry holes, which we set about putting right as the ship's company took some well earned leave. I was relieved to see HMS Avenger and my Brother arrive safely in late summer, and without delay he set about leaving the Navy and moving over to America with his wife. They stayed in a married quarter in Plymouth for a few months and then moved over to Portland Oregon. I didn't see him again for 19 years. The war/conflict in my opinion affected him badly, and with perfect hindsight there was a good chance that he was suffering psychologically from the experience. I found out later that he had struggled to come to terms with his experience, drinking heavily and finding it hard to integrate into society. At that time there was no real safety net for checking that combatants were ok prior to their being released into the world, and as a consequence he was forced to suffer alone in silence. I hope that the treatment of servicemen has improved since those days, but I doubt it.

Chapter 8

Hurry Up and Wait

To my own shame I did not really notice any problems John might have been having at the time—I was too busy with my own plans. In July of 1982 the other big occasion for me was my marriage to Anna, my by now long term fiancé from Malta. We had become engaged the previous year, and while of course the plans had been under the microscope during the conflict, as soon as it became clear that the Ariadne would not be involved, the plans forged ahead. On my return to the UK I had made arrangements for a married quarter (a flat in St Budeaux), all the necessary permissions and stuff, while Anna had done the same in Malta. The plan was to get married in the church in Kalkara Malta, have a honeymoon there, and then return as a married couple to the UK. The first hiccup was my family. I had of course invited everybody, but they all cried off due to the expense of flying to Malta—even my Mother. I had even offered to pay for her travel but she had still declined. How embarrassed was I turning up in Malta on my own to get married? They took it pretty well, although my Father-in-Law simply could not get his head around my Mother not being there for her son's wedding! Nevertheless we went ahead and had a nice service (all in Maltese of course). It was mid July in Malta and bloody hot.

I wore a suit and the service turned into a sweating contest between me and the priest. We had a nice reception afterwards, lots of hand shaking and kisses on cheeks, and then stayed for the rest of the week in a pretty grotty little hotel on the island.

Looking back with perfect hindsight, it must have been a terrible ordeal for Anna. We were both very young, me 21 and Anna 20, but we were determined to make everything work. I could not afford a mortgage on a home of our own, and I am not sure that the thought even crossed my mind at that stage, and so we had to opt for a Married Quarter. Of course we were luckier than some couples, those that didn't even have that option, but on arrival at our allocated flat it was still a bit of a shock.

We had flown back to the UK from Malta, and had had a nice welcome from the family I suppose. As always seemed to be the case in those days life just carried on whatever happened, and it was just kind of "Nice to see you both—welcome to the family Anna" kind of acceptance. I was unable to drive in those days and it seemed a good idea when my elder brother Neil offered to drive us down to Plymouth to move into our new place. Well his wife at the time, a girl called Kim was having none of it, and decided that she and their baby would come along too, for the ride and a bit of a holiday. We couldn't refuse—how could we with him having offered to drive us. Anyway we all clambered into his little Nissan 120Y (I remember it so well because I think the name plate is permanently engraved on my arse!), and spluttered off on our way. The plan (which seemed a decent one at the time) was that having arrived back in the UK sometime during the day; we would travel overnight to Plymouth in preparation for moving in to our new married quarter home the next day. To say it was a tight fit would be unfair to tight fits, it was excruciating! Neil and Kim were in relative luxury, having a seat each at the front, while Anna, me and the baby (who was dumped on us from the get-go—"Go on Anna, you might as well get used to holding a baby, hehe"), along with the nappies, bottles, baby food, spare clothing and God knows what else had the back bench seat all to ourselves. In the tiny boot and on top of the car were Anna and my entire worldly possessions, along with Neil and Kim's "holiday" stuff. The car was, quite frankly a piece of moving scrap, with the moving bit being somewhat intermittent. We did not have the nice easy to follow main roads and dual carriageways down to Plymouth in those days, and the journey was long, hot, smelly and totally unpleasant. The child had a tendency to vomit at the drop of a hat, and that was in between pooing with monotonous regularity, a course of events its Mother seemed to take great pleasure in bringing to our attention:

"Baby needs a change Anna" or "Don't worry, she/he (can't remember which) is just a little car sick"

I knew the feeling. Poor Anna must have thought she was in Hell.

Every so often one of 2 things happened. Either the car would break down, leading to an outburst of oaths, slamming doors, raised hood and banging from the engine compartment, followed by an exchange of further oaths between Neil and Kim, baby crying, and off we go again; or an argument breaking out between Neil and Kim about where we were, where we were going, how lost we were and how much longer it would be to get there. We sat there holding the baby, cramped and miserable and hoping against hope that a big articulated lorry would go out of control and bring our nightmare to an end. Although I think we had a couple of flasks of tea or coffee, there was nothing to eat and again, there was little in the way of road-side cafes to stop and rest a bit at.

It was a very long night. None of us had any sleep at all, and all of us including the baby were very snappy and tired by the time the Tamar Bridge came into sight early next morning. Our ordeal wasn't over yet though.

We managed to find the married quarter in St Budeaux where my brother John and his wife of the time Noreen were living, and rolled up outside their door at about 7 am—totally unexpectedly as we had omitted to warn them of our impending arrival. Noreen was not a morning person, and being American was not slow in making it known that she was not at all happy with the situation:

"Nice to see you guys, but shit, you could have at least phoned for Christ's sake".

Point taken. To be fair she soon got used to the idea—at least she did once she realised we were not going to be staying with her. On came the breakfast, congratulations and coo, cooing over the baby. John I suppose was more used to the unexpected and didn't bat an eyelid at our arrival—he was off to work anyway so didn't have to suffer us too long.

After we had settled down a bit, we mentioned that we would be getting our married quarter this very morning, and were due to meet some woman at the flat, as I recall at about ten in the morning. Noreen to our surprise started bristling at the very mention, and began telling us about the "March-In"—the handing over process for married quarters. In our

My Bloody Efforts

naivety we had assumed that you just signed for the thing, filled in a direct debit form and then Bob's the brother of your Mother's sister. Apparently, and to our utter surprise, it turned out that you had to accompany the Allocations Officer around the place, formally inspecting the bloody thing and noting absolutely any defect that might be present. Noreen made it very clear that this was vital for us, because when we eventually left the place another inspection would be made (imaginatively called the March-Out), and if there were any defects not on the original list we would have to pay to make them good. Having been up all night, we were far from being too happy about the whole thing.

We turned up at the flat at the appointed time, having left the other 3 with Noreen for now. From the outside the block looked pretty well maintained, and was one of about 9 or 10 on the estate. An official looking lady turned up a few minutes later, introduced herself and ushered us towards the block. Our flat would be one on the bottom floor. She was a no-nonsense sort, all business and watch-checking, and was intent in getting our signatures and being off. The flat was nice enough and reasonably clean (although Anna probably didn't think so), and consisted of a front room, kitchen, bathroom and two bedrooms, all painted a faintly dirty white colour. We had opted for a furnished flat, and indeed this one was fitted with some Government Issue standard furniture—chairs, sofa, table and chairs etc, all with bare wood and prickly covers. It was basic but since we were in no position to do anything else, it would do us for now. The battleaxe whisked us around in seconds, pointing out this or that for our attention, then pushed apiece of paper in our faces and asked us to sign it. We were not to be hurried though, and on Noreen's advice set about inspecting the place properly, producing a list of any and every defect we could see, and asking here to add each item to the appropriate part of the form. She quickly became impatient with us, quietly snorting and tapping her clipboard with a pen, which of course made us more determined to do the job properly. Anna was in her element, and as I came to find out over the years, became totally shitty with the woman trying to force her will upon us. Eventually we were satisfied that we had listed everything and signed the paper. It was good advice from Noreen, as when we came to leave the place a couple of years later, lo and behold, the very same form came along with the Allocations Officer for the March-Out, and you can bet he (it was a he this time), checked every single item on it.

The woman left us alone in the place—our place. We were dog tired, and dreading the thought of Neil, Kim and the baby coming over to join us. Although the flat was furnished, it did not have a lot of the basics like sheets, towels and stuff, and before we could even catch a bit of sleep we would have to go and get some. I had never had cause to go to St Budeaux so far in my illustrious naval career, and so didn't even know where the shops that sold household bits and pieces were! Our only alternative was to go back to Noreen's and seek a bit of grown-up advice—we would probably have to get Neil to drive us down to the town.

Noreen saved the day though—being the sensible sort, she insisted that rather than trolling down the shops now, we could borrow sheets, towels, crockery and stuff from her for the period that Neil and the tribe were here, then buy the stuff slowly as we found are feet. Simple really when you've had a full night's sleep!

It's fair to say that the next few days were very difficult for us. We had been married for all of about a week, were in a totally new environment for both of us, were trying to get to know one-another and the new place we were living in, and at the same time trying to entertain guests. Boy, and no offense to Neil, but we were mighty glad when they left.

In no time at all the honeymoon period was over, and it was back to work for me. I rejoined HMS Defiance, by now a proper shore establishment in its own right rather than an old rusting hulk, and was placed with one of the mobile repair teams in the dockyard. By this stage the conflict was over and we very quickly settled down in to a routine where our role was to assist the ship's companies during their maintenance periods alongside. For me it started as an enjoyable time, as it was a removal from the routine I had become used to as the engineer's office boy. In addition of course it gave me and Anna a solid start to our married life, and meant that in the end, I had almost 2 years on shore before being posted to my next ship. After a couple of months I was posted with Defiance to the Gas-Turbine Change Unit, a work gang specialising in the removal and replacement of gas turbine engines on the warships. Again it was a complete change for me, as until then I had only worked on steam machinery. It was interesting and challenging to change an engine, and I felt useful and interested doing the work. Changing a gas turbine unit on a frigate was quite a complicated affair. The gas turbines in use at the time on the Type 21 and Type 22 frigates based in Plymouth were Rolls-Royce "Tyne" engines, and the larger "Olympus" gas turbines—the same basic form of the engines fitted on the Concorde (a fact we never tired of telling anybody remotely interested!). To change one on a frigate involved opening an engine removal route through the ship, which in turn meant that we Stokers spent much of our time "spanner wanking"—removing hundreds of bolts holding huge removable panels in place through the ship, and then using heavy lift gear to take them shore side. This then allowed the Artificers to remove the defective gas turbine from its module in the engine room, and once the thing was de-coupled the Stokers, under the direction of the "Chief Tiff" would then haul and lift the engine through a tortuous removal path using chain blocks and cranes, finally having the 4 ton weight lifted clean out of a huge opening created in the middle of the ship. The replacement of the new engine was of course a reversal of the whole process. When I started with the unit the whole thing used to take a full 5 days, working in shifts day and night, but within a year we had got the process down to just 3 days. It was bloody hard work though.

The funniest time I remember about the whole period involved a special tool that the Tiffs used to use to align the new turbine with its output drive shaft. The tool was a big stainless steel "wagon wheel" shaped thing, about 4 feet in diameter and machined to very small tolerances, which they used to clamp to the business end of the turbine. The other side of the wheel would then be aligned by minute jacking movements of the engine. When the engine and output shaft were in perfect alignment, the engine could be "slotted" onto the shaft, and it would ensure then that there would be no vibration when the engine was driving its gearbox. All of the unit's gear used to be carted around in two 20 ton containers, which would be dumped next to which ever the ship we happened to be working on. As part of the preparation for a job, we would get all of out stuff out, including the alignment tool, and lay it out on the ground for checking prior to use. Invariably our containers would be dumped underneath one of the huge dockyard cranes, and our gear would then be spread out between the tracks on which the cranes would traverse up and down the dockside. In this instance it turned out, the alignment tool, weighing about 150 pounds, must have been a bit too close to the tracks, because unknown to anybody it had been struck by a passing crane. There was no visible damage to the tool, but the strike must have been hard enough to bend it slightly, because for the next 3 days the Tiffs simply could not get the new engine to align. We Stokers had done our bit by removing all the stuff along the route, and took great pleasure in winding up the harassed Tiffs as they sweated, scratched their heads and tried to work out what the hell the problem was. Of course the ship's engineers quickly became twitchy about the delay, and eventually even the Captain of the ship became involved, wanting to know when they could put their ship back together again. So, no pressure then. The alignment tool was a big heavy lump of metal, and nobody for one moment imagined that it could go out of alignment, but the Tiffs eventually reached the conclusion that the only thing which COULD be out was the tool. A new one was requisitioned with remarkable speed, and hey presto, the engine went straight in. There was a big finger-pointing session afterwards, the Tiffs blaming the Stokers for bending the tool, but the Chief Stoker was having none of it—neatly pointing out that if the "fucking prima-donnas" helped the Stokers unload and put the gear away in the first place, some damage to other equipment might be avoided. In the end we had the usual "we are all in the same team" pep-talk, and everybody learned a new respect for the gear we had to use.

While the work side of life was good, there remained one serious fly in the ointment. I had been back to being a stoker 1st class for about a year now, and it was looking increasing less likely that I would be promoted to Leading Hand again any time soon. The dates on the promotion roster seemed to tick along ridiculously slowly, and I worked out that at the current rate I would be about 26 years old before I was promoted. While I was waiting I could not take any further promotion exams, which in turn meant that the way things were going I would not even make Petty officer by the time I left the Navy at 40 years old! I tried to keep myself going by taking and passing my driving test, as well as taking "O" level exams in English, Maths and physics, but I was starting to get really frustrated by the slow pace of my naval career. I was now a married man, and in the 1980s everybody had aspirations of buying their own house, having a nice car and all that stuff, so why should I be any different.

It was around this period that I started seriously looking at the Fire Brigade as an alternative career move. I had always fancied that I could do the job, and had made my mind up that at 22 I needed to make a long term decision about what I wanted to do with the rest of my working life. I enjoyed the Navy very much but there was no way I was going to stay either a Leading Hand or Petty Officer for the rest of my life. There was a chance that I could be selected for Artificer training from the Leading Mechanics Career Course I would soon be attending, but that (at the time) was a bit of a long shot. I sounded out the fire service for recruitment prospects, and was informed that yes; the Devon Fire Service was actively taking on people. Before I had time to take it further though, I was given notice that I was to be posted to the Leading Stoker's Career Course in HMS Sultan within the next couple of months. I decided there and then that if I was not selected for Artificer Training (the naval engineering apprenticeship) while on the course, I would leave the Navy.

Before starting the Leading Stokers Qualifying Course, there was one more than I was notified to attend first. This was the dreaded Leading Rates Leadership Course (LRLC). This was a 4-weeks duration training course held at a place called HMS Royal Arthur in Corsham, Wiltshire. I use the word "dreaded" purposely, as the course had something of a nasty reputation in the fleet, mostly for the supposed harsh treatment of candidates and the physical exertion required for the duration of it. The physical bit I was not too worried about as by now I was reasonably fit, but not surprisingly there was considerable apprehension about the course content. One good piece of advice I was given was to exchange all of my kit for new stuff, as the dress standards on course were ridiculously high. It was a good move as it turned out.

The first problem on this course was finding the bloody place! We had been ordered to join the course on during the day on a Friday, which was really unusual. We soon found out why. As we arrived at the appointed time we were ordered into our physical training (or "fiz") kit, and told to muster outside. The pain was going to start from minute one, and without further ado we carried out a Naval Fitness Test. This consisted at the time of a 1½ mile run to be completed with a certain time, followed by measured numbers of press-ups, sit-ups and stuff, all under the screaming attention of the training staff and physical training instructors (PTIs).

"Push-out" became the new watch-word, and we were constantly being encouraged to do so!

For me the test was not difficult, but for a number of others it was the end of their course before it had even begun, and they were sent away. They may have been the lucky ones!

The course was designed to turn "Able" ratings from all branches of the service into "Leading" ratings. The process was quite blunt—put people into stressful situations, and then teach them how to handle it. This was very much a leadership rather than management course, and the onus was on "taking charge" of a group of men. The course stress was induced in a number of ways—very high dress and personal standards, physical tiredness induced through extreme exercise and lack of sleep, and by putting people normally used to being told what to do, in the full glare of the spotlight.

For all of us on the course, it was our first taste of any form of leadership training, and boy it was painful. The instructors were absolutely unbending in their ferocity towards us, and completely hammered us at every turn. From the very next morning's kit muster, where the entire contents of our lockers were thrown about the mess deck for being "fucking crap!", to the constant punishment of press-ups for any and every misdemeanour—whether we were outside in the snow, or in the dining hall at lunch. We were under a constant barrage of verbal abuse, and for the first few days it was quite draining. It was pretty unpleasant to have a great big PTI screaming into your face from a couple of inches away—couldn't have been all that hygienic either I wouldn't have thought.

The Leadership element of the course was in 2 parts. Most mornings, after the first fiz session of the day, we would attend lectures on Leadership, management and theoretical side of the process. This was followed after more fiz, or clothing changes, or mess deck cleanliness rounds, or some other bullshit by putting the theory into practice using "Practical Leadership Tasks" or "PLTs". Here, we would take in turns to be in-charge for some practical exercise—perhaps constructing a path across a "chasm" using oil drums and rope, or lifting a casualty from a "crashed" helicopter using a fag packet and chewing gum! We were supposed to conduct the exercise in a set way—briefing, ideas, construction, conclusion etc, but this was quite difficult with a number of Chiefs and Petty Officers screaming obscenities in either ear! My first PLT consisted of taking charge of a squad of men on the parade ground—something totally alien to a Stoker! Unfortunately this was no ordinary squad, but was an "awkward squad", briefed to occasionally mis-hear or ignore a particular order! I would order "quick-march", and 10 of the 12 would start moving, or order "Squad-Halt" and find the first two guys continuing! It was very frustrating (as it was supposed to be). At the same time a Gunnery Instructor or "GI" was bellowing (and boy, could the bellow!) in my starboard ear "LEADER—TAKE CHARGE OF YOUR SQUAD!!" and other much less pleasant entreaties.

While our days were taken up with exercise, PLTs and lectures, we were no less busy in the evenings and weekends. There was no leave for the duration of the course, and in the evenings we had a number of options to keep us out of mischief. Of course the upkeep of our uniforms took a huge amount of time and effort, and they required constant washing, ironing, folding and brushing. We were changing in and out of all of our uniforms about 8 times a day (it was part of the stress building process), and in addition we were needing fresh gym kit 3 times a day, as well as needing to wash the constant mud and crap out of our working clothes and boots. Well, the boots were just constantly wet. Just chuck a bit of polish over them and hope for the best. The washing and drying rooms were hopelessly inadequate, and it was not unusual to be wearing wet clothing. So long as it was spotlessly clean we could get away with it. When the washing and ironing was done, the planning for the weekends could start. Each weekend of the course we would be out in the Brecon Beacons in Wales. The difficulty of the treks would increase progressively over the course, until for the final weekend we would be dropped off somewhere in the depths of Wales, and left to find our way back to base camp. It could be done in the 3-day weekend, so long as you did not stop for anything trivial like food or sleep. For all of us this was going to be torture—the most outdoor kind of thing we had done was a camping weekend with the Scouts! There was much complaining about this aspect of the course—most of us decided that we had come to the wrong base, and had accidently joined the fucking Marines!!

The stress started to take its toll after just a couple days for some people. Many of the guys (and it was just guys in those days) were not used to much physical exercise, and before too long the strains and sprains started to show up. Most of us had some kind of injury—in my case my left ankle was giving me gyp—but we just strapped it up, took a few paracetamol and cracked on—there was no way we were going "around the buoy", or doing the course again! Quite a number dropped out over the course of the 4 weeks, and I am sorry with hindsight to say that at the time there was no remorse for them—we had enough to think about for ourselves to worry about the fate of others. They were weak, and it was their own fault for not preparing properly. Tough shit! "Let's get this fucking nightmare finished and get the hell out of here!" was the general feeling of the survivors.

Being one of the fitter guys on the course, I was "selected" to take part in another demanding "after hours" activity. This was the "Cliff and Chasm" challenge, more commonly (and accurately!) called the "Cough and Spasm" challenge. This was an Assault Course near the base, with a steep hill and chasm area, where a beer barrel filled with sand had to be traversed, using 50 metres of thick rope, all carried by a 10-man assault team. Naturally there was a fastest time record for the course, and every class passing through was invited to better it. The course record stood at around 15 minutes had not been improved for very many years. It had been set by a team of PTIs, all super fit buggers, and the likelihood of us breaking it was very slim indeed.

Nonetheless, for the entire time of the course, we 10 of the assault team spent a number of hours each evening figuring out how to run the course quickly. The barrel of sand was ridiculously heavy, and could only be carried by a couple of guys in turn, so that a constant barrel handover system was needed. The rope too was heavy and awkward, and tended to unravel as we went over and under obstacles, including a 40 foot rope net halfway along the course. Once we reached the chasm, only 2 guys, one of which was me, could take the end of the rope over to set up the hoist to get the barrel across. The barrel would come flying across the chasm and crash past us to the ground—we would then pick it up and run! By the time the next relay team took the barrel we were practically dead on our feet. We got into it over the weeks, and by the time we did the record run, we were only about 30 seconds short of the record. As it was we gave it our best shot, but on the day the record was safe in the hands of the PTIs. Looking back now, how we all managed to escape without any broken bones is incredible—that bloody barrel used to go whizzing past our ears, knees and ankles at a remarkable speed. Ah the bravery of youth!

As the course progressed, we started to become hardened to the treatment of the instructors. The guys who were not going to complete the course had mostly been weeded out by this stage, and we had started working as a team to complete the many and various challenges presented to us. As we got to know each other, we began to understand the strengths and weaknesses of each person, and adapt accordingly. The fiz, PLTs and after hours stuff all became easier, and we actually started enjoying the course. Eventually, once the instructors had got the result they desired from us, their attitude softened a bit, making our lives slightly easier. The last real hurdle was the final weekend in the Brecon Beacons. People had been binned from the course even at this late stage for failing to complete this part of the course.

It was a miserable weekend from start to finish. The weather was bloody awful from the moment we got off the bus, until the moment we were picked up. Strong winds, driving rain and the cold ensured that we were soaked through after the first couple of hours, and there was never any opportunity to dry anything out. It was all good "character building" stuff, and the only thing to do was to dig your chin into your chest and walk. My map reading skills were non-existent, so I let somebody else do that stuff. I just walked, and walked, and . . . walked. Time dragged like hell, and I constantly wondered why people would want to do this for either a career or for "fun". Every few hours a Landrover would appear, and an Instructor would ask if we were ok from behind a cloud of steam given off from the red-hot tea he would be drinking from his Thermos. I don't remember anybody dropping out during the weekend, but there were certainly times when the idea was attractive!

The Leadership course ended quite meekly really. We were each given a personal performance appraisal by the Course Manager, into which each of the instructor had an input. In my case it was complete bollocks, and I wondered if they had the right person. They said my performance had been "Just Satisfactory", and that I was not fit enough! Cheeky bastards—I had kept up with all of the physical stuff, and had been on the Cough and Spasm team. Didn't want much then, did they! I signed in agreement with the appraisal just to get out of the bloody place. It was nice to see Royal Arthur getting smaller in my rear-view mirror.

Chapter 9

Time to Put-Up or Shut-Up

The Leading Marine Engineering Mechanic's Career Course (more commonly known as the Killick Stoker's Course) as the name suggests, was the course that gave a prospective Leading Stoker the engineering skills he would need onboard a ship. It was a 12 weeks long course, and included a fair bit of academic and engineering theory, which for quite a few people was the first (and for a number last) time that they would be exposed to "classroom" training. I joined HMS Sultan for the course early in 1984, with the sole intention of being selected from the course for Artificer training. This would be my one chance for "guaranteed" promotion, and I had no intention of missing it.

Because of the really slow promotion rate at the time, and despite being titled as a "Leading Stoker's Course", all of the class were in fact still waiting to be promoted when we joined for the start. This was a "first" for HMS Sultan as normally the people on the course would be at the rate of Leading Hand, and there was initially a bit of confusion about how we should be treated—as Leading Hands, or as Stokers? In practical terms the only difference was that Leading Hands were not required to march around the place as a group, whereas Stokers were. We of course were outraged! It was not our fault that we had not been promoted—we had all passed for Leading Hand and were by now fairly experienced sailors. There would be tears before bedtime if we had to march around like new entrants, and thankfully good sense prevailed. We would be treated as "prospective Leading Stokers", having first been given the obligatory warning that we were to set an example to the younger guys in our behaviour blah, blah blah!

The course started in earnest with a few of weeks of Maths, Physics, Engineering Science and other classroom pleasures. While a good few of the guys hated it, for me it was great! I had recently passed Physics and Maths "O" levels which I had taken in my own time, and it paid off handsomely. I was usually 1st or 2nd in each exam, normally sharing the spoils with a Scottish lad, and quickly got a name for myself as a "girly swot". I was enjoying the classroom work, and was getting the marks I needed for Artificer selection. All was looking good.

After a few weeks of the classroom work, we started on the practical side of the training. The practical training was in two phases—workshops and maintenance bays. In the maintenance bays we took pieces of machinery to bits and put them back together again, the parts becoming more complicated until in the end we were required to rebuild a piece of machinery (an auxiliary or "donkey" boiler in my case) and to get the thing running. It was again straight forward for me with my recent maintenance base experience.

The problems started in the workshop. Throughout my naval career to then I had not really had any opportunity to do much in a workshop. Of course I had drilled a few holes here and there on the pillar drill, but that was about it. Our first job in the training workshop was to cut out, square off and then drill some holes in, a piece of plate metal. Now that did not seem too difficult a proposition on first view, but it soon became obvious that my brain was better than my hands! I could not saw straight using a hacksaw, and when it came to filing, it was a nightmare. We had these little "set-square" things to show you when the piece of metal was flat and square, but at the rate I was going, there would be not metal left to check! Of course the worse it went, the more panicky I became, in turn making it worse and so on . . . We had about 5 hour's workshop time to make this thing, and by about hour 3 I was considering launching the fucking thing through the nearest window. Luckily I was not alone in my despair, and quite a lot of us were having serious difficulty.

Nobody came to help us. We would appeal to the passing instructors in their nice white lab coats to come and instruct us, by they would just smile, tell us to "crack on" and wander off. After the 5 hours of sweating, swearing and creating blisters on sawing and filing palms and fingers, we were told to "down tools". I looked at the masterpiece in the vice in front of me. I had managed in 5 hours to cut out the rough shape of a square, and had spent the next 4 hours and 50 minutes filing one side in a vain attempt to get it straight. I had failed miserably. I looked around the rest of the class, and felt some solace that a lot of others were in the same boat. A few smart-arses had managed to get some holes drilled, but in general we had all done pretty dismally.

The Fleet Chief in charge of the workshop training department walked amongst us, picking up a piece of work here, a broken hacksaw blade there, and smiling benignly at out stressed, sweating faces.

"Well Gentlemen. This effort is pathetic. My 5 year old daughter could turn out better pieces than this. Looks like we have a bit of work to do doesn't it? Who here is hoping for Artificer selection?" A number of hands went tentatively up (not including mine I might add) "You had better get your shit in one sock pretty smartly then lads, because on this showing you wouldn't be selected for a Boy Scout's tent making badge!" And so the scene was set.

It was a pretty shocking introduction to the world of metalwork, and in my case made me realise what a mountain I would have to climb if I wanted to achieve Artificer selection. In fairness, following the shock tactic initially employed by the instructors, they did revert to starting from the basics and then expanding from there. They taught us how to hold files and hacksaws correctly, how to stand so that we could achieve straightness and all sorts of other stuff in an effort to get us working with metal properly. With me, the tendency is that I take ages to learn something, but once the bit of knowledge is embedded, it tends to stay there. In this environment though, time was of the essence, and the rate of increase in difficulty in the work we were expected to produce was relentless. There was never any time to consolidate, and even with the excellent instruction I was starting to struggle. I could now hacksaw a line to within 0.5 of a millimetre, and could file an edge absolutely flat, but it was taking too long—it always ended with me having to rush for the last couple of hours, making silly errors and cocking up the job.

I was starting to see my future in the Navy as a pretty short one—if I could not up my score in the workshop, I would have no chance of passing Artificer selection, no matter how well I had done in the classroom. I decided that my only course of action was a direct appeal to the Instructors for a bit of extra assistance. I targeted one of the old retired metalwork instructors, put on my best doe eyes, and asked if there was any way I could do extra instruction, in the evenings say, so that I would have some slim hope in hell of getting selected for the Apprenticeship.

The instructor in question was a retired aircraft engineering fitter, more famous in HMS Sultan for growing bon-sai trees than for anything to do with engineering! In any case he was an absolute marvel with metalwork, was remarkably relaxed in every crises presented to him by panicking students, and always had a way of recovering apparent disasters with hacksaw and file. We would spend hours without success trying to file some edge flat, and just at the point of picking a window through which the offending article would be flying, this guy would come along, take the file, and in about a minute would have the bloody thing perfect. To my intense relief he took pity on me, asking me how I had done in the classroom, why I wanted Artificer selection and that kind of thing. He said that there was no need for me to work in the evenings, as he would give me a bit more attention during the workshop sessions instead.

True to his word, this gentleman from then on did spend more time with me, correcting this or that mistake, and showing me little techniques that made my work faster and more accurate. My marks started to improve, and my confidence in the workshop with them. In truth though, the instructor was making sure that my marks were consistently high enough to achieve the selection requirement, and had he not done that I would not have even been considered, so to him I am eternally grateful. Being the self-centred sod I was at that time I don't think I even thanked him, although I did buy a little tree off him at some car boot sale. It died.

The final week of the Leading Stoker's course is dedicated to selection of Artificer Candidates. The basic criterion for selection was to achieve certain minimum marks in the areas of Academics (Maths, Physics, engineering science etc), Engineering Theory, and Workshop Practice. I had achieved the 2nd highest marks in the academic phase, 1st highest marks in the Engineering Theory, but had just scraped through with about 2% to spare in the Workshop. The final part of the selection process was to attend a pre-selection interview board. The board consisted of a Lieutenant-Commander rank engineering officer, assisted by another Lieutenant engineer and a Lieutenant "Schoolie" or academics teacher. I and 10 others had been invited to attend the board, and we would do so dressed in our best No.1 uniforms (in order to give the best overall impression). We were absolutely bricking it.

There was no swotting to be done for this test. It was a straight-forward interview where the board members could and would ask anything they wanted. We heard horror stories of candidates being asked to explain how all manner of things worked, ranging from a toaster to an aeroplane wing. On the appointed day we all turned up at the training school in our best uniforms, were herded into a classroom and told to wait. We waited in trepidation, all aware of the significance of this day to our naval futures, and all petrified that we would fuck up.

In best naval tradition we went in alphabetical order, and as was usually the case that meant it was me first. I was called out, stood up and followed the Petty Officer. I could feel the eyes of the others burning in to my back as I left. I was glad to go first—at least the ordeal would be over one way or another.

The PO knocked, opened the door and ushered me past him, closing the door behind me. The room was a small office with a window opposite, giving a view of a grassy courtyard beyond. Directly in front of the window was a long desk, the other side of which sat the 3 officers, the Lieutenants flanking the Lieutenant Commander. I did not recognise any of them, and all, like me, were dressed in their best uniforms. All 3 stared at me with neutral eyes and faces. I stood to attention.

"Come in MEM Bridgman. Welcome, relax and take a seat" Relax, yeah right!

I took the seat placed strategically in front of the table.

The Lieutenant Commander introduced himself and the others, outlined the reason for the board, and then commenced going through my course record exam by exam, reciting scores achieved and identifying for the others what he considered potential weak areas—to be investigating during the board. The others nodded occasionally, and continued to look me over. Eventually the questions started:

"Can you explain to me the propulsion system of one of the frigates you have served on?" I did so, with ease.

"I see you worked with gas turbines for some time. How do they work then?" Again, a nice easy question that I was able to field fairly easily.

This went on for some time, and was probably done on purpose (although it was never stated) to put me at ease. Then the more difficult stuff started.

From the Lieutenant engineer "MEM Bridgman, I note that you were the Engineer's Writer on a couple of ships. Does that mean you were more interested in paperwork than the machinery?"

I had been expecting this one "No Sir. Actually I was the Writer for one draft—we happened to change ships half way through the draft. I am sure you have also noted that during the time I was a Writer I was also keeping shifts in the machinery spaces, and in fact passed for Leading Stoker during that time. I don't think that would have happened if I had no interest in engineering".

"Very good—Thank you. What car do you drive?"

I was thrown by that one "Er . . . a Ford Escort Sir"

"Ok, what is the difference between the car you drive and say, a Mini?"

"Well, mine's bigger Sir!" I just couldn't help it. I thought it was funny, but the stony stares remained.

"No, I mean in terms of machinery—why is a mini different from your Escort?"

Then it clicked. "Oh yes, a Mini is a front wheel drive car Sir".

"Yes good. So what difference does that make then?"

"Well if I remember rightly, the engine is mounted sideways. That means the gearbox does not poke into the passenger space, and allows the room inside to be much larger than it would be otherwise".

"Excellent. Thank you".

Up until now the Lieutenant Schoolie had been a bystander. Clearly this was his signal to spring into action.

"MEM Bridgman—what do you think about calculators being allowed to be used during examinations?" Luckily for me we had been allowed to use them during our recent Maths and Sciences exams.

"Well Sir, it was useful to be able to have them on the desk, so that you could check your answers. For me though it remains vital that the mathematical theory is fully understood, with the calculators merely being there for confirmation". Bad move. I had fallen hook, line and sinker into his little trap.

"Yes I see. You had good marks in Maths and Physics, but I would just like to check that you can carry out mental calculations". Oh Shit! "Please calculate for me 6 times 13, divided by 4, plus 23, minus 10".

I could feel my face reddening as my brain did internal back flips. I really had not expected this kind of thing. The three officers stared impassively at me as I tried to concentrate on the numbers. Er, 6 x 13 is 78, oh God, this is taking too long, divided by 4 is . . . well, if it was 80 it would be 20, so must be 19 and a half—what's the next bit? It felt like I had been sitting there calculating for hours.

"31 Sir" I knew it was the wrong answer.

"Thank you".

The questioning continued for another 30 minutes or so—each officer taking a turn. Some of the questions were straightforward, and obviously taken from the course syllabus to test our retention of information. Others were seemingly off-the-cuff things, and extremely wide ranging. Some questions were a breeze, and some others I simply had no clue about. This was particularly the case with the electrical questions.

"Explain to me what an 'Earth' is?"

"That's the dissipation of electrical current into the, er . . . Earth"

"Yes, kind of, but how does that work on a ship then—the ship is not in contact with the Earth is it?"

Bollocks. Good question! "No Sir, the ship is . . . bonded, and so the hull is . . . earthed."

"Well not quite, but you're in the right direction. Look into when you get back to sea."

And so it went on, seemingly for hours but in reality for just over one hour. Surprisingly to me, the fact that I had struggled with the workshop phase was not even mentioned. Eventually the Chairman said:

"That's all MEM Bridgman. Please send in the next candidate". No indication whatsoever whether I was selected.

I left the room and sent in the next poor bastard.

As he went to face his doom, the rest of the guys gathered around me.

"Well, what did they ask you?"

My head pounding, I tried to recall every question I had been asked, although it was just about impossible. As I relayed the questions there was the occasional "Oh, Fuck!" and dramatic clutching of heads. As I tried to remember the last few titbits I was cast aside as people withdrew back into their own worlds in preparation for their turn.

Now it was a waiting game. While the others had the stress of waiting to go in, I had equal measures waiting to find out if I was selected. I made myself a coffee, had a cigarette (or 10), and made myself comfortable. The next guy came out, looking as stressed as I must have and was instantly surrounded by those still waiting their turn. The guy had been in there for only about 45 minutes—good or bad sign I wondered.

The process continued throughout the day, with just a 30 minutes lunch break—as though any of us could eat! The last of the 11 came out at around 5:30pm. This was it. None of us had any idea of whether we would be selected. Once again, it was me first.

I went in again, and stood at attention in front of the officers. The Lieutenant Commander spoke:

"MEM Bridgman. Your marks throughout the Leading Stoker's course have been consistently high, with the exception of the Workshop. That is not unusual though, and with the correct attitude, the hand skills can be learned. Of more concern to us was your previous experience as an Engineer's Writer, where you could have lost any engineering ambitions you might have." My heart sank. "However you have managed to convince us that you are prepared to learn, and therefore you have been selected as an Artificer Candidate. Congratulations."

A big stupid smile plonked itself on my face. I thanked the officers profusely for their trust, and assured them I would not let them down. I ran out and back into the waiting room. I was ecstatic. If there had been mobile phones around then I would have called Anna, but I had to wait.

In my excitement I had not noticed the next guy going into the room. I noticed him return though—his long face told the whole story. He had failed. We patted him on the back and offered our commiserations, but he just picked up his cap and left without further ado.

It was the same for the next man, and the next, and the next. In fact the next 8 men all failed selection. I could not believe it. The tenth man passed, but by then we were so shell shocked that the celebrations were muted. The eleventh and last man went in, and again returned unselected.

From eleven eligible men, and after all the work that had been done by everybody, just 2 of us had been selected for the naval apprenticeship. Of course the 2 of us were very pleased, but as we went back to the mess, and over the next few closing days, our joy was muted by the heavy cloud hanging over the guys that had not made it.

At the beginning of the course, we had been asked to complete the now familiar Drafting Preference Form. I had never served on a gas turbine powered ship, and having worked on the engines before starting the course, I asked to be drafted to a Type 21 or Type 22 frigate based in Plymouth. As the course finished we all started to receive notice of where our next draft would be. I was being sent to join a ship called HMS Herald, an ocean going survey vessel. At least she was based in Plymouth, so I suppose I had got half of my wish! The Herald was a diesel-electric powered vessel—about as far removed from the modern gas turbines I had requested as I could get! Worse still, I was being sent as the Engineer's Writer again, and this with me having just passed selection for Artificer training, and just when I needed all the engineering experience I could get. By now though, I was well used to the disconnect between what I would like to do, and what "the Pusser" actually got me doing!

I was due to join my new (well, 25 year old) ship in a couple of months, and in the meantime I was being sent back to HMS Drake in Plymouth to wait. Having said our goodbyes at the end of the course I joined Drake the following Monday, fully expecting to be sent down to HMS Defiance, the normal repository of Stokers waiting for their drafts. In this instance though, I was informed that I would be joining a section in HMS Drake known as the "Communal Party". This was a group of people who were either "walking wounding" recovering from illnesses or injuries and not yet fit enough to rejoin their ships, or those from non-Stoker branches awaiting their next draft. It was very unusual for Stokers to be sent here, as usually they would be snapped up by HMS Defiance and put to work doing onboard maintenance. With my having just passed for Artificer selection, and awaiting imminent promotion to Leading Stoker, it would be fair to say that my nose was well and truly put out of joint by this draft.

After the highs of the course, I was brought back to earth with a huge bump—the Communal Party was used for collecting rubbish, moving furniture, general base "husbandry", and even a bit of gardening as I recall. It was a long 2 months, and I hated every minute of it.

Chapter 10

The Herald of a New Dawn

The Royal Naval Survey Ship Flotilla was based in the South Yard of Devonport Naval Dockyard. To be blunt I had never heard of it. I had only visited the South Yard a couple times briefly in my now 8 year career in the Navy, and then only to visit one or other of the huge naval stores down there. So, another first then!

The Flotilla consisted of a mixture of ocean going, coastal and inshore survey vessels, whose job it was to carry out surveys on behalf of the Admiralty, from which (as far as I am aware) Admiralty survey maps were produced. The "H" class of survey ships were the largest at about 2,500 tonnes displacement—about half that of a Leander class frigate, and there were 4 of those, HMS Hecla, Hydra, Hecate and Herald.

Of course my part in the operation of the Herald would have very little to do with ocean surveys. I was quite apprehensive about riding this ship because of its small size. In rough weather when I was on frigates I used to suffer quite badly from seasickness, and considering the survey ship was much smaller I felt that I was going to be in for a very rough couple of years.

I was also surprised to discover that since the Falklands conflict, all of the survey ships were painted the usual battleship grey, rather than the bright white colour I had been expecting. Apparently the ships had been used as floating ambulances during the conflict, and had never been returned to their original colour. I would hear more about that role later on.

My worst fears about the size of the ship were confirmed on my first sight of her. She was a somewhat squat looking thing, with a very distinct bow from stem to stern—there didn't seem to be a straight deck anywhere on her, although there must have been because she carried a helicopter! On first view the only thing naval about her was the grey paint and flags flying forward and aft—there seemed to be a lot of cranes, winches and sea boats dotted around her decks, and there was a very marked absence of any form of weaponry on her. She seemed to have an oversized funnel for the size of the ship, and it stood out like a sore thumb. On each side of the funnel were 2 very large davits holding what appeared to my untrained eye a couple of 30 foot inshore survey boats.

I joined the Herald in November 1984. My new boss, Lieutenant Pike, was a very different man from the naval engineering officers I had come across to date. Easy-going but very astute, he knew the ship inside out, and would quite happily get stuck in when a particularly difficult defect arose—which was quite often on this ship. As soon as I joined the ship I was promoted to Acting Local Leading Stoker—his thinking being that if I had passed for the rate, and had since been selected for Artificer Training, then it was only fair I get some reward. It was a good move on his part, as it had the effect of motivating me from day one. He did wonder why it was they had sent me to the ship as the Engineer's writer, but vowed to ensure that I got plenty of machinery space time during my draft.

My Bloody Efforts

Machinery wise, the Herald and her sisters were unlike anything I had come across to date. So far the main machinery I had worked with had either been steam boilers and turbines, or gas turbines, together with twin propeller shafts. This ship had a very odd propulsion set up, consisting of a single propeller shaft driven by a very large direct current motor, which in turn was powered by a set of three 12-cylinder Paxman diesel engines. In addition to these, there were another two diesel generators providing the electrical power to the ships systems, and a number of air compressors, hydraulic systems, fuel systems and a "donkey" boiler for generating steam. She was also fitted with a bow thruster—another machine that I had not come across before. Most of the machinery was contained in the large and open engine room, while the big electric motor driving the shaft had its own separated imaginatively named "motor-room". The whole place smelled of a mixture of diesel fuel, diesel oil and that electric "ether" smell—reminded me of the smell of the London underground. In between the two main machinery spaces was the Machinery Control Room, which contained all of the remote operating equipment and systems for the machinery, and from where the shifts (or "watches") were controlled.

In the corridor above the engine room was located the Technical or Engineers Office—my main work station. It was a nice little place actually, and I had everything I needed there to run the administration of the engineering department. I was particularly taken with the window or "scuttle" in the office from which I could get a great view as we sailed along. The scuttle was fixed and therefore could not be opened, which was probably a good thing as it was only about 10 feet from the waterline. I was to find that in anything other than dead calm seas I would be getting an underwater view! Sharing the office with me was the engineering Charge Chief—a guy called Bill Withers, later to be replaced with a Warrant Officer—Ginge Young.

Both these gentlemen treated me very well during my draft, Bill Withers particularly really helping me to progress. Unfortunately I heard that he died couple of years after leaving the ship—he was only about 38 or 39 as I recall. A great shame. Slightly more worrying was that in the same corridor as the Tech office, there was also located the office of the Master at Arms. As it turned out, the chap on the Herald was unlike any naval Policeman I had encountered to date, and we got along quite nicely.

I was to find that many things that I had become used to in the "fighting" navy were very different in the survey world. I was surprised that the Senior ratings routinely called us by our first names, and found it difficult at first to get used having the engineer drop into the office for a cup of tea and a chat with me and the Charge Chief—feet on desk and hat tipped back. His cabin was located just one deck up from the office, and another first for me was that whenever I had to go to his cabin/office, he would invite me in, tell me to sit and chat away as he signed whatever I was bringing. At sea we could dress in non-naval clothing, and there was not much shoe polishing and saluting. Obviously when we were in view of the brass we did the military thing, but out in the open ocean the routines were pretty relaxed. All of that would stand me in good stead for submarines later on.

The accommodation was not too shoddy either. As usual, the different departments had their own mess decks, and the Stokers mess was a pretty good one. It was located right in the centre of the ship, so should be fairly stable, and close by was the dining hall and heads (showers and toilets). In those days I was quite interested in physical fitness, and was pleased to find that the ship had a very well equipped gym down in one of the forward holds. Over the next couple of years I would spend quite a bit of time there.

I was a bit surprised to learn that the ship carried a crew of almost 100 people. The engineering department was the largest group, with almost 30, ranging from the engineering officer down to about 15 Stokers of varying rank. As the Leading Stoker Writer, I was pretty much out of the mainstream of activities, and could pick and choose what engineering tasks I wanted to get involved in. So long as my "day job" was up to scratch, the boss didn't mind me getting stuck into anything else I thought would be useful for me to know.

When I joined the ship, she was just coming out of a maintenance period. This was always followed by a "work-up", where the crew was put through their paces before the ship was made operational once more. Up until now, the "work-ups" had been a complete pain in the ass—the Flag Officer Sea Training (FOST) staff being complete bastards. They would come onboard the ship, and then proceed to run the crew ragged with exercise fires, floods, machinery breakdowns, casualties and war games, at all hours of the night and day—usually for 7 days straight. On the frigates this process had been hard work and tiring, but on the Herald, with her being a non-combatant, it was much more relaxed. Of course we had the usual fire and flood drills, together with lots of machinery breakdown drills, but with the combat part absent, there was only so much the FOST staff could throw at us. As Team Leader of a 4-man fire fighting team, I had much more room to manoeuvre than I would on a frigate, and with lots of DC current around in the machinery spaces we were not permitted to throw any water around, so that the hoses we were using remained un-charged—lovely! The work-up was a breeze. I could get used to this.

My first trip on the ship was a fairly low-key affair. We were tasked with some survey work up around the Scottish isles. The weather was not too bad, and so long as the ship just maintained a rolling motion I was fine. For the engineering section, the survey work was pretty tedious—just trolling up and down in a "box", with the Side-Scan sonar deployed. The boys up in the map rooms then used the images to map the sea floor in the area we were surveying. We were quite close into land, and some of the views of the highlands were absolutely stunning. For me it was a time to get up close and personal with the machinery of the ship, and to establish myself in the role of Engineer's Writer. The writer job was very straightforward after my previous posting to a squadron leader ship. The engineer on Herald was not much of a letter writer, and the routine document returns and so forth were a breeze. That left me a lot of time for watch keeping and studying, which I made good use of. In addition, I had ample opportunity for my new hobby of getting and keeping fit—not always easy with the ship rocking and rolling in the sea swell. The trip was fairly short at around 6 weeks, and by the time we returned to Plymouth I was pretty well settled onboard.

Our next deployment was to be more of a challenge. We were informed by the Captain on the way back from the Scotland trip that we had been tasked with carrying out a survey of the Falklands Isles. The maps used during the Falklands Conflict had originated from the First World War period apparently, and they needed to be updated. The trip was going to be 7 months long, and would involve long passages there and back, including visiting the west coast of South America as part of the return journey.

We said our teary goodbyes and set sail in early April 1985, popping in to Gibraltar on the way, before heading off to a little island in the Atlantic called Saint Helena. This place really was in the middle of nowhere, but nonetheless it gave us a little respite from the tedium of being at sea. We all had a chance of getting ashore for a few hours, and many of us were surprised to discover that this had been Emperor Napoleons' prison and final resting place following his defeat at Waterloo. There wasn't really much to see there though, but I did manage to take the opportunity to get my hair cut. We had been at sea for a good few weeks by now, and I would rather get my hair cut by a civilian than have it butchered by the onboard "barber"—although a few weeks later there was no choice.

Spot of deck volleyball anyone?—HMS Herald off St Helena 1985

The real reason we were there though was to rendezvous with a fuel tanker, so that we could top up our tanks before the long run to the Falklands. The civilian tanker duly arrived off St Helena, and much to the annoyance of the sailors, tied up alongside us, scraping the paint on the side of the ship nicely.

Another part of my duties onboard the ship was that of being the person in charge of refuelling. The Herald was quite economic really, and usually we didn't need to refuel away from our main base. In the instances where we had refuelled previously, it had always been using a naval tanker, so we knew what equipment and procedures to use. This would be my first time using a civilian set-up.

I had a couple of Stokers to help me, and their job would be to set up the system to receive fuel, and also to "dip" the tanks as the fuel was pumped onboard. We set up the system so that all of the tanks would be filled at the same time, took on and connected up the fuelling hoses, and told the tanker to "start Pumping". I and one of the lads removed the dip-tape tube covers to start dipping the tanks, and this gave me my first indication that something was wrong. As I took the cover off, a "whoosh" of escaping air rushed past me, indicating that the tank was filling bloody quickly. I looked back at the fuel hoses and noticed that they were bulging alarmingly with the pressure of the fuel flowing through them. Stupidly, I had not asked the tanker at what pressure they normally pumped, and clearly it was a great deal more than we were used to receiving! I rushed over to the side of the ship and shouted to the men standing there:

"You are pumping too fast—lower the flow-rate!"

One of the men looked up casually, shrugged, and started ambling off somewhere to slow the rate. In the meantime the Stoker shouted from the port side:

"Steve, the bloody tank is filling quicker than I can measure—you need to slow it down!"

"Yes, I know—I just asked them to . . ."

Before I could finish the sentence, the gurgling noise from the dip-tape tubes and tank vents lining the upper deck of the ship increased to a crescendo, and huge funnels of diesel fuel stated to erupt from them!

"Shit! TURN THE FUCKING PUMPS OFF!!" I screamed to the tanker crew.

They scattered, running here and there, shutting valves and chattering away to each other.

"Steve, shall I shut the main inlet valves" asked the Stoker.

"No, if we do that, the hoses will burst" I replied. "They have to shut down on the tanker first".

Fuel continued to spurt at full pressure from the tank vents. The stink of the diesel was overpowering, and it was not long before people below decks realised something was amiss. The fuel was running down the decks of the ship and overboard through the drains, leaving an ever growing multi-coloured pool around the anchored ships. After what seemed like an age, but was probably in reality 30 seconds, the pressure dissipated as the fuel pumps were turned off on the tanker. The Engineer appeared by my side, mouth open in surprise at the stinking mess all along the scuttles and wooden decking of the top deck of the ship:

"What the hell is going on Steve?" By now the deck apes were starting to get agitated—they needed to get the diesel off the wood pretty quickly or it was going to smell forever.

"The fucking tanker pumped in too fast!" I replied, pissed off "We didn't stand a chance at that pressure!"

"Look at this bloody mess—the Skipper is going to flip at this!" As if I didn't know it. I glanced over the rail and was aghast at the sight that presented itself. There was a horrendous plume of shining diesel fuel floating off behind the ship—it must have been visible from the whole of St Helena! While not quite on the scale of the Exxon Valdes disaster, it was certainly enough to send Greenpeace into a tizzy fit!

After throwing considerable abuse at the tanker crew for spoiling my day (well, I had to blame somebody!), I set about sorting out the mess. We isolated the refuelling system, and then tried to help the sailors clean up the decks. We had the brainwave of using an industrial degreasing agent widely used in the machinery spaces at the time called "slicks" to scrub the wooden decking to remove the diesel. Unfortunately the ecological effects of either the diesel or slicks were pretty low on the priority list at the time, and it is debatable which probably caused more damage to the environment! At any rate, our priority was to get the ship clean and diesel free in double quick time. Luckily by the time the Captain came back onboard from being ashore we had finished, and there was no obvious sign of the mishap. There was still a slight whiff of diesel in the air, but hey, we had been refuelling so it could be expected. The sailor's whinged for a good while afterwards and of course the Captain got to hear about it, but since the ship was nice and clean, he did not make any fuss. The boss called me in later and gave me a bit of a rollicking, but in fairness I think he knew that it was a mistake that could have been made by anybody, so he did not want to press it.

Up until now, the weather on the trip had been pretty good. As we travelled further south though, crossing the Equator and further on down, the seas became heavier, and the skies more stormy. Our only other point of call on the entire journey down to the Falklands was to a place I had never heard of, Tristan de Chuna—a small island on the way to the South Atlantic. The plan was to stop there just for a day to pick up food and fuel, but as we drew nearer to the island, the Atlantic swell was so bad that we were not able to get alongside the pier or to get any boats alongside the ship. We had to wait for the weather to improve, and while we did so, we just had to live with the terrible motion of the ship, which even in the "lee of the land" (sheltering behind the mass of the island) was violent and nauseating. I knew it was going to be bad when even some of the "old sea-dogs" started feeling unwell, which was really unusual. For me personally it was a total nightmare without end—I couldn't eat, sleep or move around the ship because of the seasickness, and had to be content with trying to wedge myself into a corner in my office, and hope it all ended soon. Naturally it didn't, and the pain went on for about 5 days solid. It was really strange. The sky was clear and blue, and the island stood out in bright contrast—a nice looking green oasis in the middle of nowhere, and yet the swell of the ocean was causing the ship to move around like a cork in a bath tub. She was rolling over in each direction to at least 45 degrees, and after each roll, she would dig her bow into the trough of the next wave, ride up and over the wave, only to be pushed over the other way in a corkscrewing motion guaranteed to send waves of nausea washing over me and many others onboard. The Captain tried to keep the ship's head into the waves, which reduced the motion to a single direction, but of course could only go so far before needing to turn around by steering "across the sea". Before the ship turned we would be warned to hold on tight, and then all hell would break loose as the ship turned "beam-on" to the huge swell. The rolling and corkscrewing would descend again, breathtakingly violent, furniture, pots and pans, and indeed anything not bolted down would take to the air and be catapulted across compartments. Anybody not firmly anchored to something would go skating from one side of the ship to the other—hopefully not bashing into something hard on the way. If you were in a compartment with any sort of view outside, the view went something like sky, horizon, massive waves, underwater, massive waves, horizon, and sky in a mad dash. To make matters worse, the Chefs gave up trying to cook anything resembling meals after the first couple of days of this battering, and resorted to basic rations of horrendous canned sausages, and beans—for breakfast, lunch and dinner! Before very long the dining hall, one of the best places to take refuge, was awash with spilled beans, coffee and orange juice, with horrible brown square sausages floating around. It was too rough to clean the place up, so what very little appetite I had disappeared completely. I had been seasick before in my time in the navy, but this was on another level completely—it was the first and only time that I was physically sick, and the worst thing about it was that it looked like it was not going to end.

The huge swell lasted for 5 days in total, five days of complete torture for many of us onboard. Eventually though, the swell died down enough for us to restock with fuel and provisions from boats, and without further ado we turned south again. If I imagined that my seasickness problems would be solved by leaving Tristan de Cuhna though, I was in for a nasty shock. We were entering the Southern Oceans, notorious for the rough seas and terrible weather. They would certainly live up to the reputation in the coming days and weeks.

Shortly after leaving the island I witnessed a nasty accident onboard the ship. I had been helping out with some of the watches in the Engine Room, and was busy studying to pass some onboard exams covering diesel engines and electrical switchboards, and so was spending a lot of time down in the spaces—particularly when the weather permitted. On this occasion I was helping one of the guys on their rounds, and had just watched him start one of the air compressors—a pretty routine happening. As we turned away from the machine, having checked on the various gauges that it was running correctly, there was a massive BANG!, and bits of metal whizzed around us and pinged off the deck plates and pipe work. I instinctively ducked, and dived behind one of the diesels as the air compressor disintegrated loudly behind me and the other chap. The noise seemed incredible at this close range, but on glancing up at the control room window I could see that they had noticed nothing over the already deafening diesel engines. I stood up shakily and checked myself over, incredulous that I had escaped injury from the flying steel. I then looked around, expecting to see the Stoker behind some other bit of protection, but he was not immediately obvious. As I moved towards the now stopped and smoking wayward air compressor and passed around the rear of one of the big diesel generators, I got the shock of my life so far. My oppo was lying face down on the deck plates, head turned away from me but clearly unconscious. Worse still, as I approached his very still form, I noticed blood and a clear fluid at the base of his head. I knelt over him and felt at his throat for a pulse, and as I did so I saw a small round hole in the back of his head from which the blood and snot was oozing. With the vibration and noise of the running diesel engine just a couple of feet away, there was no way I was going to feel a pulse, and for a moment I was sure he was dead, and panic started to rise in my chest. He must have been hit by something flying off the machine, and fell behind me as I legged it away.

I had a smelly rag in my pocket—one that we all carried around when on watch for wiping leaks and dirty hands, and my first though was to stick this over the oozing wound in the man's head. With perfect hindsight probably not the most hygienic thing to do. I was now in a quandary—to get the attention of the guys in the control room I needed to leave the casualty, but in my own shock I was scared that if I left him alone he might come to and hurt himself even more. And hurt he clearly was. In the minute or less since I had found him, the front of his head and temple had swelled to an extent that his eyes were now hidden in the swelling, and he needed help. I fixed the cloth as best I could and ran out and up to the control room. Bursting through the door I screamed at the Petty Officer to get help—declare an emergency!! He and the Leading Stoker looked at me as though I had just landed from the moon. I took a deep breath and quickly explained, the Leading Stoker immediately jumping down into the engine room with the first aid kit in hand. The Petty Officer phoned the Bridge, and within seconds the "Emergency Stations" claxon started sounding followed by the broadcast "Casualty in the Engine Room—Medical Party Close-Up!" I took a seat in the control room and lit a nervous cigarette as the first aid party rushed past, clutching bulky medical packs and equipment.

The Herald was categorised as a "small" ship, and as such carried just a single Medical Branch Leading Hand. Of course he was universally known, as all medical branch staff were as "The Doc". We were lucky in that our Doc was a good medic, but it soon became apparent that the injuries to the Stoker were way beyond his capability to remedy. After carrying out an initial assessment of the casualty where he lay, the Doc declared that in his opinion something had struck the poor guy in the back of the head, and had entered the head causing goodness knows what internal damage. The man was still deeply unconscious and was not responding to stimulus, and to put it bluntly, if he was not gotten to a good hospital very soon, the Doc thought he would die. The swelling had also continued, and the Doc had to put a breathing line down the man's throat to keep his airway open.

Because the Doc though that the casualty had a piece of metal in his head, he requested that the ship's engines and generators be stopped, to prevent vibration hurting the man further. We of course complied, and with the ship on emergency lighting only, we put him on a stretcher and moved him gingerly to the Sickbay. Mercifully the weather was pretty good and the ship was not moving too much, but it was still a rough ride up the machinery space steps and ladders. In the meantime the ship had been in touch with the Admiralty, and they had, in no time at all, organised that he be flown off the ship on the helicopter carried onboard, and would be taken to a hospital in Peru—the country we happened to be passing at the time. As luck would have it, one of the finest brain surgeons in South America worked there, and so the chap would be in good hands.

Everything was a whirl as I helped prepare him for the journey. The Doc had been on the satellite phone to the RN Hospital in Portsmouth, and had been administering cocktails of drugs on their advice to minimise the swelling—now reckoned to be the greatest danger for the guy. Nothing seemed to work though, and by the time we carted him to the waiting helicopter, and strapped him in the best we could, his head was a huge horrendous black and blue mess, with eyes and nose closed, and a gaping tube helping him to breathe. Fortunately he remained unconscious throughout, and I think the Doc had ensured he remained that way for his own good. Then suddenly in a whirl of rotor blades and aviation fuel exhaust he was gone, leaving all of us shell-shocked and wide-eyed. My Boss asked me if I was ok. Surprisingly I was, apart from the shock of course, but throughout the whole episode I had felt kind of detached, just a spectator. Strange really. Maybe it was the training kicking in, in times of crises, or maybe I was just a cold bastard. Either way, it was to the guy's advantage in the long run—it would have been no good me panicking, so I was quietly pleased with myself that I had not 'thrown a wobbly'.

I happened to meet the Stoker about 18 months later back in Plymouth. He had been invalided out of the Navy as a result of the injury and was attempting to build a compensation claim against the manufacturers of the exploding air compressor. I tried to help him with some information about the machines onboard the Herald. Anyway he gave me the full story of what happened after he left the ship—of which he remembered little. He discovered that he had been taken to hospital where he had immediately been taken for emergency surgery. The surgeon had removed half of a half inch steel nut from his head. The piece of metal had hit him in the back of the head with enough force to fracture his skull, to pass through the bone of the skull, and then to pass around to the front of his head between the skull bone and the tough membrane that apparently covers the brain. He showed off the massive scars on his head where the surgeon had opened him up. The surgeon was surprised that the man had survived the trauma, and described the wound as "like being shot from a .22 pistol at close range". Subsequent to the surgery, the chap had been flown back to the UK by the RAF, and had made an almost full recovery, although he complained that he could no longer concentrate for long periods—although as I remember, he couldn't do that before the accident! I have no idea if he managed to make a claim for the injuries as we never met again, as was often the case with people one worked with in the Navy.

After flying off our casualty we continued down towards the Falklands Islands, entering the feared Southern Oceans on the way. The fearsome reputation was justified, and it soon became apparent that the remainder of the trip to the Islands was going to be traumatic. I was lucky enough to be in a position where I could either go to bed if the seasickness became too unbearable, or alternatively spend my time on the bridge, clinging on for dear life to the rails. Being able to see the horizon seemed to help with the seasickness—for me at any rate, and it also took my mind off it. Within a very short time after leaving Tristan De Cuhna the ship was once again battened down against the appalling weather with nobody allowed on the upper decks, and doors and hatches tightly clipped shut. As we traversed south huge waves washed over the entire ship and along every exposed deck as the bow crashed down and then through 40 foot walls of water stacked up endlessly in front of us. One moment I was staring at the blue sky as we rode up and over the crest of the wave, and the next I would be looking up at the next wall of water as the ship dropped sickening into the next trough. The ship would then plough into the mass of water with a huge shudder, shaking the whole ship, before creaking and groaning under the weight of water, climbing up the face of the wave—the whole tiring process endlessly repeating. As soon as I was forced to go below for something—sleep mostly, dizziness and nausea would wash over me, and I would sink into despair at the thought that this torture would continue, without seeming end. With a storm, at least there was the knowledge that it was likely to last a day or two at the most, but here, the weather itself was not bad—blue skies and low wind, but the swell was the problem. The giant waves marched relentlessly along as far as the horizon, and the ship just ploughed either through or over them, in constant motion. The only difference was that dependent on the size of the waves, the ship either bounced from the top of one to the next, or sailed up and over the top of the wider spaced ones—either way it was vomit inducing! The worst of all though was if the waves were coming from the stern, in which case the back of the ship would rise, and as the wave passed beneath, the ship would sit on the crest before twisting, and the violently dropping stern first back into the next trough. This was known as "corkscrewing", and was sheer hell for those of us that suffered seasickness. I was told that with time the senses adjust and it becomes easier—utter bollocks! I suffered seasickness for my entire naval service. It was one of those things, and with experience I could judge when it was going to hit me hard and could plan my life around it. It was one of the main reasons I chose submarines later on, although in my naivety I was to find that submarines themselves are not the most stable platforms.

The sea state stayed the same for almost the entire remainder of the journey down to the Falklands, and by the time we reached Port Stanley, boy was I glad to get a breather on dry land. As we sailed into the protected harbour we were able to get our first (for many of us) look at the place. On this dull grey day the town looked exactly like we had seen it on the telly, bleak landscape dotted with the colourful rooftops of the settlement houses. To many of us it looked exactly like many of the Scottish islands we had recently been surveying, the obvious difference being the military presence everywhere. Two and a half years after the conflict had finished there remained a heavy army presence, with army Landrovers and trucks all over the place, and with a huge floating accommodation unit sited in

My Bloody Efforts

the harbour, known as the "Flo-Tel", where some at least of the garrison could get some relief from the tents and porta-cabins used up until then as accommodation. Before we were able to venture ashore, an army bomb disposal team visited the ship, and warned us in no uncertain terms about the danger that still existed of anti-personnel mines, which the Argentines have sprinkled liberally almost everywhere on the islands. While the main areas of population had been cleared, some of the places out in the sticks where we would be operating had yet to be moved far enough up the "to do" list to be addressed yet. Unsurprisingly there had been a number of sheep blown up in the meantime, indicating that mines were indeed present, but mercifully no humans had been lost since the war, sorry, conflict!

We would not be staying around Port Stanley for long, so we (gingerly) set foot ashore for the first time in weeks, and look a look around the place. Most of us were content to wander over to the NAAFI that had been set up, and to top up on "nutty, smellies and fufu", or sweets, shaving gear and deodorant. The onboard canteen had long since run out of these things, and it was good to re-stock with a bit of luxury. This being the days before mobiles and emails, the queue for the few pay phones was another heavily subscribed pastime. While we waited our turn we chatted with the army lads (or "trees", or "Pongoes"), and were horrified to discover that some of them were spending up to 6 months in the Falklands at a time! Most of them were fairly pragmatic about it though, and were already planning their new cars or motor bikes with the money they would save—but even so! The guys down there at the time were from the Light Infantry, and seemed friendly enough in most instances.

After taking on stores and fuel, we were on our way again. We would be spending the next 6 weeks carrying out surveys of various areas around the

Falklands Islands—the first surveys there since the First World War, and we quickly slipped into a routine. We would arrive at a survey site, the boats would go out and land shore parties with transmitters at a number of high points, and then the ship would steam up and down for a number of days mapping an area. The Survey Recorders were in seventh heaven—this to them was "pure" surveying—no distractions from shipping or underwater obstacles, resulting in excellent maps, but to the rest of us it was absolute tedium. I managed to get away a few times as boat's crew or battery carrier, and in fairness the landscape was beautiful. When we did get ashore, we were able to approach the penguins and other wildlife without them showing the slightest fear, which was incredible, and the view from the shore back to the ship, with the snow capped landscape behind was really something. It was slow laborious work, but for me the major bonus was that most of it was done in sheltered bays, which in turn meant the ship was stable! I took the opportunity to do some more engineering studying, and with gaining experience in the machinery spaces. We were able to catch up on a bit of fitness training too, which certainly helped pass the time.

Every couple of weeks or so, we would sail back into Port Stanley for a day, to take on supplies and fuel. On one occasion we decided to offer a challenge to the Pongoes to have a Squash match. Stupid idea really—how could we possibly be a fit as the army guys? They were in an ideal environment for getting and keeping really fit, and we were on a 150ft long ship where the options were "limited". In any case, we showed up on the Flotel and made our way to the squash courts onboard. I played as 4th seed out of 5 of us, and had not played a game of squash in months. My opponent was a corporal—thin as a stick but about 9 feet tall! He obviously had played a bit, and ran me ragged within minutes! I simply could not get near the ball and had absolutely no endurance—he completely dicked me without breaking a sweat. It was the same story for the entire team, and we certainly didn't ask for a return match! On returning to the ship I decided that I really needed to improve my endurance, and immediately started training with the Marines—doing grid sprints on the flight deck and running around and around the upper deck—being sure to change direction half way around so as not to get dizzy! I think I got a bit paranoid about it. I would be out there running around the deck come hell or high water, in snow storms and lashing rain. The only thing that would stop me was rough weather, which blissfully had been few and far between in the bays. I t became a routine that I continued right until leaving the ship, and it stood me in good stead for the Apprenticeship later on.

Back out to sea again, and into another bay for a spot of surveying. This bay was a bit different though—San Carlos Water, the scene of one of the major British landings during the conflict. At the time, Herald had been an "Ambulance" ship—transferring some of the badly wounded firstly from the aid stations ashore to the hospital ship that was stationed off the Falklands for the duration of the War, and then, for the more badly wounded guys, transferring them from the hospital ship to shore in Valparaiso in Chile, from where they could be flown to the UK as quickly as possible. Re-visiting the bay brought back some memories for some of the blokes that had been on the ship at the time—a good number of casualties had been from the Welsh Guards who had been caught onboard a landing ship during a bombing raid, and who had been in some cases, very badly burned. Many were flown by helicopter to the hospital ship, but subsequently the less badly injured had been taken to Chile onboard the Herald. The guys recalled how the men were mostly suffering from "flash" burns—their faces and hands charred and blistered by the flash of the exploding bomb. Their treatment consisted at the time of slapping some evil thick cream on their faces and hands, and then enclosing the hands in clear plastic bags, presumably to prevent infection. That was fine, and no doubt from a medical point of view worked a treat, but the problem with the idea was that over a short period the cream on the faces went black, thick and gooey, making the men's heads look hideous—of course helped further by the charred skin detaching itself from their faces in big chunks. Worse still, the plastic bags containing the burned hands of the soldiers started filling with a dark brown "soup", collecting from the burst blisters and dead skin from the men's hands. Together, these two effects made the guys look like some form of alien beings. The sailors tried their best to make the wounded comfortable onboard, assisted by a medical team onboard for the duration. The soldiers (and sailors) with burns of course could not feed themselves with plastic bags over their hands, so the ship's company took it upon themselves to help them out. For some of the guys onboard, the memory of being up close and personal to some of the wounded was scarred into their brains—something never to be forgotten. They said that they could smell the stench of burned flesh and disinfectant onboard the ship for the next 2 years. I never did, but then I wasn't there.

What was there when I managed to get ashore again was minefields and quite a bit of weaponry left behind by the Argentine forces. We took a stroll along the edge of one particularly well marked mined area—we hoped it was accurately marked and looked back down into the bay. The scene before us was the one remembered from the TV three years before—the bay stretching across our front and bleak hillsides behind. The Herald, squat and grey in the bay could have been a landing ship, and at any moment a Skyraider could come streaking overhead on its attack run. We agreed that this was a crap place to be getting killed and wounded, and we felt a very long way from home at that moment. How worse it must have been for those Welsh Guards. One of the local pongoes took us to a large sheep shearing shed and showed us a pile of guns and equipment just lying around—rifles, machine guns, webbing belts, and of course the obligatory steel helmets. I was especially taken with a 20 mm canon mounted on a tripod, used as an anti-aircraft weapon. Unfortunately he wouldn't let us take any souvenirs—probably wise with hindsight! All in all it was a poignant reminder of what a nasty little war it had been.

"Come and say hello to my little friend!"—HMS Herald Falklands 1985

The six weeks of surveying came to an end, and following a final visit to Port Stanley we started on our journey back to the UK. Rather bizarrely, a half a dozen soldiers from the Green Jackets had volunteered to come back with us on the ship, and had sacrificed their leave to do so. They would act as extra deck-apes for the 6-week trip, and we thought they were bonkers! It must be said that they were not the sharpest knives in the drawer, as proved by a game of "Spoons" we had just a few days out of port. In this game, two people attempt to make the other surrender, by gripping a desert spoon in their mouths, and then tapping the other on the head as hard as they can with the spoon. Both players must have their hands behind their backs, and each is blindfolded was they await the strike. Of course it is not as simple as that, and the people in the know soon find out that some serious cheating goes on! The Green Jackets loved the idea of the game, and one guy—a very large black gentleman, was very keen to go first, naturally assuming that his enormous neck muscles would make tapping the spoon on his opponent's head very painful indeed. The Leading Chef was lined us as his opponent, and great show was made of preparing both men for the "fight". Then with both guys sitting facing each-other, a blindfold was ceremonially put on the Killick Chef—who was over-acting for Britain by this stage, and both men's hands were tied behind their backs. Finally the game started, the "guest" being invited to strike first. With huge concentration, the soldier lifted his head and "whack!", the spoon smacked onto the Chef's head—the Chef cursing as though he had been shot, then slowly recovering enough to take his turn—great acting! "My turn!" he shouted eagerly as the blindfold was removed. The blindfold was ceremoniously slipped over the soldier's head in readiness for the return blow—you could see he was confident in his power to beat the Chef. Once the blindfold was on the soldier, the Leading Chef was quickly released from his bindings, and with giggles and fingers to lips to let the other soldiers' into the joke, he produced his spoon—a 3ft soup ladle from the galley! "You ready?" he asked "Here it comes!" He lifted the ladle about 6" from the man's head and let it fall. There was a loud "Thwack!", and roars of laughter from the crowd as the ladle bounced off. The ladle was quickly hidden as the Chef retook his seat and pretended to still be tied up.

The soldier's blindfold was removed, and as he surfaced he looked around in slight confusion at the smiling faces around him. Clearly that hit stung a bit, but there was no way he was going to say so in front of all these Matelots. "You want to give in mate?" asked the Chef sweetly "or do you want to carry on?"

"We'll carry on. My turn" replied the soldier. His mates tried gallantly to look serious.

"OK, but not so hard this time eh?" said the Leading Chef, rubbing his head in mock pain, and having the blindfold slipped on.

Once again, the man raised his head, spoon in mouth and brought it down as hard as he could on the sailor's head. The Chef leapt around like a wounded buffalo, roaring with pretend pain!

"OK, my turn" He again made a remarkable recovery, and set himself up once more. This time the ladle was moved about a foot away from the soldier's head, and brought down with enough force for the crowd to give an involuntary "Oooh!"

Again the blindfold was removed, and the man looked around with a slightly dazed expression. I think I could see the start of a lump on the side of the chap's head, but again he did not realise what was happening, as most people would have done by now. You could see that he couldn't quite understand how the little Chef was producing so much power. Anyway, he wanted to continue, and so we did—for about another half dozen smacks on the side of the head! Finally, one of his mates took pity on him and let him into the trick. He was furious, and wanted to rip the Chef in half—which he looked quite capable of doing! We scattered! Eventually he calmed down and managed to see the funny side of it, as did his mates. The episode was a good ice breaker between us and we all got along just fine for the whole trip. In fact, the Sergeant of the group became quite a good Uckers player by the end of the trip, and our parting gift to him was a board and a set of "bits". I recall that the black guy had a nightmare with seasickness for a lot of the trip back to the UK, so I and he had a lot in common!

The start of the trip back to Plymouth, which would be something like 5 weeks long, was incredible. We had sailed southwards from the Falklands and back around the tip of South America, again through horrendous weather and seas, and were now heading towards Chile, where we would be visiting a Chilean Naval base at Valparaiso. To get there though, we had to pass through a beautiful mountainous area called the "Tierra Del Fuego" or Land of Fire. The scenery was absolutely stunning—flat sea surrounded by lovely green mountain ranges stretching far into the distance, each one so high that the tops were covered with snow and ice. Beautiful to look at, but a true wilderness in all other senses. It took us three days to sail through, and for all of that time I don't recall seeing a single dwelling of any sort.

We got the surprise of our lives going into Valparaiso. We were apparently the first official visiting British Navy ship for years, and my goodness were we made welcome. As we approached our dock, suddenly a Chilean naval band marched around the corner, accompanied by what looked like a company of armed marines, all in their best bib and tucker. We had not prepared for this at all, and were standing around in our normal working clothes, getting ready to bring on fuel and stores, but not much else! The band stopped on the quay and played away—"Rule Britannia", "Hearts of Oak" and good old favourites, while the marines marched up and down, chucking their rifles around and giving us a very smart display of military precision—we could have learned a lot from those guys!

It was pretty clear that somebody had cocked up somewhere. We really had no idea that we would be getting any sort of reception, and the poor old Captain looked dumbfounded by the proceedings. As quick as we could, we got the bunting out and rigged, while some of the sailors got dressed in their blues to line the ship's side. We put the fuelling gear away and tried to smarten the place up a bit, expecting that some party or other would want to come onboard. As we got nearer to the dock, we could see a reception committee gathering there—lots of brass and scrambled eggs amongst them. The Chilean officer's uniforms were very ornate, even from some distance, and it was difficult to tell the level of the gentlemen waiting, but my goodness if gold rings and tassels were anything to go by, we must have had the entire Chilean naval high command there!

With perfect hindsight maybe we should have expected something like this. The British and Chilean navies were on pretty good terms as I recall, and certainly the Royal Navy systems and traditions was the basis of the Chilean one, even down to the style of uniform worn by the personnel, which certainly at rating and senior rating level were identical to ours. As I looked around the naval base, I was also reminded that the South American navies had been the recipients of a number of ex-RN ships. Across the way I could recognise a couple of ex-Leander frigates, and an old County Class destroyer. I had been told that the Chileans even had one of our aircraft carriers and a "Tiger" class cruiser, although they were not in evidence. I wondered whether there was any intention to sell them any of the newer warships like we had done to Argentina a few years previously. Look what had happened with that deal!

That was not my problem though, and for now I was just enjoying the spectacle. Eventually we got tied up and the reception committee came onboard and straight to the Captain's cabin. The rest of us mingled around with the Chilean Marines and sailors, us showing them around the ship and generally being hospitable. The Green Jackets and our own Marines were loving it, swapping stories and showing the Chilean soldiers how the British drill went and so forth. It was a nice welcome, and we soon found out that a tour of the Chilean capital Santiago had been arranged for us, along with a reception at the British High Commission, and a rugby match against a Chilean navy side. I didn't even know the Chileans played rugby! "We don't much" I was told "it is only a few who play—just for fun you understand".

The tour of Santiago was nice, and the reception at the British residence better. Come the day of the rugby match though and we were in a bit of a pickle. We were only a relatively small ship's company, and the number of rugby players was limited, together with which, none of us was probably fit enough to play a full game in any case. I was not much of a player in any case, and so gladly gave up my place to become sponge man and supporter, and the Army boys chipped in as well, becoming honorary sailors for the day. On the day in question a bus arrived for the team, and off we went. We didn't know where the ground was of course, but it became apparent that the Chileans were taking the game a bit seriously as we drove in through the gates of the Chilean Naval Officers College, a grand old building somewhere off the base. On arrival at the ground, impressively set out before some very important and old looking college buildings, we were a bit surprised to find that a number of stands had been erected around the pitch, and as the boys started warming up in readiness for the game, we suddenly heard the all too familiar band striking up again somewhere off in the distance.

We looked at each other nervously as the sound of the band came drew closer, and then to our utter disbelief, marching briskly towards the rugby pitch came first a full band in dress uniform, followed by 3 divisions of naval officer cadets, ranging in age I would guess from around 16 to early twenties, and all dressed in immaculate 18th century military uniforms, consisting of dark blue tailed jackets, a lighter blue trousers with stripes down each leg, and all topped with tall black caps—very impressive it was too! As the divisions reached the stands they came to a halt, were dismissed and made their way up to the seats, chattering loudly amongst themselves. Two of the divisions were on the far side, while the third came to our side of the pitch. It got better though, as the boys detailed to our side had also been detailed as "British Navy" supporters! As soon as they were seated, British flags appeared and were waved about, and cries of "Come on British!" started ringing out. There must have been about 500 supporters all told, and the lads started looking a bit green at the prospect of keeping this lot happy!

As the crowd settled into their seats, on came the Chilean rugby team, bounding on to the pitch to the cheers and shouts of encouragement from the stands. They were a fine looking bunch! All looked very fit and tough, and had clearly played a bit before. They gathered into a huddle, and quickly our team captain called our players to do the same. As we grouped up, some nervous glances passed around as the guys realised that far from being a "friendly" match, this had become the Chilean Navy versus the Royal Navy. The spotlight was well and truly on then!

Our Team Captain was a Stoker Petty Officer from the ship called Benny. That was not his real name, and the nickname came from a bumbling character in a TV show of the time called "Crossroads". Our Benny, like the TV character was a slow talking brute of a bloke, which was where the similarity ended. Benny quickly realised that a bit of Leadership was required, and finished an inspiring team talk with the exultation to "Dominate your opposite number early—show him who's Boss, right?!" "RIGHT!" came the enthusiastic reply from 14 throats. We were ready to rock and roll!

I stood nervously on the sidelines, sponge bag at the ready as the game kicked off. The Chileans were fast and aggressive right from the off, crashing into our players with resounding thuds. They were clearly much fitter than our guys, but we were giving some back though, and for the first 20 minutes it was a hard fought battle without any score. The cadets loved it, cheering and shouting their heads off. I began to relax and enjoy it too, as it became clear that our boys were up to the challenge.

It starting going wrong after about 25 minutes. It had been a clean game up until then, but our boys were running out of puff and starting to lag a bit. Benny was in his element, encouraging and bullying his way around the field in fine form. He must have realised that the forwards particularly were struggling a bit, and started trying to whip them up. "Come on Boys, take charge of the bastards!" At the next line-out, rather than going for the ball he chose to concentrate on his opposite number, and roughly pushed him out of line in the air. Bad move. The guy was massive, and rather than retaliating, he just noted the move. At the following line-out Benny and the guy jumped together, but the bloke neatly whipped his arm backwards, connecting his fist squarely in the chops of Benny, who went down like a sack of potatoes. I rushed on to the pitch.

Benny was on his hands and knees, blood pouring from his nose and lips. I slapped the sponge over his face and started wiping blood. "Benny, you ok mate?" I asked. He didn't look ok. He turned his head towards me and it was immediately clear that he was still seeing stars. I indicated that he needed to be replaced, and with the assistance of a couple of others I got him into a seat as the game continued. The bleeding did not stop, and I was also worried that he might be suffering concussion. I lost all interest in the game, but it was about to get much worse.

Taff Reece was playing at winger. He was a Stoker with a bit of a mean streak in him. Onboard he was a pain in the arse in the Mess, always moaning about having to clean up, and generally bullying the younger guys. On the rugby pitch he tended to try to use the same tactics, which was fine if you could back it up by being a talented player. He was not. So far in the game, he had taken a swipe at his opposite number at any opportunity, catching the man a few times in the process. Again to his credit, the Chilean had shrugged off the attention and concentrated on playing well instead. I guess enough was enough though, and a few minutes after Benny had come off, there was another ruck, with bodies flying in from all angles. As the game moved on it was clear that a guy was lying prone in its wake, and he was one of ours. I left Benny still bleeding and dazed, and ran over to the guy. It was Taff and he was out cold.

I got the sponge going and tried to bring him round. Eventually he opened his eyes and immediately clutched at his mouth and jaw, wincing loudly in pain. I told him to lie still, and on feeling around his jaw found a large lump under his right ear. It was obvious to me that he had broken or at least badly damaged his jaw, and I told him to put his hand under the jaw and not to move. I signalled the referee, and he immediately stopped the game. The Chilean sponge-man ran on the pitch as well to lend a hand. We sat Taff up, and the Chilean, who apparently was a proper medical person of some kind, wrapped a bandage around Taff's head in such a way that the jaw could not move. We got him off the pitch and plonked him next to Benny.

I didn't see the rest of the game. I now had two walking wounded and needed to get them back to the ship for attention. Meanwhile though, the Chilean medic had other ideas, and had organised some transport to the base Sickbay. It seemed like a good idea to me as it was much closer, and there was probably a doctor there, while onboard all we had was a Medic, who while he was very good certainly did not have any x-ray facilities and the ability to fix potentially broken jaws. We loaded both men, who were in a lot of pain by now into the car and off we went.

It was all very organised. We got to the Sickbay, and waiting for us was presumably, a Doctor—white coat and stethoscope, and a couple of male nurses. After a quick examination of both, it was decided (by hand signals mostly) that Benny just needed a few stitches in his mouth, and a good rest, but that Taff was going to need some x-rays on his jaw before they could decide what to do, and since the base did not have an x-ray machine, he would have to go to the local hospital. Great! The sponge man left us with the medical people, who indicated that they would take us—with an armed guard!

We left Benny there, to be returned to the ship later, and got back into the car. They had given Taff some sort of pain killer by now, and he was getting decidedly whoosey, resting his head on my shoulder as we travelled along. At the main gate of the base we stopped, and in jumped a military policeman armed with a sub-machine gun of some kind, as well as a 9mm automatic pistol at his waist. "Ola's" were exchanged all around like this was a Sunday afternoon pick-nick, and we set off towards town.

We arrived at the hospital 20 minutes or so later, and piled in through the main door. The military policeman went in first, helmet on and looking very fierce, and talked heatedly to somebody at the reception. There was lots of hand waving and glances in our direction, with a crowd of patiently waiting Chileans looking on. I had the distinctly uncomfortable impression that we were jumping the queue, and this was confirmed when we were ushered past all of the waiting people and into a treatment room. I uttered "Sorry, excuse me" to people as we passed, but they just looked on with resigned indifference—maybe they were used to this kind of thing happening. Once in the treatment room, the now decidedly sleepy Taff was taken away, still covered in mud and dirt, to be x-rayed while I waited. After a while a person in a white lab coat came out and gestured to me to join him. We went through into another treatment room, where Taff was sitting back in a dentist type chair. The man took me over to where another two people in white coats were looking at x-rays on a viewer. None could speak English, and the one who had fetched me started talking very fast in Spanish, gesticulating at the x-rays. "No ablo Espanola" I said as he rattled on, clearly frustrated that I could not understand. "OK, look" he said, pointing at the x-rays and then to his own jaw "Is broken!" I looked more closely at the frame, and there was quite clearly a crack in Taff's jawbone under his right ear. "We fix" the man continued. I must have looked confused, "We fix, like this" he indicated some wire, tongs and other implements on the stand next to Taff, and it clicked—they wanted to wire Taff's jaw closed, and they were asking my permission. They must have thought I was his boss or something. Oh shit! I felt three pairs of eyes boring in to me.

I really didn't want to be the one to say it was ok to wire the guy's jaw up. I went over to Taff, lying almost out of it in the chair. The dentistry instruments lying next to him looked very menacing close up.

"Taff, Taff, wake up. Do you know where you are?" His eyes lazily focused in my direction

"Steve, how you doing mate?" me mumbled through the bandaging "I was playing rugby".

"That's right Taff; do you know where you are now though?"

He looked around the room lazily "Sickbay is it?"

"That's right. Look Taff, you've broken your jaw. The Doctor wants to wire it up. You ok with that?"

He looked at me a bit more focused "How the fuck will I eat?" he said, a rather good question that I had not even considered to be fair.

I looked at the white coats, and made stupid hand to mouth movements. They knew what I was talking about and to my horror indicated quite clearly that they were going to remove Taff's front teeth before wiring the jaw!

"Taff, they need to take out some of your teeth so that you can still eat with the jaw wired" I should maybe have held my tongue.

"No fucking way!!" Taff spluttered through the bandage, now wide awake again and trying to climb out of the chair. The three white coats rushed over and pushed him back down, chattering in Spanish and trying to soothe him. "Get your fucking hands off me!!" he shouted, wriggling and writhing in the chair. I thought he would do himself some serious damage.

"OK, OK, no teeth OK" shouted the man from before, indicating to Taff that he would leave his teeth alone.

This was getting out of hand now. We were away from the ship in a foreign hospital where they wanted to knock my friend's teeth out, and then wire his jaw closed! This was way above my pay scale and I decided that the decision should be from somebody higher than me. I asked if I could borrow a "telephono".

I had long ago (well, since being stranded in Spain a few years back!) taken the habit of noting the number of the gangway when we were abroad, and in this instance it was a good move. I rang the ship and the Quartermaster answered. I asked him to bring the Officer of the Day to the phone—he could make the decision.

After a moment a new voice came on the line, and my heart sank. Just my luck! The Officer of the Day was Midshipman Lewis, the youngest, lowest and most inexperienced "officer" onboard. This should be fun.

I explained the situation in any case, and then asked what he wanted me to do, emphasising that if Taff's jaw was wired, he would be eating soup through a straw for the next six weeks! There was a long silence.

"Er, what do YOU think we should do LMEM Bridgman?" was the eventual response.

"Well Sir, I don't think there is any choice really, he has to have the jaw wired up. What other option is there?"

"Er, do you think it can wait until the Captain or First Lieutenant get back—just to be sure?"

"How long will that be? The guy is in a lot of pain and this is no private clinic—the doctors are keen to get it done".

"I don't know when they'll be back—they went off with the High Commissioner".

"Is there no way we can contact them? They must have left a contact number surely".

"Er, well, they did, but I should not disturb them unless it is an emergency".

"Beg your pardon Sir, but I would suggest this incident is probably in that category". Then it clicked—he didn't *want* to phone them. He would see that as some kind of failure, maybe of him not being able to make a decision. OK no problem.

"OK Sir, decision time, what do you want me to do?" There you go Cocker, your decision, your move.

"Right Leader, they can wire up the jaw, and then you and he return to the ship" No shit, genius.

At least I felt better as I returned to the treatment room—the decision was out of my hands. I passed on the instructions to the doctors as best I could, and had a chat with Taff, mostly to assure him that he would not be losing any teeth! He didn't look convinced as the medics approached him ready to set to work. I swiftly left the room as needles, wires and pliers started appearing. I certainly didn't need to see the actual process, and took a seat outside.

About an hour later he was done and dusted. He was a bit groggy but able to walk, and a car was waiting to take us back to the ship. Taff at this point was quite up about the wiring job, and proudly showed off the wiring passing here and there in his mouth, and the pair of wire snippers he had been giving so that he could cut the wires if he were sick or choking! Nice touch, but better I suppose that having half a dozen front teeth knocked out. He would not be so chirpy once the pain killers wore off, and his mood would deteriorate over the coming weeks on his forced diet of liquidised everything. On the day of the rugby match Taff was about 15 stone, but over the duration of the trip back to the UK he must have lost about 4 stone, despite the best efforts of the chefs to keep him beefed up. On the up side, it was a lot quieter in the Mess! To make matters even worse on the day, the rest of the rugby team, after having been soundly but bravely beaten, had been given a rousing reception in the Chilean Officers College Dining Room—full dress dinner, drinks and all, and had all come back onboard in the wee small hours, pissed as farts and pleased as punch with the World. I don't think I even had a can of beer that day!

Thankfully there were no further incidents in Valparaiso, and we sailed away with fond memories of the place (well, some of us did anyway!). It was a bit of a surprise that Taff was going to stay onboard, as most of us thought he would be flown back to the UK. We only had very limited medical facilities and thought the powers-that-be would not accept him staying. Still, he was fine in himself—just a bit quieter actually, and it wasn't long before he was being ribbed mercilessly about his injury and his crap strategy for "dominating his opponent".

After leaving Chile we sailed up the side of South America, heading for the Panama Canal. By the time we arrived there we were in our tropical uniforms, and were working hard on our tans. We got a chance to have a look around Panama City, and then took on fuel and off we went through the canal. We were a tiny ship compared to some of the massive ones passing through, and the efficiency of the transport through the giant locks was very impressive—some of the super-tankers and container ships were passing through with just a couple of inches clearance on each side, the little locomotives chugging along rails on each dockside tugging their huge charges along inch by inch. The journey through the canal itself was very pretty, high ridges on each side and tropical foliage spread out in front of us. This was a time before serious terrorism threats, and we were able to flop out on the flight deck and forecastle, beer in hand and catching some serious rays.

We passed into the Atlantic and then up and along the east coast of America, finally crossing the Pond and heading back to Plymouth. We had been away for more than 7 months in total, and it was great to be back. I always loved the coming home bit in the Navy. There was an expectation that started a week before arrival in port, and that grew with each passing day as home came nearer. We always strained to see the first sight of the English countryside, no matter what time of day or night that might happen. In the later years, people would know we were getting closer to home when their mobile phones started to detect signals far out to sea. In submarines it was a bit different, and it was only by popping one's head into the navigation plot on the way on watch and thereby seeing the track of the boat with the southwest foot of England slowly growing on the map that you could tell where you were. When the boat surfaced it was generally about 24 hours travelling time left to Plymouth. I still maintain that there is no feeling better than reaching home after a long deployment and being welcomed by the family. It's almost worth the grief of the trip. Almost.

The only lasting effect from that trip was one of cold weather. We had left the UK in the March of the year, i.e. at the end of winter but not yet spring, had travelled to the South Atlantic—in the middle of their winter, and had returned to the UK at the start of November, just in time for winter. We had been lucky enough to get a couple of week's decent weather on the way down and again on the way back, but in general terms had to suffer 3 winters in a row. I had skin the colour of a plucked chicken, which tallied nicely with the name that Maltese people such as my wife called the tourists there—plucked chickens. Very apt.

Shortly after returning to the UK I received notice that I would be starting my apprenticeship training in early 1987, about a year away. I had already been waiting for well over a year, and so by the time I started the course I would be 26 years old! Any normal apprenticeship would start at age 18, but then if I had the qualifications I could have done a normal apprenticeship in the first place, so I couldn't complain (too much!). Along with the notification came some nice pre-course study material—mostly maths of course, and in very small writing a notice informing students that the previous practice of promoting those joining the course to Acting Petty Officer would no longer apply. Unless you had now passed a promotion board for the rate, you would remain a Leading Hand throughout 2 and a half year course, and then be promoted. This was a major blow to me and now meant that I needed to sit and pass the examination for promotion to Petty Officer Stoker as soon as possible, so that there was a chance of getting some promotion while I was on the course. On checking the promotion roster, I could see that the waiting time for promotion was up around the 2 year mark, so that if I did the exam right now, I might get promoted one year into the course. This was crap! I and many others complained bitterly about it to no avail. Just my luck—as usual.

In reality, it was going to take me a good 3 months to prepare for the promotion examination, and I set about doing the work reluctantly. In the long run I was going to get on course and be promoted one way or another, and I found it very difficult to get motivated. To prepare for the exam, I would have to first get qualified as a "Control Room Petty Officer Stoker", and "Switchboard Watch keeper", and both positions would be new ones for me. In addition there was a whole load of disciplinary stuff to learn, as well as rules and regulations that I didn't have to deal with at Leading Hand level—quite frankly I would rather prepare properly for the Apprenticeship! Nonetheless, within a few weeks I had passed the switchboard test, and also after plenty of time in the machinery control room, had been ticked off on that one too—probably made a bit easier by everybody sympathising with my plight no doubt. All that was now left for me to do was the exam itself; consisting of a 3 hour written paper followed by the obligatory "Fleetboard"—this time in front of my own Engineering Officer Lt Pike, a Lieutenant Commander from the base, and the Flotilla Engineering Commander. I still had a few weeks studying to do before that though, but the date was now booked so there was no more time to be messing about. I got my head into the books.

All the time that this was going on, the ship was preparing for, and then setting sail on, the next trip out. On this occasion we were only going for 3 months or so, surveying off and around Gibraltar. We would be spending a lot of time at sea on the trip, which for me, so long as the weather was fine, would be a good chance to get the studying in. The plan worked for most of the time, and by the time we were preparing to return to the UK once more, I felt confident that I knew enough to pass the Fleetboard.

Before heading back to the UK, we had a stop in Gibraltar so that we could blow off the cobwebs and have a well-earned beer or three. By now, Gibraltar for me was like a second home base. I have been there on numerous occasions already, and was well used to the potential of the place to get a person in deep trouble. The bars were plentiful and cheap, and on a nice warm spring day it was very easy to sit, chat, drink, chat, drink and then drink some more. It was the younger chaps who normally fell into this trap, and Paddy Shaw was no exception. He was a good young Stoker, a high spirited Southern Irish man as friendly and funny as you like; hard working and with a good potential for the future in the Navy. He went ashore with a group of the boys as usual. They did the usual pub crawl along the Main Street, ending up at the well-used "Angry Friar" pub. That's when he disappeared. It wasn't considered unusual for that to happen, as sometimes when somebody got pissed they would wander off somewhere—normally back to the ship in fact, and that's what his mates thought had happened to him. It wouldn't be allowed to happen somewhere dodgy, but Gibraltar was a pretty safe place to be alone, so the guys rightly thought nothing more of it. I happened to be the duty Leading Hand onboard on the day, and was awoken at about 2 AM by a messenger from the gangway. When I got there, I was confronted by two Navy Policemen, and Paddy standing, well swaying, between them, hands behind his back and handcuffed. I called for the Officer of the Day, and all of us went to the Stokers mess. The "Reggies" explained that Paddy was being released to the custody of the ship, but would require to be presented at the Criminal Court in the morning, charged with maliciously damaging 11 cars! We looked at his small frame and friendly face. What?

The allegation was that Paddy had drunkenly stolen a car, and then proceeded to drive the thing up one of the narrow roads in Gibraltar, bumping off cars parked along the sides of the road as he went. We were dumfounded! Finally, he had smacked into the last car, had stalled and then been dragged from the car by passersby and held until the police arrived. Again we looked at the skinny little thing in front of us. Clearly he was very drunk, but nicking cars and then going on a destruction derby? There was not a mark on him, either physically or on his clothing which seemed remarkably clean for somebody supposedly dragged from a car. I wasn't even sure if he could drive for goodness sake. The Officer of the Day voiced the obvious question—"Are you sure this is the right man?"

"Sir, we have to go by what the police are telling us. That's what he has been arrested for, and they say there are witnesses who say it was him" replied Crusher No.1. Like they gave a shit.

Paddy was then signed over to our custody. Of course he was in added shit by the fact that he had also been "brought back onboard drunk", an offense in itself in naval law. Of course people always came back onboard drunk, but usually under their own steam. The fact that he had been brought back by the military police meant that he was "officially" drunk, as it were. We put him to bed anyway, but somebody had to sit with him all night to stop him either drowning if he vomited, or escaping now that he was under house arrest.

He was awoken early next morning in good time to get him ready for his court appearance. He was genuinely surprised and shocked at what had happened, and claimed to remember none of it. No matter. He had a court appearance to attend to, and we would see what would happen from there. It didn't take long, and within an hour he was returned to the ship once more, looking something like a little boy lost. He had been remanded to the custody of the ship once more while investigation were underway, but he had been warned by the judge that he was looking at a possible custodial sentence if the initial reports of damage were true. It's fair to say that he and we were gob-smacked by this turn of events, and were still finding it very difficult to believe that Paddy was capable of the carnage that was being described, but without any independent witnesses we didn't have a leg to stand on in his defence. Over the next few days the initial furore quietened down some, but with the Sword of Damocles hanging over him, not surprisingly Paddy withdrew into his shell.

About four days after his court appearance I happened again to be duty. Paddy was by now settled down into a routine onboard, just doing his normal work, but having to report to the Duty Leading Hand about 5 times a day to ensure he remained on board the ship. Of course being such a small ship the formally involved in the process fizzled out almost immediately—after all, we all lived together and so there was no need for the formal reporting stuff. It was the same with me, and I just occasionally saw him wandering around or sitting in the mess, so took it for granted all was well. During the evening, Paddy was going around the mess selling some of his possessions—t-shirts, music cassettes and such like, to pay he said for some things to take with him if he ended up inside. Seemed sensible to me, and I think I even bought a couple of cassettes from him. Things moved on and I promptly forgot all about it—until a rude awakening the next morning that was!

When I awoke next morning, all hell had broken loose. Paddy was missing from the ship! We did a full search of the ship, and sure enough he was gone. In those days the border with Spain was closed, which meant that he was either still on Gibraltar, or had flown out of the place—which he could not do since his passport had been seized while he was under open arrest right? Er, no actually—were we supposed to be doing that, or the Police? Ah, slight problem. They thought we had done it, and we thought they . . . you get the picture.

Paddy was long gone. He had been very clever indeed. Clearly he had hatched the plan as soon as he realised on-one was going to take his passport. He had told absolutely no-one what he intended, and had not shown any intention at all in the way of packing bags or anything obvious like that. The only give-away was when he needed to raise money by selling his things, but no-one had clicked onto the real reason. Then, having bought the ticket by phone, he had jumped ship sometime between midnight and maybe 3 am, gone to the airport and jumped on a flight off the Rock. The flight had been to Dublin, and as an Irish citizen he was untouchable by the British authorities so long as he did not step foot onto British territory. Secretly we were delighted, as we suspected something amiss with the whole set-up here, although of course we couldn't show it. The police were translucent with rage, and questioned us all intently. They could not prove any collusion though, and were frankly embarrassed by the whole episode, so let it drop. We sailed away from Gibraltar minus one Stoker, but at least he wasn't in some stinking Gibraltar gaol. We received a postcard from Paddy about 3 months later, apologising for putting us through the grief. He got home ok in the end, and we were happy for him.

This had been my last major deployment on the Herald, although there were a couple of small trips thrown in between maintenance periods, before I was to leave the ship to commence Technician training. My last major hurdle before going was to take and pass the promotion exam for Petty Officer Stoker, so that hopefully I would be promoted to Petty Officer prior to finishing the course. I would hate to still be a Leading Hand at 29 years old!

I had been doing quite a bit of studying for the fleetboard part of the exam process, but in reality was pretty confident that having been selected for Artificer training that the entire episode would be a "tick-in-the-box" affair. I did the written exam without any difficulty, and was then presented, as was becoming fairly routine, to a Commander, a Lieutenant Commander and my own Lieutenant Engineer to be bombarded with what I thought would be the "standard" engineering questions. They were no fools though, and knowing that I was already selected for Technical training, decided that they would hammer me on the other aspect of promotion to Petty Officer—leadership. For the next hour I was asked how I would deal with a bewildering variation of disciplinary situations, ranging from somebody failing to obey a lawful order, to somebody found using drugs, to how I might deal with a homosexual encounter! The Lieutenant Commander particularly felt it necessary to take every scenario to "nth" degree, and never appeared completely satisfied with my answers. The other two by contrast seemed to be going through the motions in many respects, and were keen to get it finished with. After an hour or so I was told to wait outside while they made a decision. A few minutes later I was called back, told I had passed the exam and wished the best of luck in my new career as a Marine Engineering Artificer. I would still have to wait nearly 2 years to get my promotion though. Blow up the balloon—and then burst it! It's the navy way.

I left the Herald soon after passing the exam for promotion, and in truth I was sorry to go. She had been a good ship for me, and despite a few hairy incidents onboard I had enjoyed my time with her. The Herald proved to be my last posting to a surface ship during my career, although I did not know that at the time. Within a few months of leaving the ship myself and my wife Anna had upped sticks and moved from our married quarter in St Budeaux (or "Budo" as it was commonly known) Plymouth, to a little 2 up, 2 down terraced house in Gosport Hampshire, just across the river from Portsmouth, which we had saved and scraped to buy. We like many people in those times had decided that we didn't want to live in married quarters forever, and needed to get on the property ladder. I was still only a Leading Stoker and after paying off the mortgage, bills, insurance and Christ knows what else, we were left with fifty pounds a month to buy everything else! Still, it was the same for everybody and things of course improved with time. The main focus of my attention was on the upcoming Artificer Candidate's Course (ACC), otherwise known as "Mech's Course" or "Tiff's Course" and I would be joining "ACC No.18" starting in February of 1987.

Chapter 11

There's a Brain in There Somewhere!

By the time I rolled up at the Main Gate of HMS Sultan for the start of my course, I was completely ready for it, and had been for the previous 2 years! I was chomping at the bit to get started, but as always in the Navy it was a case of "Hurry-up and Wait" again. The course introduction was going to take the whole week, and bizarrely included a tour of HMS Sultan—like none of us had been there before! There was also a "meet and greet" afternoon where we firstly got to know the guys who would be our class-mates for the next 2 and a half years and also some of the department and section heads who ran the place. Throughout the week we were subjected to a barrage of "this is the start, not the end" and "you'll get out what you put in" speeches from everybody ranging from the Commodore of Sultan, down to our individual class officers. It became tedious very quickly indeed. The one highlight of the week was when the "foreign navies" students showed up on the final Friday. We had about half a dozen from Kenya, and some more from a few other places, and they had the good sense to miss all the start of course bullshit. They were not big on discipline, as we were to find out in spades as the course got under way. They were mostly a friendly bunch though, apart from one guy called "Shadrack"—apparently, so the others said, his Dad was some high-up back home, which made him a bit special. No matter—we would soon put him right on that score.

The course started in earnest the following week, and it was straight into maths and physics. The entire first year of study was based on the academic stuff, and included all the favourites—maths, physics, chemistry (which I loathed!), engineering science, and the totally new subjects (to me) of electronic and electrical theory. The pace was relentless from the off, and included the dreaded Phase Test every week. I very quickly got into the routine of studying every evening, and depending on what day the exam was, I could be up to around 2:00 am at the books. It came as a total surprise to me to find that I enjoyed the studying, and even more of a surprise to discover that I was pretty good at the exams too. In pretty short order I was regularly coming in the first 3 for most exams, usually to be beaten by another Scottish lad who seemed to have a brain the size of a planet, and who swore that he never studied—who knows?

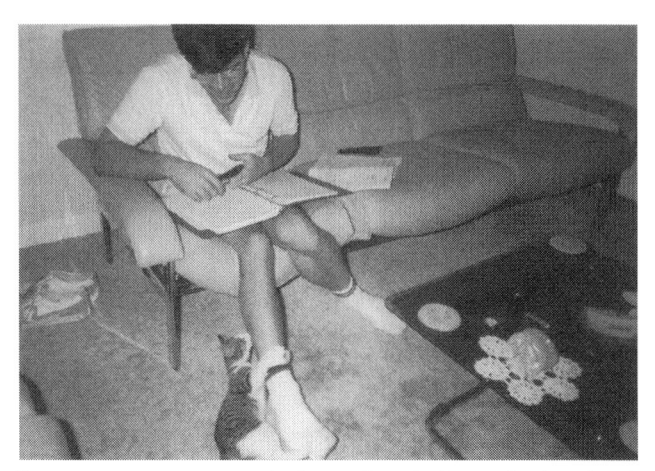

"Molly, I am trying to Study!"—A break from the books during Apprenticeship 1987

My Bloody Efforts

Along with the academic stuff there was the usual "naval general training" or "NGT", the parades and the normal naval bollocks. We were required to attend a full parade (usually for some class or other "Passing Out") about once every two weeks, and that was in our best bib and tucker. In addition there was a weekly Tuesday morning divisions in working clothes (perfectly turned out of course), and this one was a pain in the arse. The Gunnery Instructors (GI's) loved parades as you might expect, as it was their opportunity to have a good shout and scream at everybody within range. For the guys on Artificer Candidates Course this regular parade was used as a bit of NGT, in that one person from the course would be chosen to be "Parade Commander". This poor sod would have to stand the other end of the parade ground and scream out the orders for the entire parade—no easy task for two reasons—there were a shit-load of orders to remember, in the right order, and on-one could ever shout load enough for the satisfaction of the GI's! The final thing that the Parade Commander of the day had to do was to "judge" the classes as they marched past the saluting stand, and decide whether they should "go-around", i.e. carry on marching around until they were smart enough. This was a two-edged sword, as they guy really didn't want to piss off any of his mates in the classes, but on the other hand, didn't want to get it wrong in front of the GI's, who would be watching to make sure he picked up the crap marching. My turn came about 3 months in to the course, and it was terrifying standing in front of a thousand men and shouting your head off. In fairness the Chief GI stood behind me and whispered the orders, which made life a bit easier, and I made about 5 class's go-around—I couldn't give a toss if I upset them—they should learn to march properly! The upshot of this though was that there was always one of us in a state of extreme apprehension building up to each Tuesday Divisions. It was something that stayed throughout the course, and by the time the course finished I think I had done it about half a dozen times. It never got any easier!

In addition to the academic training, we also embarked on an entire year of "specialist" branch training. In my case I was earmarked to be a "Fitter and Turner", and so commenced in-depth metalwork training, which included filing, use of workshop power tools, and a load of "turning" on a lathe. The first months were merely about working metal by hand, and were a continuation of the Leading Stoker's course really. Once again the pace was crippling. We had to work to technical drawings, and produce each piece within a given number of work hours, and to very tight specifications. The marking scheme was prescribed for each piece, and the marks were very hard to squeeze out of the Instructors. We started off by just producing flat and perfectly square plates, then plates with precise drillings or milled areas, and then moving on to square blocks within blocks and so forth. In each case you had to score above about 60% as I recall, and if you failed a piece, you would have to do it again out of working hours. I really didn't want to do that as I had enough studying to do as it was and couldn't afford to be stuck in the workshop every evening. Within the first few days my (and everybody else's) hands were in ribbons, and I began to think that I would suffer the same woes with filing and cutting that I had in the past. Remarkably though, with the concentrated work at the bench, I fairly quickly became quite proficient, and found that I could actually hacksaw and file straight. I was never going to become a master metalworker, but was managing to keep my end up so far. As always, there were people who seemed to have the magic touch with the equipment, and I became firm friends with one of them—Paul "Happy" Day. We had not met prior to the course, but seemed to hit it off straight away on it. He was very good at the metalwork and helped me out a lot.

We (and our wives) remained good mates throughout the course, but as is usual in the navy, went our separate ways at the end of it. He to Destroyers I think, and me to submarines.

Life was good on the domestic front as well. Since we had been married, the longest myself and my wife had spent together had been about 3 months in a single spell. Now though, we were like a "normal" married couple—me with my effectively 9 to 5 job, and her doing the "domestic goddess" thing around our own home. It couldn't last though, and within a relatively short time we were finding it very hard to get by. The mortgage was crippling us and we had to make some hard decisions—either Anna goes out to work, or we move back into married quarters. Anna insisted though that she wanted to get a job, and in short order was hired as a Care Assistant. That helped the money worries, but others soon surfaced.

We had bought our little terraced house in a single weekend visit from Plymouth to Gosport—with perfect hindsight a bloody stupid thing to do. In mitigation though, we had no-one to ask for help looking around the place, or on how you even buy a house, so we did our best. The house had all the right bits of paper, surveys and all that good stuff, which had failed to identify any problems with it, but almost as soon as we moved in we started noticing that we had rising damp. All of the walls on the ground floor were discoloured up to about a metre high, and the skirting boards were falling to bits when they were touched. I called in a specialist who poked around with some instrument (the needle of which swung alarmingly into the red zone and beeped every time he did it!), and then finally declared that yes, we had damp, dry rot and goodness knows what else, and it was going to cost £6000.00 to fix. We were living on fifty quid a month! Where the hell would we find that?

I didn't really need this crap right now just then, but we were stuck. We couldn't sell the place like this, and we couldn't find six grand anytime soon. We couldn't even decorate because the wallpaper would just slide off the wet walls, and so we were stuck in a 1960s time warp with bloody awful flowery walls and rock hard brown paint. What a disaster!

The situation was salvaged more through luck than judgement. I had seen a leaflet somewhere from the local council advertising subsidized loft insulation, and had gone to the local council office to find out the details. While I was chatting to a person there, and basically draining down on them about my knackered house, they happened to mention that the council was running a scheme whereby they assisted owners of "old" houses to modernise them. My ears pricked up in a second. I grabbed a bunch of application forms, filled them in there and then and went away smiling. I expected that they might front up with maybe a couple of thousand pounds, but in the end they gave us almost two-thirds of the cost of the repair work—almost four thousand pounds. We had to live upstairs for a couple of months while all of the plastering was stripped off all the downstairs walls, some horrible smelling chemical injected into the walls (it made everything in the place, clothes, furniture, bedding, everything stink for weeks!), left to dry, and then the walls re-plastered. It was a living nightmare and the mess was incredible—but we had little choice. I wish I could say that we learned a lesson for when we bought future houses, but we didn't!

The course at least was progressing well. I was doing ok in most areas, except for Technical Drawing the exam of which I failed first time around. Following further instruction I managed to scrape through with my lowest score of the entire course. On the workshop front all was going fairly well, and we had by now moved on to working with lathes. On first introduction I imagined that I would never understand how to control the thing, and they were pretty scary too. They whizzed round at very high speed and bits of metal flew off at all angles as the job in the chuck was cut to shape. They had a peculiar smell too—hot oil and machinery, together with the metallic smell of the metal actually being cut. How nobody was seriously injured in the first few weeks was beyond me. We started the machines with chuck keys still in, with jobs not tightened in the chuck, with cutting tools loose, and with all sorts of other misdemeanours going on. There were tools and chuck keys and all sorts of things flying about all of the time, and every now and then would come the cry "Duck!!!" as another piece of tooling went flying.

It was pretty clear that we were all a bit scared of the lathes. The Instructors realised this very quickly and decided to put a little show on for us to demonstrate that we were not going to break anything on the machines. They set up a 6" diameter piece of metal in one of the chucks, and then proceeded to take the biggest cuts out of the metal that they could with the cutting tool on the lathe. Huge swirls and twists of metal flew off the lathe, and when they stopped the cooling fluid the machine smoked and coughed, but kept turning. Larger and larger cuts were taken, the lathe jumping and vibrating violently as the cutting tool bit into the steel until finally, with a huge thump, the machine stopped dead. The instructor turned off the power, withdrew the cutting tool and restarted the lathe—it turned perfectly and without apparent damage. "There you go gentlemen. Believe me you are not going to break one of these machines! OK, crack on then". It did the trick and we felt much more comfortable chopping and turning. It allowed us to concentrate more on the work process than operating the machine and that was a weight off our shoulders. Within no time we had the things whizzing around turning out jobs. On the lathes we had an added bit of pressure in that we were now required to produce work plans for each piece we needed to create. This thing consisted of a blow-by-blow intimate description of each step that we needed to take in the process of making whatever it was, and had to include a technical drawing of each stage as well. For me the descriptive bit was fine, but my technical drawing was atrocious! I was forever in trouble with the instructors for it. The problem on the lathe was that the marking system was all arse about face. You started with 100%, but then had marks deducted for each mistake or infringement, and since the pass mark in all cases was 65%, you didn't have a lot of room to manoeuvre! It was becoming normal for me to lose between 5 and 10% of each job just for the work plan, and whatever I did; I could not seem to get better at the drawing. This handicap stayed with me throughout the metalworking phase, and cost me a lot of marks during the final Trade Test.

Along with every other posting I had in the Navy, there was the usual requirement, even on a career training course, or having to do "duties"—that is extra work over an entire 24 hour period once every 6 days or so. I could understand the necessity for it on a front line ship which obviously needed to be manned all of the time, but had found previously that the shore bases seemed to feel it necessary to invent jobs so that everybody was subjected to one kind of duty or other, and HMS Sultan was no exception. The duty roster for our class meant that a person would end up doing such entirely necessary extra work as being "Security Leading Hand", or "Duty Leading Hand of the Mess" or other such interesting jobs—this when we were subject to almost weekly exams. What was more irritating was that there were people drafted into those jobs at Sultan, yet were somehow too busy themselves. Ridiculous.

I and "Happy" Day thought that we had found the perfect 'out' though. Sultan like all other shore bases had its own "Internal Security" or 'I.S.' platoon. This was made up of people on the base who in times of emergency would form a rapid response unit, armed to the teeth and ready to repel any attack, from any quarter! In reality, the platoon was more "Dad's Army" than "Modern Army", and when we visited the Armoury to get some information, we found that the equipment they used was all 1945 vintage, right down to the pudding dish helmets and gaters! The webbing was the stuff you used to see in World War 2 films, and the Self-Loading Rifles (SLR) had not even been taken out of their wrapping by the Rock-Apes manning the place. We spoke to the Gunnery Instructor Petty Officer "in-charge" of the IS platoon, who told us that they met once every now and again to talk about hand grenades or something, or to run around dressed as trees, but that was about it. He noted also, that if you volunteered for the IS platoon you were exempt from duties! I and Happy looked at each other—perfect! Where do we sign?

All was well with this arrangement for about 6 months or so. We would wander into the Armoury once a week or so, have a chat with the guys in there for 5 minutes and then wander off again—duty done. One week though, we received a message that we were required to muster at the Armoury on a certain day and at a certain time—very unusual. We turned up and mingled around in the muster hall with a whole load of other people we had never seen before—presumably the other members of the elusive internal security platoon. We chatted amongst ourselves for a while, and then got the shock of our lives as two Royal Marines sergeants stomped into the room, dressed in combat gear and looking very menacing!

"Right, Listen in!" shouted the first, a bit blond chap—square jawed and tough looking.

As we settled down, the second guy, smaller than the first but fitted with the obligatory moustache that the trees seemed to favour, chipped in:

"We are the new Internal Security Platoon Leaders. You may have heard that the government has decided to beef up the IS platoons in all of the Navy and Marine bases, and that's why we are here. Things are going to change I can assure you!" The last was added with a rather nasty look in his eye.

It turned out that these gentlemen had been in Sultan for a number of days, checking out the Armoury, the platoon, its equipment and so on, and drawing up a plan of action to get the security of the place "up to standard".

We were given a straightforward option. We could go back to doing duties, or stay with the IS platoon on the understanding that we would be subject to some "proper" military training—Royal Marines style. Me and Happy decided that it might be interesting to stick around and opted to stay, but about 10 guys (mostly the fat bastards actually) opted to return to normal duties and promptly disappeared.

Our infantry training started straight away with some physical fitness stuff—which we would now do for the first 45 minutes every time we mustered. This was not too bad and mostly consisted of us running around in squad formation looking hard, and in any case we were all fairly fit anyway. The two Sergeants were still in Royal Marines Lympstone (or "Limp-dick" as we hilariously called it) mode though, and were very quickly christened "Sergeant Death"—the little one with the mad eyes, and "Sergeant Shut-UP!"—The Blondie with the big gob. For the next couple of sessions they bawled and shouted at us, and tried the aggressive approach that they presumably used on new Marines recruits. It mostly fell on deaf ears though, and we frequently reminded them that if we had wanted to crawl around in dirt, hide behind trees and paint our faces black, we would have had our brains removed and joined the Marines. That usually got a bite! The standard wind-up after a session of training was that we were "sweating like a Marine in a spelling test!" That usually got us an extra 20 sit-ups too, but it was worth it.

After the initial mutual distrust had worn off, we settled down into a routine that in truth suited all of us. Sergeants Death and Shut-Up eventually realised that as keen as we were to learn about killing people and blowing stuff up, we were never going to be real soldiers, and once they had got to that understanding things ran much more smoothly. They eventually managed to get us modern camouflage uniforms; boots, helmets and webbing, and that made us take a greater interest in the whole thing. It was still a struggle for them though, as we had absolutely no "natural" soldiering instincts—a case in point was our first vehicle search instruction session.

Sergeant Death mustered us outside the Armoury while Sergeant Shut-up drove up in his beaten up old Ford Cortina.

"Right then, Bridgman and Day, I want you to search this car".

"Alright Sarge, anything particular we are looking for?"

"What the fuck do you think you would be looking for, chocolates and flowers?"

"Point taken." Me and Happy stepped forward and started opening the boot, bonnet and doors, glove compartment and anything else that opened in the car, poking around and looking here and there—nothing!

"Nothing here Sarge, the car's clean" I announced after a couple of minutes fruitless search. Happy nodded in agreement.

"You sure?" replied Death. We looked at each other, shrugged agreement and nodded that we were.

"Fucking incredible!" Sergeants Death and Shut-up approached the car.

"First. You do not open anything right? You get the owner to do it while you stand behind him. If the fucker has booby trapped the handles he is unlikely to want to open it himself is he?" Good point.

"Second. How are you supposed to search the car properly if you don't have a torch? You got fucking x-ray vision Bridgman or what?" Fair comment.

"Third. See that bit of kit over there (pointing a small wheeled platform like mechanics use to look under cars), you use that to look under the car for anything that might have been attached there—like a fucking bomb! Did you two clowns even look under the car?" I and Happy took on suitably sheepish facial expressions.

"The "search" you did was crap. If you had done it properly you might have noticed this!" From under a wheel arch he unclipped and removed a 9mm pistol.

"And this" said Shut-up, as he drew out another 9mm pistol from where the spare wheel goes in the boot. I had looked there—shit!

"And if you'd bothered to look under the car you might have seen this!" A large block of plasticine posing as plastic explosive was retrieved and laid next to the 2 shining pistols.

This process continued for another couple of minutes as the Marines produced magazines from here, or cartridges from there, and at one point removing the petrol filler cap and pulling up a bag of goodies on a string from the petrol tank. Finally they finished, and we surveyed the surprising large pile of weaponry at our feet.

The Marines looked pretty pissed off at the end of the exercise, and it may have been at this point they realised that their work was cut out for them. In any case it was a wake up call for us, and we did make an effort in future to take it all a bit more seriously.

Myself and Happy stayed with the IS platoon throughout our training at Sultan, and overall it was a good laugh and made a nice change from the study routine we were under. Shortly before we left the platoon we took part in quite a large exercise on the base, where we were going to be attached by a bunch of SAS troops, to test our readiness.

By then we had received quite a bit of military training, and considered ourselves fairly proficient in most aspects of the job—arrest techniques, weapons control, personal and vehicle searching and patrolling. For this exercise, for the first time, we were provided with a couple of magazines of blank ammunition to use as well, and so we were all pretty excited about it. The exercise started about 5 pm and was due to last all night, with us patrolling around the base and dealing with any incursions that might, or might not, happen. Initially we walked around, sticking to the shadows and doing all the good military stuff, while we waiting for the "enemy" to strike. The novelty wore off for me at around 3 am the next day though, having been wandering round for hours in the cold and wet, and having not seen a bloody thing!

The tedium continued until about 6 am, when there was a report of a couple of enemy soldiers having been spotted across the other side of the base, near to one of the old Second World War hangars. At that time I was part of the QRF or "Quick Reaction Force", and we were ordered into the attack!

We quickly grabbed our gear and started off in the direction of the hangar. We would need to cross the parade ground to get there, and so Sergeant Shut-up reminded us to use proper military technique while we were crossing the open ground:

"Work in pairs, one moves forward while the other covers him, then vice-versa" he shouted as we raced off.

We slowed as we reached the edge of the parade ground, the Sergeant's words echoing in our ears—until someone spotted a couple of figures in the distance:

"That's the bastards—get after them" someone shouted, and totally forgetting all of our rigorous training we dashed off in a mob in the direction of the "enemy", loading up our weapons with a magazine of blanks as we went.

At some point during the dash, somebody fired off a blank round in the direction of the figures. This had a remarkable effect, and within seconds, not knowing where the shot had come from, we all dove to the tarmac of the parade ground and started blatting away with our self-loading rifles. The noise was deafening, but strangely you could still hear the "tinkling" of the spent shell cases hitting the ground. I fired off first one then the other magazine in about 5 seconds, like everybody else, at nothing in particular. It was probably just frustration from the long night doing stuff all.

Within seconds Sergeant Death was among us screaming "Cease Fire, fucking Cease Fire, NOW!"

"What the fucking are you firing at? There's fucking nothing there you dickheads!" he screamed at us, livid with rage.

"How many rounds have you got left?" pointing a one then the next guy, and getting either "don't know" or "none" in reply.

"You fucking matelots are fucking useless!" he stomped off back to the Armoury.

It turned out that the SAS had not visited the camp at all, and that the "enemy" we had seen was a couple walking their dog the other side of the perimeter fence—poor buggers must have had the fright of their lives!

There were a couple more exercises during our time with the platoon, but nothing really ever as big as this one had been. The Sergeants' became something of fixture at Sultan and went on to create a really quite professional Internal Security platoon there—later on they even became involved with the daily and weekly parades, acting as Gunnery Instructors, and we saw them a few times in the future dressed up to the nines in their ceremonial kit, waving their pace sticks about and screaming out orders to all and sundry. They loved it!

Back in the world of becoming an Artificer, we had by now completed the academic phase (I came second overall), and had also completed the final "Trade Test" in the workshop. This had consisted of making a fire fighting hose nozzle from scratch—producing the worksheet as well. I think it was 50 hours to make the thing and it involved all of the skills we had leaned over the last 1400 hours in the workshop. You were provided with a billet of metal with a trade stamp on it, and if you had to do some work where the stamp was removed (cutting or grinding or something), you had to go to the staff and get the metal stamped somewhere else—failure to do so meant an automatic loss of 2% I think. I must have lost 5% right from the off thanks to my rubbish technical drawing, and straight away I lost another 2% failing to move the stamp before cutting! All was going well for the next couple of days, until in a complete brain fart I managed to round off a couple of edges of the body of my nozzle in the lathe. I was devastated! Within seconds I had a crowd of instructors gathered around my machine, huffing and puffing, measuring this or that and working out the damage done. There was no case of "what can we do to salvage this?", but more of "how much shall we deduct for this cock-up". Finally it was agreed that the mistake would cost me about 10%—phew! The loss in percentage was building up though and I really had to be careful.

I eventually finished the nozzle, using every last second of the time allocated. I was very unhappy with the finished product and very relieved to have passed the trade test with 4% to spare—my score was 69% and the pass mark 65%. Some of the better "hands-on" guys had achieved scores of up to 90%, including Happy who had got about 85% as I recall. There was a big ruckus around this time, because some of the foreign navy guys had passed the test, when it was abundantly clear that their work was way below standard. It had been the same throughout the workshop phase, when a lot of their pieces were not very good. They blamed it on their limited understanding of English, but most of them spoke better English than all of us, and they never had any problems with the language during the academic work! In any case it didn't affect my pay scale, so I couldn't give a toss personally. I was just relieved to have got this major hurdle out of the way—I was now on the home stretch. Overall I had done some 1500 hours at the bench or on the lathe, and in my remaining 14 years in the Navy I never touched a lathe again—such a waste really.

We were now on the home run of the course, with just the engineering systems and components bit to do. This was the most interesting area for me, and I enjoyed it very much. We learned about steam systems and different types of oils, and how air compressors worked and so forth. The best part though was that the pressure was off us now that we had passed the academics and workshops phases, and we were left well alone. At last we were being treated as grown-ups, and were now allowed to pretty much do our own thing—no more divisions either! It was a very nice time for all of us, safe in the knowledge that unless we did something very, very stupid, we were going to leave Sultan as Petty Officer Artificers.

At the time of our apprenticeship there was a character on TV known as "Loadsamoney", who captured the "spend, spend" attitude of the times. Our very own versions of the character were the submariners with us on the course, who took each and every opportunity of emphasizing the higher rates of pay they received for submarine service—even when they were on a 2 and a half year training course! They drove around in nice cars, had all of the gadgets and "bling" (although it wasn't called that in those days), and seemed to be allowed to get away with a lot dress code violations and petty discipline stuff—a button carelessly undone here, single word answers instead of "Yes, staff", hair slightly longer than necessary, and a general "who gives a shit!" attitude. I had never seen anything like it before, and I suppose I was impressed.

During the course I had got along with everybody really, but had struck up closer friendships with Happy Day, and a guy called Dave Sutton, who I had first met years before on the Ark Royal. When we had gone our separate ways form that ship, he had been drafted into submarines—very much against his will at the time. He had settled into it though, and through fate we had ended up on the same "Tiff's" course. We had spoken a lot about life in submarines—he had served on a number of boats (as submarines were known—from being called "submarine boats" when they were first introduced into the navy), and gave me a lot of inside information on life onboard. I had come to the conclusion that volunteering for submarines was a way I might go—it was different from anything I had done before, and in truth I liked the sound of the extra dosh!

My decision was finally cemented by the arrival at class one day of the submarines drafting team, brought in to each class as they approached the end of course to try to illicit a few volunteers from the newly qualified technicians. They talked the service up of course, selling the submarine fleet as the "elite" of the Royal Navy, only accepting the best candidates, providing the highest quality training blah, blah. By then I think I had already made up my mind, and applied to join there and then, together with a couple of others. The change of attitude towards us amongst our peers was instant and quite ferocious, and we were immediately ostracised from the "skimmers"—even Happy Day cooled off towards me, which was quite odd. Still, I had made my decision and that was it. I told Anna that I had been drafted to submarines—she would not have been too happy had I admitted I had been a volunteer!

A couple of weeks after volunteering, I was finally promoted to Acting Petty Officer Marine Engineering Mechanic—almost 3 years after passing the promotion exam! I was now 28 years old, and it had taken me 12 years to get this far, although in fairness I had waited a total of nearly 6 years for different promotions, having passed the exams in good time. We were now just 6 weeks from the end of our course, at which time I would be changing my uniform to that of Acting Petty Officer Artificer! I still had to sew on the badges of Petty Officer Stoker though, only to remove them again later.

In the final few weeks of the course we started receiving our drafting orders for our new postings. Most people received what they had asked for—a surprise in itself! As expected I was drafted to HMS Dolphin, the submarine training school, for 4 weeks of basic submarine training—known as Part 1 training, before coming back to Sultan for another 8 weeks of submarine engineering training, or Part 2 training. After that, I would join the 2nd Submarine Squadron in Plymouth where I would be assigned to a boat for my Part 3 training. I and Anna started making preparations for selling our house in Gosport and moving back to Plymouth.

"Do try to look impressed" Artificer Course Prize giving 1989 with Anna Mum and Step Father Mick

The final couple of weeks at Sultan were basically a holiday. Everybody was promoted to either Leading or Petty Officer Artificer, depending on whether they had passed the PO's exam before joining—some had not, and we all felt a bit stiff and awkward in our shiny new peaked caps and suits. There were lots of parties to celebrate our passing the course, and plenty of goodbyes to be said. The course culminated in a "prize-giving" ceremony in front of our families, and I was lucky enough to receive an award for coming 1st in the engineering systems phase of the course—a nice tankard and forty quid's worth of tools! In the afternoon there was our "Passing Out" divisions in best uniforms, where the top engineering admiral was to say some nice things and send us on our merry way into the fleet. Unfortunately, and this was August for goodness sake, the heavens opened and 2000 sailors and a number of visiting families got absolutely drenched. The prats made everybody stand there for 2 hours in the pouring rain! It was so wet that the dye from the uniforms started running—every bloke had a puddle of nice dark blue around his feet, and we marched past the equally dripping admiral on his dais, arcs of spray flying off swinging arms, and hundreds of feet splashing through pools of still water. Incredible! All of the uniforms were totally destroyed, and later we were given permission to order new ones—for the already new ones that were trashed, all 2000 of them. Expensive parade.

So ended the apprenticeship. I was now a fully spammed-up, proper engineering technician—I even had a City and Guilds Certificate and Engineering Council Ordinary National Certificate to prove it. I was a Petty Officer as well, and with being promoted to PO Stoker, then PO Tiff, as well as basic submarine pay to come, it meant that my pay had effectively doubled in the space of a couple of months—things were really looking up!

Apprenticeship – Bah! It was a breeze!

CHAPTER 12

Make Sure You Keep Blowing!

I JOINED HMS DOLPHIN, the submarine training school late in December 1989 for Part 1, or "basic" submarine training. Dolphin was located in Gosport, and was also the base of operations for the dwindling "conventional" (i.e. non-nuclear) fleet of Porpoise and Oberon class of submarines, or "P & O Boats" as they were more commonly known. These were more akin to the Second World War U-Boats that everybody was familiar with from war films than to any "modern" submarine, but were in fact fitted with some very sophisticated equipment. The problem was that the hulls themselves were getting pretty old, and from a personal point of view I wouldn't fancy working in them—they looked very small, and the hygiene conditions onboard pretty basic. In any case at that time no new crew were being drafted into the P&O boats, and that suited me fine.

The basic submarine course was four weeks long, and really was basic. The instruction was very relaxed which felt a bit odd for us guys coming straight off the apprenticeship, and consisted mostly of "sea stories" from the instructors on their experiences in boats. The formal bits of the course consisted of showing us how submarines surfaced, dived and manoeuvred, as well as the major components of a boat. In addition we had a personalised tour of the impressive submarine museum, where the tour guide really brought home to us the history, and it must be said the danger, of the new career we were embarking on.

An idea of the spirit of some of our forebears was demonstrated to the senior ratings on the course when we were required to host the annual "Submariners Association" visit to HMS Dolphin. We at first wondered why we had to be the hosts—we were not even qualified submariners yet, but we could only get the response that "You'll see!" and "Whatever you do, do not try to keep up with the buggers!" The visit traditionally took place over a complete weekend, so we were a bit less than enthusiastic when the date arrived.

The function on the Friday evening would be a mess dinner. We dressed up in our best uniforms and turned up at the nicely decorated dining hall, to be met by about a hundred ex-submariners, all dressed smartly in blazers and ties, standing around chatting quietly. We mingled in and got to know a few of the guys, their ages ranging from probably mid-fifties, to a couple of octogenarians, and probably everything in between. It was all very nice and relaxed, and we anticipated a pleasant evening listening to stories starting with "When I was on the . . ."

I have never been much of a spirits drinker, and so resisted the constant invitation to "Have a tot" from the old boys. They on the other hand had no such reluctance, and most if not all of them were knocking back neat Navy Rum by 9:00 pm, having already been quite liberal with the beer, and then wine and port through dinner. It was pretty clear that these gentlemen were taking the opportunity to really let their hair down (well, those that had any!) and as the evening progressed they got louder, and the stories more outrageous. I must admit I enjoyed the stories, and some of the older chaps had seen war service, and told of events that would make your hair curl—being depth-charged, or sinking a ship, or surfacing at night to remove a depth-charge caught up in the casing. It was impressive stuff.

The old boys could take a fearsome amount of alcohol, but obviously at some point it was going to catch up with some of them. By around midnight the sensible ones had gone to bed, pacing themselves perhaps for the long weekend ahead. As always with these things though, there was a hardcore that wanted to party on, and that expected us to party on with them. I had drunk much more than I would normally, but was relatively ok and agreed with some of the other hosts to stay, while the rest could clear off home. It was a bad move. I finally got into the swing of the evening, and carried on drinking, staying with the old boys probably until about 4 am, when I just had to go. It was too late to get a taxi so I staggered all the way home in a drunken stupor, arriving at about 5 am. Thank goodness it was the weekend! My wife was disgusted, and gave me an additional earache to the headache I already had from the hangover later. Luckily that was my input to the weekend finished, but the old comrades continued to party at that pace for the entire weekend—we poor wimps were not able to keep up with them, although several tried and failed. We found out later that it was not unusual for one or two of the comrades to die over the weekend—it had happened on several past occasions. Luckily no-one died this particular weekend, but it certainly gave us an insight into the character of the submariner—boy, could these boys play. We were to find out that they worked just as hard too.

The crowning glory of the course was the submarine escape tower training. The escape tower was about 40 metres tall, and dominated the skyline of Dolphin, reminding us new boys everyday that we were drawing nearer to having to face it. The tower building contained the 30 metre deep pool of water where the submarine escape training would take place, at the bottom of which was the chamber in which the pressurised part of the training happened. The "wet" part of the training took place over 3 days for new recruits, with the first day being an introduction into the world of submarine escape and the pleasures of the "bends".

On the first day of the escape training we were subjected to a morning of basically horror movies. These were of people suffering from the bends—that is gas in the bloodstream expanding and coming out of solution, caused by people rising from underwater too quickly. The physical effects on the people were often extreme, causing some very nasty disabilities and even death. One video concerned some very fit people carrying out trials on submarine escape equipment, where they set a new world record of escaping from something like 600 feet. They were all super-fit PTIs though, who had also received a great deal of specialised training, and yet a number of these guys had ended up with ruptured stomachs and the like. What hope was there for us "normal" people then we wondered?

One of the most memorable parts of that training for me was when we were allowed to listen to a recording made during the sinking of the US submarine USS Thresher during the 1960s. This was a secret recording, made as part of the analysis of a post-refit set of trials the submarine was undertaking. The boat had already done a number of test dives, and was embarked on the final "deep dive", a dive down to the maximum designed diving depth of the boat. Something had gone wrong during the dive, resulting that the boat was sinking with no way of being able to surface again. As the boat sank deeper and deeper, communications had been maintained between the control room and the "mother ship" on the surface. As the submarine got into deeper and deeper difficulties, the strain in the voices becomes palpable, until eventually, as the submarine crew realise that they are going to die—crushed to death by the pressure of the outside water as the boat sank deeper and deeper into the depths, the exchange changes from military reports to simple human despair, with the voice on the microphone asking calmly that his wife should be told that he loved her. He then incredibly calmly reads off the depth of the submarine as she sinks, and that the nuclear reactor has been shut down. One can hear in the background bulkheads collapsing, and men screaming and crying. Finally, there is just static on the line as the boat implodes. It shook us up tremendously and made the training we were about to undertake deadly serious. In all of our minds though was the realisation that it was fine having all of this safety gear onboard, but it only worked to 600 feet—what about beyond that depth? The simple answer was that below that depth you were dead, plain and simple. It wasn't a pleasant thought and most of us just put it aside—what else could we do?

Day two was the first day in the escape tank. We were straight into swimming trunks, and the first exercise of the day was a simulated "rush escape". This would be where the submarine had sunk, and was filling with water so that there would be no time to prepare for a controlled ascent to the surface. We all dressed in the bulky and cumbersome escape suits, went into the simulated escape compartment, and waited for all hell to break loose. On the order, water started rushing in, and the lights went out. We had to one at a time duck under the escape tower lower rim, as though we were going to escape. Quite frankly it was mayhem, and gave us some idea of the panic that would set in if it were for real. Also, the water flooding in was warmed up a bit—certainly it was a great deal warmer than the water would be if a boat sank anywhere near home waters! The next part of the training was the first time that our heads would actually be under water. We were required to carry out a "free ascent" in the escape tank, from a depth of 9 metres. This didn't sound too bad, but before we could do it we needed to do yet more listening. We were given another tour of the tank, this time from the top, from where it looked very deep indeed. The "swimmers" then gave us a demonstration of ascending from various depths to the surface, in an attempt to convince us that by expelling air all the way to the surface, there would be no danger of anybody getting the bends or otherwise damaging themselves. Next they indicated a line painted onto the floor, where we would be required to stand on surfacing—so that the instructors could monitor us for signs of the bends for a mandatory 10 minutes. Finally, in we went, to practise a nice controlled blowing action that we were to adopt the whole way to the surface—how stupid did we feel hanging on to the side of the tank, mouths at surface level, pursing our lips and blowing? We were told in no uncertain terms that we were to continue blowing all the way to the surface whatever happened, and whether we felt like we had run out of air to expel or not. It all seemed a bit serious now. We also knew that over the years a few people had died doing this training. No-one wanted to be the next casualty.

I was in the first group as always (alphabetical of course). We all donned vented lifejacket, goggles, nose clip and strange belt with a couple of handles hanging off it, and were herded into the "9 metre chamber"—a little sealed room leading off from the 9 metre point of the escape tank.

The watertight door clanged shut, and immediately the chamber started filling with water making my ears feel pressurised, and causing me to need to keep equalising them by swallowing. The water level was soon at my knees, and then waist, and then my chin, me being one of the smaller ones, making me have to tip-toe to keep my mouth above the water. From the escape tower behind us, another underwater door then opened, so that we were now effectively in an air bubble connected to the main tank. Now each of us in turn moved to the entrance to the main tank, turned around, took a deep breath, ducked under water and then felt a couple of hands grabbing us by our belts, yanking us out into the escape tank. Once out floating free in the tank, I straightened my body out, hands behind my back and head up as instructed, and once I felt a tap on the forehead I started blowing out. The instructors swimming around me then checked I was blowing properly before releasing me to float towards the surface of the tank. It was all very surreal. To start with there was little upward motion when I was released, and as my lungs started to empty of air, I wondered if I would run out before reaching the surface. All of a sudden though, I could feel myself floating with greater force upwards, and just as I started to struggle to continue blowing out I broke surface and took a huge breath. Within seconds I was assisted out of the pool and was standing on the white line—several pairs of eyes staring at me intently, looking for any signs that I was about to collapse. Every now and then someone walked along the line "You OK?", or "Did you enjoy that?". After 10 minutes, I was released and sent off for a cup of tea, and in those days, a cigarette. We were all very excited afterwards and couldn't wait to do it again! The chance came very quickly. In no time we were preparing to do it all again—only this time from a depth of 18 metres! Our minds begin to think about how we nearly ran out of lung capacity from 9 metres—how would it be from double the depth? We were assured that it would not be a problem, and that our lungs would re-inflate on their own. We were pretty sceptical, but by then trusted the instructors not to tell us fibs. The routine was the same as for the 9 metre ascent, except that the pressure on the ears was greater. As I am pulled out into the escape tank and start blowing, I can't help but to look wide eyed at the depth markings painted on the tank wall and it seemed an awfully long way up to the surface. I started to chase the bubbles as they rose rapidly to the surface, and the temptation to kick upwards with arms and legs is almost overpowering. As the 9 metre mark goes by, I am straining to continue blowing—my lungs seemingly emptied of air. Then, remarkably, my lungs fill to overflowing with new air, seemingly from nowhere, and I had to blow out with renewed vigour to empty them again—this was the gas in my lungs expanding as the weight of water on my body gets less as I near the surface of the tank. The feeling of the lungs expanding on their own was incredible, and quite unlike any other sensation—quite shocking in some ways as this was the first experience of those kinds of physical effects. On surfacing I am once again made to stand on the line for 10 minutes. We have all survived the free ascent, and all that remained on the last day was the 30 metre "tethered" ascent in the submarine escape suit. We all enjoyed the experience and wanted to do it again. This apparently was the normal reaction from the students.

Next day we arrived bright and early, and ready for the day's trials. As had become normal, the first couple of hours were taken up with briefings and dry runs, and then it was on.

First we dressed in the submarine survival suits. These are bulky "dry-suits", bright Day-Glo orange in colour and with a built in lifejacket and zip-up hood attached. We had worn them on the first day of the course, but this would be the first occasion where we actually needed to don the hooded part—zipping a plastic bag over my head did not feel totally comfortable.

From there on it was very much a one at a time exercise, and the person undergoing the training had the full attention of the entire training staff—this became very apparent when my turn came.

After donning the suit, I had to clamber into a small chamber at the bottom of the escape tower. This chamber was directly underneath a complete replica of the escape compartment hatch onboard a submarine. Once in the chamber I could feel the legs of an instructor already in there, at a level somewhere above me. As already instructed, I plugged a pipe located on one sleeve of my escape suit into a connection on the inside of the escape tower, and instantly air was pumped into my lifejacket, and from there into the hood of my suit. The instructor above me spoke:

"You ready down there"?

"Ready Staff"

"Remember, once I start flooding the pressure will come on quickly—make sure you stay ahead of it. If you cannot clear your ears, tap me on the legs and I will slow it down ok"?

"OK—Understood"

"Right lets go. Remember to breathe normally all the way up. Enjoy the ride"!

Without further ado a deafening hissing and roaring started as the instructor manipulated the valves which allowed water to begin flooding into the small compartment. Once more I felt the water level creeping up my body, flattening the escape suit to me. My ears immediately became pressurised and I had to continually swallow and pop them—we had been warned that in a real escape there would not be time to regulate the flow into the chamber, and that our eardrums would almost certainly rupture. Now though, panic started to rise in me as my ears ached as I struggled to keep up with the rapid rise in pressure, and I frantically tapped the instructor's legs so that he would reduce the rate—to no apparent effect. Soon though I other things to worry about as the water level reached my chin. Suddenly the buoyancy of my suit lifted me off the floor of the chamber, so that the now fully inflated hood bashed against the underside of the escape hatch. It was remarkable—I was fully submerged in the escape compartment, but my head was dry and I was breathing normally inside the hood of the escape suit!

As the pressure inside the escape compartment equalised with that of the escape tower on the other side of the closed hatch, two things happened. First my ears stopped aching—a great relief! Second, in a whoosh of escaping air and bubbles, the hatch above me started opening. As it did so, my super buoyant suit drove me upwards through the hatch, at the same time releasing the pipe from the charging connection in the tower. As I emerged wide-eyed into the bottom of the escape tank, one of the swimmers stopped me from shooting the surface by grabbing me in a bear hug, as a second swimmer attached a belt I was wearing to an anchor point somewhere around the rim of the now fully open hatch. I was now tethered to the bottom of the escape tank, bouncing around as the air trapped in my suit and hood tried to fight its way up to the surface 30 metres above.

My head was still dry inside the hood of my suit, and now that the excitement of the exit from the escape compartment had waned slightly, I could get a good look around through the clear faceplate of the hood. I was facing the side of the tank with the depth painted on it, and the large "30 Metres" painted there brought home my position. I looked upwards to see the sparkling surface so far above me, the outline of the people waiting for my ascent clearly visible through the water.

The swimmers were busy fussing around me, checking this or that. Finally, one hooked me up to a fixed cable that ran from the bottom of the tank to the surface. Being tethered with a sliding hook to this cable would prevent me bouncing off the sides of the tank as I went up, so I was pretty interested in making sure they attached it tightly! Finally, one of the swimmers came face to face with my faceplate to get a good look at me to see if I was alright. He then smiled, backed off and gave me an exaggerated thumbs up, which I returned with gusto! Standing well clear, he then released the catch on the anchor holding me down, at which point the fun really started.

I shot to the surface quite literally like a cork from a champagne bottle. The depth markings on the side of the tank sped by in a flash, and I think I even accelerated the nearer I got to the surface—it was brilliant! The finale was that on reaching the surface of the escape tower, the force of the ascent was sufficient to expel me from the water to a height of about 6 feet, then to splash down again, and to float on my back held in place by the lifejacket built into the suit. I quickly unzipped the now deflated hood and beamed up at the instructors gathered around the top of the pool.

"That was BRILLIANT! Can I do it again"?

"Just swim to the side Petty Officer Bridgman"

"Wow! Yeah!—That was COOL!!"

"Petty Officer, swim to the side of the tank"!

I leisurely swam to the side and was helped out, chattering like an excited schoolboy. As I moved to the now familiar white line, still chattering away, the knowing little smiles of the instructors showed that this response was not new to them. I stood and watched the rest of the guys follow suit, each one whooping and excitedly chirping as they were helped out and assisted onto the line. Everybody got through without any drama, and we were now ready to move on to the final bit of training before becoming "proper" submariners.

About six months later a guy died doing the same training. But for the grace of God . . . etc.

Chapter 13

Black Silent Messenger of Death...
After Some More Training!

After the part 1 training it was back again to HMS Sultan for the Part 2 training, or "Nuclear Systems Course" as it was otherwise known. In the meantime I had been informed that I would be joining the Second Submarine Squadron (or "SM2") in Plymouth on completion of the training, and Anna and I had set about selling our house in Gosport and finding a new one in the South West. Selling the place in Gosport proved no problem at all, and I recall that it was sold for the asking price to the first viewer. Rather stupidly we bought our new place in a single weekend visit to Plymouth, although in fairness we had spent a lot of time before the visit going through the details of loads of places that had been sent to us. In the end we visited 12 properties in 2 days, settling finally on a nice terraced place across the river from Plymouth, in a place in Cornwall called Saltash. The front had great views across the Tamar valley and right across to Dartmoor, while a 15 minute walk to the rear took us to great views right down into Cornwall and particularly some lovely countryside of the Duchy of Cornwall. We loved the place and stayed there happily for 13 years.

The Nuclear Systems Course was a career technical course for Petty Officer level Artificers, and lasted for 8 weeks. The course took place in the dedicated submarine engineering block, known as Rutherford block in Sultan. This was a proper introduction to most of us to the engineering systems on a British nuclear submarine. At this stage, the nuclear engineering input was very minimum—just a fairly vague description of how the heat from the reactor boiled the steam for the turbines and generators, as our jobs onboard would be mostly involved with the conventional aspects such as engines, gearboxes, fridges, air-conditioning and so forth. The machinery we were talking about was in fact very similar, in terms of the engine room layout particularly, to that of a steam driven frigate—indeed the engines themselves were the same as those on a frigate. For many of us, this part of the training was again just going over stuff we already know. In any case, we went over the construction of the steam, high pressure air, hydraulics and others systems on the boats, as well as some familiar and not quite so familiar types of machinery we would come across onboard.

One part that was new was the concept of the "Shut-Down Senior Rating". This was very much a submarine thing, and was not anything we had heard of before. This was a form of duty where Petty Officer technicians and above would be required to man the Machinery Control Room, known as the "Manoeuvring Room" in a submarine, while the boat was in harbour. That didn't seem too bad until we found out that as well as controlling the normal control functions in harbour, the nuclear reactor might well be either being started or being shut-down, which then became part of the responsibility involved in the duty. In order for us to get an idea of what that might be like, we were put through a series of Manoeuvring Room simulator training sessions, which became progressively more difficult as the course progressed. The simulator was new to all of us and seemed very unfamiliar and frankly, terrifying. It only seemed to consist of alarms ringing, bells flashing, and voices all speaking at once, and with us expected to know what the hell was going on—I for one certainly did not! The work in the simulator seemed to be lots of studying of emergency procedures, which were then practised in "real" conditions. The culmination of the course included a simulator assessment carried out by the senior training officer which we were all dreading. On the day we all passed, more through luck than judgement I suspect, but once again it was another eye-opener of things to come.

I rejoined the fleet in the shape of the Second Submarine Squadron in Plymouth in early 1990, over two and a half years after leaving HMS Herald, the last surface ship (or "skimmer", or "Target") as I was now to call anything that floated on the surface! I had left as a surface fleet Leading Stoker, and was now rejoining as a submarine Petty Officer Artificer, and qualified metalwork Fitter and Turner. I couldn't wait to get stuck into my new role, and joined SM2 full of expectations.

If I thought I was going to be accepted with warm greetings and happy smiles I was going to be very badly disappointed. I turned up at the Coxswain's office (he would be equivalent to a Master at Arms of a surface ship) at the appointed time, all enthusiasm, to be told that all the squadron's boats were out at sea, so I would have to wait for one to come in to get onboard. In the meantime I was to get myself familiar with the shore facilities of the base, and help out where I could. Oh yes, and from now on I was a "Part 3", that is somebody yet to complete the third and hardest phase of the submarine training. Part 3's were, to qualified submariners, the lowest of the low, whether they were able seamen or Commanders, and were to be treated with the utmost disrespect until they had become fully qualified, and therefore useful members of the submarines crew. This process started from the very first day of joining the squadron, where despite my rank badges so hard earned, I was allowed by the Coxswain to be talked to like a piece of crap by the submarine qualified writer in the office. This was something I would have to get used to, but boy it was hard that first day not to punch the little shit's head in!

It was going to be a couple weeks before a boat came back to base, so in the meantime I was sent away on "5th Watch", and told to come back a couple of days before the boat. I had never heard of this 5th watch thing, and it was certainly not something we had in surface ships. It worked like this. A normal submarine crew consisted of about 115 people. Also onboard of course would be quite a number of trainees in different stages of completion of training, taking the crew number up to anything around the 125 mark. When these guys got qualified, it meant that there was an extra person available to man the position, which in turn allowed one of the previously qualified guys to take a bit of leave until the newly qualified bloke was drafted off to another boat. It was a good system, and was a bit of an incentive for the guys trying to get the trainees qualified to push them a bit harder—the sooner they were trained, the more 5th watch time was likely to be forthcoming.

The first squadron boat to return to Devonport was HMS Tireless, a Trafalgar Class boat—the newest boat in the squadron at that time, having been launched in 1897. I wasted no time at all getting down there to take a look at a real live nuclear boat. I watched her steam up the Tamar, looking black and menacing—the epitome of the "sleek black messenger of death" as the popular description of the time went, and then rushed down as soon as she got alongside her fenced and security accessed berth.

As I approached the sentry and blithely started walking past, he held up a restraining hand:

"Pass please PO"

"Pass? What pass—I'm just popping down to take a look around the boat"

"Not while she is in Plant State A you're not—unless you have a pass"

"Oh right. Er . . . when can I get a look onboard then?"

"Well it normally takes a day to shut the reactor down, so come back this time tomorrow. When she is in Plant State B it is normal access"

Feeling very much the new boy I walked away, and made plans to return the next day. Going back to the squadron offices I found some text books to try to remind myself of these "Plant States"—I had a vague memory of them being mentioned during the systems course, but it had not really sunk in I guess. A quick read though reminded me that there were 3 main Plant States associated with the reactor, each of which described its state of readiness for operation. Actually there were 4, but the 4th was a refit condition and not usually referred to during operational service of the boat.

"Plant State A" was where the reactor plant was at normal operating pressure and temperature, in preparation for taking the reactor itself "critical"—that is, withdrawing the control rods and releasing the nuclear energy of the thing. In harbour this was the most difficult condition to maintain, as obviously it took a lot of the limited electrical power that was available to the boat, thereby limiting the amount that could be used for other things onboard. This problem obviously disappeared once the reactor was critical and the onboard turbo generators were supplying the ships powers. Controlling Plant State A in harbour, as I was to find out, was a nerve-racking proposition for the newly qualified guys. When a boat came alongside, the reactor itself was shut-down relatively quickly, however the pressure and temperature of the machinery supporting it, and the reactor vessel itself, had to be reduced slowly in order to avoid the possibility of "fatigue cracking" of the components due to excessive heating and cooling or "thermal cycling" during reactor starting and stopping.

"Plant State B" could more or less be considered as the normal state of the machinery plant when alongside in harbour. In this state the reactor systems or "primary plant" were cooled down and its pressure lowered to much less that that required for reactor operations. In this way the primary plant was basically dormant, awaiting the next warm up process. This allowed routine maintenance to be carried out on the machinery, and it also allowed all of the shore electrical power to be utilised throughout the boat.

"Plant State C" was a machinery plant state where the pressure and temperature were reduced even lower so that primary system specific maintenance tasks could be executed with the submarine alongside its berth, rather than having to put the boat into a dry-dock.

Having reminded myself of what was happening on the boat I went home with expectations for an interesting next day. I was not disappointed.

I turned up next morning to find that the sentry had now disappeared, and that all that stood between me and my look around the boat was the Quartermaster (or "Upper Trot") standing in his little sentry box now fitted over the main access hatch to the boat. I walked onboard over the trailing mooring lines and various cables and pipes running over the casing:

"Can I help you mate"? With gritted teeth I managed to stop myself snapping "Its Petty Officer, not mate"!!

"Mind if I take a wander around the boat?—I just joined the Squadron"

"Yeah, fill your boots Pal—just leave me your ID card though" I passed over my card and made my way down the much wider than I had expected main access hatch vertical ladder.

Reaching bottom of the ladder and looking around, I found myself space that led off in 3 directions. Immediately behind me was a small space containing a large number of valves of varying sizes, large pipes and a number of gauges. A large tally above the entrance identified the area as the Fuel Filling Space. To my left was a heavily armoured oval doorway with a round operating wheel at its centre—heavy strengthening bars emanation from it, and with a small round viewing window at the top of the door. This I recognised from training as one of the doors of the "tunnel forward airlock"—part of the access system to the after end of the boat where the reactor and other main machinery was located. I would visit there later.

Turning right, I was faced by a short corridor leading forward directly in to the Control Room of the boat. As I walked forward I passed on my left hand side the "Radio Shack" or as it was formally known, the Wireless

Transmissions, or "WT" Office, home of the Signallers or "Sparks". This office was one of the Restricted Access areas onboard and in 12 years on boats I don't recall ever going into one. Directly opposite was the one and only single person cabin onboard the boat, that of the Commanding Officer. This was the "Skipper's Cabin", another place rarely visited by ratings—again visited by me only 3 times in 12 years. Twice for family bereavements and once on leaving the Tireless for good.

Moving on past the Skipper's Cabin, I could either go down to 2 deck via a ladder to my left, or straight on into the Control, past a large chart table on my right. Carrying on forward, I entered the Control Room proper. To the front left of the space was the Ship Control Console, and alongside that the Planesman's Position with the aircraft type "steering wheel. The console and panels in front of the planesman's position were a sea of levers, buttons, dials and gauges, few of which meant much to me at that time. There seemed to be depth meters of various types all over the place, as might be expected here I supposed. Directly behind this area was the conning position and Captain's chair, next to the two periscopes on the boat—the "Search" scope, and smaller (as seen on the surface) "Attack" scope. I recall being surprised at how large these pieces of equipment were in real life—the periscope "wells", into which they fitted when lowered, disappeared beneath me for a distance of about 15 metres, while when raised, the body of the scopes into which the officer stared, rather than being a couple of handles and an eyepiece as was normally the case in films, was in fact a piece of very technical equipment with a diameter of about 2 feet, on to which cameras could be attached, and which gave outputs in infra-red, night vision and all sorts of other tricks. Oh yes and I never once saw anybody turn their hat around before looking into one either!

Stretching back along the centreline of the Control Room were wells for the other masts and aerials that could be raised out of the top of the conning tower of the boat, or "fin" as it was called. These included the induction and exhaust masts for the diesel generators, the WT mast, a radar mast, and something called the "ESM" mast, that had something to do with picking up signals emanating from other craft—don't ask me how that worked! Then, along the port side of the Control Room were a bank of 4 sonar repeater screens that would be manned at sea by the Deck-apes. At various positions around the compartment curtains were positioned that could close off the different areas in total darkness when required. At the moment, with only me and the "Lower Trot Sentry" in the place it looked quite large, but I knew that at sea, it would be filled with at least 8 or 9 people, giving very little room to move around. Looking forward again from the area of the control panels, there was another little passageway. Entering this, I found to my left the entrance to the bottom of the conning tower (fin), with ladders disappearing upwards to a watertight hatchway around 10 metres above me. Further forward again were the doors to the restricted access Sonar Room and Radar Room. On each was a list of those personnel permitted to enter—my name was not among them. Strangely, at sea anyone could take a look inside, but not while we were in harbour.

As I turned to leave the Control Room, a telephone started to ring on the Nav Table to my left. I looked at the Lower Trot but he was on another phone, and gave me a good ignoring. Unusually for me I was being totally indecisive and couldn't decide whether to answer it or not, when a small, bearded Lieutenant-Commander came bounding up the stairs, grabbed the phone and said:

"Tireless Control Room, MEO" he glared angrily at me as he held a swift conversation, and then put the phone down.

"You fucking deaf or what"? His angry eyes bored into me.

"Er, no Sir. I'm not ship's company"

"I don't give a fuck who you are PO. You hear a phone ringing then you fucking answer it alright? It might have been somebody reporting an emergency"! With that he clomped off back down the ladder and disappeared.

It occurred to me that if somebody had been reporting an emergency, the last person he would want to hear would be an unqualified trainee, but thought perhaps this might not be an ideal time to mention it. I found out that the officer was the Marine Engineering Officer, Lt Cdr Hogan, who I would have occasion to meet again.

I next ventured down the same ladder as the MEO, leading down onto 2 deck. As I reached the bottom I was facing the passageway into "Officer Country"—the officer's bunkspace and 2-man cabins, leading around a corner into the Wardroom, a place I was destined not to visit with any regularity for another couple of years yet. To my left was the entrance to the Junior Ratings Mess (JR's Mess), a space about the size of a single bedroom in which about 45 people would have to eat, watch TV or play cards whilst at sea. Further along 2 deck passage was the Galley, the size of one you might find in a decent sized caravan, where the four Chefs and PO Chef would turn out 3 meals a day for 120 people. Every time I looked in there it amazed me how they did it, but however they did, it was much appreciated. The passageway then continued around a corner, heading forward and past another entrance to the Wardroom, and the entrance to the Senior Ratings Mess. Similar in size to the JR's Mess, the main difference with the Senior Rates Mess was that it was fitted with a bar in harbour! Further on still, was an entrance to a place called the "Sonar Cabinet Space", an electronics compartment containing all of the operating electronics for the Sonar arrays. This was the land of the "Pinkies" or electronics engineers, and normal people stayed well clear. Across the passageway from the Cab space was the Laundry, basically a cupboard with a washing machine and tumble dryer inside, operated by the forward Stokers. Just up from the Laundry along the right hand side of the boat was then located the Junior Ratings Showers and Heads, and forward of that the Senior Ratings Showers and Heads. In the JR's heads there were 3 toilets and 3 showers, whilst in the Senior Rates there were 2 of each. This didn't seem like a lot for the number of people onboard, but I don't recall any great difficulty finding an empty toilet or shower, although there were sometimes queues for the sinks in the morning!

Next to the entrance to the Senior Rates Heads there was a ladder going upwards, behind which a hatch and ladder was leading downward. The upwards ladder lead to an area known as the "Upper Bunkspace", and was the main Senior Ratings sleeping area, with 18 bunks, or "racks". Next to the bunkspace was a small "Pinky" workshop, full of test gear and soldering irons—again not a place frequently visited by most of us. The hatch and downward ladder led into what was probably the largest space in the forward end of the boat, the Torpedo Compartment or "Bomb Shop". When you first see a torpedo it is quite a shocking experience. They are massive things, and totally unlike the common "U-boat" version, they are not manhandled into gaping torpedo tubes by sweating bare-chested torpedo men. In reality the Mark-48 and Spearfish torpedoes the Tireless was fitted with at the time have a diameter of over 2 feet, and are about 25 feet long. They are stacked up on both sides of the Bomb Shop, one above the other, on moving platforms that line up with the remarkably old fashioned looking torpedo tube doors—the design of which in fact has hardly changed since the very first torpedoes were used, apart from the addition of lots of interlocks to ensure the inner and outer doors cannot be opened at the same time. That would be really bad. I would get to know the Bomb Shop pretty well in the coming months—it would be where I would be sleeping as a new trainee!

Climbing back out of the Bomb Shop and turning to my right, I came across one of the two main watertight bulkheads in the submarine, known as "29 Bulkhead". In the event of any emergency this bulkhead, along with one at the aft end of the boat known as "76 Bulkhead" would be "shut-down", meaning that the bulkhead was sealed in case of flooding by shutting a number of openings, mainly those for ventilation. Access through the bulkhead was by means of a large hydraulically powered door, normally open, but closed and heavily latched in emergency. Because of the importance of this bulkhead to the watertight integrity of the boat, at sea one person was nominated as "29 Bulkhead Sentry", whose entire existence was dedicated to ensuring the bulkhead was shutdown when required. Once through the bulkhead and heading forward again, I found myself in the Junior Rates Bunkspace, an area packed with bunks stacked 3 high, where all of the Junior Ratings "racked-out". The Stokers were lucky in that they all had their own "racks", whereas most of the "Crumple Zone Commandos" (another name for the Deck Apes, or Sailors, or Ballast, or Oxygen Thieves and lots more) were forced to "Hot Bunk"—that is share the rack with another person. One person would be on watch while the rack was in use by the off-watch guy, and vice-versa. Not really my cup of tea, and thankfully I never had to do it. The bunkspace filled the full width of the submarine, but there was still room to include another hatchway leading down into the boat's refrigeration machinery space and the fridges themselves, and one more ladder leading up and upwards, into the Forward Escape Compartment at a position as far forward in the boat as one could get.

Climbing up into the "Forward Escape", the space was dominated by the bottom end of the now familiar escape tower itself, surrounded by gauges, operating levers and peripheral equipment. In the area surrounding the tower were also incredibly, located the 2 main "dry" stores onboard, together with a tiny stores office and canteen. Dominating the front area of the compartment was the massive "Weapons Embarkation Hatch"—large enough when opened to allow the loading straight into the Bomb Shop of the huge torpedoes. The entire Forward Escape was filled to overflowing with lockers containing escape suits and equipment, as well as Oxygen Generators and emergency CO_2 scrubber units, leaving very little room for much else. It was noticeable in fact that throughout the boat were an inordinate number of fire extinguishers or all types, emergency breathing mask lockers everywhere, notice boards, storage cupboards and all sorts of bits and pieces in all and every available space. Some of the lockers were of ingenious shapes to fit into every nook and cranny onboard such that there was hardly a single area of free space anywhere. The Emergency Breathing System (EBS) pipework spread through every compartment onboard like some kind of friendly and reassuring weed, and every 9 inches or so an instantaneous connection sprouted, into which an EBS mask could be plugged in the event of the atmosphere onboard the board becoming un-breathable. In emergency or at Action Stations each man carried his own personal EBS mask and extension hose, and would plug into the system when required. In exercises the wearing of the masks became a real ball-ache—the were hot, uncomfortable, gave you a nasty face rash, and meant you were restricted in movement by the length of the extension—in real life though they could be the difference between life and death. Part of the training onboard for the new guys was to know where the "nearest EBS" connection was at all times. Eventually it became second nature to look for the nearest connection to you, wherever you were and whatever you were doing.

Making my way out of the Fwd escape, back through 29 Bulkhead and along 2 Deck Passage, I ventured down the ladder outside of the JR's Mess and down onto 3 Deck. At the bottom of the ladder was the door to the "LP Blower" compartment. This was a huge fan effectively that was used to bring the submarine buoyant after surfacing—it would suck air in through the induction mast and fill the ballast tanks, saving the high pressure air in the storage bottles which is what is used to initially make the boat start to rise. The HP air gives the boat the initial "Oomph" to get up (with the hydroplanes helping to drive the boat upwards too), and then the blower finishes the job in a more leisurely manner. It was a very large machine though and made a hell of a noise when it was running, making life in the Senior Rates Lower Bunkspace next door difficult. The Lower Bunkspace or "Crypt", was the repository of the "After-Endees", the machinery space Senior Ratings. It was a space about the size of a small single bedroom (only not as high), which was packed with 15 bunks in groups of 3, and with small lockers in between. At sea the space was in perpetual darkness due to there always being somebody off-watch trying to "rack-out". I would eventually be allocated the top rack of the 3 "fuck-sake" bunks—i.e. those just behind the entrance door to the place, which would be bumped every time the door opened or closed, hence the name—every 5 minutes it was "for fuck-sake", as somebody again banged into the bunk and woke the incumbent up! We learned to dread the broadcast or "pipe" of "About to Run the LP Blower". The thing started up and ran with such a din that our entire bunks would vibrate madly, and it would be impossible to even think straight, let alone sleep, so that it meant whenever the blower was running we would be forced to get up and go for a coffee or something. It always struck me as strange that the entire complement of the machinery spaces Petty Officers and Chief Petty Officers were billeted in the same space—in the event of an emergency, the potential would be that you lost all of them in one go. A bit daft really.

Next to the entrance to the Crypt was a hatchway down again into the battery compartment of the boat. As a back-up power supply the boat carried around 109 lead-acid battery cells—the same as those used in cars, but each about 20 times the size. In the event of the nuclear reactor shutting itself down for any reason, the batteries were able to propel the boat for a set amount of time, dependent on how well they were charged! The biggest problem with the batteries was that as they were charged, they gave off hydrogen gas which of course is very flammable. The boat had a very good hydrogen ventilation system around the battery compartment, and meters showing the hydrogen content—we were very careful to keep it low!

On the other side of the blower entrance was located the combined Coxswain's and Ship's office. About the size of a decent cupboard, this place was the administrative centre of the boat, and also housed the submarine equivalent of a surface ship Master at Arms, or ship's policeman. The Cox'n was in charge of discipline onboard, as well as being usually the most experienced active Planesman, usually taking the helm during entering and leaving harbour, and during difficult manoeuvres. Unlike their surface fleet brethren, Coxn's were usually quite approachable, and so long as we were doing our jobs properly tended to leave us alone. This was particularly the case with the "Afties", where discipline was generally left to the Charge Chiefs of the various sections to sort out.

Along again from the Coxn's office was the Air Purification Space or "APS". In here was located all the machinery necessary to create oxygen from seawater while underwater, and to dispose of the carbon dioxide that would build up in the boat as well. Oxygen was manufactured by machines called Electrolysers, where effectively, the oxygen and hydrogen bits that constituted water (i.e. H20) were split, with the oxygen (O2) becoming part of the atmosphere of the submarine, and the hydrogen (H) being pumped over the side. Along with this, CO2 scrubber machines would then use a chemical process to remove the carbon dioxide from the air already circulating—this ensured that the levels of oxygen and carbon dioxide (as well as many other gases) remained at the correct levels in the boat. Too much or too little of either could be real bad news, and the levels were monitored very closely by the medics onboard.

The only other compartments on this level of the boat were "Pinky" spaces—little workshops used by the Pinkies to hide away in during action stations. That just left a ladder leading down to a machinery compartment used by the Fwd Staff to locate the forward trim pump and some other bits and pieces. In reality the space was mostly used by the smokers, and in time became the only place that smoking was permitted in the fwd end of the boat.

Impressed at the size of the submarine, I made my way back to the main access hatch, and prepared to get a look at the after end—which would be my workplace onboard. On reaching the bottom of the ladder into the boat, I turned and faced the first of 4 Reactor Tunnel airlock doors. These were heavy armoured doors with chunky lugs which could be operated with a locking bar to seal the door tight in emergency. The doors were hydraulically operated using "Dead man's Handle" type levers which stopped the door moving when released. To prevent both airlock doors from being opened at once and thereby reducing the reactor containment boundary, they were interlocked so that only one could be operated at any time. Because of the shape of the doors, there was a natural tendency for the people operating the doors to rest their hands on the locking lugs while it slowly opened. This was a very bad idea though as when the door opened there was about 3mm clearance between the lugs and the door edge—a lot of people had lost the tips of their fingers in the doors! I remembered the warning and kept my fingers to myself as I opened the first door and went into the fwd airlock.

This space was also crammed with gear—mostly sailors stuff like flag poles and flags and stuff. I moved on quickly and opened the inner airlock, which opened into the Reactor Tunnel itself. Rather strangely, the "tunnel" also served as one of the fire and repair party muster stations, and the first thing that struck me was the incredible amount of breathing apparatus and fire fighting gear stuffed into the red lockers lining the port bulkhead of the place! On the opposite bulkhead was located the huge Reactor Compartment Access Door, or the "Plug Door", so named after the shape of the thing when open. The plug weighed in the region of a ton, was over a foot thick and was shaped like a massive sink plug standing on its side. The door opened into the tunnel, and took most of the space in the place when it was open, as it was now in harbour to allow access to the reactor compartment below. There must have been people in the reactor compartment, as a sentry was in position at the entrance, dressed in the typical "nuclear" white overalls, fetching cap and overshoes. I asked him if I could take a peek into the reactor compartment (universally known as the "RC"), but he declined since I was not in the right clothing. I moved on—there would be plenty of time to see the place in detail later.

In the centre of the tunnel deck was a small hatchway affair underneath which was located the "RC Window"—a glass window about 8 inches in diameter (and about 10 inches thick!) from which one could look into the RC when the reactor was running. Looking through the window now, I could see down into the RC, and via 3 mirrors forward onto the top of the reactor itself and at both steam generators—one on either side of the compartment. To me at that stage it was just a mass of white lagging and stainless steel components, and white dressed technicians bustling around looking busy.

Moving further along the tunnel, I found that there were 2 small annexes at the rear, one on the port side and another to starboard—these were known as Reactor Services Compartments or "RSCs". In the starboard one was located the Primary Sampling Sink, from where water samples from the reactor core could be taken for analysis—a daily event both at sea and in harbour. On the port side were located a number of remote operating valves for some of the reactor systems, known as "top hat" valves. In time, I would have to learn to find and operate these valves blind-folded, such was their importance. For now though, they were just about the right height for a person to smack their head into—which I managed to do with gusto! It would not be the last time.

Rubbing the nice bump on my head, I made my way through the much smaller after airlock into the Manoeuvring Room Flat. I was now well and truly in the back end of the boat amongst the machinery that I would eventually be in charge of. For now though, I was pretty much in awe of the structures around me—steam, air and hydraulic pipes or all sizes running this way and that, as well as huge bundles of electrical cabling traversing along various parts of the ceiling (deck head). Additionally there were large grey lumps of machinery and control panels placed all over in the space, the purpose of which to me at this stage was totally unknown. As I looked around I recognised the Main Steam Stop valves—one in each forward corner of the space that shut off the steam from the generators to the machinery spaces. They were very large, and together with the operating equipment took up a lot of space. Moving around the back of the electrical panels, I came to a little room which doubled as the Sickbay and Reactor Health Physics laboratory, where the primary water samples and air samples were analysed. Again I would get to know this place and the 3 Medicals Assistants onboard pretty well in the future. Further on, and rounding the back of some more panels I came across the entrance to the Manoeuvring Room itself—the heart of the machinery control systems onboard.

In harbour the compartment was manned by one senior rating—the "Shutdown Senior Rate", and one Junior Rating—the "Shutdown JR". The control panels themselves looked much like the ones I had seen at HMS Sultan, with the addition of some extra electronic read-outs in the back corner. The real compartment seemed much more cramped that the training one, mostly due to the extra storage lockers that seemed to be jammed into every available space, which in turn were crammed with books of reference, training guides and all sorts of other paraphernalia.

People in overalls were constantly in and out of the place as I looked on, asking the questions or permission to do this or that. In the 5 minutes I was there the telephone must have rung half a dozen times as well, and in between the Senior Rate had to answer or make "pipes"—broadcasts on the intercom system to either the whole boat or a particular machinery compartment. It looked very busy!

Just behind the entrance to the Manoeuvring Room (or "Manoeuvring" for short) was a hatchway and ladder down into the Switchboard Room—I headed that way. As the name suggested, this was the located for all of the electrical distribution throughout the boat, split into "Essential" and "Non-Essential" switchboards, circuit breakers and switchgear. Along the forward bulkhead of the compartment there was located 2 "racks" of reactor protection electronics cabinets—something to do with a system that automatically stopped or "shut-down" the reactor if it detected certain parameters outside of the required settings. I didn't need to worry about that for now. As was now usual, the remainder of the compartment was stacked up with extra stowage's, lockers and firefighting equipment, so that there were just slim walkways that could be followed around the space. It was quite tight down there, but remarkably, at sea later on we managed to install a rowing machine between 2 of the switchboard so that we could get a bit of exercise!

Below the hatch leading into the Switchboard was another, leading down into the "Diesel Generator Compartment" or "Diesel Room". This was without doubt one of the most dangerous places on the ship, containing as it did two 12 cylinder diesel generators, each the size of a large 4x4 truck, two "motor generators" two very high pressure hydraulic oil pumps and associated machinery (called hydraulic plants), and any number of high pressure air lines, steam drains and positive pressure primary water pumps. It was, even with the submarine machinery shut-down, a noisy, smelly, hot, cramped and uncomfortable place to work in—so imagine then doing the same with a couple of pounding V12 diesels throbbing away, as I would have to! I was not looking forward to that part of the job.

Climbing back up from the Diesel Room and through the Switchboard I re-entered the Man Room. Just like at the forward end of the boat, there was another watertight door and bulkhead separating this area from the Engine Room, known as "76 Bulkhead". Just as was the case forward, this bulkhead could be "shut-down" to make it completely watertight, and the heavy armoured door could be closed to seal off both side of the bulkhead.

Stepping through the open bulkhead door, I entered for the first time the place in the boat that I would be working in when I was eventually drafted. Directly through the door heading aft one stepped on to the "After Escape Platform" or "After Escape". This area was dominated, like its forward counterpart by the huge submarine escape tower placed squarely in the middle, and by its supporting equipment in dedicated lockers surrounding the place. At this end of the boat, the escape area also doubled as a kind of workshop, with a full size lathe, pillar drill, bench grinder and fitting bench taking up most of the remaining space. On the machinery side, the Aft Escape was kind of the meeting point for the machinery spaces, where everybody gathered during operation—its main feature being the large tea-urn and sink placed smack-bang in the middle of the place!

At the far end of the platform, normally closed at sea and with a ladder leading up to it, was the "Engine Room Access Hatch" which obviously gave direct access to the machinery spaces when the boat was in harbour. Leading onward and looking aft, was the Engine Room itself. Directly in front of the two main steam turbine engines was the "Local Throttle Control" position, with two large silver wheels from where the engines could be controlled in the event of loss of remote control from the Manoeuvring Room. The heavily lagged engines themselves—the same type as used in the old Leander frigates—stretched out into the engine room space, leaving walkways along each side of the engine room for access. Behind the engines was located the single double-reduction main gearbox, clutched to the main engines, and leading on to the single propeller shaft disappearing out of the stern gland at the rear of the boat. On the port side of the gearbox was bolted on the Emergency Propulsion Motor (EPM), a direct current driven back-up drive used in the event of a loss of steam if and when the reactor was shut-down. On either side of the main engines, outboard of the walkways were located the two steam driven turbo-generators, used to supply all of the boat's electrical power when steam was available with the reactor operating, but now in harbour sitting quiet and cold. Finally on this level were the Secondary Sampling Sink where boiler water samples were analysed each watch at sea, and the "Tech Office", where the 5 Charge Chief Petty Officer Technician's planned the maintenance and repair of the boat in harbour. It was the size of a small garden shed but had 4 chairs in there somehow!

Leading forward from the Local Control Position, there was a kind of mid level space, known as the "Freon Flat", where there were four quite large "freons" or chilled water coolers. From these plants, chilled water was distributed throughout the submarine through pipework to cool all of the electronic equipment, and via "ATUs" or Air Treatment Units, to cool down the crew too. Outboard of the Freons were the two high pressure

Air Compressors onboard, used to keep the onboard reservoirs of vital compressed air full. The access down in this area was very cramped, for as well as the large machines dotted around, there were masses of pipework, electrical cabling, control panels, firefighting and damage control equipment, and tool lockers and spares. Leading down once more, and to the very bowels of the engine room was a long ladder. This took me down to the "Lower Level" of the engine room. Down here was a noisy and smelly place, inhabited by the poor Stokers onboard. At sea it was incredibly hot and noisy, and housed things like the lubricating oil pumps and tanks, the main condensers and water extraction systems for the main engines, and the main feed water systems and pumps for the "boilers" (as the Steam Generators were known). In my first couple of years onboard a boat I would be spending a great deal of time down here learning the ropes—I became particularly fond of the "Braby's"—the fresh water making evaporators on the boat—which were particularly temperamental and tended to "throw a wobbly" at the drop of a hat! For now though, all was quiet and cold down there.

The final part of the machinery spaces to look at was the "After Ends". Behind all of the main machinery, gearbox and shaft was a little area that I learned to dread visiting. This area contained the "After Hydraulic Plant" which supplied the power to operate the massive rudder of the submarine, as well as the equally huge hydroplanes. So, important was this system that in fact there were two motors, one AC and the other DC, so that in the event of an emergency, the hydraulic plant would always have power so that the boat could steer and manoeuvre. In the same space where the operating rams for the rudder and 'planes, as well as the "Stern Gland" where the propeller shaft left the boat. There were occasions when we would have to operate the rudder and 'planes from this space in local control, which was always a nightmare. The mixture of seawater leaking in from the stern gland and the hydraulic oil leaking from the hydraulic plant, when hot, gave off a stench that used to make me gag, so that in rough weather (which was when they always seemed to practice local control) it would be quite literally torture to work there.

I made my way back through the engine room, up the engine room ladder and out of the hatch—back on to the submarine after casing. My first real visit around a nuclear Hunter-Killer submarine had made me both apprehensive and excited at the same time—I wanted to get a draft as soon as possible.

Chapter 14

At Last, The Respect I Deserve—NOT!

My chance came to join the Tireless about 6 weeks later. I had been working onboard the boat as part of one of the repair gangs, and had discovered that in reality the best way to get onboard a boat was by way of a recommend from one of the Charge Chiefs onboard, and I had set about getting one. I made a point of always being around, taking interest in as much as I could, and basically being in the faces of the onboard engineers. It must have worked, as eventually I was asked if I would like to join the boat as one of the new trainees. I jumped at the chance.

If I thought I would be joining as a qualified Petty Officer Technician, I had a rude awakening coming. On my first day onboard, I carried down the boat my hold-all containing what I thought was the minimum gear I needed—3 pairs of overalls, 2 pairs of No.8 working gear, 3 sets if white shirts and black trousers, my No.1 uniform and so on. I was then shown my sleeping arrangements—a rack under a torpedo in the Bomb Shop—and there was no locker for trainees, you had to literally live out of a bag while your uniforms hung from a washing line strung across the rear of the compartment. It was going to be tough!

It was made very clear to me that I would be joining the boat as a Part III Trainee, or "Part—3". In this post I would have 2 tasks initially to perform—that of becoming a qualified submariner and of becoming qualified in what would be my normal place of work onboard, that of "Engine Room Upper Level Watch keeper", or "Upper Level". My first priority I was told was to pass the Part III. This could normally take up to 6 months (some guys took much longer), but just to build up the pressure on me I was told that they wanted me qualified by the end of "the next trip"—about 4 months time! The engineers of course considered the Upper Level qualification more important, and were equally keen to get me qualified as quickly as possible in that position! This was going to be a tough trip!

As the departure date for my first trip in a submarine drew ever closer, I began to get a grasp of the magnitude of the learning tasks ahead of me onboard. The Part III qualification was quite simply a nightmare of epic proportions. The requirement of the individual was that he be knowledgeable, to quite some depth, on all departments, equipment, machinery, processes and procedures onboard the boat. The way this manifested itself in practice was that the trainee would be required to follow a task book for each department, where he would have to get a whole number of practical and theoretical tasks completed and signed off by Petty Officers or above (mostly above in fact). That did not sound too bad, and certainly in the after end of the boat most of it could be achieved while I would be on-watch. In the crumple zone though you had to remember that the guys worked 6 hours on and 6 hours off at sea. This meant that they were busy while on-watch, so did not want to be showing trainees around, and you would not dare ask them to do it off-watch! In addition to the "routine" tasks, trainees would be roused from their beds to witness every and any evolution, from "ditching gash" to loading a torpedo, for the whole time they were a trainee and whether they had seen it once or a hundred times. This, coupled with the normal shift pattern, and the fact that I as a Technician was also expected to witness every single machinery evolution as well as the whole ship ones, meant that sleep would be a precious luxury in the coming weeks. The final part of the qualification process consisted of 2 practical, and 1 oral examination. The 2 practical tests consisted of a "forward walk-round" and an "after walk-round". These were dreaded by all the Part III trainees, whether they are Officers or the lowest ratings. The walk-round consisted of quite literally a walk through each compartment in either the fwd or aft end of the boat, where the trainee was accompanied by usually, a very experienced and senior person—it could be a Lieutenant or a Chief. As the trainee wandered along, the examiner would ask questions:

"Where is the main hydraulic bulkhead isolating valve"?

"Here Chief"

"How many EBS connections in this compartment"?

"Er, 12 Chief"?

"Where is the nearest one to you right now"?

"To the side of the locker over there Chief"

"How and who would you report a fire in this compartment"?

"There is an internal comms panels just to the right of the door. I would select the toggle switch to 'Main Broadcast' and pipe 'Fire, Fire, Fire, fire in the Sonar Cab Space!'"

"What would you do then"?

"Attack the fire with one of the CO2 extinqishers, and wait for the Attack Party to back me up"

"So, who is in the Attack Party, and what is their job"?

And so the exhausting process would go on. Most walk-rounds could take anything up to 8 hours in total, usually spread over a couple of days. Then, on successful completion of both walk-rounds, there would be the final Part III exam to be sat before one of the engineer officers and the Executive Officer—usually another marathon of several hours duration, during which a trainee would be taken through the whole process of sailing, some emergencies at sea, and then returning to harbour—with pretty much anything in between! All of these joys awaited me in the coming months.

Along with the Part III training, I would also have the joys of becoming qualified in my place of work. For me this was in the Engine Room, and later as Shut Down Senior Rate—much later hopefully, as learning my day to day job would be enough for now. I wasn't too worried about the Upper Level job, as the machinery was in many respects similar to some of the stuff I had dealt with before—at least the steam system side was at any rate. Where I would have to put a lot of work in was in the area of submarine routines like diving and surfacing and the machinery operating routines—that would come with time and experience though. Also, before

I could qualify as an Upper Level Watch keeper I would also have to spend a lot of time in the Lower Level to learn all about the machinery and systems down there too. I could feel a tough time coming, and I was excited to get stuck in!

The change onboard since my last visit was remarkable. In a few short weeks the place had been transformed from a bomb site into a sleek, tidy and seaworthy submarine. Making my way onboard once more, I was greeted without any nonsense and told to settle in for a day, but to then get to work on qualifying Part III. I was required to conduct the obligatory "joining routine"—visiting many of the different departments and getting my card stamped for this and that—including the pillow and sleeping bag which I could now set up in the Torpedo Room. Going "back-aft" to the machinery spaces, I was introduced to my fellow trainees and the guys that would be teaching us—and eventually making way for us in the shift patterns. They seemed friendly enough at this stage. The pace was hotting up though, and I was told that the next day I was expected to attach myself to one of the Upper Level Watchkeepers for the day, as the engineering department made preparations to "flash-up" the reactor. I was told it would be a long and busy day for me—there was a lot to see!

Unlike the remainder of the ship's company, for the "back-afties" the start of a deployment was actually about 4 days before the boat sailed. This was the commencement of the "flash-up", the process of starting the nuclear reactor. It all started with a "line-up" check. Clearly the reactor itself was a relatively minor individual part of the entire submarine propulsion system, but of course was supported by a whole range of systems starting from the primary water circuits, i.e. the cooling medium for the reactor core which in turn carried the heat to the steam generators, through to drainage systems, secondary water systems, main steam, auxiliary steam, steam drains, feed water, make-up water, lubricating oil, HP air, hydraulics and goodness knows what else. In each system were a large number of valves to direct the medium to different areas and before the reactor could be started the position of each individual valve had to be verified. The machinery spaces were split into sections, each the responsibility of a CPO, a PO, and then with the Stokers split between all. On the Primary side, the valves line-ups in the reactor compartment were carried out by the MEA's of the Watch, the mechanical Chief Technician's, while all of the line-ups outside the RC were normally done by the Upper Levels. It was a pretty simple process, just following and checking the position of an entire listing of the valves on a particular system—so long as you knew where all the valves were! In the meantime the electrician's were doing a similar process of testing all of the electrical systems and equipment in the machinery spaces too, including the reactor protection system. To me it looked like something form a space ship in the Manoeuvring Room as bells and buzzes sounded, lights flashed on and off and people spoke into microphones and headsets, seemingly all random, but in fact to a very organised set of checklists.

I was seconded to "Bungy", a Petty Officer Stoker and one of the Upper Levels, so that I could follow what he was doing. He picked up the valve line-up checklist for the Main Steam system and off we went. We did not hang around, and he was not really big on waiting for me to keep up.

"Right Steve, we'll start in the Tunnel with the steam drains there" he was off!

We passed through the after airlock and into the Tunnel. He then disappeared again—into the stbd services compartment:

"Look, here. This is SD 1241, and SD 1243. They are the upstream steam range drains. Cycle the valves and then record the final position on the checklist. Ok?" I was still looking for the handles as he zipped across to the other side of the Tunnel:

"These are the same valves on the port side, SD 1240 and SD 1242. Same thing goes. OK, let's go!"

He was through the airlock in a flash, me close behind. In the Man Room Flat he went straight for the stbd Main Steam Stop valve:

"This is MS 401. It is closed now, and stays that way until we get steam down the range. You'll have the pleasure of testing that later" In went the tick and off we go again.

For the next 2 hours I had a whirlwind tour of the submarine's main steam system, and certainly sighted every single valve in it. The problem was that after about half an hour I was totally confused which valve was what, and despite the encouragement of Bungy that "You'll soon remember every single one!" I was not convinced. After completing the line-up, Bungy went back to the Man Room and signed for the check. Nobody was now permitted to alter the position of any valve in the system without the permission of the Engineer Officer. Bungy grabbed the next system checklist in the pile, this time the main lubricating oil system, and we repeated the process.

The valve line-up check took most of the day to complete. With that done a process of warming up the reactor and systems would now progress, where internal heating elements slowly raised the reactor core temperature and pressure to its normal operating limits, prior to the reactor control rods being pulled out to make the reactor go "critical" nearer to sailing. This would take a full day to achieve, and was done so slowly to avoid "thermal shock" to the reactor and systems. The only real worry during this period of operation was the use of electrical power, since most of it being brought onboard would now be needed to power up the heaters, meaning that there was now very little for use with anything else. The ship's company needed to be constantly reminded that if they wanted to start anything bigger than a kettle, they first needed to get permission!

In normal circumstances, the non-duty staff would be released for the "warm-up" to go home for the last time before sailing, but because I was a trainee I was required to stay and learn! I spent the whole night sitting there watching one pressure gauge and one temperature gauge, indicating that the reactor was warming. I got to bed just in time for the guys to come onboard in the morning—talking, banging things around and generally being noisy twats! Oh, and of course the lights in the Bomb Shop never went off in any case, so sleep was out of the question. I would have to get used to it.

Overnight the reactor had slowly been warmed up in preparation for testing the machinery prior to sailing. This process had now altered the submarine "Plant State" so that we were now in a condition called "Plant State A" where the temperature and pressure of the reactor were at normal operating levels—all that remained was to take the thing "critical" now, so that heat from the nuclear chain reactor could be used to make the reactor self-sustaining, that is, operating under its own power.

As a lowly trainee I was required to witness the whole process, so up I got again and trooped bleary eyed to the Engine Room. There was no way

My Bloody Efforts

I was going to get into the Man Rm, as this was now occupied by the complete "steaming watch", as well as goodness knows how many others carefully watching the needles and dials as the reactor control rods were slowly withdrawn from the core—it was all a bit of an anti-climax really. I was kind of expecting lots of whistles, bells and flashing lights as criticality was achieved, but the only outside indication that anything had changed was a bland announcement from the Engineer of the Watch that "The Reactor is Now Critical". Oh, right, so what now then?

Well, now it was time to bring the engine room to life. With the reactor critical we could start producing the steam for driving the turbine generators and main engines. Before we could do that though, the complete steam system would have to be slowly warmed up and pressurised—a process taking at least another 4 hours, of course happening again overnight. I had been up all day once more watching all of the operations going on and we were sailing the next morning. I had heard one of the other trainees ask for permission to go home for one last time before we went, only to be told that he could—if he was not interested in getting qualified, and didn't want to be a team player, and wasn't committed to the boat etc etc! I didn't dare ask and had to be content with a quick phone call to my wife to say goodbye. Then it was back to the engine room for another long night of training.

All of the drains in the steam system are checked open, and then steam is slowly released into the system to start a long warming process. Initially water comes out of the drains, slowly getting warmer and then hot as the metalwork of the pipe systems warms up and expands. In a short while the temperature in the engine room increases and the atmosphere gets sticky and humid—we do not have any power to start more cooling yet, so we just have to live with it. Eventually after a couple of hours the water from the drains has turned into steam and we can start closing the valves to bring up the pressure in the system in readiness for getting a turbo-generator "flashed up"

Before we can do that though, we need to test the automatic steam stop valves. These allow steam to pass from the boilers to the steam system. In certain emergency situations these valves would slam shut automatically to instantly stop the flow of steam. That was fine, but although they closed automatically, they had to be opened manually using a huge ratchet spanner. As part of the testing programme, each parameter that caused the valves to shut had to be tested, which meant that the valves required to be wound open about six times—guess who had the job of doing that? It was about midnight when this process started, and it was back-breaking work—you wind open the valve, and 'bang' it slams shut again. You are told to open it again—five minutes of heaving; sweating action, then 'bang' it shuts again. I was exhausted at the end of this, but there is never any reprieve. "Wet the tea Steve, there's a good lad—we need a break in here"—sniggers from the panel watchkeepers. I bite my tongue and make the tea, with added dripping sweat in each cup for extra flavour. Enjoy chaps!

After the Main Stops have been tested its time for a generator to be started. The turbo-generators, or "TeeGees" are the main sources of electrical power onboard a boat and are large steam turbine driven alternating current generators taking up the length of the engine room on both port and starboard outboard sides. They are very large machines, and as with the Main Stop valves, have a number of parameters that would make them stop in an emergency. Once again, following extensive pre-start checks, the process is to get the machine turning by opening a large and awkwardly sited throttle valve, run it up to a certain speed and then "trip" it by simulating a fault condition, which then causes the throttle valve to slam shut. After this, the throttle valve has to be wound back in to reset it, and the process all starts again until the trip parameters are tested correct. Again, the trainees are the best work horses for the manual labour and I became rather more familiar with the TG throttle valves than I would have like. I was shagged!! Nonetheless by the end we had a TG running which meant at least another air conditioning plant could be started, and the engine room could cool down a bit.

By now it was about 4 am—we were sailing at 8 am this very morning. With the TGs on-line a whole process of starting bits of machinery here and there played out now that we had ample electrical power. At the forward end of the boat they could now test all of their gear too, and the boat came alive with pinging sonar, rotating radar masts, rudders and hydroplanes testing and all of the other preparations for getting underway. All that remained at our end was the testing of the main engines, gearbox and propeller.

The engines were warmed through in much the same way as the steam system. Steam was gently introduced into the engines to slowly warm them, while the turbines were slowly turned using small electrical motors. This process was used to prevent the turbines from "sagging" as they expanded to their normal operating limits from the hot steam hitting them. After a "soak" period, the main throttles were slowly opened and the engines spooled up under no load to make sure they were operating correctly. As they slowed down the gearbox clutches were engaged and then, first using remote throttles from the Man. Rm, and then "local" manual throttles from the engine room, the main engines, gearbox and propeller were turned ahead and astern to check they operated correctly. As the astern revolutions of the shaft came on, the boat bounced and heaved around, indicating the immense power of the main machinery of the submarine.

I was finally released to go and get some breakfast at around 7 am—just one hour before sailing time. I was dead tired and hungry, but just had time to wolf down some food before being called back on duty to help with final pre-sailing preparations. As I stumbled back to the engine room I was called to assist with the final bringing onboard of all the hoses, pipes and ropes connecting the "Service Patch" to the boat—these supplied all our water, air, oil and other stuff while we were in harbour, and then lowing the gear and patch through the engine room hatch to be secured onboard, by which time "Harbour Stations" was being broadcast.

Harbour Stations was the call for everybody onboard to be up and about, and in their allotted sailing position on the boat. As a trainee I did not have a defined position, but was expected to hang around the engine room as the last flurry of pre-sailing activity got underway. Names were checked off on lists, reports that this or that section or compartment was "closed up at Harbour Stations", equipment "secured for sea", final machinery checks carried out, and finally, the after escape tower and engine room hatches closed and latched shut. Finally everybody seemed to be either sitting around on the after escape platform or standing facing the main engine telegraph order receiver, in anticipated of getting under way.

Suddenly through my headphones I hear "Standby on the platform for revolutions order".

"Standing by" responded the upper level. From the Man Rm I hear a buzzer and the revolution order indicator jangles around, resting on "24" revolutions. This is now the maximum speed that would be set on the propeller shaft at the order "Half Ahead" (or astern). At "Slow Ahead" (or astern) the shaft speed was always 15 RPM, while if we received the order "Full Ahead" (or astern) we would whack on as many revs as we could get out of the engines—although that was very unlikely. This was unless we were under "Captain's Rules" where a full engine order was restricted to 65 RPM to prevent unnecessary stress to the machinery, but that's a different story, more of which later. Man, there were a lot of rules and regulations to learn!

"24 revs set" reported the upper level to the Engineer of the watch

"24 revs set on the platform Roger. Standby to obey telegraphs"

"Standing by"

"Platform Manoeuvring—Obey Telegraphs"

"Obey Telegraphs—platform Roger". The telegraph order receiver moved to "Slow Ahead" and the throttle operator opened the ahead throttles to start the turbines rotating. The upper level watchkeeper stayed near to the local handles in case of remote failure, and suddenly we were moving.

For the next 20 minutes or so the telegraph orders came thick and fast as the submarine was expertly manoeuvred away from the wall and turned in the river. Previously on surface vessels I would have been able to see at least some of this, but now locked up in the bowels of the boat I could only guess by revolution orders what was happening topside. Every now and then there would be a broadcast "Passing South Yard", or "Passing Plymouth Hoe" to give us an idea of where we were. Eventually the revolutions order changes slowed down, indication that we were now on a steady path out of the dockyard and past the Plymouth breakwater, and out into the Atlantic ocean—on my first trip onboard a British Nuclear Hunter-Killer submarine. I was too knackered to be excited.

Chapter 15

Life's a Piece of Shit, When You Look at It!

I HAD BEEN TOLD during the flash up that the first 24 hours at sea were normally very quiet, to give everybody a chance to settle into their watch systems, and to allow those guys who had been busy with machinery a chance to catch up on their sleep. That was true—except if you were a trainee! As the boat was stood down from Harbour Stations and the off-watch guys headed for their racks, I was none too gently informed that I was now on watch for the next 6 hours and had better start following systems so they could be ticked off in my training log.

To make matters worse, we had now sailed past the Plymouth breakwater and out to open sea. I had kind of naively expected that we would dive straight away, and was gutted to learn that we would stay on the surface FOR ANOTHER TWO DAYS!! Unbeknown to me at the time, and never mentioned before, was the fact that a submarine had to be in a certain designated diving area before diving for the first time after being in harbour—and this area was two days steaming away from Plymouth! I was gutted! One of the reasons for my transfer was to avoid seasickness, and yet here I was in a round shaped vessel on the surface of the Atlantic.

This was not going to be pretty. The submarine did start moving around, rolling quite a lot as might be expected, but also dipping nastily into waves as we got further out to sea. At first the movement was not too uncomfortable, but as time moved on it started to wear me down so that it wasn't long before I was feeling rough. It seemed like the end of my first watch at sea was a long time away.

Unlike when I was on a surface ship, I could not any longer run away to my bunk when the sea became too rough. As a technician, and more particularly a trainee I would be expected to front up for my watch come hell or high water, so it was in my interest to try to build up a bit of resistance against seasickness if I could.

I was very grateful when my time came around to go off-watch. I had been awake for the best part of two full days and really needed to be reacquainted with my rack in the Bomb Shop. I figured that a solid 6 hours of sleep would put me right, and allow me to regain some drive for the continued uphill climb towards qualification. As I headed through the reactor tunnel and into the forward end of the boat, neither the smell of food nor the taunts of "Bloody trainees—off to bed already? We've only been out a couple of hours, you should be studying, not sleeping!" could deflect me from my bed. Even though the lights were fully on and people were moving about, I collapsed onto the rack and was instantly asleep.

After what seemed mere minutes, but was in fact 5 and a half hours later, I felt a hand shaking my shoulder "Up you get Steve, you're on watch". As a lay there staring up at the two tons of explosives directly above my head I instantly felt that the motion of the boat had increased while I slept. Even as I rolled out of the rack and climbed into my overalls my head was already spinning. It was going to be a very unpleasant 6 hours for me that was for sure.

As I wended my way back through the reactor tunnel towards the machinery spaces I passed the HP Lab. Poking my head in I asked the Doc for some seasickness tablets, hoping for a bit of relief for the growing symptoms. Pills I got, sympathy though was non-existent:

"There's no point taking them now is there? You should have taken them before we sailed".

"If I had known it was going to be rough I would have, wouldn't I!"

"Rough? This is just the swell. You think this is rough, you've got a bit of a problem Pal".

I swallowed the pills in any case—they might kick in later. On arrival back in the engine room it was straight back to business. The on-watch upper level (a PO Stoker in this case) instantly sent me to the Lower Level of the engine room to begin tracing systems. I didn't mind, I figured the lower down I was the better—at least it wasn't so far to throw up into the bilges from!

As I reached the bottom of the long ladder, turned and faced the main condensers and condensate extraction pumps, the lower level Stoker walked past making notes on his log board. He stopped, and did a double-take look at me:

"You alright mate? You look like shit"

"Bit seasick"

"Listen, if you throw up in the bilge, you'll be cleaning it up, right? If you are going to vom, use a bucket. Best thing to do is get busy—takes your mind off it". He wandered off towards the feed pumps.

"Yeah, no shit" This kid must have been about 18 years old and was giving me, an old seadog with 14 years surface experience fucking medical advice! I tried to take it lightly, but was rapidly finding that if you were a part 3 trainee on a submarine, every bastard considered it fair game to treat you like a dimwit. Then again, maybe I was just getting paranoid.

In any case I collected myself and headed aft towards the lubricating oil tanks and pumps—bad move. The smell of hot oil in the air set me off dry heaving, and I hastily beat a retreat. It was hot down on the lower level and I was sweating heavily just moving from one place to another. Having been on the lower level for less than 10 minutes I heard through my headphones "Petty Officer Bridgman, come to the upper level".

I made my way to the upper level to find that I had been volunteered to make the tea for the guys in the Man Rm. Again this was fairly standard practice, and part of the game of seeing how far the new boy could be pushed. It was imperative that one did not "bite", and I put on a cheerful face as I took the orders from the team, made the drinks, and retreated back to the lower level. In a way it probably helped, as indeed my mind was taken off the seasickness for a while. I tried to remain in that state of mind for the rest of my watch as I traced this or that system, or matched one or another valve or machine to the training documentation. I was very glad again though to see my bunk, and again missing "scan" or food, I went straight to bed to sleep.

I was a bit happier on waking for my third shift, knowing that on this one, the ship was due to dive—some relief at last. It would be a huge and welcome break to have this bloody boat still!

As was becoming routine, my first job going on watch was to wet the tea. I was starting to remember without asking who took what, and a bit of chatter was starting with some of the guys too. There were a few offers of help in finding certain bits and pieces in the spaces, and other advice of the best way to study, where to start from and the like. I was starting to realise it was a learning process for the crew too—I was a brand new untested bloke they had never seen before, and they had to learn what I was like before they wasted any trust or energy on me. I also had to remember that they were always training up new guys, some of whom turned out to be useful and others of which ended up as "oxygen thieves"—in other words useless, who either were carried as ballast or who returned to surface ships. I could start to see that the enthusiasm for training people might wear thin after a while. For my part I just needed to keep my mouth shut, get stuck into the training and get qualified as soon as I could—it was the only way to fit into the crew without too much stress. It was sometimes hard to take crap from some of the crew, but you had to go with the flow. My time would come later, of that I was convinced.

Some way into the watch came a broadcast for "pre-diving" checks to be carried out throughout the boat. The upper level, another Petty Officer Stoker called Ross, told me to join him for his checks because "You'll be doing these yourself soon enough!" Basically the checks revolved around making sure everything was ready in the engine room for the boat to submerge—we went around checking the position of valves, pistons and machines, and then signed that everything was as it should be.

The next order we got was to "Uncotter No.3 and No.4 Main Vents", which meant nothing to me at the time, but involved us unlocking the big vent valves that when opened from the Control Room, would allow the air in the main ballast tanks to escape, causing the boat to submerge. These were physically locked closed in harbour and on the surface for a passage to prevent inadvertent diving of the boat, and the padlocks had to be removed, and again signed for. With the vents unlocked, both those, and the "Main Blows" were cycled from the Control Room to ensure they worked properly. The Main Blow Valves controlled the passage of high pressure air into the ballast tanks to help surface the submarine, and made an incredible noise when they opened allowing air to whoosh into the tanks—the boat buffeted around as they opened and closed, again giving an indication of the huge forces in operation. In the meantime, all around the boat other safety checks were being done by the crew to ensure a safe first dive after maintenance. Finally, when the boat was almost ready to dive came a broadcast over the public address:

"Hands to Diving Stations, hands to Diving Stations, shut down 29 and 76 bulkheads". This resulted in a flurry of activity as people closed up in the different compartments and made reports to Ship Control. Once everybody was where they should have been, and each compartment was shut down in case of flooding when the boat when submerged, the next broadcast that came out was:

"Diving Now, Diving Now!"

I again was expecting some great fanfare of action and noise as the boat dived, something along the lines of a U-boat crash-diving to escape the depth charge attack from the circling Tommy destroyer, but nothing seemed to change initially. Then, the revolution orders were increased and the boat all of a sudden took on a quite small downward angle as she was driven under the surface. At last the depth meters started to register some movement as the boat crept beneath the surface, and to my great relief the movement of the boat started to diminish as she went under. As I watched the depth gauge the needle swung around to periscope depth. I commented to one of the blokes that it had seemed to take a long time to get underwater—clearly a comment he had heard from new boys before:

"You're not on a fucking U-boat mate! You have to remember that in a war, this boat would slip out of the harbour, dive straight away, and then not be seen again for the next 6 months! We don't have to keep surfacing you know, like they did in the old days, and the only reason we even go to periscope depth is to catch radio signals! Fair point.

"The submarine is at periscope depth. All compartments check for leaks and report to Ship Control". One by one the closed compartments reported themselves free of leaks.

"Carry out long post diving checks"

Once again I followed the Upper Level around, reading off another long checklist as we again ensured everything was in the correct position for the submarine being submerged. We remained at periscope depth until the entire set of checks was completed throughout the boat. Everything was fine though, and after about an hour we were ready to continue. For the next part of the first dive after maintenance, we would dive in stages to our maximum operating depth, just to gain confidence that she was working fine. For my part I was already feeling much better now that the motion of the boat had almost stopped, that I really didn't consider any danger associated with deep diving. The guys though had rigged up a demonstration of how compressed the boat becomes on diving by rigging a rope across the length of the engine room. The trainees were instructed to watch it as we dived.

From then on the boat dived deeper and deeper, in 50 metre stages, to the maximum operating depth—which is DEEP! There was no messing about as we went. We would angle the boat down by 10 degree and just drive on down. At each stage, the boat was levelled, and then searched for leaks—as soon as none were reported, off we went again. It was fascinating to watch the demeanour of the crew change as the boat got deeper—from almost carefree familiarity at or near the surface, to a very businesslike professionalism the deeper the boat got. It was pretty clear that we were in dangerous territory down in the depths, and the fact was that should something go badly wrong down here then there was little hope that any of us would survive. It became very tense indeed. I had been watching the rope stretched across the engine room as we dived, and had seen it transform from a tight line at periscope depth, to a sagging one as we got deeper, indicating that the boat was being crushed by massive pressure as we dived—this was a machine constructed from 3" thick hardened steel! The boat had reduced in diameter by about a foot as we dived! It was impressive and scary at the same time. It worked out that for each 10 metres depth, the pressure on the boat increased by 1 bar (one atmosphere)—it was only now that the meaning of that statistic became clear. Everybody was relieved when we returned to a more normal depth.

Having completed the deep dive everybody not on watch could go back to bed, and from then on the boat would surface and dive as a normal operation only requiring the on-watch people to be involved. Much to my disgust the guy I had spoken to earlier was correct in that even nuclear submarines spent an inordinate amount of time at periscope depth, whatever the sea state on the surface, in order to receive or send communications messages. It was a blow to me as it meant the sea-sickness would continue if I happened to be on-watch at the time. Still, it was something I would need to get used to, although it remained a bugbear for the rest of my career.

The next few days went by in a daze of studying, eating, sleeping and tracing systems around machinery spaces. Within a fairly short time I got into the routine, and time became something of an abstract idea. The time that my watch said it was really didn't matter—the lights were always on in any case where I slept, but its amazing how quickly the body adapts. Luckily I am a fairly inoffensive person most of the time so I was just minding my own business and working my way through the training book—the idea being that the quicker I became qualified the easier life would become. For some of the other trainees I think it was not so easy. A couple had a nasty habit of answering back or contradicting what they were being told, much to the annoyance of the crew! One junior officer in particular was getting up people's noses by giving it the "big I am" and in consequence was ending up doing some really horrible tasks—cleaning the bilges, de-lagging the dusty pipework to fix steam leaks and stuff. In the end, his white officers' overalls were put into the washing machine with some red towels "by mistake" so that they came out pink. He had to wear them and looked lovely. We kept advising him to keep a low profile until he was qualified but he wouldn't have it—still, it took the spotlight off the rest of us, so good luck to him!

In the machinery spaces of the boat I felt that I was making good progress—the Upper Level part of the training was going particularly well, as a greater part of it was very similar to what I used to do on surface ship engine rooms—taking machinery readings, looking after the engines, and normal watchkeeping stuff. I was unused to some of the machines—the air compressors and refrigeration plants being cases in point, but a lot of it was a steam frigate shoe-horned into a submarine hull. I was getting to know the engine room Stoker and Technician Petty Officers and now that they had got to know me a bit more, they were starting to loosen up a bit—apart from one little shit. One guy, a young Petty Officer Tiff, had taken it upon himself to treat all of the Part III trainees like dirt, whatever their background. I had tried to explain to him that I had been around a bit and that he could cut out the attitude—just tell me how things work, let me try it on my own, and then if he was happy he could sign off the task in my training log. Well, rather than do that he decided that he had to verbally abuse me (and others) every time he spoke to us, talking to me as if I had just crawled from under his steaming boots. This had happened a few times now, and quite frankly, on top of the general distain everybody else was showing anyway, it proved the straw that broke the camel's back. Early one morning halfway through the Middle watch, after a couple of hours of taking crap from this kid, I had decided enough was enough and was going to take the guy somewhere quiet and just explain that he needed to back off a bit. Unfortunately it didn't work quite like that though. I had been asked (told) to once again make the tea for the watch, a task I never really minded as it gave me a break too! On dishing out the tea, about 5 of us were sitting around on the After Escape Platform when the Upper Level pulled out a packet of biscuits and offered them around to everybody—except me. He offered them my way and as I reached out for one he pulled them away saying "Fucking trainees don't deserve food.

You can have one when you're qualified!" To their credit, nobody else saw the funny side. For my part I squirmed in my seat with embarrassment and rage.

About an hour later I decided that I had stewed enough. I went down to the Freon Flat beneath the Escape Platform, and then make a broadcast for the Upper Level to come to the same place. I had every intention of just talking quietly to the guy, but as he rounded the corner with a stupid smirk on his face I just couldn't control myself and smacked him straight in the gob. As he fell backwards more in surprise than pain I grabbed him by the throat and we got real close and personal. "You listen very carefully fuck-head. If you fucking talk to me like that again I am going to rip your fucking head off! Is that clear!?" He nodded quickly, blood now dripping from a split lip. I thought he might put up more of a fight, but at the moment there was only fear in his eyes—no resistance at all. "I have been in the Navy for nearly 15 years and I do not need little shit-heads like you talking down to me. I suggest you learn some fucking manners! One more snide little comment from you and we will be repeating this discussion, now fuck off!" He dashed away.

I automatically assumed that I would be deep in trouble now. I thought the little tosser would run straight to the Man Rm and report me to the Officer of the Watch. I would then be arrested and charged with assault, put in military prison and hey presto, career over. I sat nursing my sore hand and waiting for the call from the Man Rm, but silence reigned. I sat for about half an hour bitterly regretting my actions (for purely selfish reasons!) and yet still no call. I made my way to the Escape Platform which was deserted, and looked into the Man Rm to see the watchkeeper in there talking to the Charge Chief and Officer of the Watch, all of whom looked my way.

The Charge Chief motioned me to come and see him and as I stepped through 76 bulkhead and into the Man Rm I could see that the guy's lip was nicely swollen.

"Steve, Nick's bumped into a pipe and split his lip—you wouldn't know anything about that would you?"

"No. That's unfortunate—there are a lot of things to bump into out there".

"Yes, it was a bad one alright—even left some red marks on his neck!" I felt all eyes burning into me. Please don't look at my hand!

"Anything you want to say Nick?" All eyes swivelled to him now. This was it—make or break.

"I will have to be more careful in future". This said looking directly at me.

"Yes, and so will you Steve. Now get back on watch, both of you".

As we got back to the Platform I said simply "Thanks"

"Fuck you" came the reply.

He came around eventually, and we learned to get on just fine. The event had the effect of clearing the air in the machinery spaces for me though, and from then on a lot of the bullshit was resolved. People understood that I was not a baby Tiff needing to be kicked up the backside to get motivated, and started talking to me like a grown-up. It was very refreshing and as a result I was flying through the training.

The same could not be said for the forward end of the boat. It was natural for there to be a certain rivalry between the engineers and the sailors, but unfortunately this had transformed into a real animosity when it came to training each-others staff for Part-III tasks. Apparently it had got out of hand before I joined the boat, in that the forward staff were making the engineers do ridiculously difficult tests to pass the Forward Walkround, and the engineers were doing likewise for the forward staff when they visited the machinery spaces. The poor old trainees were piggy-in-the-middle in this game, and were being expected to learn about the systems and machinery in incredible and unrealistic detail. On one occasion one of the Charge Chiefs would not pass somebody on an Aft Walkround because he could only remember 4 ways a batsman could be out in cricket! One of the Stokers was failed on a Forward Walkround because he didn't know normal and alternative frequencies for the different types of Sonar onboard. Absolute nonsense. When I started to look around the forward end of the boat I found that the required level of knowledge depended very much on who I talked to, but that in many cases the guys at this end of the boat were no less helpful that those at the back. I really didn't encounter too much grief, and so long as I showed willing to learn, then most people were happy to take the time to teach.

Life carried on much the same way for the next couple of weeks. The boat was making its way out to the Atlantic where we would be doing some exercise prior to disappearing into the Barents Sea later on in the patrol. On the way out we had pretty much daily machinery space drills and whole ship evolutions, like exercise fires, floods, high pressure air bursts, hydraulic bursts, loss of ship control and all sorts of other stuff. In real terms this meant that when people were off watch they were being awoken by alarm buzzers and then having to rush off, dress in firefighting gear and get stuck in—at least they could then go back to bed, whereas we poor trainees usually had to hang around afterwards for some other thing we needed to witness. By that stage I was probably surviving on 4 hours sleep a day, and it was starting to have an effect on my motivation and performance. It had very quickly been established that trainees were only allowed in the mess for food—visits for any kind of recreation were banned, as it was seen a slacking off from getting qualified. Whenever we did venture into the mess at mealtimes, we were met with a constant barrage of abuse throughout our meals which was, by now wearing very thin. We were all trying desperately not to rise to the bait, and when one of the others dared to speak back to one of the forward Chiefs, it resulted in a serious dressing down to the man—not the bastard giving the trainee so much grief, but to the trainee for "daring" to talk back to the qualified guy!

It seemed a bit of a harsh way to put pressure on the new men, but I suppose it was a well proven system that did have the effect of ensuring that only those who really wanted it would finish. I wasn't too bothered by the temporary hard life, as I knew that once I was qualified life would become a great deal better. The only thing that got through to me was rudeness—something I personally despised and took great exception to, particularly when it was from the younger guys who, even though I was "just" a trainee should show at least a modicum of respect for the rate and the work I had put in just to reach this stage. I did make sure though that they were left in no uncertain terms that "what goes around, comes around", so that if they chose to talk down to me then I would extract my revenge at a later date. I just wanted fairness, and after a while onboard, for the most part I got it.

After 3 or 4 weeks onboard I had reached the point where I was ready for qualification as an Upper Level Watch keeper, but it was decided that although I could "take the watch" and do the work of the guy on watch, it was not right for me to get qualified in the position until I had passed the Part III training. Therefore, I was now released from position training to concentrate solely on the Part III stuff, and within another couple of weeks was ready for the "back-aft" walkround. This I did with one of the Charge-Chiefs. It took about 5 hours in total and I really enjoyed it—the guy was a mine of information, and I felt like I had learned more in that short time than I had in the entire previous couple of months! Anyway, I passed and was now ready to really get stuck into the forward part of the boat.

For the next few weeks I would be dedicating myself solely to the forward end of the submarine, and was not permitted to "go aft" at all until I had become qualified forward. One might imagine that this would be a good thing—nice and cool, close to the mess deck and racks, could hear yourself think and so on, but in reality it was a nightmare of epic proportions.

As I may have mentioned, being a trainee on a nuclear submarine is not a fun experience. At least at the back of the boat I was among "my own kind" and could look after myself to a certain extent because of my, albeit limited, machinery knowledge. In the "crumple zone" up front, I was totally in the dark about sonar, radar, ship control, radio communications and such like, making the learning curve that much steeper. In addition, the sailors, pinkies, cooks and bottle washers really took the "give the trainee constant crap" regime to the extreme, laying on the abuse at the slightest perceived infringement of what they considered appropriate trainee behaviour. If you dared try to get a cup of tea from the mess, or spend more than 10 minutes eating, or god forbid, attempted to watch a movie one evening, you would be on the end of so much abuse you wouldn't do it a second time!

By now I was a hardened trainee though, and knew most of the ways to avoid too much crap. I simply got stuck into the training manuals, got the torch out and spent my time wandering around the forward end of the boat, finding some valve or piece of kit, checking the operation of this or that, or questioning somebody about a procedure or process. I didn't seem to getting on too badly with everybody, and certainly didn't have any problems getting the advice and mentoring I sorely needed with a lot of the gear.

I was relieved to learn that in reality the depth of knowledge expected of new guys on the machinery and systems in the forward end of the boat was not as deep as I had feared. There remained a lot to learn though and I particularly struggled with some of the sonar and periscope concepts. Everybody thinks that a submarine has just one periscope—the Captain turns his cap around, shouts "Up Periscope!", rests his hands on the handles and swings around looking for the menacing enemy destroyer. In reality there are in fact 2 periscopes, called the "Search" and "Attack" periscopes, both of which are remarkably complicated pieces of machinery. Both have sophisticated optics, infra-red and thermal cameras, all sorts of measuring stuff, external camera attachments and goodness knows what else. As well as those, there are also a whole range of other "masts", ranging from Electronic Countermeasures, to diesel induction and exhaust, to radar and other fancy stuff. Each of these things had a set procedure for raising and lowering, and in the case of the diesel masts needed to be emptied of water and blown through with air to dry them out before use. While we were not expected to know every bit, we had to have a good overall knowledge of them all! Then there was the Torpedo Compartment where I was sleeping. Up to then it had just been a large space full of torpedoes and sleeping men. Now though, I needed to learn about the Mark 48 torpedo, its wire-guided control from the Control Room, opening torpedo tube doors, checking torpedo tubes were not flooded, ensuring the torpedo batteries were not overheating and all sorts of other stuff I had not even dreamed of. All of a sudden the torpedo I was sleeping under seemed a lot more dangerous than before! The comment that "If you get any torpedo motor fuel on you, it will burn its way through your body without stopping" didn't help much—might have been more useful information about 2 months ago, sprung to mind!

All the while this was going on there remained the continual round of drills and exercises, ranging from fires to a casualty appearing somewhere. We the trainees continued to be called for each and every one of these, whatever time of day the event happened. This had by now become very much the normal routine, and we were by and large used to surviving on little or no sleep. After being at sea for about 3 months I had reached the stage where I could do the forward walkround, but failed on the first attempt, my knowledge of many of the systems there not being deep enough to satisfy the Chief walking me around. I wasn't too disappointed though and had kind of expected to have to do it again. I learned a lot again from the experience, and set about filling in the gaps in my forward knowledge straight away.

The training programme had always been tight, and after failing the forward walkround it became apparent that I would not be qualified quite as quickly as my superiors would have liked. We were on the homeward leg of this my first trip now, and it was reluctantly accepted that it would not be until the second trip that I could expect to pass my Part III and Upper Level qualifications. Even if that were the case, I would become qualified in probably about 6 months, when it was not unusual for newcomers to submarines to take up to one year to be fully trained—I couldn't see the problem myself, but for the guys who would now be missing out on a bit of extra leave (or 5th watch as it was known), my name was shit. Well, it was tough—there was only so much a bloke could take in at one sitting.

It was fairly common in those days for boats returning from patrol to pop into Gibraltar for a bit of R+R prior to the leg back to Plymouth, and this occasion was no different. We surfaced and sailed in, tied up alongside and started shutting down the machinery, the smell of fresh air making us gag as the hatches were opened up for the first time in 3 months. There was (from me at any rate) this romantic notion that once the hatches opened, the fresh air would smell wonderful after the manufactured stuff we had breathing for so long, but in reality it was rank, smelling of pollution, fumes and goodness knows what poisons. What was stunning though was the view up the Rock from the casing of the boat. We had to shade our eyes from the incredible brightness after being shut away for so long, and it took our eyes ages to adjust to the idea of looking further than about 4 metres—as we had done for what seemed a lifetime. Another thing I noticed on going "topside" was that my overalls, clean on from the washing machine this morning, stank to high heaven of what I would come to recognise as the "submarine smell"—a mixture of hot oil, machinery, food, sweat and dankness that permeated every piece of clothing ever taken onboard. It didn't matter how "clean" something was, it got the smell and stayed with it for as long as it was owned. You became used to it.

There was no way that 115 people could live on a submarine alongside (at sea half of them were asleep), and so it was normal for the non-duty crew to be accommodated in a local hotel. Rather than a luxury this was a necessity and quite often the hotels used were not much better than "ok". That was not usually a problem though as most people just needed somewhere to rack-out after a good piss-up—particularly the first night after a patrol! As the boat started to quieten down after tying up as first the sailors and then others left the boat for their hotels, in the machinery spaces work continued to ensure that the hot machinery cooled down correctly and the systems were de-activated in the right order. Eventually as the processes were brought under control the Stokers and Tiffs not duty on the first day were released, and disappeared. As the numbers dropped we trainees started getting restless and wondered when we too could go ashore, get a shower, change and then have a pint or three! Our hopes were soon dashed:

"You guys need to stay and watch the reactor shut-down—you will get ashore when that's finished"

I knew that the reactor shut-down and cooling down process would take well into the next day, and so resigned myself to my fate—another all-nighter watching pressure and temperature gauges!

Some of the others took the news more badly that me, and complained bitterly to the Charge Chief that all of the forward trainees had been released to go ashore and relax a bit. He was less than sympathetic:

"Joined the wrong fucking branch then didn't you! If you don't like it go and see your Divisional Officer and become a fucking Deck Ape!"

It was an unfortunate fact of life that in the engineering department somebody had to start the machinery before we left port, and to shut it down when we returned. It was a pain in the arse but somebody always got the short straw of being duty first night in port, and we as trainees would most certainly not receive any sympathy from the men on duty tonight. The phase "get qualified!" was the usual repose to any moans from us on that score.

Our fate therefore sealed, we got on with helping our and learning about a machinery and reactor shut-down to "Plant State A". This was where all of the machinery was now stopped in turn to reduce the load on the reactor, and then where the reactor control rods were fully inserted to shut the reactor down. In this instance though, since we would only be in Gibraltar for a few days, the reactor primary systems remained "hot and pressurised" to minimise the thermal stress of cooling down then heating up again. The only problem with Plant State A was that it was incredible heavy on the limited shore electrical power available, which in turn made it hard work for the shut down watchkeeper, who had to keep a careful eye on power. For me particularly it was an opportunity to learn some more of what would be my eventual job in the Engine Room, and then to get a chance to sit in the Manoeuvring Room and find out what goes on in there, now that the five people who normally inhabit the place had been reduced to one.

At about 6 o'clock in the evening I was sent forward to the Senior Ratings Mess for Supper, to find that there was a "getting alongside" party in full swing. Quite a number of the Senior Rates were merrily having (quite) a few beers before going off to their hotels. This was not an unusual occurrence apparently, for one because the booze was cheaper on board that in the hotels, and secondly because they just fancied a drink after a long patrol. It was generally tolerated by the Officers so long as nobody got out of hand, and again it was not unusual to see a couple of the officers in the Mess at the invitation of the Mess President during these times. Of course I came in for some of the usual stick as I sat down at the table reserved for the duty guys to eat, but it was mostly good natured banter, accelerated in a few cases by the alcohol—nothing to worry about, but I didn't hang about for any after dinner sherry!

Following dinner I made my way back to the Engine Room and continued trying to get a grasp of a reactor shut down in between the usual making tea and carrying out the tasks the qualified guys disliked, and it was not until about 1 am the next morning that I got forward again to freshen up—I would be required to stay aft all night. I took a shower and then went to the mess for a cup of tea, thinking that surely I would not be harangued at half one in the morning with the boat in foreign harbour—there was only the duty guys onboard right?

As I walked into the mess I found that about 8 or 10 of the more experienced Senior Rates were still there drinking. They had been there since early the previous afternoon and were still going strong! I immediately came under full strength condemnation for daring to enter the mess as an "unqualified aftie bastard" from the forward Chiefs there, including the Mess President who happened to be the Chief Weapons Artificer.

"Sorry to interrupt, I am just getting a cup of tea and I'll be out" I said

"Get your tea back aft. You can come in here when you're qualified" was the response.

I could see that they were all pissed as farts, so there was little point in arguing. I left and went back aft.

For the rest of the night I sat in the Manoeuvring Room watches gauges and dials, and asking endless questions of the changing watchkeepers. By 7.30 am I was knackered and hungry, but finally released to go and get a shave, shower and breakfast. I needed it having been up now for almost 2 full days, and wearily trudged forward.

Having washed up I made my way to the mess, opened the door and was astounded to see 4 of the drinkers still propped up in the corner, glasses on the table in front of them, and the mess stinking of stale beer. It was usually the case that whoever was in the mess at breakfast time set the tables for everybody, but of course this had not been done. I set about doing it as the shutter to the serving counter opened, and the other three back aft trainees came in the mess.

"Oi Trainee! What the fuck are you doing in the mess? You should be out getting qualified!" This came from an old Weapons Chief that I had nicknamed "The Lorry Driver" due to his lank greasy hair and fat beer gut. His 3 mates tittered loudly at his hilarious joke.

"I've been out training all night actually Chief and I've come in for my breakfast".

"Actually chief" he mimicked mockingly "You fuckers don't deserve any breakfast".

I couldn't stop myself and under my breath said "Yeah, not like you ah?" Unfortunately the other trainees heard me and laughed quietly.

"Did you say something you little fuck?" From the same man, and as I looked all four had become belligerent and wide eyed with alcohol induced outrage.

"I said Yes, I would like to Chief" Again my companions laughed at my bravado.

"Just eat your breakfast and then fuck off out of here".

We did as we were told and served ourselves decent helping of Full English. All the while we felt four sets of eyes boring into us. This seemed to spur us on, and we made loud conversation, intentionally I think, interspaced with jokes and laughter, just to piss the bastards off. We had all been treated like shit for the last few months which was okay when we were in the working environment. We had silently collectively agreed that we were not going to take it from some drunken twats—forward drunken twats at that!

The Lorry Driver spoke soon after.

"Oi you" pointing at me "you can go visit the skimmer in front of us and buy a barrel of beer—we've run out".

"Sorry Chief, I have important training I need to do this morning. I need to get qualified". Titters from the trainees.

"That wasn't a request Son, I'm fucking ordering you Pal" Nods from the drinking team.

"You can order what the fuck you want, and the name's Bridgman—it's written right here on my name tally!" No laughter this time.

"Right, I'll tell you just this once *Bridgman*, get your useless trainee arse over to the ship next door, and get us a barrel of beer—it's on the orders of the Mess President!"

"Listen. I am not taking orders from a drunken Chief for one thing. For another, senior rates do not order each-other around in the Mess—there is supposed to be no rank while we are in here. Also, I don't see the Mess President here so he is ordering fuck-all too. If you want some more beer, go get the fucker yourself!"

"You cheeky little bastard" He struggled out of his seat and came over to lean on the table we were occupying "Who the fuck do you think you are talking to?" He leaned over me, angry bloodshot eyes staring at me and stale alcohol breath washing over me.

I should have been intimidated—he was a big man and could probably knock me unconscious—if he were sober! Now though, I was pumped up with exhaustion and outrage at these fucking clowns. There was no way I was going to take a step backward (I couldn't anyway, the bulkhead was in the way!), so I stood up and went face to face with the twat—not what he expected, and he took a step back just as the door to the mess opened, and in walked the "NUC1"—the senior back aft Technician. He stopped, took the scene in instantly and said:

"What the hell is going on here?"

The Lorry Driver looked confused for a moment and said "I just gave this little fucker an order and he refused. "I'm going to have him trooped!" He looked back at me "Report to the Coxswain's office!"

"Fuck you!"

The NUC1 looked at me "Shut it!" He then looked at the Lorry Driver "What was the order?"

I replied for him "He told me to go to the ship next door and buy the mess a barrel of beer!"

"You trainees—go back aft and continue with your training, now!" We disappeared.

Shortly after, we saw the four senior rates leave the boat and disappear into town, and found out they had been invited to get out of the mess, so we assumed a small victory. We were quite wrong though, and when the NUC1 came aft he got us all in the Tech Office:

"Listen carefully. You guys are nothing until you are qualified. I don't want to hear about you, see you or even know that you exist, right? If I hear that any of you are involved in arguments in future I will remove you from this boat".

"But Charge, we didn't do anything, he just laid into us, he . . ."

"Zip it! Grow up and get over the playground shit! If it happens again, walk away and get something to eat from the galley door. Now get on with your work."

Later I was called to see the Mess President. He took me aside:

"I heard about the little spat this morning with the Chief Weapons Artificer. Get one thing straight, you do not speak to a senior mess member in that manner—ever. Got it?" He was red in the face and livid. I recalled the briefing from the NUC1. Clearly there was no point in arguing my case.

"Yes, got it Chief".

"Your mess punishment is that you are banned from the use of the mess for 4 weeks. You do not even step in the mess to eat—clear?"

"Yes Chief". Well, not much difference there then I thought as he wandered off. I was totally pissed off with the unfairness of it all, but hey, what could I do. The next time I saw the Lorry Driver he gave me a slimy little smirk, just to indicate he knew what had happened. I nodded politely while hoping the fat bastard suffered a heart attack while taking a shit! Get over the playground? NEVER!

We worked through that day, but were finally allowed to go ashore in the afternoon. The boat was sailing the day after next, which meant that I would actually get one day ashore before I needed to be back onboard for the flash-up. I had all plans to get out that evening and have a few pints, but once I had settled into my room at the hotel, I took a lovely long soak in the bath, laid down "for a few minutes" on the bed, and woke up not knowing where I was almost 10 hours later! It was 4 am and pitch dark, so it was an easy decision just to stay in bed. It was almost mid-day by the time I surfaced again. I had slept for close to 18 hours straight, and boy had I needed it. I was now starving hungry and set about sorting out some food.

The last time I had been to Gibraltar had been several years previously by now, but the place always seemed to remain more or less the same. I stopped by in a couple of the pubs I used to frequent, had a pint or two and something to eat. I couldn't go mad though, as I had to be back onboard that evening and would probably be awake all night for the flash-up. I had missed my one chance at getting wrecked by sleeping through it, but looking at the state of some of the men who had been out the night before, that was a good thing. By the time I had wandered around the streets, bought a few "gizzits" or presents, and the obligatory "been there, done that" tee-shirt to add to the collection, made the phone call home, and got my stuff together, it was time to return to the boat. So, that was Gibraltar then.

On returning to the boat it was back to what had by now become the usual routine. I assisted the duty guys in getting ready for the machinery flash-up, then with the warm through of the steam range and testing of machinery. By the next morning, with little sleep overnight for we trainees, the boat was ready once again for sea. She became alive once more as the shore services were one by one disconnected, the hatches clanged shut and the noise and heat of the operating machinery invaded every waking moment. Without fuss, but with tugs in attendance we pulled away from the jetty and manoeuvred our way out into the Straights of Gibraltar, where we hung a left out towards the Atlantic Ocean once more. One of the good points in that area of the World was that it was generally quite good weather wise, which in turn meant that staying on the surface was relatively pleasant, and seasickness free. A day or so out of Gibraltar the boat dived for what should be a nice relaxed transit back to Plymouth. Over the next week or so I would have the opportunity to crack in some good training at the forward end of the boat, and hopefully pass at least the forward walkround.

After three days at sea I again took the forward walkround, and after a 6-hour marathon with the forward end Engineer Officer I managed to scrape a pass. I was never going to be an expert on the electronic gubbins on the boat, but at least I knew how to shut down 29 bulkhead and isolated most of the systems at the front of the boat should I need to. It was a good feeling to have both walkrounds in the bag, and now all I needed was to pass the Part III board. That would not happen though for another few weeks—We were close to getting home now so it would be at the start of the next trip. Nobody was interested being this close to Plymouth, so I would have to wait. I was told though to make sure I "boffed-up" or studied carefully the routines onboard, as I could guarantee that I would be asked about most of them during the oral exam.

Pretty soon we were back alongside the Second Submarine Squadron wharfs in Plymouth, and while most of the ship's company managed to disappear within a couple of hours of being there, the back-aft shut down was taking place, once again with the trainees required to assist and learn. It was harder to stay focused being this close to home, but it wasn't as if there was any choice in the matter! We were finally released late the following morning, and given a couple of days off. I went home exhausted and promptly turned in for almost a day. It was great to be home though.

It was actually quite a bizarre feeling coming back from a 3 months deployment—life of course had moved on, but everything was hustling and bustling just as it had before departing, and it was as if I had just disappeared for 3 months only to re-appear suddenly, interrupt my wife's routines, and just get ready to do it all again! Being used to being awake for long periods at sea, I found that I could not sleep properly at night. I would be wide awake at 3 am, and want to chat with Anna, and then at 10 am I would be falling asleep on the bus to Plymouth to do something normal—shopping! I would make her turn off the vacuum cleaner, the noise of which I found suddenly really irritating. I returned to the boat a few days later tired and jaded, somewhere between the sea-going hyper state and the domesticity of normal family life. That would pass once I got comfortable with a full nights sleep at home, but in the meantime it was hard work.

Back onboard the lads were getting stuck into carrying out the normal routine maintenance onboard, and with fixing many of the defects that arose during any operation of the boat. While I was in training I wasn't really expected to help out on the engineering side much, but now that I had passed both Part III walkrounds it was considered that I should become involved with my "Part of Ship". This was a person's working area when the boat was in harbour and for maintenance and defect repair at sea, and in my case was the "Auxiliary Machinery Section" or "Auxiliaries" for short. There was a Section Chief who would be my direct boss, and above him the "Nuc 2" or propulsion Charge Chief, and then one of the Assistant Marine Engineering Officers, leading finally to the Engineer Officer himself. I had to keep all of these people happy or suffer the consequences. In practice I usually only had to deal with the Section Chief and that was fine with me.

Our section responsibilities were quite wide, and we had to look after all of the secondary steam systems, all air systems, air compressor machinery, all pumps including main water feed, lubricating oil, condensate water, water and oil storage, and not forgetting the main turbo-generators and diesel generators onboard. As the new boy I was initially given fairly small jobs, just to ensure I could handle the work in a professional and competent way, and I made absolutely sure that every single job I did, no matter how small, I did as perfectly as I could manage—using the correct tools, procedures and standards, and afterwards ensuring that the repair site was cleaner than I found it.

It wasn't long before I was being trusted with some of the more complex jobs, and I really stated to enjoy the work. I had the opportunity to work on "live" steam systems and other bits of equipment, and could easily immerse myself for the entire day taking bits apart and then putting them back together again.

We were only alongside for a few weeks and of course they passed in a flash. Within no time at all we were once again starting to prepare the boat to go back to sea—another cold-war patrol around the Barents Sea, looking for Russian boats or military items of interest. Soon it was goodbye time once more as I joined the boat a day and a half before sailing to witness the reactor flash-up and machinery trials prior to sailing. Thankfully none of the work I did on the steam systems leaked—that would have been disastrous!

For this trip we were sailing with only one spare Upper Level watchkeeper, the supposition being that within a couple of weeks at sea I would have completed the Part III oral board, and be qualified as a watchkeeper too. So, not pressure there then!

As it turned out they were right, and within being at sea for a week I was sitting in front of the Marine Engineering Officer and the Executive Officer, desperately trying to remember the sequence of events for various evolutions that happened around the ship. The oral exam took place in a cramped compartment at the front of the boat, and began with my being asked to describe all of the processes involved with getting the boat to sea, from an engineering and whole ship perspective—a massive memory test. As I stumbled my way through the process the officers would each throw in a curve ball now and again, interrupting the flow. I would say that for instance the diesel generators would be started to help with the electrical load, after which the Engineer would say "Imagine that as the second generator was started, a cylinder head blew off and a fire started—what would happen throughout the ship?" I would then be sidetracked into describing the entire ship's reaction to a fire onboard, and afterwards come back to the original description of getting the boat to sea.

This process continued for about 4 hours, with me going from the ship sailing, processes we might undertake while at sea, and then the boat coming back alongside after a trip. It was exhausting, and when I had finished and was asked to stand outside the room, I was sure that I had failed. To my utter relief though I was called back in and told that I had passed, and congratulations, I was now a fully qualified Royal Navy submariner. I was ecstatic! and walked around as though I was 6 feet tall for the next few days. The congratulations came from all sides, and remarkably, the hazing stopped from that very moment, which was weird to start with.

Of course I was no longer a trainee, which in turn meant that I had no particular job onboard. That wouldn't last long and after a day to recover from the Part III exam, I was assigned to the Engine Room for dedicated Upper Level training. I would be attached to one of the watchkeepers for the next couple of weeks and would stay with him until I qualified as an Upper Level Watchkeeper. It shouldn't take long as I had effectively been working the area for a good while now and knew my way around.

The next thing on the agenda for me to move out of the Bomb Shop and into the Lower Bunk Space, or "Crypt" as it was known. For the first time I would have my own personal locker, and could stop living out of a bag! The locker was tiny in reality, but for me it was wonderful—I could actually find stuff for the first time on boats—luxury!

As an engineering trainee life was much easier, but still involved some hassles. Although I was now in a dedicated bunk space rather than the continuously lit Bomb Shop, my rack was far from being the best. I had the upper one of three "fuck-sake" racks, i.e. those on the inside of the entrance to the Crypt. This meant that every time the door was opened by somebody entering or leaving the Crypt, it would smack against the side of the three trainee bunks, resulting in a "For Fuck Sake!!" from anybody trying to sleep there. For me though it was an improvement from sleeping on several tons of high explosive, and in any case I would not be there for long.

I was much more comfortable with the Part III training now behind me, and very quickly got into my element back aft in the Engine Room. I was really enjoying the studying to qualify in what I considered to be my element, and before long I was once again sitting in front of a couple of examiners, explaining the intricacies of double to single main engine drive, clutch in or clutch out, steam pressures and feed water pump speeds and combinations, starting turbo-generators and uncottering main vents for diving. I pass the oral test without any difficulty at all, and within a couple of days found myself undergoing the practical examination too. In this instance I was basically testing for a whole shift on the various evolutions that the Upper Level would be expected to perform, from reacting to a nuclear reactor shut down, to main gearbox clutch operations to transfer from turbine drive to the emergency propulsion motor and back again. Finally after a harrowing 4 hours, I was called to the Lower Level on the pretext that the watchkeeper down there needed my help. I was then called to the ladder to the Upper Level, looked up and was hit by about 3 buckets of water thrown by the guys from the top! This was the traditional back-aft way of telling someone they had passed a test. I was soaked but ecstatic—I had made it as a fully qualified watchkeeper on a nuclear submarine. I had a cup of tea—made by somebody else for the first time—and a cigarette, and got ready for my first watch alone. They did not hang about, and I would slip straight into the schedule that evening.

My first few watches were a bit nerve-racking, but I managed to get through them without any major mishaps, and soon settled into a routine. I soon found that the qualification part was just the start really, and took it upon myself not to rest on my laurels when I was on watch. I couldn't just sit around when it was quiet, and needed to keep looking around the Engine Room and back-aft generally to satisfy myself that I knew all I needed to about the machinery in my charge. I read a lot on watch too, which was initially frowned upon by some of the Chiefs and Officers. I managed to persuade them that I was still doing my rounds and stuff, and eventually they got used to the idea of studying on watch. It helped to have the books around, and I could mix the theory and practice in real time that way.

Now that I was finally there, things onboard started going my way a bit more too. As a qualified submariner, I now had a pay rise of about ten pounds a day, which was the first bit of good news. Then a few days later the Cox'n told to me to report to the Captain's Cabin! I tentatively knocked on the door, and was greeted with a gruff "Come In!" I slid open the door, and to my surprise there was the Captain and Engineer, waiting for me to enter to be "officially" qualified. This was a tradition dated back to the very first boats, and entailed me being handed a glass of what I could smell to be whisky, containing a submarine badge (or "Dolphins") and being told to drink the whisky and to catch the Dolphins as I drank. It was a very large tot of whisky, and went down very well! I caught the Dolphins too, and have then to this day. I walked around the boat all day in an alcoholic buzz, but nobody seemed to mind and once again congratulated me on qualifying. Now, I truly did feel part of the crew.

Chapter 16

Onward and Upward

For the next couple of voyages I had the opportunity to settle down into my new life as a fully qualified submariner. I had quickly become familiar with the machinery for which I was responsible and with the routines that I was required to perform in my duties. The first trip after qualifying saw me alone on watch as one of the 3 Upper Level watchkeepers, which in turn meant that I had moved from the "fuck-sake" racks down in the Crypt into the much more comfortable dedicated Upper Level racks. I was now for the first time getting a good sleep during some of my off-watch time, as well as now being able to use the Senior Rates mess without hindrance. Life was good.

Of course it could not last. In due course I realised that far from being completed, my training was really only just starting! At my stage, as well as qualifying in my watchkeeping position, I would also require to qualify in another 2 areas before I could rest easy as a Petty Officer, and indeed before I could hope to progress to the dizzy heights of Chief Petty Officer Technician. These were the positions of Diesel Generator watchkeeper, and Shut Down Senior Rate. The former I considered to be a walk in the park, the latter was something else though.

The boat carried 2 diesel generators, used as a back-up electrical supply for the motor-generators in the event of a reactor automated shut-down, and for when extra electrical supply was required, such as during reactor start-up when huge amounts of energy were needed to get heat into the core. The diesels were normally aspirated Paxman 12 cylinder beasties, which of course meant that they needed air to operate, and hence could only operate when the boat was either surfaced, or at periscope depth, when air could be drawn into the boat, and exhaust gases expelled from the boat, through movable masts in the Conning Tower or "Fin". These masts were known as the Snort Induction mast and the Diesel Exhaust masts, and had to be raised and then drained of water before they could be used. This process was highly choreographed to ensure that no water flooded into the boat by accident, and so that the diesels were not "dead-headed" on starting which would result in the entire submarine being engulfed in diesel exhaust fumes—a very unpleasant situation! The process required teamwork between the Control Room, Manoeuvring Room and Diesel Compartment to run smoothly. With time you could tell a well drilled boat—just watch the diesel starting process when submerged. If it went well, they were a good team!

There were two aspects to becoming diesel qualified. The first was to know about the machines themselves—how they operated, their operating limits, starting and stopping etc—which for me, with my previous survey ship background was very straightforward. With exception of a few changes because of their operating environment, the diesels were pretty much the same as I had come across before. The second and different part was learning the operating procedure for the diesels onboard a nuclear submarine. On surface ships we did not have to worry about the induction and exhaust masts being raised and emptied, it was just push the starter button and off we went! Here though, we had to prepare the engines while the forward staff prepared the masts, and while the sailors brought the boat from deep to periscope depth. While they were doing that we would open up the oil, fuel and high pressure starting air to the engines, and open the individual cylinder "purge" valves, and "inch around" the engines, that is slowly rotate them to ensure there was no water in the cylinders which of course would be bad news. Usually by then, the ship would be a periscope depth, and the masts would be up and drained. At this point came the order to start the diesels. We would close the purge valves and hit the starter button. The engines would rumble around, catch and roar into life, with us desperately hoping that the governor would catch it correctly at 1200 rpm—if the previously person had not reset it, it would carry on and have to be tripped which really pissed of the Boss! If we had visitors, we would deliberately leave one purge valve open. It was really impressive when a huge flame shot out of the valve and scorched the bulkhead! We would then say "Whoops, sorry, missed that one!" We were easily entertained.

When they were up and running the diesels made a horrendous clatter. You could not hear yourself think, even wearing ear defenders, and watchkeeper on them got boring very quickly. The diesels had solid mountings and bashed themselves to bits as they ran, so it often wasn't long before one or the other was leaking something—most of the time oil, but occasionally a jet of diesel fuel would erupt from some pipe or other.

The normal way that the diesels were stopped was for the boat to carry out a "crash-dive". This would give the sailors a chance to practise their drills, but was a nightmare for the watchkeeper. The way it was supposed to work was that as the boat took on a nose-down attitude and passed through periscope depth, the induction and exhaust masts would go underwater. This would cause a back-pressure in the masts which should trip the diesels. In practise the Boss hated the diesels being tripped like that because they should have been run on no load for 10 minutes before stopping to allow them to cool properly, so he would take them off load on the nod from the Control Room that a crash-dive was coming. The guy watching the diesels though would hear the change in the noise they made as the load came off, so would know that something was coming. It was quite clever really and helped the guy watching the engines to anticipate the crash-dive, and then to take the right actions and make the right reports every time.

It did not take me long to qualify as a diesel watchkeeper, and a few months later I lived to regret qualifying so quickly when I came close to having my head cut off by a low flying lump of metal!

The starting sequence for the diesels had by now become fairly routine, and on this occasion the engines had been running for a while when I took over from another guy. As had become normal practice, I took a walk around the engines to make sure all was well, and then went and sat down at the front of the engines, from where I could easily watch the banks of dials and gauges showing all of the various temperatures and pressures I needed to monitor. It was hot, noisy and smelly in the diesel room, as always, and I set myself up directly in front of a ventilation outlet blowing nice cool air directly at me.

The best place to sit was on the side of another machinery plant known as the Main Hydraulic Plant. This machine was about the size of a small family car, and provided hydraulic power to the entire submarine via pipe work and valves, and operated things like the heavy powered bulkhead doors, periscopes and masts and pretty much anything else that used hydraulics inside the boat. It was normally run in automatic mode and just sat there squeezing oil. The only reason we ever took any notice of it was because the bloody thing was always leaking oil, which of course constantly needed to be cleaned up. Apart from that, it just sat there "fat, dumb and happy" as we used to say—just doing its job and bothering no-one.

There was a nice flat bit on the side of the plant, on to which we would put a small padded seat we had made for the purpose, sit there and keep an eye on the diesels. I was doing just that on this day when "BANG!!!"

There was a huge metallic bang from behind me, much louder than the sound of the diesels which was already deafening. I instinctively, through surprise and fright, must have ducked my head where I sat, and as I did so I felt a "whoosh" of something heavy just passing my left ear. Out of the corner of my eye I saw something whizz past me, hit the steel deck plates and bounce up to hit the port diesel control panel, smashing a number of gauges there before disappearing over the diesel and somewhere aft in the compartment. This had hardly registered before a torrent of hot hydraulic oil flooded over me, soaking my overalls and body and making the deck plates slippery and dangerous.

I was instantly terrified that the hot oil would burst into flames, but somehow the training took over. I grabbed the PA microphone, pressed the transmit button and remarkably calmly, broadcast to the entire ship:

"Hydraulic Burst, Hydraulic Burst, Hydraulic Burst in the Diesel Room!"

Of course the Control Room would have probably known that they had lost hydraulic power from the main system already, judging by the amount of oil that I was wearing, but would not have known where it was leaking from—they did now!

My broadcast was repeated by the Control Room, with the addition of a warning claxon, and the order for the ship to go to Emergency Stations. I knew now that back-up would be on its way.

As I waited for the cavalry to arrive, again training took over. There were a number of fire extinguishers in the compartment, and I emptied a couple of foam ones onto the oil that was everywhere—particularly that which had got onto the running diesel generators which was already smoking ominously.

Both diesels were still running, although the port one was now leaking oil and water through its broken control panel gauges, so I decided without further ado to shut them both down. I quickly used the PA to inform the Manoeuvring Room of my intentions so that they could offload the machines, and then pulled on the emergency shut-down cables—you had to keep the cables pulled until the engines stopped fully, or they would restart on their own again.

By now I felt the boat putting on a downward angle and assumed we were diving down to our "safe depth" so we could sort ourselves out in safety. I quickly checked that the diesel induction and exhaust valves in the mast had been shut as we dived, and even though we had no main hydraulics to close them, the back-up accumulators had done the job for us thank goodness. It would be real bad to dive with great big 12 inch holes fully open in the masts—we would fill up pretty quickly!

My Bloody Efforts

All this had happened in the space of about 3 minutes, although it seemed much longer. As I stood soaked to the skin in hydraulic oil, fire extinguisher in hand, hoping that there would not be a flash fire, the first of the cavalry arrived. This was a fire-fighting team, fully booted and spurred in breathing gear and "wholly-bear" fire suits, climbing through the hatch carrying fire hoses and thermal cameras. I stood aside and let them in. Basically in a situation like this, if there had been a fire, it was fully understood by all concerned that I was expendable, and that the main concern was to save the boat. I would be dead basically.

Eventually it was agreed that the risk of fire had passed, and that we could put all the fire gear away and start to clean the place up and find out what had happened. A relief watchkeeper was sent down to relieve me, and I was told to go report to the Boss.

The shakes started as I got to the top of the diesel room ladder. I couldn't control my hands, and as I got to the back of the Man Rm, the Boss saw me drenched as I was, and took pity on me.

"Go get a cup of tea on the Platform PO—I'll talk to you a bit later. Well done by the way"

I went and sat on the platform bench. Somebody offered to make me a cup of tea, and as I smoked in those days, I fumbled around in my overalls pocket for my cigarettes. The packet though was mush, soaked through with oil. I took a cigarette from somebody else and took a deep puff. The tea arrived, but I couldn't hold it with my shaking hands. Phew, that was close!!

Eventually I calmed down. Investigation showed that a valve in the main hydraulics plant had failed, causing a spike in pressure in the system. This had caused a 15 lb brass isolation valve to catastrophically fail. This was the thing that had whizzed past my ear, had smacked into the steel deck plates with enough force to leave a 3 inch dent in them, and had then smashed 4 gauges to smithereens on the diesel control panel. If my head had been turned to the left when it happened, I would have been without a face! It was a scary thought and put all of us on our toes. Certainly I was much more wary of where we sat when running the diesels from then on.

Life goes on though. My overalls and boots were ruined, and had to be changed, but apart from that I was expected to carry on as normal. I went off watch, had a shower and a sleep, and then went back on watch as normal. The hydraulic plant and diesel gauges had been repaired, the place cleaned up and all that showed was the dent in the deck plates. It remained a reminder for the next eight years of my time onboard.

Becoming qualified as a Shut-Down Senior Rate (SDSR) was an entirely different matter. By now I was very comfortable in the Engine Room, and could pretty well do the job without any drama. This meant that I could now start thinking about studying towards SDSR, and was encouraged to do so without delay. The position, as the name suggested, was needed when the boat was alongside. The Manoeuvring Room was manned 24 hours a day, every day, from the moment the reactor was installed onboard, until the boat was decommissioned. The reactor still needed cooling and pressurising even when it was "shut down", and therefore needed constant monitoring—this was the main function of the SDSR—the reactor control rods were fully in, but the plant still had to be controlled.

Up until now, my studies and experience had been purely non-nuclear. I had learned about the boat, the propulsion machinery, hydraulics, HP air and so on, but hardly anything about how the reactor worked. Now I had to have a crash course in nuclear physics, thermal dynamics, radiation, Health Physics and goodness knows what else to get me ready for shut down duties. In addition there were a whole new load of machinery plant states, reactor protection and fire, flood and famine rules to learn about. Another mountain to climb!

As the book-bashing progressed, life onboard went on pretty much as usual. For me the routine was fine—I worked a "1 in 3" system where once in every 3 days I would get an "all-night-in", that is, a full night's sleep—unless it was interrupted by some whole ship exercise or another. The watch I hated the most was called the "Morning", that is from 0300 to 0700 hrs. I could never sleep before the watch because I hated being woken at 0250 in the morning, so usually stayed up to watch the midnight movie. By about 0500 though I would be drained, but then had to fight through to 0700. After that it was a big "fat boy" breakfast and straight to bed, waking up at about mid-day with raging heartburn! Healthy lifestyle it was not! That was during something called "Patrol Routine" when there were not too many fire drills, machinery drills, and flood drills, loss of control exercises, wars, and torpedo firing drills or countless other evolutions which might spoil my beauty sleep. If we were on a "Work-Up", or exercising with other submarines or surface vessels (or targets as we liked to call them!), then sleep more or less became impossible. You got used to it.

During the next few months I continued in a routine of studying and normal watchkeeping. The patrols we were doing at the time were really a throwback to the years of the Cold War. We would sail from Devonport, and usually turned north. On the way up to Scotland, usually sailing past the west of Ireland, we would do quite a bit of whole ship training to blow the cobwebs off. We would usually pop into Faslane for a couple of days to fix any outstanding defects and to take on our last few supplies, before slipping out and heading North once more. Once we were on patrol we were not usually able to do any exercising as it was too noisy a practice when of course the whole idea was to be quiet. We mostly passed between the Iceland/Faroes gap and head up into the cold waters up in that part of the World. Once there we would follow set patrol routes searching for originally Soviet, but then Russian missile submarines passing out into the Atlantic Ocean. The sailors and sonar geeks found all this terribly interesting, but with some rare exceptions, to us at the driving end it really didn't make a huge difference where we were—we just kept the boat moving along.

It wasn't too often we came across something, but it was really good when we did! When the message came back that something had been found on sonar, the boat took on a different persona. It was as if the entire boat was suddenly sneaking up on an enemy. The lights would be dimmed as a signal to those waking up that we were on to something and to be quiet. We would turn off any machinery that was not immediately required, there would be no noise allowed in the messes, and even doors would be tied open so that nobody could accidently slam them shut. Once all this had happened, the boat would slowly and carefully try to sneak closer to the other boat so that it could be identified, and then if possible, we would follow them and log their track, so that in time of war we would know that the "enemy" used a certain route which could be intercepted. Of course the idea was that all this happened without the opposition knowing, but that worked both ways. The Soviet "bombers" normally went around with

2 "guard-boats"—that is Soviet hunter-killers whose job was to clear the way and to always keep the bomber out of harm's way. In the depths of the Cold War there had been instances where the guard boats had been known to aim straight for US and UK boats upon detecting them, only turning away at the last instant, thus forcing them to turn away from the bomber. There had been known collisions between UK and Soviet hunter/killers, a famous one being where a British "S" boat out of Faslane had been rammed by a Soviet Akula class boat, resulting in the S-boat having its conning tower knocked clean off. Luckily there is a pressure tight hatch at the bottom of the conning tower, so no water got into the boat. The boat had to be brought back into harbour though at night, and with a scaffold structure manufactured in place of the missing fin and covered with tarpaulin to fool inquisitive onlookers. Must have worked because it never made the papers!

During my time we were never actually physically attacked. By then there was an unwritten (I suppose) agreement that if the Russians knew we were there and wanted us to know they knew, they would light up their active sonar and aggressively "ping" the boat. It was a pretty obvious signal because submarines hardly ever use active sonar (it tells everybody for miles around exactly where you are!). That was our signal to move away, and it happened a few times while I was onboard. It made you wonder what it would be like in a real conflict, after all the Soviets/Russian had something like 200 nuclear boats to our (UK not US) 10 or 11 at that time. Best not to think about it.

By the end of a couple of trips I was in a position to have a go at the SDSR exam. By then I had spent ages in the books, and had spent an entire period alongside in the Manoeuvring Room alongside any SDSR who happened to be on watch, picking their brains and just watching what it was they actually did while they were there. What I hadn't taken into consideration was the machinery simulator, which would be the first thing I would have to pass, even before taking the oral test.

As the name suggests, the simulator is a mock-up of the submarine Manoeuvring Room. It was a real time simulator, meaning that the entire thing had every single gauge, dial, lever, switch and button that the real thing had, and could replicate every evolution that the real thing could perform. The simulator was operated by a group of Charge Chief Petty Officer Artificers—all very experienced submarine technicians, and my introduction to them and to the simulator itself was very scary! We had briefly used a simulator during the submarine systems course, but then it had just been a laugh—nobody was really singled out or had to specifically perform. This time though, it very quickly became apparent that it was for real—fail the SDSR assessment, and potentially my submarine career was over. No pressure then!

From the very start I hated the bloody thing! My problem was that unlike a lot of people, I could never treat the thing as a game. Put simply, something happened in the simulator—a fire, or flood, or some kind of machinery breakdown, and the SDSR had to react by following some kind of emergency procedure. People who were good in the simulator were able to remember exact sequences of action, and then press the right buttons etc. I on the other hand wanted to accept that everything that happened in the thing was "real" and had to analyse every single aspect of everything that happened, and then try to formulate a response. It's fair to say that the response was normally right, but just took too long to put into action. I instantly hated the instructors too. They insisted on putting on these silly voices when they were responding to broadcasts by the guy in the simulator. If it was the Control Room they were pretending to be, the voice would be posh—supposedly an officer there, while if you were talking to the Shut Down Junior Rate he would have a ridiculous school-boy accent. When you were already struggling just to comprehend what was happening, silly voices just made the situation worse (for me at any rate). They also had very little sympathy for the guys undergoing training, which I suppose they had to do, but for me they could have been a little more helpful, especially for the guys just starting out. Finally there was the simulator itself. It was supposed to be the same as a T-Boat one, but again, it was not quite the same. Of course it didn't move, unlike perhaps an aircraft one might, which was ok for the shut-down stuff. Later on though when I got higher up the food chain, I found it ridiculous to do an emergency surface without moving at all—didn't really work for me! In addition the alarms, bells and buzzers did not sound the same in the simulator as they did onboard—they were deafening for a start, and they just sounded different—every time I went in there I had problems recognising which alarm was for what, something that never changed throughout my time as a nuclear technician.

Well, for all those faults, the fact was that I would have to pass the thing if I wanted to continue with my naval career—it was as simple as that. The system was not going to change for me, so I would have to roll my sleeves up and get on with it. The way it worked for the assessment was that as a new guy, I would get 3 training sessions in the simulator before doing a final assessment run. The training was brutal—even though I had of course studied the emergency procedures, and had done touch-drills onboard Tireless, doing it in real time was very different. I had not really considered the peripheral stuff that needed to be done either. For instance, if one of the lubricating oil pumps failed, I would have to carry out the emergency drill, which was fairly straightforward. On top of that though, I would have to order the Shut Down Junior Rate (SDJR) to investigate the failure, and then inform the Control Room of the situation. That I would do, but then there would be responses—the SDJR would make a long and detailed report back (in a stupid school-boy accent!), which I had to listen to while still watching the meters and carrying out actions myself. Then the phone would ring and the "Duty Engineer" would want to know what was happening, then the Control Room would come back with a question. It was the management of these non-direct actions, rather than the emergencies themselves that I had real problems with.

Practice makes perfect though apparently, and although I got plenty of practice I felt a long way from being perfect when the day came for my assessment. For a start I would have to do the assessment in a shirt and tie—again something out of the ordinary, for who wears a shirt and tie normally on watch?

For the assessment you went in, they closed the door behind you, and off you went. Waiting for the first scenario was like waiting for some kind of dreaded axe to fall, and to "ease you in", the first alarm to ring would probably be something simple like a bilge alarm. Even though I was expecting it, when the bell rang I almost jumped clean out of my skin I was so nervous, but managed to overcome the nerves and to respond correctly. It continued like that for some while, one small incident after another, clearly in a vain attempt to engender some confidence in me, which to some extent worked. As I correctly responded to each small occurrence my confidence did start to increase, and with that the assessment started to ramp up. Suddenly from a single small problem, a larger one would arise—I would receive a report of a smell of smoke in say, the diesel room, followed by the loss of electrical supplies to the port non-essential switchboard. Both indications were supposed to lead me to the conclusion that there had been an electrical fault in the diesel room, as a result of which I would have to broadcast for a fire team to close up, while electrically isolating the defective switchboard and preserving electrical supplies to the reactor essential services. In the meantime somebody would be on the phone asking what had happened to the lights at the forward end of the boat. It was frantic, but exciting, and I found that much to my surprise I could handle it pretty well. I was far from perfect at this stage in the game, but was good enough to achieve a pass. It was strange but after all of the nervousness during the training and practice sessions, I found that during the actual assessment I had managed to find a calmness which allowed me to perform adequately. This became a feature of pretty much every simulator assessment I attended for the remainder of my career—I would suffer terrible nerves during the training, but somehow almost always managed to pull it together for the assessment phase. I don't think I ever became "good" at operating the thing, but luckily my bosses got to know that I was much better in the real place!

Having passed the simulator (which I would now have to re-pass every year as a SDSR), I was subjected to a long oral test. As usual, this consisted of being bombarded with scenarios and questions concerning what my duties would be while I was on watch. Again as usual, the exam dragged on for hours while the engineer officers went through their checklist of every conceivable situation I might find myself in, and tested my reaction to each. They particularly concentrated, understandably I suppose, on the various things that could go pear shaped while the reactor was at its most vulnerable in harbour, that is when the plant is in a condition known as

Plant State A—with the reactor "hot and pressurised". In this condition the reactor is fully up to operating pressure and temperature but without the control rods withdrawn, and hence with the reactor "sub-critical". The problem in this state was that the pressure and temperature were being artificially maintained using heater banks which sucked up pretty much all the electricity available alongside, so that if you lost shore supply for any reason (like somebody starting a large machine without permission) you would lose the supply to the heaters and the reactor might cool down too fast, causing thermal damage to its structure. I was closely questioned on my understanding of this condition, and what I would do if this or that happened. After about 6 hours of questioning I had the familiar "stand outside", while my future was decided. I was called back in and told that I had passed, but still "had a lot of studying to do". I was already fully aware of that!

During my first watch as the lone SDSR I sat staring at the meters and gauges in trepidation, expecting alarms and bells and buzzers to erupt into noise at any moment, just as they did in the simulator. The watch though, like 99% of all shut down watches I undertook from then on, passed by without incident. Another hurdle successfully leaped!

By now, as a fully qualified Upper Level and SDSR I was feeling properly part of the submarine crew. I felt that I was now at last being treated as a competent Petty Officer, and my confidence as a result was flying high. The way it worked in the machinery spaces was that I was now a member of a "watch" consisting of the Marine Engineering Artificer of the Watch (MEAOW)—a Chief Petty Officer Technician, myself the Upper Level Watchkeeper at Petty Officer Technician or Stoker Petty Officer level, and the Lower Level Watchkeeper, normally a Stoker 1st Class or Leading

Stoker. In the Manoeuvring Room but still part of the same watch worked the electricians, consisting of the Reactor Panel Operator (RPO)—a Chief Petty Officer "Greeny" Artificer, the Electrical Panel Operator (EPO)—a Petty Officer Greeny Artificer or Stoker Petty Officer, and the Throttle Panel Operator (TPO or "Throttle Jockey")—a Leading Stoker Greeny. The Engineering Officer of the Watch (EOOW) and Nuclear Chief of the Watch (NCOW)—normally a Charge Chief or Warrant Officer Technician would differ on each watch rotation, as they worked a 1 in 4 system as opposed to the 1 in 3 system we were working.

As a watch we each got to know one-another very well during trips away from home. The members of a watch tended to work together, eat together and to be awake and asleep when each other was. It was inevitable that competitiveness would build up between the watches, and each watch would be desperate to be the best at all the drills and machinery evolutions that were always taking place. Also, wobetide any watch that passed on a defect to the following one if they were supposed to fix it on their shift. Their name would be mud for a long time afterwards, and it took ages to shake off a bad reputation in such close confines.

Watches tended to stick together whenever we happened to get ashore too. The MEAOW and the RPO were normally the eldest and took on the role of watch leaders, both onboard and ashore, and it was usually their character that set the mood of the entire watch. If they were happy people, then the watch tended to be a happy one, and vice-versa.

My most memorable MEAOW during my time as an Upper Level was "Baz". He must have been a few years older than me at about mid thirties, and to look at was precisely what you might have imagined a submarine engineer might be—tall, scraggy hair accentuated by a full face beard, untrimmed at sea. He always looked untidy, even in his best uniform, and quite frankly, couldn't give a shit! He would sit on the bench on the After Escape Platform puffing his ever present pipe (which made him look older still!), and say very little. What he did say, when he chose to speak, was always to do with either engineering or making tea, and he simply did not "do" small-talk. He was a very good technician, and I cannot recall any mistakes he ever made, and he taught me a great deal, but as a socialite he scored absolutely zero. I liked him, but really knew nothing about him personally.

On one trip we would be visiting, for one night only, the US Groton submarine base in Virginia. We were all looking forward to it and were anticipating a good "run-ashore" after being at sea for quite a while, on this occasion involving us being a target boat for some US ships, on their torpedo firing ranges. It had been a difficult trip, and on a couple of occasions the dummy torpedoes had actually struck the boat, making a huge "clang" and making the whole boat vibrate violently. We could easily imagine their effects if they had been live!

By the time we pulled into Groton, we were all ready for a night on the town. We had entered a US submarine base with more submarines than our entire navy, all stretched out either side of our berth as far as the eye could see. The base itself was bigger probably than Plymouth, and contained every amenity any US sailor could ever need, including a huge Senior Rates Club.

As a watch we had decided to hit the club rather than being bothered to go and find the local town. Luckily the Yanks were not too familiar with UK navy ranks, and we just told them we were all, including the Junior Rates with us, Petty Officers and above. To our surprise Baz said that he would be coming along with us. Baz NEVER came out with us!

Anyway we all went ashore and into the club. As usual in America the place was massive and he drink was cheap. We got stuck into the alcohol and just chatted amongst ourselves, just enjoying each-others company and having the night off while some other poor watch had to stay onboard.

As the evening progressed Baz became more and more chatty. This was unheard of by us previously, but we were glad he was taking part and maybe coming out of his shell. He told us about his home, wife and "normal" stuff. He was clearly pissed as a fart, but hey, we all were. That was the plan!

The crunch came much later when to our surprise (as we had never come across it in the States before) somebody started setting up karaoke equipment on a large stage at the front of the hall. It was a very professional set up with large speakers and a screen onto which the words of each song could be projected. We looked on in amusement—wouldn't catch us standing up and singing in public—no way!!

As you might expect, at first singers were reluctant to come forward. As the evening went by though, more and more people took their turn to bang out their favourite song—some were quite good too, but most were at best, enthusiastic amateurs! The crowd were treating everybody, good or rubbish, with good humour, which was making the whole experience good fun. Throughout the evening Baz had apparently taken little interest in the karaoke, but then suddenly, to our utter amazement, he stood up, announced "I fancy a go at that" and stomped off in the direction of the bloke running the show! We sat there in stunned silence as he chatted with the guy, got up on the stage, picked up the microphone and waited patiently:

"Ladies and gentlemen, now for your pleasure, all the way from Plymouth England and representing the British submarine HMS Tireless, is Baz singing 'My Way'".

Our chins dropped to our boots as the music and lyrics came on and Baz started belting out "And now, the time is near, the time to face, my final curtain . . ." Not only was he singing, but he was also doing the actions—down on one knee, arms outstretched sweeping across the audience, who by the way seemed to be loving it!

Our table had been in silent shock throughout the performance, but as it came to a crashing finish with "I . . . did it . . . MY WWAAYYYY . . . !" we joined the rest of the audience in clapping furiously and hollering our approval in that over-the-top way the yanks do. It had been so out of character that we were still amazed and laughing as he rejoined us, sat down, picked up his pipe and started puffing away as though he had just come back from a visit to the toilets.

Well, his lead and the response from the yanks in the hall, hollering and whooping as they liked to do, encouraged the rest of us to get involved too. We went up one by one to have a go—I was crap by the way, then in twos to do duets, and then as a gang with some of the yanks to sing something else. All the while the audience egged us on, and by the early hours of the next morning all of us, including Baz were suffering from sore throats from shouting and laughing so much. We made our way back to the boat tired, pissed and happy. It had been a great night ashore—full of surprises and laughs, and Baz had turned out to be a hoot!

We were sailing in the morning—now only a few short hours away, so there would be no lie-in for us today. We were soon up and on watch again, and incredibly Baz was straight back to his old self. Usually there would be a re-run of the previous evening's festivities, but while the rest of us laughed and reviewed the songs we had sung, Baz was back to sitting quietly and puffing on his pipe, lost in his own world once more. I never saw him loosen up again in all the time I knew him, and I don't think he ever mentioned his short singing career again. You get some strange people on boats!

By now I had been onboard Tireless for about 14 months, and considered my position to be fairly well consolidated. I was qualified in all the positions I needed to be, and by now had a good few trips under my belt. I was by now pretty familiar also with most of the whole boat routines, and life had become pretty stable for me. Naturally my thoughts started to turn towards promotion.

As an Artificer, I could expect pretty much automatic promotion to Chief Petty Officer (CPO) level, so long as I didn't do anything stupid. I had so far proved myself to be capable and competent onboard, and my appraisal reports were all positive.

In order to be promoted to CPO a person had to have been a Petty Officer for 3 years, and to be qualified in all the positions I had achieved to date, that is Part III, Lower Level, Upper Level and SDSR. The 3 year period could be reduced by an amount of time, called "accelerated advancement" a person was awarded for marks gained during the apprenticeship—in my case this was something like 20 weeks or 5 months, meaning that I would only have to wait a total of 2 years and 7 months. Since I had already been a PO for about 8 months even before joining the boat, it meant that in theory I could be a Chief in less than a year's time! I started to look much more closely at what the MEAOW did for a living as basically, I might be doing that myself soon.

Before that though there were 2 obstacles to overcome. The first of these was the Petty Officer's Leadership Course, which everybody had to do before they could be promoted to CPO, and on top of that was the 15 week long Nuclear Operator's Course, which I would have to successfully complete if I wanted to progress further up the ladder. The "Operator's Course" was an in-depth introduction to the nuclear engineering theory I would need as a CPO Artificer, and as always, took place at HMS Sultan in Gosport Hampshire.

An opportunity to attend the Petty Officers Leadership Course, or "Management" course as they had started calling it in this PC age, presented itself during a Docking and Essential Defects rectification period (or "DED" for short) later that year, and came as a short notice announcement one morning:-

"Steve, there's a PO's leadership course starting next week—fancy it?"

Considering I had been onboard a boat for well over a year, meaning that my fitness level was nowhere near good enough for this tough course I said:

"No, it's too soon—I need to get fit"

"I'll take that as a yes then. You are already booked to attend—better start training mate!"

So, that was that then. I spent the next couple of days at least ensuring that my uniforms were of a decent standard—changing a number of shirts, trousers and bits and pieces. If I wasn't fit enough, at least I could be smart enough! I also started attending the lunchtime fitness training conducted by the base Physical Training Instructors and much to my surprise found that I wasn't as unfit as I expected. That is to say, I managed to survive the sessions without either throwing up or dying!

I arrived at HMS Royal Arthur on the Monday of the start of the course, and as expected went straight into a welcoming fitness test. In those days the latest big thing was the "beep" test. You had to run to each end of the gym, reaching the end and turning to a rhythm of a set of beeps, the time interval between each reducing steadily until you simply could not keep up any longer, at which point your fitness was measured. I was measured at about average I suppose, but enough to stay on course which had been the first objective.

For the rest of the day we were bombarded with the usual crap they came out with on these things—"We will turn you into leaders!" You will get out what you put in!" "This is the first step to becoming an effective Senior Rate!" and so forth. Most of us were more or less used to this kind of thing, and many of my comrades were pretty experienced senior rates by now, and were only here because some shiny-arse had decided they needed this training to become Chiefs. Opposed to that group were the

21 year old newly promoted Petty Officer Tiffs, full of themselves and keen as mustard. It was going to be an interesting course.

The course was being heavily publicised as a "Management" as opposed to the Leading Rates "Leadership" version of the same thing. It was kind of hard to tell the difference for me though, as this one just seemed like a hyped up version of the former course. Lots of physical activity involving physical training (PT or "fizz") and practical leadership tasks again, just like before. Myself and the other submariners present wasted no time in pointing out that our opportunities for PT onboard a nuclear submarine were somewhat limited, but were simply told to "zip-it-fucking submariners!" As with the Leading Hands course, a number of people fell by the wayside in the first week or so, mostly due to injuries caused by lack of fitness. I was surprised and proud that none of them were submariners, although we had all struggled. The young Tiffs by this stage had proven that they were all super fit bastards, bounding through all of the tests without being out of breath, but that was to be expected—us older generation would huff and puff our way through, hacking and determined to get it done. Then we would stop, have a fag and a cup of tea, and catch our breath ready for the next torture. As the kids would go bounding off into the distance we would stay as a bunch and help each-other through. This was the proper teamwork the instructors were looking for, and we had to laugh to see the youngsters getting a bollocking at the finish line for not staying at the speed of the slowest (usually and thankfully for us one of the Wrens) and helping us geriatrics through!

The course continued in this macho and manly way for the next 4 weeks, and while it undoubtedly improved my fitness, I felt that overall it was a complete waste of time. I didn't feel that I was either a better manager or better "Leader" as a result of the course, and just had a lingering resentment of all of the force-fed bullshit the instructors had come up with, which to me bore no resemblance in any form to what I did in my day-to-day work. None of the instructors had ever stepped foot onboard a boat, and to tell me then that I should stand up straight, take charge and bellow orders at people was utter bollocks. It simply did not work like that, and if I had tried that onboard I would have been laughed off the boat. On a boat you led by imposing your personality on people. You earned their trust by being professional and competent, and if you needed to either tell somebody twice, or to shout at somebody you were not doing it right—simple as that. The only time voices were raised was to prevent an accident from happening, or to reinforce an order during tense situations.

That was also evidently the consensus of my superiors. When I returned onboard I was not even asked for the end of course report, but simply welcomed back and sent back straight into the shift system. Course done, move on to the next one.

CHAPTER 17

Nuclear Fission . . . and All That

THE NEXT ONE was not long in coming. Following a couple of more incident free patrols I was told that I had now gained enough experience to become a TG Tiff at Chief Petty Officer level, and was being sent away to HMS Sultan to do the Nuclear Propulsion Operators Course (NPOC)—more commonly known as "Operator's Course". Unusually I would be re-joining Tireless after the course. I had effectively completed my first draft to the boat by going on the course and you were not usually drafted to another boat until the completion of the course, but in my case I had been asked if I would like to come back to the same boat and I had immediately agreed—it would for one thing save me having to repeat some of the Part III training on a different boat, and also meant that I would return to the systems and routines I was already used to. I would lose a bit of "shore time", that is time in a base between drafts, but it would be much easier in the long run.

I joined HMS Sultan for the start of the course in January 1992. This was my first time there as a "proper" senior rate and straight away the entire experience was totally different. This time we had the free run of the senior rates mess, and since I had been there a couple of years earlier the cabins had been upgraded into large comfortable rooms. At last we were being treated as adults in the place and it was really quite pleasant. I would have to commute to Plymouth every weekend but that was part of the baggage in this game—at least there were no duties for us to have to carry out, so we would get away each weekend.

The operator's course itself was pretty heavy duty. There were about 12 of us on the course, and for each of us this would be a stiff introduction into the dark arts of Nuclear Physics, Nuclear Chemistry, Health Physics, water chemistry, and the construction and operation of a pressurised nuclear reactor and associated mechanical and electrical systems. In the very first week we did nothing but maths revision, which was a shocker for most of us. The first couple of exam results were serious wake-up calls, particularly for those who came on the course expecting it to be a "jolly". We very rapidly found out that we couldn't burn the candle at both ends, and believe me we tried!

A couple of weeks into the course we returned to our accommodation block to discover that the entire top floor had been taken over by a whole senior rates complement of Pakistani Navy personnel, over to take over some frigate or other for their navy. They seemed a decent bunch—a bit noisy but hey, they were just settling in. We had the shock of our lives the next morning a about 4 am, when some twat started doing the Islamic praying bit at full volume, followed by the shuffling of feet as the rest of the buggers joined in. I, along with everybody else on our floor walked out onto the corridor scratching our heads and trying to clear blurry eyes, as one of the Chiefs muttered "fuck this!" crashed through the end of corridor doors and disappeared upstairs. Next thing we hear is:

"Oi, keep the fucking noise down! There are people trying to sleep downstairs!" Evidently he was ignored as the Imam continued the incessant wailing.

The Chief crashed back through the double doors on our level:

"Bastards are all out in the corridor on their fucking mats. I'm calling the Officer of the Day!"

15 minutes later a young sub-lieutenant turned up, sleepy eyed and irritated at being called out. We explained that we knew how he felt, and aimed him at the top floor. Off he went with the Chief, but within a couple of minutes they were back, even more pissed off:

"Sorry guys. They are Muslims, and their Imam reckons that the first prayer of the day is at this time. He says it will only last for half an hour maximum". With that, off he went back presumably to his warm bed as we got a brew going.

The same thing happened every day from then on, and until the end of the course. At first we were absolutely outraged at having to be woken up at 4am every day, and even though we tried to get other accommodation, it soon became evident that we were stuck with it. It was most annoying for those of us who liked to study into the early hours, especially before an exam, but we soon learned to go to bed early, get woken by the Imam, and then study until breakfast. We also soon learned that the Pakistanis liked to go back to sleep after early morning prayers, so of course we would turn the music up to max while they were praying to drown the wailing, and then to keep it loud while we studied before breakfast. Hopefully it pissed them off as much as they were doing to us—in any case we got some shitty looks from them whenever we bumped into them, but what goes around, comes around. When we got speaking to some of them they were apologetic about it all. Apparently they could have held their morning prayers at a more friendly time, say 6 am, but their Imam was a bit of a tyrant and insisted they be held early!

The new subjects and ever present exams kept on coming as we progressed through the course, and for the most part the new stuff was interesting and the exams fairly straight forward. There is always an exception to every rule though, and for most of us that was the subject of reactor chemistry. I for one found it totally baffling from day one, a situation not helped in this instance by the instructor. I had never done any chemistry in any previous courses I had taken, and the Periodic Table might have been written in Chinese for all the sense it made to me. The Instructor was a Lieutenant "Schoolie", or career teacher, and while he could undoubtedly tell you the square root of anything you might like to know, he was irritable and lacked any patience. He would tell us some complicated chemical reaction once, and once only—if you didn't get it then tough as far as he was concerned. We pointed out this flaw to him on several occasions, but he insisted that at our career stage we "should know the basics" of chemistry, but to us, what we were learning was far from basic chemistry—it was nuclear chemistry for a start, and he had already told us that normal chemical rules did not apply when chemicals came into contact with radiation!

The crunch came at the first chemistry Phase Test. 9 out of 12 of us failed the test, and the other 3 only scraped through by the skin of their teeth. After the test the Lieutenant was livid—of course a poor result reflected badly on him too. He got quite upset about it and accused us of trying to make him look bad! We attempted to explain to him that he needed to go over the concepts in more detail because we did not understand them, but he simply could not lower his teaching method to our level. We had to take the Phase Test again, after supposedly receiving extra tuition, but again we failed the test. This second mass failure caught the attention of our bosses, who then set about finding out the cause. They called us all together without the presence of the Teacher, and we explained what our problem was. For the next few classes there was a second officer sitting at the back of the class, and to start with, the Lieutenant's attitude improved. He would carefully explain some chemical reaction using the Periodic Table, patiently pointing out some unusual twist caused by this or that type of radiation interaction, and answering questions from the class without being irritated. After a week of further tuition, we all took and passed the first Phase Test at the third attempt, and while nobody scored very good marks, it was clear that we could pass the exam when properly instructed. Old habits die hard though, and within a few lessons without the other officer in the room the old demons reappeared. Short tempered, huffing and puffing and getting worked up, he soon returned to the old ways, and once again we had to zip it, sit back in our chairs and let the stuff just roll over the top.

This could not continue and so we took matters into our own hands. With the second Phase Test approaching we all agreed that nobody would pass the test, even if they could! We had decided we had had enough of the guy, and so everybody failing would be a wake-up call to our bosses that we needed somebody else to teach us.

In due course the exam came along, and sure enough we all failed—some on purpose but most of us without having to pretend. The Teacher was livid, and again got all bent out of shape believing that we were trying to get him into trouble—in this case rightly!

Sure enough, within a couple of days we had a new instructor. We simply turned up for chemistry as normal to find the course Warrant Officer waiting for us:

"Right gents, today you have a new chemistry instructor. Lt Ward requested transfer to another block, which has been accepted" he lowered his voice "I know what you bastards did to get rid of him, and if I could prove it I would throw the lot of you off course. Try that again gentlemen, and I will be down on you like a ton of bricks—be warned!" We sat staring innocently up at him.

The new instructor was more like it—he was much more reasonable, and fully understood that we were not clever! While none of us could ever claim to have fully grasped the intricacies of nuclear chemistry, we all eventually managed to get past the exams—just, in my case with the lowest marks I scored in any exam after my apprenticeship. Still, a pass is a pass, and that's enough for me.

We had by now been on course for a good few weeks, and I was aware that it must be getting near to my being up for promotion to Chief Petty Officer. Nobody had mentioned anything though, and so I thought that since I was on course, I would have to wait until I returned to the boat to be promoted—I had certainly never heard of anybody being promoted while on a relatively short training course in any case. I resigned myself to waiting—it made no real difference anyway, I would eventually get the back-pay which was the main thing. Much to my surprise though, about a week later I received a notification that I would be attending Captains' Table in Sultan for promotion to Acting Chief Petty Officer. I was thrilled! After 16 years of being in the Navy, I had finally made it to Chief. It had been a long hard road, but now in my mind at least, I had reached the furthest I was going to get. My pension was safe, and I would now be on a good pay scale for the rest of my time in the RN.

The Captains' Table was a bit of a farce really—simply because I was away from my boat, and so didn't really know any of the people there. The Divisional Officer from Sultan said some neutral stuff about me being 'dedicated' and 'professional' and all that good stuff; and the Captain said a few nice words of congratulation and the usual "you are out of the rig of the day Chief" stuff they seemed to find hilarious at every promotion ceremony, and that was it—I was now a Chief Petty Officer Submarine Artificer. If I had bothered to get a few 'O' levels at school I could have been one about six years earlier, but they, that's the way the mop flops as they say.

The course continued, and was now coming towards its conclusion. As was becoming normal now, the last week consisted entirely of Manoeuvring Room simulator training. In this case we would be taking on the role of Reactor Panel Operator for the assessment phase of the training, and for me, as always; this was the most stressful part. It was assumed that by now we were all proficient in the role of Electrical Panel and Throttle Panel Operators in the simulator, and so no time was expended in bringing us up to speed in these areas. The guys I was in the simulator with were all Greenies, and had subsequently spent all of their time onboard there, and so were very good in the damn thing compared to me who had spent most of my time in the machinery spaces. For the first couple of days they spent a lot of time instructing me on the basics of what should be done on those panels in the event of a reactor scram, so they we all could actually get some training done on the Reactor Panel! I fairly quickly got the hang of what I needed to do with the generators and to protect the essential electrical supplies when the reactor automatically shut-down or "scrammed", and so armed, was able to spend some more time trying to figure out what was happening to the reactor when it all went wrong.

The assessment phase of the reactor training consisted of the person being assessed sitting at the Reactor Panel, and being supported on the other panels by the other 3 people in the team manning the other panels. The instructors would then instigate a reactor scram, or a series of other failures on the Reactor Panel to see how the guy being assessed handled it, but for the guy being assessed to get his actions right depended on the others doing all the right things also, so it got pretty tense. We all made cock-ups of course, and it was very frustrating when having done the drills on your panel correctly, the exercise was a failure because somebody forgot to shut a valve or to take a generator off load or something. It was for me a real eye-opener on how important teamwork was in the Manoeuvring Room, and for all of us it was a lesson in how careful and thoughtful you needed to be when you were operating the panels in there—one incorrectly placed switch could really mess everybody up. In any case we all passed after much stress and late night studying, and soon we were saying our goodbyes once more and heading off back to our boats.

The thinking at the time concerning returning from courses to the same boat was pretty much that it should not happen. Well for me it was a big bonus—I would only have to do a mini Part III requalification as I had been off the boat for less that 6 months, and of course I was familiar with the machinery, procedures and most of the personnel onboard, although a few had changed since I was last onboard.

I was welcomed back onboard—especially by the MEAs of the Watch who wasted no time in starting the on-the-job training bit. They of course wanted me qualified as quickly as possible to add another body to their number, thus increasing the chance of them getting a bit of extra leave—couldn't blame them for that!

It wasn't too long after rejoining that the boat slipped out again on patrol. The part of the MEAOW in the reactor and machinery start-up was much more intense than that of the Upper Level—I was involved in the process of checking the status of the primary systems and valves prior to the flash-up. Their position was obviously much more critical than those of the valves in the machinery spaces, as once the reactor was started there was no further entry into the Reactor Compartment. As part of the pre-requisites for the reactor start every single valve in the Reactor Compartment and Reactor Services Compartments had to be checked, which meant that every one had to be found, the locking wire and "position tag" checked intact and where a valve had been moved in the maintenance period, it had to be physically cycled to the correct position, capped and then wired locked and tagged. It was a laborious but vital business, and it was always done in pairs. Then as the reactor and systems warmed up there would be a need to discharge water from the primary circuit to dockside Primary Effluent Tanks (PET), another complicated a task for which the MEAOW was responsible. The discharge hoses were made of rubber, and the consequences of bursting one by discharging too fast did not bear thinking about! Discharging primary effluent was something that I would have to learn to do at sea as well—it was required following a reactor scram. It was much easier at sea!

It was decided that I would sail as an Upper Level Watchkeeper, with a PO trainee in attendance, and then when I and he had qualified in our positions, I would move up into the MEAOW position while he took over my Engine Room tasks. It was a pretty sound plan and meant that we both had a bit of a push on to get qualified as quickly as possible.

My new job at sea was quite a step-up from the Upper Level job. When I had been a Petty Officer I just had the engine room machinery to look after and that was it—when I was on watch I would never step further forward than 76 Watertight Bulkhead door. Now, as MEAOW I firstly had an overview role in charge of the Upper and Lower Levels, but as well as that I would now have responsibility while I was on watch for all of the machinery stretching from the Fuel Filling Space outside of the most forward Reactor Tunnel door, right through to where the propeller shaft left the boat, including controlling and operating all of the reactor systems and equipments. A big part of that was doing the hourly boiler water chemistry checks, and the daily primary water test, where we extracted some water from the reactor which the Health Physics boys tested to make sure all was well within the thing. This involved operating something called the Primary Sampling Sink which was a piping system connected directly to the primary water loop and hence the reactor itself. It was a bit scary to start with knowing that you could potentially drain a whole load of primary coolant into the reactor tunnel, getting contaminated and irradiated in the process, but like anything, having done it a few times I learned to relax a bit, although I like my colleagues was always wary of the thing.

Another aspect of the new position was the interaction I now had with the people in the Manoeuvring Room. When I was on the Upper Level, I never really had any direct contact with the guys on watch there, apart from being the waiter when I used to make jacket potatoes during the Middle watch using the main engine throttles as the ovens, and the only communication was through the PA system. Now though, I was spending quite a lot of time there, conferring with the Nuclear Chief of the Watch or the Officer of the Watch on some procedure or piece of equipment, or passing on the results of the various water tests. It was a new experience to see the panels during full operation at sea, and it was great to be able to range around the whole of the back end of the boat when I was on watch. It was interesting too, and it gave me the opportunity to look more closely and in details at all of the electrical and reactor protection equipment located in the Switchboard Room below the Manoeuvring Room.

It didn't take the new Upper Level too long to qualify, and so I was able to concentrate fairly quickly on learning my new role. We relied very heavily on the idea of on-the-job training in the Navy, and so I spent the next few weeks shadowing one of the more experienced guys. In reality I was also supposed to re-qualify Part III training, but since I had not been away from the boat for too long all I needed to do was a forward and aft walkround, which I did in the first week back at sea.

It was also quite remarkable how life changed domestically onboard for me now that I was a Chief—even if I was still a trainee. Probably because I was already known onboard, I didn't have to suffer any of the standard trainee bullshit as a MEAOW trainee, and slipped back straight into mess life onboard. In the Crypt I was now far removed from the "fuck-sake" racks, and in fact now had one of the choice racks in one of the 2 Chief's "Gulches"—curtained off little areas of complete darkness and relative quiet, where some quality sleep could be had. Ah, the privileges of rank! Life had become easier during practice and real emergencies too, since now my position would involve me being free to range around the machinery spaces as an engineering "trouble-shooter", rather than having to dress in the "wholly-bear" fire-fighting suit and sweating my bollocks off!

I was finding that being a Chief really did put you on an entirely new level, particularly in the engineering World. Whereas previously as a Petty Officer you had another level to pass problems onto, I was now suddenly a supposed expert on all things mechanical. Becoming a Chief was considered to be where the Technician came of age, and so when you were asked a question about the machinery or systems, you were expected to know the answer.

As an Upper Level Petty Officer there had been two particular machines that I really could never get along with. These were the Evaporators down on the Lower Level—temperamental things at the best of times and particularly so the deeper the boat got underwater, and a horrible bit of kit called the Submerged Signal Ejector (SSE)—a kind of underwater missile launcher the we used to send up flares, water temperature sensors and escape signals. At the time it wasn't really an issue because I would simply ask the MEAOW to fix whatever problem I had with them, but now that I was going to be the MEAOW I really needed to get my head around the bloody things!

In the case of the evaporators, and after many hours crawling around pipework, reading manuals and playing with different valves settings, I finally managed to get some sort of vague understanding of their control. Their operation was very simple in theory—you simply boiled seawater, and then condensed the freshwater steam from the boiling seawater. This could then be pumped into the boat's freshwater tanks. In practice though the process, which was supposed to be automatic, seemed to be adversely affected by almost anything—boat too shallow, too deep, dive angle to steep, seawater too hot or too cold, and all sorts of other things. The Lower Level watchkeeper would regularly call for the assistance of the MEAOW whenever the "dirty water" alarm was set off in the Man Rm, and because the alarm was there, everybody would be watching the effects of any action taken by the MEAOW to get the evaporators (or 'Brabys' as they were known) making good water again. When I first started going down to assist, I would frantically turn this or that valve, adjust this flow rate or that injection setting, tweak this hand wheel or that sensor, and then hope that would do the trick. Eventually though, I realised that what I was doing was panicking and not really seeing the effects of my actions. Finally I got used to going down to the lower level when called, standing back and having a smoke for 5 minutes, seeing if the boat had changed either depth or angle in the last 10 minutes, and then, only if I REALLY needed to, very slightly adjusting a single parameter, then leaving it alone. 98% of the time the Brabys would start making good water again on their own once the boat had settled onto a new track, and it turned out that the easiest way to stop the things making bad water was to stop the bloody Stokers playing with them! I found that what had been happening was that the Stokers would see the alarm on their panel, and then frantically tweak the controls, every time the boat changed position! Once I had got them to get used to the idea of waiting for 5 minutes after a boat depth or angle change, we had (on my watch anyway) hardly any problems with the evaporators. Trouble was that after this I was known as a bit of an expert (or 'wheel') on the Brabys and tended to be called every time a real problem came up on them!

The Submerged Signal Ejector (SSE) was a different matter. The equipment consisted of basically an 3.5 inch tube that passed through the submarine hull, with a hull valve on the outside of it and a breech valve on the inside of the boat through which the missiles (or 'Stores') were loaded. It was a kind of mini torpedo tube I suppose, and high pressure air was used to eject the store from the tube. It was actually a weapon of sorts, and because of that it was maintained by the weapons guys, but operated by the engineers, usually the Upper Level Watchkeeper. When I was an Upper Level I had suffered nightmares with the damn thing. To fire it, you had to make sure that the hull valve was shut before you could open the breech to load the store, and this was ensured by the use of interlocks between the two valves—just like on a real size torpedo tube. Unfortunately though, the interlock sometimes failed to work, which meant that potentially you could open up an 3.5 inch hole in the side of the boat every time you used it! In addition, some of the stores we used were either flares or smoke grenades, about 4 feet long and pretty awkward to handle. The SSE was located in the deck head (ceiling), and you had to ram the flare almost all the way into the tube, remove a safety pin from the end, and then push and twist the thing to lock it into place in the tube, shut the breech, flood and equalise the tube, and then fire the thing with a great "whoosh" of high pressure air. Many of the flares and grenades were seawater activated, and so as soon as you started flooding the tube, you had only a few seconds to get rid of the thing before it went off—it sometimes got pretty tense! There was a particular exercise where we had to fire off flares of different colours in quick succession (to indicate torpedo attacks I think), and so we had a pile of red and another pile of green flares laid out on the after escape platform, unpacked and with pins out, being loaded one after another. With perfect hindsight it was a recipe for disaster, and we were fortunate not to have had a nasty event.

There were frequently problems with the interlocks and electronics on the SSEs, which while I was an Upper Level I could just palm off onto somebody else. Unfortunately I was now that somebody else, and so I needed to get more knowledgeable on the things. I asked the weapons guys to come along and give us a briefing on how to use them properly, and soon enough we were all standing around the thing being lectured by the two weapons Chiefs on how to use an SSE without causing a jam or other snags. The two guys were being pretty condescending to us in their manner, and I could see some of the lads getting a bit restless. The spell was broken though when one of the Chiefs was making a point about ensure that the store was twisted into place as it was loaded into the tube "or else you will be wearing it!" Sure enough, as he turned away from loading the store, out it slid and the bottom edge smacked straight into the back of his head. We all involuntarily flinched and mouthed "Ouch!" as the dummy store floored him. Served the smartarse right. As with the evaporators though, I found that once I had bothered to invest a bit of time in actually finding out how the things worked properly, they became much easier to use, and although I was always very wary of them, never really had too many further problems using them.

Along with the training the patrols continued apace. We were persisting with the Iceland/Faroes Gap and Barents Sea runs most of the time, but occasionally we would be tasked with other, more exciting jobs. Once such new role was that of being the release boat for 'sneaky' operations; that is, carrying Special Forces troops into action. Up until recent years that task had been one for the conventional boats, the nuclear boats being considered too big and clumsy to get into shallow water close to foreign coastlines, but with the demise of the old Porpoise and Oberon classes ('P & O boats'), and the failure of the new T2400s to live up to much (and subsequently to be sold to the Canadians), we had ended with no conventional boats left, but still with a requirement to offload the SAS and SBS forces when the need arose.

It was decided that the Tireless would be a test boat for the embarkation and off-loading of Special Forces, and we were sent to Gibraltar to carry out some warm-water trials. The way it was supposed to work was that the boat would creep underwater as close to land as she could safely manage, then raise the back end of the boat out of the water sufficiently to allow the engine room hatch to be opened and the Special Forces guys to leave the boat, open and inflate their rubber dinghies on the after casing, get in and then float off as the submarine submerged beneath them. This called for some pretty clever submarine handling, as the nuclear boats were very heavy and not designed to bob up and down within fine tolerances at the surface. They tended to respond to small changes in buoyancy like wallowing elephants, unlike the small and relatively light P & O boats which could control their buoyancy much more easily and effectively.

This limitation was quickly recognised by the high command, and the first trials would take place in deep water to prevent any risk of the boat striking the sea bed as she tried to 'catch a trim', and be in a state where we could find the ideal boat condition for just staying afloat as the soldiers left the boat, and then submerging in a controlled way once they had left. For a number of days we carried out dry runs, creeping up to the surface, slowly semi-surfacing and trying to hold the boat steady in that position for a few minutes before stealthily submerging again. From where we were in the machinery spaces it felt like the sailors were struggling to get it right as the boat took on steep angles and high pressure air blasted into ballast tanks, and was just as quickly released through ballast tank vent valves. Clearly it was a difficult balancing act for such a large vessel designed to spend most of its time underwater, and even to our untrained senses, the boat felt awkward and sluggish as the sailors fought to hold her steady at very low speeds and so close to the buoyancy limits.

Eventually they got as good as they were going to and we embarked some SAS guys and their kit to do some real tests. They bought with them a couple of inflatable boats tightly rolled up to fit through the engine room hatch, air bottles, weapons and all sorts of gear that could be strapped to their bodies on webbing harnesses, and off we sailed to the exercise areas once more.

I would be part of the team in the engine room that would help to pass the gear out of the hatch, and back in when we recovered them. The boats took 4 men to lift, and we would have to pass them above our heads and up and out of the open hatch, along with 4 large outboard engines, fuel and air tanks etc—there would be a couple of SAS blokes pulling from the top, having passed through the hatch and onto the after casing first. Health and safety was not big on the agenda for this one, as we would be carrying out he exercises at night, which meant that the engine room lights would be off so as not to shine out of the hatch once it had been opened. The whole process of getting the 8 SAS men and their gear out through the hatch, and getting the hatch closed again should take no more than 2 minutes. We spent the time between sailing from Gib and getting to the exercise areas practising shifting gear with the SAS men. They, not surprisingly, were all business, and spent a lot of time looking around the egress route to familiarise themselves with it—even asking us to turn out the lights so they could feel their way around in the dark. They were not great talkers but were generally ok with us—one even commented that we must be 'nuts' to work in submarines. This coming from guys kitted and armed up to the eyeballs, painted with black camo, waiting to exit a nuclear submarine, inflate a boat and then zoom off to kick somebody's ass! Horses for course I suppose. Anyway in a quiet spot a couple of them showed some of us around their weapons and gear, and it was pretty plain that they knew their stuff. None was particularly big, but they were all of a solidness you kind of expected—you could see it in their hands and necks—all muscle. You got the impression that you wouldn't want to be on the wrong end of an attack from these guys, and we were glad they were on our side!

So, there we were at 'stupid-o'clock' in the morning, waiting around in the dark of the after escape platform and engine room for the sailors to get the boat comfortably settled at periscope depth, and then to creep slowly to the surface. Right from the 'get-go' it was plain that they were still having trouble keeping a good trim at these slow speeds and the boat was tipping this way and that as they struggled for control up front. Eventually though the boat seemed settled down and we got the order to open the engine room hatch and offload the green death.

The hatch opened with a rush of fresh air and a small amount of water. Silently we started to heave the gear up and out of the hatch as the soldiers clambered up and through the hatch on to the after casing, which they reported was only a couple of inches above the sea level, rather than the normal 4 feet or so when we were fully surfaced. The engine room hatch was never open at sea usually so we were all pretty uncomfortable gazing up at the stars from the footplates. The gear seemed to be endless as we carried out passing it up, and soon we were being hassled by the Manoeuvring Room to get the engine room hatch shut. The two inflatable boats were out and being inflated on the casing and we had just passed up one of the outboard motors when suddenly we felt the boat lurch at the back end. Almost instantly the rear end of the boat started to sink and within seconds water was pouring in through the open engine room hatch, washing straight down into the engine room and into the electrical fuse and control panels all over the place down there. As the boat continued to submerge backwards the rush of water through the hatch increased until it was so strong that on-one could climb up and close the hatch. The backward and downward angle on the boat increased very quickly at an alarming rate, until eventually the boat must have been down at the stern by at least 20 degrees. We could feel the boat moving backwards too as the water crashed in through the hatch, and looking at the depth gauge it was clear that we were heading down backwards. Luckily, and it really was pure luck, because had the boat submerged level it would not have happened, due to the hinge on the engine room hatch being towards the front of the boat, the fact that we were submerging stern first had the effect of causing the hatch to fall shut under its own weight, a phenomena speeded up by the weight of water rushing past the hatch. As the boat seemed to pass through 10 metres on the depth gauge the inrush of water finally subsided and we heard a resounding 'clang' as the hatch slammed shut. Panic reigned still in the engine room though as fuse panels and starter boxes, supposedly water tight, arced and sparked and machinery ground to a halt. Somebody at last turned on the lights so that we could survey the damage and assess the amount of water taken on. All the time the boat continued to sink backwards, until at about 80 metres the sailors blew air into the after ballast tanks, and moved the telegraphs to 'half ahead' to arrest our descent and to level out the boat. Finally the boat settled out at about 100 metres, and we set about pumping out the tonnes of water we had taken onboard, and to begin the clean up operation in preparation for restoring all of the lost electrical services.

Throughout the drama everybody had forgotten about the soldiers who had been up on the casing. At the time the boat had started sinking they had all been up on the casing either inside the inflatable boats which were lashed on to the deck, or milling around sorting out their kit and stuff. We later learned that on finding the boat sinking beneath them, they had, all except one man, jumped into the boats, cut themselves free and then simply floated off the casing. Since they had no engines they decided just to wait for the boat to surface and find them later. One guy though, a Sergeant I think, had got himself caught in one of the ropes and was dragged down by the submarine "fucking deep—if I'd been there much longer I would have needed gills!", before managing to cut himself free, rise to the surface and rejoin his comrades. When we got them back onboard after surfacing later, he had a huge red wield around one wrist and his neck for his pains, but shrugged it off as "Shit happens!"

It was later determined that the boat had hit a patch of much less dense water which are common in the Mediterranean, which had caused the sudden loss of buoyancy. It was decided that for future operations the boat would rise further out of the water on surfacing, to give us a bit of freeboard while having the engine room hatch open We continued the trials for a couple of weeks, and the sailors finally got the hang of controlling the boat within such tight parameters. Back aft in the engine room, after drying out all of the damp fuse panels, we too learnt our lessons and for future operations ensured that all of the electrical boxes were tightly latched shut and sealed, and from then on we had huge plastic sheets covering as many of the panels as possible while the hatch was open, just in case of a repeat performance.

Within a relatively short time I had gained enough on the job experience to be ready to take the examination for Marine Engineer Artificer of the Watch (MEAOW), which as usual consisted of a 'walkround' and oral examination board. The walkround by the senior Charge Chief was pretty much a formality, although as ever the guy doing it was a mine of information, some of which I knew and some of which I didn't. At Chief level the oral examination now took on a new seriousness and for the first time the Senior Engineer Officer and his deputy, both Lieutenant Commanders, took part in the oral examination. The majority of the questioning, again for the first time for me, revolved around how the nuclear reactor and its support system operated, both from the theoretical nuclear fission, materials, forces and stresses side, and the practical system operating point of view. It was a pretty intense examination lasting most of one day, but I was considered good enough to pass.

As was the case with the lesser positions, the first couple of watches on my own were a bit hairy, but I was soon able to settle down and get on with the work. As well as being a fully qualified MEAOW, I had also been moved into the 'Primaries' Section for maintenance and defect repair duties, which was the section that had the responsibility for the nuclear reactor, its support systems (primary water, make-up water, reactor high and low pressure air, primary sampling sink and chemicals, steam systems in the reactor tunnel) and for some odd reason the diesel generators. The equipment on the primary side was totally different to the secondary steam valves and other gear, and so now, rather than thinking that I could take a break from the studying for a while, I had a whole new set of manuals, drawing and plans to look at and get familiar with! Pretty soon I was heavily involved in the numerous and continuous small defects that always occur at sea, always trying to ensure that the small defects remained just that—small. We were intensely aware that many previous accidents had originated from small defects that were allowed to fester and grow bigger, or had masked much larger problems, and so we made it a point to attack the smaller defects aggressively and repair them completely every time. Of course we could only carry so many parts and spares onboard, so there would always be cases where something wasn't working for a long period, or had to remain broken. You just had to work around those.

I was finding too that I was starting to have a much bigger role to play during the machinery breakdown drills we were frequently running. It was vital that we all practised what we needed to do when there were major machinery failures at sea. The top level failure was the 'Reactor Scram', where the reactor would automatically shut itself down due to its own electronic protection system detecting one of the key parameters being out of tolerance. The protection system was quite a complex logic sequence, which monitored a number of important operating parameters, and provided first warnings, and then taking action to insert the control rods if the parameters were exceeded. When that happened, support systems automatically closed a number of steam valves to maintain the heat inside the reactor so that once the fault was cleared the reactor could be restarted relatively quickly, but in so doing of course removed the steam supply to the main engines, and just as importantly to the turbo-generators. That in turn meant we lost propulsion and AC electrical power.

The main battery would provide us with limited power via the motor generators, and we also had an electric motor as a back-up for propulsion, which needed to be engaged from the engine room for us to regain some propulsion. The process of engaging the electric drive involved a gearbox clutching sequence, controlled from the Manoeuvring Room, which was overseen by the MEAOW and carried out by the Upper Level Watchkeeper. As well as the on-watch guys there would also be safety numbers around the spaces to make sure nothing went horribly wrong, and these would normally be the off-watch MEAOWs.

I had always only really seen the effects of a scram from outside in the machinery spaces, but now, I could stand at the back of the Manoeuvring Room and watch the guys in there do their stuff. Even when they knew a scram was coming in got pretty tense in there, and I hadn't realised how totally focused everybody had to be to get their drills right. I would find out later that you left the place completely drained when there were machinery drills taking place!

Along with the reactor scram there were a whole load of lesser drills that had to be regularly practised, ranging from electrical failures, to single main engine drive, to turbo generator trips and lubricating oil pump failures. Pretty much every single day (except when we were actually on patrol) we would exercise a number of drills, and while it was a pain in the butt at the time, it stood me in good stead form later events. As well as the practise drills there were of course the real machinery breakdowns to deal with also. These tended to develop much more slowly in real life than when we practised them, and gave us a 'feel' for how the machinery operated in the different configurations that needed to be adopted sometimes to fix defects. On a couple of occasions we were required to adopt either single loop—where only one side of the reactor water circuit is producing power, or single steam generator—where steam is only being produced from one of the two steam generators, in order to rectify a defect or fix a steam leak. These were considered as extreme configurations due to their affect on the water flow through the reactor core, and we were all pretty wide eyed when we needed to do them! On one memorable occasion we suffered a nasty steam leak from one of the two main steam stop valves located in the Manoeuvring Room Flat. It had been calculated that if one of these valves failed totally, the Manoeuvring Room would be steam drenched and all the people in it scolded to death within about 5 seconds. There was a lot of breath-holding going on when the repair was completed and the valves re-pressurised! Luckily the repair was a good one.

The patrols kept on coming and before long we were informed that our next one would be a trip under the polar ice cap to the North Pole. The idea was that it was known that the Russians would transit into the North Atlantic by going under the ice, and so we and an American boat would conduct a patrol under there to see if we could pick anything up, follow it and see where it went.

Very few of us had operated under the ice before, and soon we were hearing horror stories of boats getting trapped under there, being unable to surface through the ice and sinking into the abyss. These stories always seemed to appear from nowhere before any patrol we did, so we pretty much ignored them. What we didn't ignore though was a visit by an American 'Ice-pilot' who would be joining us for the cruise, and who was an expert in under ice navigation. He gave us a briefing on how that worked, and to the relief of many of us explained that contrary to popular belief, the ice on the way to the North Pole was not a solid sheet, but had weak points, where the ice was much thinner, running throughout it called 'Polynias'. These were very important to submarines because should we suffer a major incident while we were under the ice, there was a possibility that we could surface through one of these weak points to do whatever we needed to do to recover. Normally of course we had the option of emergency blowing our ballast tanks to get to the surface quickly, but now we would have to learn a new skill of surfacing straight upwards and breaking through (hopefully) a thin sheet of ice to get to fresh air—it was going to be a testing time.

We started our preparations for the trip by having to re-write many of our emergency drills. Any drill that ended with the action "Emergency Surface, Full Ahead telegraphs, emergency blow all main ballast tanks!" had to be amended for ice operations, so that now they ended with "Follow directions of Ice-Pilot to nearest mapped polynia, and surface when able". In addition cameras were fitted on the fin and casing so that the sailors could see the bottom of the ice, and upward-looking sonar was also fitted to gauge the thickness of the ice above our heads. In the machinery spaces we had our own preparations to make. The temperature of the water where we were going was much lower that we were used to, and so we had to fit special heaters around the small pipework running everywhere to stop the water freezing inside. Condensation was also going to be a huge problem for us, and so we used the good old plastic sheeting to create double glazing around some of the more exposed bulkheads. Apart from that we took onboard as many spares and consumable bits and pieces we could hold, well knowing that there was not going to be any way to resupply during our long periods under the ice.

We finally sailed and once out at sea did the normal post sailing work-up to get us back up to speed with all the equipment and procedures. We soon got ourselves into patrol routine though, and within a couple of weeks were in the areas where the Northern ice floes started. At first all that could be seen on the newly fitted cameras were small blocks of ice dotting the surface of the water here and there, but within a few short hours the blocks were becoming the size of houses! It felt odd to be looking upwards from inside the submarine and not a little creepy too. Normally we would be sailing along in blind ignorance to whatever was above and below us, but to be seeing the bow of the boat, several hundred feet underwater was weird. Within a couple of days the ice above our heads had become a continuous sheet, but the water was still clear enough for us to peer upwards through the cameras, to see the roughened bottom of the ever thickening ice flow seemingly a few metres above our heads. Human beings are remarkably adaptable creatures—after the first few days of being very aware of the ice above us, surely preventing us from escaping in an emergency, we accepted our fate and just got used to the situation. I don't think anybody every actually forgot that the ice was there, but in the stoic way of submariners we just got on with our jobs and hoped nothing went wrong. Passing through the Control Room when going off watch became a bit of sport—we would stick our heads into the navigation's niche and watch the Ice Pilot mapping Polynia's on his ice map (which to us looked like a sheet of white A3 paper!). The upwards sonar would ping out a signal and then he would stare intensely at the read out before marking the map. We would teasingly ask him how far it was to the next 'breathing hole' and whether we would make it if the boat was flooding. "No problem guys" would always be the answer. We were not so convinced, particular so since the breathing holes seemed to be further apart the thicker the ice became.

We spent the next few weeks patrolling around under the ice trying to pick up the trail of any passing opposition bombers, but to no avail. One of the most remarkable things I remember from that trip was lying in my bunk and listening to the whales 'singing'. It was an incredible experience, and to be able to hear the creatures through the outer plating and boat's hull just went to prove how deathly quiet it was under the ice. It gave us a warm feeling too—if the whales were around it meant that there must be breathing holes around, which in turn meant we had somewhere to head for if the shit hit the fan.

About halfway through the patrol it had been decided that we would rendezvous with an American submarine at or near to the geographic North Pole, by surfacing through the ice. In order to do this we would have to find a suitably thin bit of ice to breakthrough with our steel reinforced fin, and the surface directly upwards, like we had learned to do previously working with the Special Forces. The American boat would have to break through in the same area, and the co-ordinates were passed across using the underwater telephone. On the day of the races the American boat would break through first, followed soon after by ourselves. With the cameras fitted to the fin and the hull we were able to watch the American boat, at that time several hundred feet above us and looking for the entire world like a tiny toy submarine, rising up and then smashing through the ice without any apparent problems. Then it was our turn.

Once we had achieved positive buoyancy the engines were stopped and we started drifting towards the surface. As we neared the underside of the ice pack I looked around the engine room and instantly had a flashback to the old World War 2 films of U-boats being depth-charged! Every face was turned upwards towards the deck head as though the guys could see through the steel hull, and as though they were expecting a great sharp lump of ice to break through any second. The boat juddered and shook as the top of the fin came into contact with the ice, and then even harder as more high pressure air was forced into the ballast tanks in an effort to force the fin through. The boat rocked this way and that until eventually, with a rending tear noise the fin broke through the ice. As the boat rose we could hear the lumps of ice scraping along the sides of the fin, and finally the casing breaking through with a 'thump' of more ice hitting it. The broadcast "Submarine surfaced" came through the speakers, closely followed by "Anybody interested in a cricket match on the ice make yourselves known to the Cox'n". We had been cooped up under the ice for several weeks—of course we wanted to get off the boat for a bit!

It was no surprise to us to find that the boat carried very little cold weather clothing. There were a few pairs of padded overalls and some wholly hats, but that was about it. Not to be fazed though, we set about 'improvising and adapting', and in my case I dressed in two pairs of overalls, a fire fighting suit, and wrapped a towel around my head before making my way up the ladder and on to the casing. Stepping out of the boat was like walking straight into a very deep freezer, and even with all the clothing I was wearing the stiff breeze cut straight through me—it was freezing!! The sailors had rigged a ladder down from the casing and on to the ice flow all around us, and before long we were wandering around by the side of the boat at the North Pole—how brilliant is that? The ice was fantastic to look at—the top was of course white with snow, but when you brushed the snow away the ice beneath had several beautiful shades of blue running through it. The extreme whiteness all around us was blinding and many of us had to go back onboard and dig out our sunglasses for a bit of eye protection. I noticed on going back onboard that they had placed a sentry with a rifle on the top of the fin to keep an eye out for polar bears—I didn't think they were that far north, but better safe than sorry I suppose.

Fairly soon we got to start mingling with the yanks off the submarine which had surfaced about 100 metres away from us. Of course every one of them had a nice arctic "Ice Station Zebra" hooded parka, padded trousers and mittens to wear, making us feel ridiculous in our mixture of civilian jackets, fire fighting suits and towels, but hey, we had beer onboard and they didn't so they dare not laugh at us too much! Some bright spark suggested a game of cricket, resulting in confused looks from the yanks, and so we agreed on a game of baseball (or 'rounders' as we preferred to call it). The game disintegrated after about 15 minutes though—frozen British sailors stopped play! Apparently an RAF Nimrod had flown overhead while we were doing this, and later my wife showed me a press cut-out showing us all standing around on the ice. We had a look around each-others boats—we were surprised at the basic nature of the American boat, and they were equally surprised that ours was so luxurious (compared to theirs that is). We swopped some beer for some American ice-cream (yes, they had an ice-cream dispenser onboard!), although we kept that at senior rate level because the yanks would have been in deep trouble if their officers knew. After a couple of hours on the surface though the heat from the boat had started to create a pool of clear water around it, making it increasingly difficult to climb back onboard, so the decision was taken that we had to leave. We bid our new friends goodbye and a safe trip (they had already been away for something like 5 months compared to our 2 months, and still had about 3 months to go!), closed the hatches and blew the ballast tanks to dive straight down. Once more it was remarkable to watch the surface slipping away above us through the TV cameras. We had been so impressed with the cameras during this trip that the Captain asked for them to remain onboard after we returned to port. They remained for the rest of my time onboard the boat, and never lost their fascination—there was nothing like walking through the Control Room with the boat at periscope depth and watching the waves washing over the periscope and seeing the bow of the boat with the deep blue abyss beneath—stunning.

We spent another couple of weeks under the ice in a fruitless search for real or imaginary foes, and then turned around and started heading back towards base. We cleared the ice-pack without any incident, but then about a day or so further along, and as we got on with removing a lot of the extra tape heaters around some of the smaller diameter pipework, we had a nasty reminder of what could have happened under the ice.

The boat was quite deep and I was working in the engine room, helping the Upper Level to remove tape heaters. I was removing a particular difficult to remove one, and so had resorted to tugging on the damn thing in an effort to pry it loose from around a quarter inch pump balance pipe. I tugged even harder and then 'bang' the tape came free having snapped the pipe. Water under very high pressure spurted out of the now open pipe, hit me in the chest and flung me backwards and on to the deck. The water was pouring in, and I got very close to hitting the nearest flood alarm, but resisted as I was still in 'under-the-ice' mode in my mind. I rushed up to the Manoeuvring Room and shouted that we had a flood in the engine room. At first they were incredulous and did not believe me, but then seeing me soaked through with still freezing cold water, they finally reacted. I was asked what side the water was coming from, and on answering saw the Nuclear Chief of the Watch lean over and shut the starboard main circulating system hull valves, instantly stopping the water coming into the boat. The boat then went to Emergency Stations and we got the amazingly large amount of water out using the big ballast pumps. It was a sobering lesson on how such a small opening in the boat could potentially lead to disaster—the pipe had been quite badly corroded inside, and the action of my tugging the tape heater off was enough to sever the pipe!

The next few trips were relatively quiet ones for me, and provided the opportunity of consolidating my new position. I really enjoyed that period on the boat—I had reached as far as I needed to go career wise, and any further promotion would be by selection and aptitude basically.

At long last there was no pressure on me to do anything other than my job, and re-qualifying in the simulator each year as SDSR, and I was enjoying the freedom. Once I had settled into the position of MEAOW the job was fairly easy and straightforward, and when we were alongside the wall, all of the tasks I had to perform on the reactor and its support machinery were done by following a written procedure authorised by a panel of experts, so that as long as I followed the procedures word for word I really couldn't make any mistakes. The Primary Section was the most high profile one onboard naturally, and being in charge of it meant that I was constantly under the spotlight while carrying out work there, but I enjoyed the attention. My stock seemed to rise during that period with the engineering officers, and before long I was being encouraged to attempt selection for Sub-Lieutenant Engineer myself.

In order to do that I had to volunteer and to be approved to become what was known as a 'CW' candidate. This meant that I would be more closely watched by the officers, would occasionally be given particular projects to perform, and would be 'written-up' or appraised every 6 months instead of the usual yearly, as a potential officer candidate. The actual selection process to become an engineer in those days consisted of a written examination covering practically every engineering theory and practice currently in operation in the Navy (the syllabus consisted of reading some 58 naval books of reference!), followed by a selection board who would pick people (only a couple a year though) based on their exam scores and the 6-monthly appraisals. The exam had a reputation of being particularly tough, and pass marks less that 50% where not even considered by the board. At the time I was a CW candidate, in order to even take the exam you had to be the rank of Charge Chief Petty Officer (it later changed to

CPO). I of course was still a CPO, and so if I was serious about it I would have to seek promotion first.

The rank of Charge Chief Petty Officer Artificer on nuclear submarines was a strange middle ground rank which was neither CPO nor Warrant Officer—it was somewhere, usually undefined, between the two. Later the rank was more formally recognised when it became Warrant Officer 2nd Class, but at the time I decided I would go for it the only advantage was a slight increase in pay—we still wore the shoulder tabs of a CPO and there was no difference in the pension rate for instance.

The one big difference between a CPO and a Charge Chief was in the amount of responsibility that a Charge Chief had to bear. The Nuclear Chief of the Watch (NCOW) was a Charge Chief, and his job at sea was basically to be the right hand of the Engineer Officer of the Watch (EOOW), and to take over control of the entire propulsion system, from reactor core to propulsor hub in the absence of the EOOW for whatever reason. The NCOW had to be qualified in every lower watchkeeping position, but also had to be able to carry out every Emergency Operation Procedure (EOP) to a standard at least equal to that of the EOOW. It was a daunting proposition for me as in Artificer terms I was really still quite junior—I had been a senior rate for about 4 years at that stage, but with the commendation of the Marine Engineer Officer ringing loudly in my ears I embarked on my new and most challenging adventure. It was decided that before I went for Charge Chief course (or 'Nuclear Systems Charge Course' as it was formally known) I should study for and pass all of the examinations for every electrical watchkeeping position onboard, so I started with Throttle Panel Operator, would then work up to Electrical Panel Operator and then finally cover the Reactor Panel Operator positions—all this while I kept down my day job as MEAOW. In between this I would start to study some of the books of reference I would need to eventually take the Sub Lieutenant's exam—I certainly did like a challenge!

Of course this was all peripheral to the main task of the boat, that of patrolling the northern wastes looking for other submarines. It was around this sort of time that we embarked on a particular patrol that would end up with us being at sea for almost double the standard patrol duration, and the Captain being awarded the Order of the British Empire medal (OBE) for his, and our efforts.

The trip started pretty much like any other—loading stores and food, preparing and then starting the reactor and machinery, leaving port and diving a couple of days later, followed by the 'work-up' to get us back into sea-going shape before we entered our patrol areas. After that we slowed down, went deeper and commenced patrolling along set route to try and locate 'enemy' submarines. After several weeks of this with absolutely no result we fell into a lethargy routine of going on watch, eating, sleeping and watching the odd movie or reading a book (or several in my case). It was going to be a long boring patrol by the looks of it, and we would be glad to tick off the days in our 'days to go' calendars—we all had them taped to the side of our racks!

We still had the cameras fitted to the boat from when we were doing under-ice ops, and I had taken to the habit of sitting in the Control Room for 20 minutes or so when I came off watch, chatting to the Crumple-Zone Commandos and watching the camera monitors. I would occasionally see a fish swimming by, or would watch the luminescence of the sea water as it flowed over the boat. I found it relaxing.

We were in the final 2 weeks of the 3 month patrol when I was sitting in the Control Room chatting away one day. There were a couple of Part-III trainees wandering around with their task-books when one of them pointed to the TV monitor and said:

"What's that on the screen Chief?"

We looked up and noticed that there was a strange line that had suddenly appeared across the bottom right corner of the screen. We all got up and in turn peered closely at the screen, wondering what it could be. Somebody said:

"It looks like a rope or hawser of some kind"

"Naw, probably a piece of crap on the camera lens"

"Maybe some water has got into the camera"

We continued to peer at the screen from various angles and distances, trying to make sense of the image. Somebody called over the Officer of the Watch (OOW) for his input, and he joined the huddle. Finally after watching the image slowly growing more defined on screen he announced:

"Shit! That's a towed array cable! Call the Captain. Sonar Room, do you have any contacts on screen?"

"Sonar Sir, no contacts".

The Captain came bounding out of his cabin at the end of the Control Room and took a long look at the screen. He asked the OOW if there were any contacts, and then announced:

"Control Room, Captain. We are going to follow this cable and see what is on the end of it! Adopt the Quiet State throughout the submarine". That meant that every piece of machinery not in use was to be turned off, including the DVDs in the messes. This must be serious! The lights were dimmed to indicate that we needed to be quiet.

As the Control Room slowly filled with sailors closing up at their stations I was pushed to wards the back and out of the way, but could still see what was happening. The Captain was manoeuvring the boat to slowly inch forward along the cable, using the cameras to guide him. It was superb ship control and amazing that we could even see the thing, let alone use the cable to locate the boat towing it! Towed array cables could be up to 2 kilometres long and we didn't know how far along it we were, so the boat could still be quite some distance away yet. Whatever boat it was, it was remarkably quiet, and as yet absolutely nothing was showing up on the sonar screens.

We continued creeping along the cable for the next half an hour before finally:

"Control, Sonar. We have a new sonar contact" came from the Chief Sonar Operator.

The Captain and OOW disappeared into the Sonar shack to take a look. They stayed there for several minutes before coming out looking confused.

"Control Room, Captain. We are following a very large target, one that the sonar computers are unable to recognise. This could well be a new type of submarine we haven't come across before. Keep your wits about you as we approach. We are directly astern of her and in her baffles, so with any luck they should not know we are here."

All eyes remained on the TV monitors as we continued along the seemingly endless cable, until finally, over an hour later a new shadow started to appear. The Captain slowed the boat further as we crept up towards the rear of a massive submarine—quite clearly visible through the fin and forecastle cameras.

The first thing noticeable were 2 huge slowly rotating propellers. One was turning clockwise and the other anticlockwise and they must have been 25 feet in diameter. In between the rotating propellers was the gigantic rudder and aft hydroplanes, both slowly moving one way then back to keep the boat on track. The towed array cable was attached to the outer extreme of the port hydroplane. The hull of the huge beast disappeared into the distance ahead of the propulsion, and it was clear by the size of the thing that this was a type of boat not seen before. We later got to know that it had been identified in harbour previously, and was known throughout NATO as a 'TYPHOON' class of Soviet intercontinental ballistic missile submarine. At the time though, it was just a big new boat that we were going to have to follow and gather intelligence from. It was all very exciting!

At that moment we were in an area behind the Russian boat known as her 'baffles'. This is an area directly behind a submarine, where the noise of the propellers and steering equipment means that the boat is unable to detect anything. There are no aft looking sonar's either so if you are able to get into the baffles of another boat they should not be able to detect you. This is a well known phenomena, and what usually happens is that when the boat is on patrol, every now and then a sharp right or left turn is initiated just to 'clear the baffles', i.e. to use the side sonar to check that there is nothing behind you—we were expecting the Typhoon to do that at any time.

Another thing we were expecting to happen was for us to be 'pinged' by one or other of the Russian escort submarines which surely must be accompanying the Typhoon. One of their tasks would be to sweep the towed array cable and baffles of the big boat, and pretty regularly too, so we might expect active sonar at any minute to bounce off the boat, letting us know that they knew we were there. For some strange reason this had not happened yet, and again there were no further contacts on the sonar plot. The Control Room team were taking advantage of their absence though, and gathering as much intelligence as possible on this new boat as they could before we were bounced.

The bounce never came. We sat there waiting, but no alarm was apparently raised. The Typhoon moved majestically onwards, neither clearing baffles or indeed conducting any sudden changes of course or depth. We stuck like glue behind her, making sure not to make any noise or to do anything which might make her aware of our presence, while the sailors continued to plot her course and to gather whatever intelligence they could. Hours stretched into days. To ensure that we would not be detected by noise, we had more or less stopped any activity which might require any discharge to be made from the boat. We could therefore not dispose of any of the rubbish (gash) through the normal ejector (gash gun), meaning that it was starting to pile up in the gash gun compartment, and no matter how much we attempted to seal the plastic bags, the smell was starting to waft through the boat. We were getting to be a bit smelly ourselves as in an effort to cut down noise the showers were put out of action. And of course we were starting to get a bit bored now, after several days not being able to watch DVDs, listen to music (apart from through personal headphones) or even play Uckers due to the slapping down of 'bits' on tables! The toilets too were only to be used for peeing during the periods we were close to the Typhoon for fear of their flushing giving us away.

We got into a routine of moving away from the back of the Typhoon once during each day to allow us to carry out 'daily routines'—ditching gash, showering, pumping bilge tanks and so on, which made life a bit more tolerable. Long queues would form for the toilets and showers while we were away, and if you were on-watch tough luck—it would be your turn tomorrow!

By now we had been following the thing for about 10 days, and were distinctly aware that by now we should have been making our way back to Devonport at the end of patrol. Speculation spread around that we would be following the Typhoon for another week or so, which caused a collective groan from the crew, but the Captain stayed silent and just told us to maintain our focus on not being detected. After another week of dark passageways and silent operation we still had not heard what the future was, although it was clear we were not going back to harbour yet.

We continued in the same vein for another 2 weeks. By now we were pretty much used to this 'ultra quiet' operating routine, interspaced with a few hours away where we could catch up with dailies and stuff, but were totally unprepared for what came next. During an exchange of signals at the latest 'routines' rotation, we received a signal from the Admiralty directing us to remain tracking the Typhoon until it either returned to base, or we ran out of food, whichever came first. The (non-commissioned at any rate) crew morale took a nosedive at this news—we had already been at sea for nearly 3 months, the last 3 weeks of it in perpetual darkness and numbing silence, and we were going to continue that for a further indefinite period—nightmare!

The routine continued seemingly ever onwards—we would closely tail the Typhoon, gathering intelligence on the boat's speed, course, operating signature and such like for about 20 hours of each day, then pull back a good distance to carry out our daily routines before slowly creeping back in again. The Russian boat never seemed to make any indication that she knew we were there, although there was the occasional change of course, speed or depth to keep the sailors on their toes. The work was particularly tough on the sailors, as they were the ones who, when they were on watch had to constantly man their stations. Normally during a 6-hour watch they would get the occasional break from their sonar screen or ship control consoles to grab a cup of tea and a smoke, but with us so close to the Typhoon they had to remain totally focused for the whole watch. They looked dead on their feet. For the 'Back-Afties' on the other hand, the routine had become really boring. Normally on patrol we would have maintenance and repairs to do, and even on-watch procedures for testing the standby machinery and so on, but since we were running ultra-quiet, we could do nothing except push the boat through the water—somebody had even shoved a rag into the telegraph order bell so that it did not ring so loudly when the sailors ordered a change of speed. Things livened up a bit when we pulled back and carried out all of the stuff we would normally do over a 24 hour period, and it got to the stage where people would come back aft to help out with the routines when they were off watch—just for something to do!

We had pretty soon realised that what we were doing was as close to being at war that most of us would like to experience. We were sneaking around following what could potentially be an enemy submarine, gathering information about the routes the Russian intercontinental ballistic missile submarines might use during a conflict, and trying very hard not to be caught doing it! We had surmised that this new boat was probably on a trial cruise, or was maybe doing a post build workup, and so had not really needed the usual 2 escorts that came with Russian 'bombers'. Either that, or this boat was so quiet (and it was extremely quiet for such a massive machine), that their hierarchy had decided that escorts simply were not required since the boat would never be discovered by a potential foe. In either case, we were certainly getting the full experience of what life might be like for a submarine crew during a real conflict, and it certainly was not pleasant.

After about a further 5 or 6 weeks into our new deployment the shortages started to bite. It was normal for the boat to be provisioned food wise for quite a considerable period longer than a normal patrol would last. That was indeed the case with us, but of course what they don't mention is that the extra provisions are of a somewhat lesser quality that the usual fare. By then we had of course run out of anything remotely fresh like eggs or flour for making bread, or vegetables and fruit, and had worked our way through the stuff at the front of the freezer. Our meals were reduced to either frozen everything or frozen meat and canned vegetables, and if we were on a good day, some tinned fruit salad for desert. Normally on a boat the food was the great morale builder, but 4 and a half months into the patrol the meals were just about as bland as the rest of the experience following what had become 'that fucking Russian boat'.

The Captain had taken the decision a few weeks back that we could start watching DVDs again in the mess, but with the volume at minimum. We found ourselves watching the same DVDs over and over, simply to kill time. Novels became prime currency, but even with a decent library onboard eventually all of the spare books had been read from cover to cover. For me, initially I had plenty of studying to do, and whiled away the off-watch hours hitting the Books of Reference and tracking this or that electrical system, or trying to work out the intricacies of a 1 out of 4 reactor protection logic system. Eventually though this became very samey, and I needed a break from the books, except there was no break to be had. For the smokers, including myself at that time, things were becoming tense. Usually the handing out of cigarettes was a reflex thing—if you wanted a smoke, you offered the packet around, but no more. Cigarettes were now jealously guarded. We knew that the supply was running dangerously low, and rationing had already started. We could buy a packet from the canteen every 3 days or so, and so of course the packet had to last! If you were a heavy smoker life was going to get very uncomfortable very soon. By then cigarettes were about the only thing left for sale in the canteen—all of the sweets (or 'nutty') was long gone. There was very little interest in the baseball caps and t-shirts!

Eventually we started to go a bit stir-crazy I think. People were looking for projects to undertake to kill time, and in my case I had decided that I would restore the deck in the Manoeuvring Room Flat—as you do! The deck consisted of a layer of plastic and rubber tiles, which over the years had been polished over and over again so that now there was a thick layer of congealed floor polish around the edges of each tile. I concluded that if I removed this old polish, and then built up a new layer, the floor deck would shine like glass—it would be brilliant! Nobody questioned why I wanted to do it—they mostly went "Shit, wish I'd thought of that!"

Each off-watch I would get down on my hands and knees with my little penknife and start laboriously scraping a little corner of one tile clean. It was kind of cathartic—mindless manual labour while the mind wanders off somewhere warm and fuzzy—others were doing similar things—scraping this or polishing that (even though we were not supposed to be carrying any polishing chemicals onboard). Some of the more clever ones took to drawing or even knitting! Anything to break up the tedium. Over the next few weeks the Manoeuvring Room deck was slowly transformed—one side dark and mangy looking, the other clean and like new, and waiting for its new coating of polish. It was strangely satisfying to my slightly deranged mind, and I think I even got annoyed when people used to walk over it in their dirty boots!

By getting on for 5 months away from home we had had about enough. We had been following the Typhoon for over 2 months, and the damn thing still didn't look like it was going to stop plodding along towing its array around behind it. It still had not made any sudden movements or rapid changes in direction, speed or depth, and we must have pretty much exhausted the intelligence gathering bit too by now. The situation on board had worsened too of course—no cigarettes, tea or coffee, really crap food, and being even more bored to death if that was possible. Finally we moved astern for the usual daily routines and radio contact with base, and were at last told to expect a relief submarine to come along and take over from us. It was brilliant news and cheered us up no end.

The relief boat took about 2 weeks to get to us. We rendezvous'd well away from the Russian boat, wished them good luck and set about getting home double-quick.

The trip home was pure luxury. We were effectively back to normal patrol routine, and could shower, watch movies at normal volume and carry out all of the stuff we had taken for granted pre-Typhoon, minus the nice food we were used to onboard. On the way back the submarine received floods of congratulatory signals from the various departments of the Admiralty, all of which were relayed to the entire ship's company—we had found and tracked a new class of potential enemy submarine, and the Powers That Be were seriously chuffed with our effort. Likewise when we actually returned to harbour we had a high level reception committee waiting to come onboard and drink some of the Captain's booze. Most of this happened at the front end of the boat, but at least we at the machinery end could bask in some reflected glory. From our side we had a visit from the Senior Squadron Engineer, who jokingly criticised the Boss for allowing the hull to become covered in marine growth! It was too! All that slow speed following stuff had allowed the sea life to get a hold on the hull—we looked like a rust bucket rather than a sleek black messenger of death! Nobody mentioned the nice sparkling polished Manoeuvring Room deck either. I was most disappointed.

After shutting down the boat we at last were released for a bit of well earned leave. We were all long haired louts by this time, and I for one wanted to get to the nearest barber and get rid of the excess hair. It was strange walking around after being cooped up for so long on the boat, and we found that for the first couple of days our eyes were unable to focus on distant objects like traffic sign and such—we had been warned not to drive for the first day back to allow our eyes to readjust. Going home after being away for nearly seven months is an incredible experience. Of course the family is delighted to see you, but in an odd way you kind of interrupt their routine! You don't really notice any changes in yourself while you are away, but in my case my wife was incredulous at the amount of weight I had lost and my general poor physical shape—she actually referred to me as looking like a 'plucked chicken' with me being so pale and skinny, and set about beefing me up in no time. Boy, it was great to be home.

The physical effects of the trip wore off quite quickly, and a few months later we were delighted to learn that our Captain had been awarded the OBE (or 'Other Buggers Efforts as we preferred to call it!) in reward for the ship's company efforts. He had left the ship by then and we had a new Skipper—we told him that he could 'dream-on' if he fancied the idea of repeating the process so that he could get a gong too! The thing that did remain (with me at least) was the memory of how tough life would become if we ever got involved in a real conflict with a serious foe. In many ways, although submarine technology has evolved an incredible amount over the years since the Second World War, the weak point remains the human beings of the crew. A nuclear submarine can in theory stay underwater and in action, machinery wise, pretty much indefinitely, but the physical and perhaps more importantly the psychological degradation of the crew, if that patrol was anything to go by, would eventually be the limiting factor—especially under the increased stress of the threat of somebody really trying to kill you. It was yet another sobering thought.

I had by now qualified in 2 out of the 3 electrical watchkeeping positions, and just had the Reactor Panel Operator (RPO) position to pass before being sent away for Charge Chiefs course. I decided to attack the qualification during the next patrol and set about the task with gusto.

The Reactor Panel Operator, as the name suggests is the Chief who monitors and control the operation of the nuclear reactor, along with the maintenance of the control equipment and reactor protection systems. As I was to find out, the operation of the reactor was actually the relatively easy part of the job, and the much harder bit (for a mechanically minded dork like me) was the comprehension and then control of the reactor protection system.

The protection system consisted of a matrix of 4 'guard lines' monitoring a number of key reactor and system parameters. In simple terms, what was supposed to happen was that should 3 out of 4 guard lines detect one of the key parameters outside of its specification, they would first issue an audible warning, then drive the control rods into the reactor to restore the parameter to normal, and finally if the parameter remained out of tolerance, cause the reactor to automatically shut-down or 'scram'—all of this was totally independent of any operator action and was designed purely to protect the reactor from exceeding operating limits. Of course there were occasions where we didn't want the reactor to suddenly shut down and remove all of our propulsion and electrical power—such as when we might be in action, and so there were a number of 'overrides' that could be operated to prevent certain conditions from causing a scram—most of these could only be operated on the direct order of the Captain, and had little plastic covers over them to prevent accidental use.

Part of the RPO's job was to conduct daily tests of the protection logic system, where they would input test signals into the system to ensure the correct indications were given as each parameter was simulated as being exceeded. On first watching this process I was totally lost as the RPO, speaking to the guy on watch through his headset, pressed series of buttons, watched resultant indications and confirmed correct sequences with his partner. In a couple of the tests, 2 guard lines were tripped together for test, meaning that should another be tripped either for real or by mistakes, then the reactor would scram! The guys looked tense when they did this test, and they knew what they were doing!

It was a massive learning curve for me, and it soon became clear that to become familiar with the job was going to take a lot more time than I had first thought. In the meantime I had my 'day job' to attend to still, and for most people that would have probably been enough. I was enjoying the challenge though, and was at that stage where I wanted everything! I had at this stage got a new Upper Level Watchkeeper who was pure entertainment on watch, and who had made it a complete pleasure to go to work.

The man's name was 'Brum' Jenkins, from Birmingham. A tall skinny bloke, he was one of those natural comedians who come along now and then in your life—just to cheer you up. From day one he was pure magic—always cheerful and smiling, and with a hilarious story for each and every occasion, and more importantly the character to get away with murder, which in Brum's case came in his tendency to er . . . well, dress up!

I first came to know about this tendency after we had been a team for a couple of months. We were sitting down on the bench on the After Escape having a cup of tea, when I noticed that Brum seemed to be scratching a lot—mainly around his crutch area! In fact it was bloody irritating and so I said:

"For fuck sake Brum, you got the crabs or something?"

"Naw, my knickers are a bit tight, that's all"

"We call them 'knicks' mate, not knickers!" I laughed.

"No, no, I mean my knickers, look!"

With that he opened the front of his overalls and turned towards me. I gaped at the sight of a red and black bra, matching knickers, suspenders and stockings. A greasy hand went in and scratched at some itch in the depths of his crotch. I quickly motioned him to do himself up.

"What the fuck is THAT!" I asked, stunned.

"What's up? I just like the feel of them that's all. Don't worry, I'm not queer or anything"

"How long you been wearing that stuff on watch?"

"I always wear it. I think I need some new stuff—this is getting tight"

So, that was that. My Upper Level was a transvestite, stocking wearing weirdo. I had known about the weirdo bit for quite a while, but the cross dressing was a new twist! Still, nobody was surprised when I mentioned it later, and it seemed that I was the only one not to know!

Later that year we were sent out on patrol at Christmas, at very short notice, and Brum once again managed to cause a stir. A few days out of harbour I had just arrived on watch and was just sitting waking up when much to my amazement Batman, mask, cape, utility belt and all sat down beside me.

"Alright Brum?" I said

"Alright Steve, want a cup of tea?" Brum replied, bat ears twitching on the top of his mask.

I surveyed him as he squashed the tea bag. He was dressed in the complete rig—tight trousers, bat shirt with large circled bat motif on the chest, utility belt, flowing black cape, green gloves with spiky cuffs, all topped off with the half face mask with bat ears on top. It was very good, and only slightly spoiled by the steaming boots his feet were stuck into!

He bought over the tea and sat down next to me. I looked at him:

"You planning on wearing that the whole watch?"

"Wearing what?"

"Wearing what? The fucking Bat rig, that's what!"

"It's Bat Man. Anyway I had no clean overalls"

"You must know they won't let you get away with it, surely"

"We'll see"

A few minutes later, "Upper Level Watchkeeper come to Manoeuvring" came over the tannoy—calling Brum to report to the Engineer of the Watch. He didn't move.

"Brum" I said "That's for you"

"They're not using the right signal to call me"

"Upper Level Watchkeeper come to Manoeuvring" came again.

"Brum, they're calling you. Come on move it!" I repeated, getting annoyed now.

"When they use the right signal I'll go"

"What do you mean the right signal?" I asked, exasperated

"They have to use the Bat torch—I left it with them"

"Upper Level Watchkeeper come to Manoeuvring—now!" The Boss was getting annoyed now too.

He wasn't going to move, so I got up and headed for the Manoeuvring Room. As I walked in I was met by an angry looking Engineer and Charge Chief, and 3 sniggering panel watchkeepers:

"What the fuck is Brum doing Steve? Tell him to get his arse in here sharpish!"

"Er, he says you have to use the Bat torch to call him"

Silence

"He's rigged up a torch with the bat silhouette, you know, like in the Batman films, so it can be shined like a spotlight to call him" I couldn't believe I was saying this!

They both stared at me, blank faced. More titters from the front row.

"So, if you just shine it out into the Engine Room, he'll come running" I finished

"Are you shitting us?" asked the Charge Chief

"Go on—give it a go Sir" laughed the RPO.

The Engineer looked at me, and then slowly picked up the 'Bat Torch'—a standard 'Pusser's Right Angle' with a bat outline drawn onto the face with a marker pen. He clicked it on and shone the beam into the Engine Room. Brum instantly rushed out in a swirl of his cape;

"Batman to the rescue! How can I help the people of Gotham City Mr Mayor?"

"Brum, drop that crap and remember where you are!" said the Engineer "The costume is very nice but you can't stay on watch like that, go and change into your overalls!"

"Aw come on Sir" from the RPO "he's not doing any harm"

"Yeah come on Sir" this time from the Electrical Panel Operator "you have to admit it's different!"

"It's not a problem for me Sir" said the Charge Chief "so long as he can do his job ok"

"Can you Brum?" asked the Engineer

"Yes Sir no problem"

"You alright with this Steve—you'll have to keep an eye on him"

"No problem for me Sir, I'm used to the silly bastard!"

"OK then—but only for this watch, clear?"

So that was it then. He stayed dressed as Batman for the whole watch, and had a Lieutenant Commander Engineer calling him using a Bat torch every time he wanted to speak to him. It was the talk of the boat for weeks to come, and made his reputation as a first class nutter. I continued to serve with him for the next year or so, and it was a continual challenge—but in a good way.

Not quite so happy was my experience while a Chief of a family member passing away. It happened for the first time in 1993 when my younger sister Karen died. The boat was in Scotland doing another 'work-up' following a maintenance period, and in fact it was quite lucky that we had not sailed on patrol yet as I wouldn't have made the funeral. At the start of any patrol the crew were individually required to state whether in the case of the death of a member of the family they preferred to be informed at the time, or on return from patrol. I had always opted to be informed at the end of a patrol, as I considered that since there would be nothing I could do in any case, there was no point in knowing until the end.

In this instance we had been out for a few days, and on return to harbour I was called to the Captain's Cabin—a very unusual occurrence which instantly put me on edge. On entering his small cabin, I found him sitting at his desk and he invited me to take a seat on the bench which doubled as his bunk at sea.

'Chief Bridgman, I am afraid I have some bad news to pass on to you. I am very sorry to inform you that we have received news that your sister Karen has passed away. Please accept my condolences" he said without prelude. The best way I suppose.

The words washed over me, and left me confused. Karen dead? How could that be, she was only 25!

"Was it an accident Sir?" I asked—just to say something I guess.

"We have no details I am afraid. We have arranged for transport for you to get home, so pack your gear and don't worry about anything here"

"Er, right Sir. Thanks"

As I left the cabin I was met outside by the Coxswain. He escorted me to the bunk space and stood by as I packed some things and changed into civilian clothes. My mind was all over the place as the news sunk in and I was walked to the jetty and into a minivan which would take me to the train station. The sympathetic eyes of my colleagues followed me off the boat. A few muttered "sorry mate" as I passed—there were no secrets on boats. I managed to do the stiff upper lip bit until I was on the train heading south, but then had to shed a little tear for her passing so young.

I made it home in time for the funeral, and in time to hear the sorry tale of her death. She had been depressed apparently and had overdosed on her prescription medication. It was such a pity, and more so because had I known she was suffering perhaps I could have helped her. Another problem with being in the forces—you are never there to help out anyone. The funeral passed in a blur and before I knew it I was back onboard sailing for another patrol—one sister less. It was surreal.

At least I had made it to her funeral. In the case of my Step Father I couldn't even manage that! It happened a couple of years after Karen's death. We returned from a patrol, and once again I was called to the Captain's cabin to be informed that my Step Father had died—6 weeks before! Once again I was provided with transport home, rushed there in grief only to find that the funeral had taken place 5 and a half weeks before, and everybody was doing their level best to carry on with their lives. My delayed bereavement was now unwanted and very much out of place—I felt a total fool! It was very strange—when we had sailed I had a Step Father, but when I returned he was gone, and had been gone for a long time. I felt very much the outsider.

Life goes on of course, and I was expected to crack on with things on returning to the boat after these incidents—it was normally a case of "You ok Steve?" to which the answer was always "Yes", and on we went with everything.

I had got myself into a situation by now where I could take the examination for the Reactor Panel Operator. The first practical part of the test was terrifying—to actually sit in the seat and operate the reactor! Thankfully there was a fully qualified guy sitting very close behind me, and several pairs of eyes very carefully watched EVERY move I made for the 4 hour watch. I left that seat quite sweaty for the next man, but managed to survive and even to sound like I knew what I was talking about! The other part of the practical test was for me to conduct the daily reactor safety checks from the Switchboard Room. Once again I was heavily supervised but even so, standing there with the headset on, throwing switches and watching for the correct light sequences, I had the distinct feeling that with every switch I threw, the reactor was about to shut itself down! Once again the completion of the test sequence without any particular problems was a giant relief, and off I went for the theory part of the test. In this instance it was taken again by the Engineer and one of the Engineering Lieutenants, who put me through the mill—most of the questions designed to test my knowledge of the reactor protection system and its many and varied configurations. They both knew that it was my intention to try for Charge Chief, and took the opportunity to see how much I knew about the reactor theory and chemistry that I would need to pass the Charge Course. It was safe to say that while my knowledge was adequate to achieve a pass as RPO, I would need to 'boff-up' on the heavy stuff. They also made it clear that they were being easy on me on this occasion since I wasn't actually going to be watchkeeping as an RPO, but when I returned to do the exam again in preparation for Charge Chief, I would get the full treatment! This felt tough enough to me as it was! I was now qualified in all of the watchkeeping positions, and therefore ready to be sent away again to undertake the Nuclear Charge Course—the last and most demanding course I would take during my naval career.

While I waited for a slot to appear for me to attend the Charge Course, there was the small matter of the examination for promotion to Acting Sub Lieutenant to take. It had now been decided that potential officer candidates no longer had to be at the rank of Charge Chief to take the exam, and anybody at CPO and above could now do it—so much for all the hard work to qualify towards Charge Chief then! I had done quite a bit of studying in the year or so since I had decided to go for it, but of course 'a lot' never seems to be enough, particularly with all the other stuff that had been going on during the day job. Nonetheless, I sat the exam for the first time in 1993, but managed to fail by a couple of percent on that occasion. One thing that I did learn though was that this particular exam was a crippler—it lasted a mere 3 hours, which was shorter than most of the promotion exams I had sat to date, but the questions seemed to require about 3 hours EACH to answer! The skill in passing seemed to need a particular skill in being concise and very accurate. I would crack it next year! I consoled myself in the thought that out of about 15 people who took the exam that year, only 2 passed, so I wasn't alone.

Chapter 18

Bitten Off More Than I Could Chew?

As an official Charge Chief candidate I was sent back to HMS Sultan in 1993 to attend the Nuclear Propulsion Charge Course (or simply 'Charge Course'). The course was described by the instructors as the 'Premier Non-Commissioned Officers Course in the Navy', and right from the get-go we had it drummed into us that we were the 'chosen ones'. The course itself was another 15-weeker, and dealt with yet another higher level of nuclear physics and chemistry, but now with the added ingredient of the concept of machinery control, and taking charge of the entire propulsion system from the Manoeuvring Room. In its most basic form, the role of the Charge Chief was to take over the running of the entire nuclear submarine propulsion system in the absence or incapacitation of the on-watch engineering officer. This course set about teaching us how to do that.

The first couple of weeks were pretty straightforward, just revision of most of the subjects we had been taught on previous courses, or knew from our own onboard experiences. After that though, the pace picked up at an incredible rate, with the emphasis hanging from system knowledge to system and personnel control on the boat—it was expected that by this stage in your career you knew all about the machinery and equipment, and so not too much time was wasted re-hashing what should already be in the memory banks! In my case my electrical and reactor protection knowledge was barely adequate, and I had to spend a lot of time studying those subjects, while for many of the 'Greenies' the case was opposite—they needed to 'boff-up' on the machinery in the spaces since much of their time onboard would have been spent in Manoeuvring.

For all of us, the step up from Chief to 'bloke in Charge' was proving to be more challenging. From the start of the course we had been encouraged to really get to know the "Standard Operating Procedures' (SOPs) and perhaps more importantly the 'Emergency Operating Procedures' (EOPs), as we would need to know how to find specific ones quickly during the simulator training to follow later. We were all of course aware of SOPs and EOPs—they were the volumes the officers and Charge Chiefs referred to onboard all the time. There was always one or other volume open on somebody's lap in Manoeuvring, and some list or other was always being followed during operations. We out in the machinery spaces had extracts from the books for the specific actions we had to take during different operations, but I had never really seen the whole thing, and boy, there was lots of it!

In the case of the SOPs it wasn't too bad—mostly we just needed to know where to find the procedures for adopting the different machinery configurations that were possible. The change from one to another during normal operations was always done in a controlled manner, following the appropriate SOP. Our job in that case was to control the change, monitor the progress and be ready for any unexpected problems.

For EOPs it was entirely different. As the name suggested the procedures were designed to be followed during emergency situations. The idea was that when an emergency occurred, the engineering team would respond instinctively to make the situation safe, and then refer to the appropriate EOP to ensure all the actions that SHOULD have been carried out, HAD been carried out, and that the danger no longer existed. This meant that we all had to remember by heart the immediate actions for every known machinery emergency that might occur, and where to find the remainder of the actions to be carried out in the volume. It was a memory test from hell!

Still, not the entire course was pure study. About halfway through we got a bit of a field trip to get some background on nuclear reactor construction up at Rolls Royce in Derby. It was a 3-day visit and we got to look around their plant there. The place was enormous, and we were suitably impressed at the production techniques used there. It was particularly interesting to visit the local hostelries and to sample the strange Northern cuisine, and we came away from the place with a much deeper understanding of the variation and strength of the beer industry there too! It made a nice break from the books for a short while.

Reality soon came crashing back in though with the start of the simulator phase of the training. On the Charge Course there is a great deal of practical instruction, with each of us taking turns to be in charge during first normal, and later on, emergency situations 'onboard'. As always, it started off fairly gently, just to get us in the mood, but then rocketed upwards at a tremendous rate! It was at this point I suffered my first 'wobble' in my Charge Chief training programme.

The pace of the course had been pretty hectic from almost the start, a situation not aided for me by the constant expectation from the instructors that we were somehow 'better' for even being there. I think the pressure started to get to me then, and I started to have doubts about my own abilities. There were eight of us on the course, and all of the others were much more experienced senior rates that I was, even those Tiffs who were still many years younger than me had been senior rates for much longer than me. I had only been a senior rate for 4 years, and a Chief for less than 2 years and I was beginning to think that maybe I was rushing it—the rush of information coming at me seemed to be insurmountable and I was starting to lose my self-confidence.

It came to a head during the first simulator week. During this week the idea was to make sure we could all operate any of the machinery control panels in the Manoeuvring Room, so that when we were taking turns as the Charge Chief directing operating the panels could be manned by anybody. In theory I was qualified in all of the positions, but the difference between a paper qualification and actually sitting at the panels and operating them in every situation was enormous. I was ok with the electrical panel and the throttle panel, but the reactor panel was a whole different kettle of fish. After the first couple of scrams, loss of electrical power and single loop drills it was clear that I (and to be fair, the other mechanically based guys) were well behind the Greenies in the practical operation of the Manoeuvring Room. With perfect hindsight it was obvious that would be the case—they sat in there all the time while we were out in the machinery spaces!

In any case, it was decided that we mechanical chaps needed extra-curricular machinery panel instruction to get us on a par with the Greenies, before the 'proper' simulator training could continue. The training would take place in the evenings and into the night in some cases, and would continue until the instructors were satisfied that we were good enough to continue.

The training started soon after with one panel at a time, the instructors throwing defects onto the system and then us working out what the problem was, before attempting to clear it. The other 2 guys seemed to be benefitting from the extra training, but I was finding the going tough—I just couldn't seem to get my brain to work fast enough. I seemed to constantly be slower than the others in identifying the fault, and then deciding the action required to rectify it—my morale took a nosedive and I requested to see the Training Officer.

By the time I got to see the Training Lieutenant Commander I had managed to persuade myself that I was not good enough to be a Charge Chief, and that I would request to voluntarily be removed from course—it was the best option all round. I had been up most of the night, firstly in the simulator (another crap session) and then in my cabin pacing around loaded with nervous energy wondering what to do with myself.

The instructors are no fools and knew what I wanted to see the Boss about. It was clear to them that I was struggling with the simulator, and it was also quite clear that the whole thing was seriously depressing me. They had obviously briefed the Lieutenant Commander and he had in turn done a bit of background work on me, so that by the time I ended up sitting in front of him, he probably knew all about me.

Anyway he greeted me in a very friendly way and asked what the problem was. I tried in my inadequate way to explain my feelings of inadequacy and so forth while he listened quietly. When I had finished he seemed to be considering what I had said before replying.

"Steve, you are here on this course because there are a lot of people who think you are good enough to be a Charge Chief. I have been reading your career record, and while yes, you have not been a Chief for very long, while you HAVE been a senior rate you have proven yourself to be very capable. My instructors know that you have been having a hard time in the simulator, but listen, most of the mechanical guys we get through have similar problems because you don't have much Manoeuvring Room time—that's why we are giving you extra time in there, not as some kind of punishment ok?" It was probably what I needed to hear, and I felt a bit better as we chatted for a while longer before he said:

"Listen, it's almost the weekend. Go home, have a good rest, leave the books alone and come back on Monday refreshed and ready to go. See how you feel about it all then. You have come a long way in a short time—it would be a shame to give all that up now".

I went away for the weekend and did have a good rest without the books for once. I had decided over the weekend that I would continue with the course and see what happened. My wife told me to stop thinking about how crap I was and start thinking positively—if I was that bad I wouldn't be here now would I?—Easier said than done sometimes, but it did seem to help. I had a life-long tendency of inferiority, and I really needed to start to realise that I was at least as good as the rest of the guys on the course. Back at work and in the simulator things started to come together at last, and I was managing to keep my end up most of the time, although it remained a mighty struggle I can tell you. Nothing more was mentioned of my wanting to quit by either my classmates or the instructors.

The culmination of the course was a complete 'dummy' Charge Chief's Qualification Examination consisting of an assessed simulator session as Charge Chief, followed by an oral examination by the Training Lieutenant Commander and one of the Training Lieutenants—just as it would be onboard, except that the one onboard was held by the Squadron Engineering Commander. For me, the simulator part went surprisingly well, no major problems at all throughout the simulated machinery breakdowns. The session ended with the obligatory reactor scram, which I managed to deal with, getting the reactor re-started and main engines back on line within the required 30 minutes or so. The oral part of the exam took about 3 hours—much less than it would do onboard, and covered all of the major topics as expected—reactor start-up, how the water flowed through the reactor core, and reactor thermodynamics during different machinery configurations and so on. Nothing unexpected, but as the Board President quite correctly pointed out, it would be VERY much more difficult for the real exam onboard the boat. I believed him!

Once again I managed to rejoin the Tireless as a trainee. This would be my third continuous draft to the same boat—a very unusual situation, but one for me which was of course to my advantage. Since again I had not been away from the boat for more than 6 months it meant that I could immediately dispense with the Part III bit again—a small bonus in what would already be a difficult enough qualification process.

There was never any place for pure passengers onboard any submarine, and so I joined as a Charge Chief trainee, but with the position of MEAOW while I did my training. It was a position I was already qualified for, and so I could slip straight into the Watchbill. It didn't make the training regime any easier, but it was agreed that once I had qualified once more in all of the other watchkeeping positions, I would be released from other duties to concentrate solely on the task of passing the Charge Chief Examinations. It was a situation that suited me perfectly.

It did not take long for me to get back into the routine onboard as the patrols continued apace. While I had been away the boat had been in an extended maintenance period, and the first trip on my return was yet another post maintenance work-up. A pain in the butt but absolutely necessary to knock us back into shape after a lengthy break. For me this particular work-up had a new significance as it would be the first time that as a trainee Charge Chief, which meant that I would have a new role during action and emergency stations (unless I was on watch). The job of the mechanical Charge Chiefs was that of Attack Party Leader, whose job was to co-ordinate fire fighting, damage control and system isolation actions in the machinery spaces during emergencies. This was a totally new role for me, and as was usual practise I was thrown straight in at the deep end! I was attached to one of the Charge Chiefs for a couple of exercises and then equipped with anti-flash gear, endless systems maps, a long emergency breathing hose and portable radio and told to get stuck in at the next fire exercise. Sure enough at the next fire exercise—a fire in the engine room—I rushed headlong to the scene, and was promptly pronounced as overcome with smoke by the umpires. I had forgotten to put on my breathing mask before entering the supposedly smoke filled compartment. A stupid mistake that now meant the fire fighting team also had a casualty to deal with. They were not very happy bunnies I can tell you! As the work-up progressed though, I started to get the hang of it a bit more, making the required reports to the Damage Control Headquarters (the Wardroom), isolating systems and directing fire-fighting teams. It was a more exciting task than I used to have as the MEAOW, and I enjoyed it (apart from when I was being bollocked by the First Lieutenant for not reporting quickly enough of course!). It was exhausting work though as the pressure was always on to get the situation under control as quickly as possible. In addition for every emergency the ventilation would be 'crash stopped' and the doors and hatches closed, which meant that within a very short time the compartment became hot and airless, causing us to sweat our nuts off! After a few days of almost continuous emergencies, I was finding myself absolutely shattered.

I spent as much time as I could in the Manoeuvring Room both on watch and again off watch, trying to take in as much as possible of the ambience and routines in there. As a Charge Chief training I was finding that the officers and Charge Chiefs took a much deeper interest in my progress towards qualification, and never missed an opportunity to hit me with almost constant questions—some instantly requiring a response, but many needing some degree of research. The Engineer was the worst—deep questions about how the reactor plant reacted to this or that configuration, what happened inside the core while the plant was doing this or that, or how I would report some machinery problem to the Control Room or directly to the Captain. It was testing but really useful stuff, and certainly got me thinking much more deeply about what I had let myself in for. Another aspect that I needed to get used to was the operation and use of the whole boat communications and Machinery Broadcast systems. Obviously in my previous positions I had used the machinery broadcast (or 'gob-stick'), but usually merely to report something to Manoeuvring, or to respond to some order or other. Now though, I would be the one explaining things over the broadcast, or making sometimes quite long reports to either the Control Room or over the whole ship broadcast—it was very different when you were trying to think and talk sensibly at the same time. My superiors onboard recognised this and wasted no time in getting me using the systems from the Manoeuvring Room communications console. The more familiar I was with it, the easier the whole thing would be later. Initially all this new stuff felt like some sick torture, but it was remarkable how quickly things I had never done before became almost routine.

The first patrol after Charge Course gave me the opportunity to re-qualify in all of the positions except for Reactor Panel Operator, which I knew would be a much more testing proposition that it had been on the first occasion, which seemed like a very long time ago now. The patrol itself had been a very quiet one for the back-afties, and had been something of a routine one for the crumple-zone commandos too—just mooching around trying to track something interesting. For me personally it had been pretty busy on the studying front, and had seemed to pass very quickly. On return to Devonport I had taken that year's Sub Lieutenant Exam, and was very surprised a couple of weeks later to learn that I had passed it! It really was a surprise too—I really hadn't put that much work into preparing for the exam this time, although I had certainly made an effort to make my answers concise and to the point. Must have worked. I was disappointed to learn that I had not been selected for promotion that year, but now that I had passed the exam it was just a matter of time right? Wrong—the very next year the entire selection process for promotion to engineering Sub-Lieutenant changed. There would no longer be a written exam, but candidates would now have to attend a 2-day selection process at the Admiralty Interview Board (AIB). All that work to pass the exam now counted for nothing! I felt cheated and refused to attend the AIB.

Childish really, but I didn't see why I should have to prove myself yet again. That was the end of my ambitions to become an officer, and I reluctantly withdrew my CW papers.

I used the next patrol to concentrate totally on learning how to be a 'proper' Reactor Panel Operator (RPO). I was still at sea as an MEAOW, but now in my on and off watch time I had only to concentrate on collecting the knowledge I needed on the reactor panel. Of course I knew what each meter and gauge was showing, and what the limits of operation were for each one, but what I really needed to find out was all the background stuff about the reactor and systems—the real deep theoretical and actual construction of the thing and how fission really worked,

I am a simple man and liked to break theories down to nice simple processes in order to have some kind of understanding. The way I learned to think of the reactor and its operation was kind of like this:

The reactor core itself was about the size of a wheelie-bin—the rest of it was casing and radiation shielding—and contained the fuel bundle where the nuclear fission process took place. The fuel was arranged on modules forming a crucifix shape in the middle through which the control rods could pass up and down to control the rate of fission. As the primary coolant (water) flowed over and around the fuel bundles, pumped around using the huge Main Coolant Pumps (MCPs), slow neutrons collided with the fuel atoms, making them 'unstable' and causing an increased rate of decay of the fuel atom, which resulted in the fuel atom disintegrating and releasing some more slow (and fast) neutrons to perpetuate a chain reaction, some 'fission fragments' (which were bad—these were irradiated particles which gave off much of the environmental radiation on the boat), and most importantly to us, heat. The entire primary circuit was maintained under high pressure so that the heat (from billions of reactions constantly taking place) was used to raise the temperature of the primary coolant to a very high level—much higher than the boiling point of water. The primary coolant was then circulated around heating elements in the steam generators, where the heat from the primary coolant is used to boil the water which would be turned into steam to be used to drive the boat's main engines and turbo-generators for the production of electrical energy. The density of the primary coolant determined the rate of fission once the control rod positions were set—the cold, dense (in relative terms) water returning to the core from the steam generators contained more slow neutrons than the heated water leaving the core, and so the reactor was known to be 'self-regulating' at steady powers. If we wanted to reduce the rate of fission then the control rods were driven in using leadscrew motors on the top of the reactor, and the material of the control rods would 'soak up' the slow neutrons causing the fission, thus reducing the rate.

That was the basic process, but of course that simple (simple?) system required a whole array of back-up and supporting systems and procedures. There were a myriad of ways that the process could go wrong, with the worst case scenario being something called a 'Loss of Coolant Accident'. This was the thing that had happened at Chernobyl and 3-Mile Island, and was where the primary coolant was lost for whatever reason, leaving absolutely no way of controlling the fission process, leading to an uncontrolled increase of the core temperature, the reactor melting, which in our case would be through the bottom of the boat. We would all be toast in that event, and there would be a major 'nuclear event' resulting wherever we happened to be in the world.

That was worst case, but there were many lesser things that could go wrong too. In reality, the reactor and its systems comprised of numerous radiation protection equipments, making everything bulky and difficult to use, endless pipe work and electrical cabling, sensors, sampling gear, valves and protection logic circuits, all of which I would need to get to know inside and out. It was a daunting task requiring me to spend hours in the reference books, looking around the systems and equipment, and picking the brains of the Chief, Charge Chiefs and Officers who specialised in controlling the thing. It was endless and pretty much thankless too. I had thought I knew the back end of the submarine to a very great detail but quickly realised that what I knew was just the mechanical half—the electrical bit took up much less space, but had a much greater role in the control, and much more importantly, the protection of the reactor.

It wasn't only that aspect of the job that the Charge Chief and Officers (or 'Cat A's' as they were collective known) wanted me to know though, and from then on everything I did was laced with needing to know the 'wider aspects'. It was not enough for me to know how for instance a turbo-generator worked, but now that I was a Charge Chief candidate I also needed to know what happened when a generator tripped, what electrical supplies would be lost, how the steam generators would become unbalanced, how much extra load the remaining generator could handle, what sequence to restore electrical supplies, what instructions to give the Upper Level watchkeeper, how to restart the generator, what to report to Command. And this was for every piece of machinery and situation that might arise onboard—including those ones which were purely seamanship issues, like coming to and returning from periscope depth, surfacing and diving, floods and fires in other parts of the submarine and such like.

The Cat A's were very keen for me to get the lesser qualifications out of the way so that I could concentrate solely on the Charge Chief bit, and within a few short weeks of sailing I was once more sitting in front of the Engineers taking the RPO exam. This time was very different from the last time I has sat the exam, and I was pretty much brain dead at the end of the 8 hour marathon. In fairness it had been as much a transfer of information from the Engineers to me as much as an exam, but by the time they had finished with me I couldn't tell if up was down or black was white. Nonetheless it was yet another barrier passed, and the way was now open to finally concentrate on the goal of becoming a Cat A watchkeeper.

I spent the remainder of that trip, and the whole of the next in very intense studying, watchkeeping and on-the-job training in the Manoeuvring Room and on return to Devonport once more felt that I was ready to take the very intimidated Charge Chief exams. I would get a chance of some practice in the dreaded simulator before the exam, and as had become normal, the exam would consist of an assessed simulator session followed by an oral exam, this time chaired by the Squadron Engineering Commander, which would basically take as long as he decided it would take!

Marine Engineering Commander Jackson was the 2nd Submarine Squadron senior engineer. I had not had much to do with the man—why would I, but knew him by reputation to be a bit of a fire-breathing monster—particularly during examinations for which he was Board President. He was known not to suffer fools gladly, and was said to have a very low flash point. Rumour said that he was apt to dismiss candidates during exams summarily if he was dissatisfied with their responses, and had a tendency to bang tables to make a point! I had a bad feeling about this.

Still, I set about the simulator training with a will, buoyed up by the knowledge that I had done the drills many times now, but on live machinery onboard the boat. Of course I needed a team for the exam, and the guys selected from the onboard teams were excellent in backing me up in there. It didn't take long though for the old simulator gremlins to come creeping in, and in pretty short order I was back to struggling in the bloody thing! As was normal for me by now, I had problems with the bells, whistles and alarms in the thing, and just couldn't equate the simulator routines with what I knew to be real onboard. I worked my and my team's butts off to try to get it flawless, but could not get rid of an occasional tendency to cock-up now and then, having missed some indication or some spoken clue from the team that I should be doing something. It was about as good as it was going to get though, and no amount of additional training would get much of an improvement. Luckily my Engineer knew that I was better with the real thing, and told me that he would make that point to the Commander on the day of the race.

Before the actual exam, I did a full dummy with the officers from the boat, both in the simulator and with the oral bit. In the simulator I was brilliant, if I must say so myself! I was taking charge of everything, making good decisions and controlling the machinery systems well. For perhaps the first time ever, everything came together, and I was just totally on top of my game. I realised that the simulator really was just an actor's stage—what they wanted to see was a character in there, shouting, pointing, ordering and being in total control. On that day I was that man! This was followed by the full Monty with the oral exam, going from walking up to the boat in the morning to flashing up the reactor, sailing, diving, suffering myriad kinds of machinery and propulsion and whole boat catastrophes, to getting back alongside and shutting down the reactor. It was mind bending stuff, but again I sailed through it with confidence. The Engineer was satisfied that I was ready for the real thing "Have a day like today Steve and you'll piss it!" where his actual words as I recall . . .

It started to go wrong a few days later. I was on a high following the success of the dummy exam, and now had a date a few days hence for the real thing. As the day approached I began to feel the nerves a bit, but remained quietly confident. A day before the exam day, I was told there would be a delay for a couple of days as the Commander had some other engagement. No problem, keep cool, don't let any of that knowledge drain away (don't tilt your head in my case!). A day before the new date there was a further postponement for a week. I was starting to panic a little now. Do I look at the books a bit, just to do a little light revision? It had been almost 2 weeks now since I had been in the simulator, and I could feel my confidence slowly ebbing away. I had found through experience that for me to be good in the simulator I needed to be in it as much as possible. I managed to persuade the simulator instructors to wedge me into a slot the day before the exam—bad move. I was crap!

Finally the day came for the exam and I was like a cat on a hot tin roof. All the previous day everybody had been wishing me luck, and their expectations weighed heavily on my shoulders. The nerves were terrible as I entered the simulator like a condemned man. As I waited for the session to start the Commander and my Engineer walked in to brief me and the team. It was the first time I had met the man, and straight away I felt intimidated by him. He was small in stature but seemed (to my terrified eyes anyway) to have a perpetual scowl on his face, and certainly made no effort to put any of us at ease, but then why should he? We got the standard 'do your best Chaps' briefing, and before we knew it we were at 80 metres, half power state, 50 revolutions, waiting anxiously for the first 'shout'. I felt VERY alone and exposed!

The session started with the obligatory engine room bilge alarm, and pretty much went downhill from there! As the complexity of the breakdowns increased from simple loss of lubricating oil pumps, to single main engine drive, leading to single steam generator followed by loss of a motor-generator, I initially felt like I had a handle on things. I seemed to be making the correct responses, and the team were clicking pretty well—helping me out too with little reminders and nudges to finish bits off and to make briefings and such like in between the drills. It came to a head though when we got to the reactor scram. This was the usual end to a session so maybe we kind of drew a breath too early, thinking that the session was coming to an end. Whatever happened though, we had a nightmare. We took too long to get the steam valves shut and the turbo-generator off line, so that we allowed the temperature of the reactor to fall too low to allow us to conduct a quick recovery. That meant we were into a procedure called a 'full' recovery, which in real time took about 4 hours to achieve, and which subsequently meant that it was NEVER done in the simulator! I had no choice though other than to follow the procedure and start the process, hoping that what I had done so far would be enough for the Commander. It wasn't. Once I had us propelling on emergency propulsion and heading towards 'periscope depth', I decided that I would make a report to the Engineer. When I picked up the phone I found to my surprise the Commander at the other end of it—usually it was one of the instructors:

"Make your report Chief"

I reported what I thought had happened, and what we had done to rectify the situation.

"How did you end up at so a low core temperature Chief?" the Commander asked

"Well Sir, the RPO was a bit slow closing the Main Steam Stops, and none of us noticed that the stbd TG was still turning". I replied.

"Chief, you are the man in charge in there. I didn't hear you reprimanding the RPO—it is HIS job to do those things, right?"

"Yes Sir"

"Right Chief, report your intentions"

"Sir I am returning to PD using the Emergency Propulsion Motor—I have 3 and a half hours of battery life. My intention is to run the diesels at periscope depth, and commence a warm up of the reactor in accordance with SOP 101, reactor delayed start-up".

"Very well. Carry on".

I relayed the message that we would be continuing to the team, and I could see their shoulders slump at the news. We had been in the simulator for a couple of very intense hours now, and the thought of going through the delayed reactor start up procedure was a shocker. But there was to be one more surprise!

As I opened the books at the correct page, I picked up the microphone to the Control Room.

"Control, Manoeuvring. Permission to return to periscope depth and to prepare the diesels for running".

"Stand by Manoeuvring"

"Manoeuvring, Control. Permission to return to periscope depth and run diesel generators denied".

Denied? How could it be denied? If I couldn't run the diesels I could not restart the reactor. Shit, this wasn't supposed to happen! I picked up the phone to the Control Room:

"Control Room—Officer of the Watch" came back. It was the Commander again.

"Nuclear Chief of the Watch here Sir. Sir, I need to get to periscope depth and run the diesels so that I can make a reactor restart"

"Captain's orders Charge. We are not able to go to periscope depth for at least 4 hours due to tactical reasons. Please brief me on power options available for propulsion".

"Stand by Sir, I will report back in 5 minutes with options"

"No Charge, I want a briefing NOW!"

"Er, Roger Sir. Without the ability to run the diesels Sir, it will be necessary for me to completely shut down the steam systems to retain as much reactor heat as possible for the eventual start up. In the meantime I will need to ensure that we stop all unnecessary electrical equipment to reduce electrical load as much as possible to ensure we achieve maximum battery life. The battery life will be extended much more if we can reduce the Emergency Propulsion Motor revolutions Sir".

"Very well—carry on"

As I replaced the telephone, mentally ticking off those equipments I could afford to lose, suddenly the lights came back on, and "SIMULATOR STOPPED" came from the back door. It was over.

The Engineer stepped in, and dismissed the rest of the team. I thanked them as they left. They had been pretty good whatever the outcome. The Engineer told me to go and get a cup of tea and have a fag, and to report for the oral exam at eleven o'clock—in about half hours time. I was bricking it!

I managed to gulp down a coffee and to smoke a few cigarettes, but then found myself sitting in front of the Commander, my Boss and his Deputy, waiting for the torture to start. I was in my No.1 uniform, and the first order of business from the Commander, to my surprise, was for him to say:

"Relax Chief; we are not going to eat you! Loosen your jacket if you like".

"Thank you Sir". I undid my jacket and tried to relax.

Thus far he had proven to be far from the ogre he had been painted, and as the oral exam started in earnest, he seemed to have little interest in the proceedings.

The exam started with a debrief of my simulator performance, the Engineer leading the questioning. My decisions about this or that machinery breakdown were taken apart one by one and assessed, the Commander butting in with the occasional question, but otherwise seemingly quite bored with the proceedings.

Finally the Commander announced "That's enough about that—move on MEO", signalling the next phase of the exam. We moved on, just as we had during the dummy exam a couple of weeks before to the boat starting up and then sailing, and had just got to the 'starting the reactor' bit when the Commander decided to break for lunch.

"So far so good Chief, see you after lunch what?'

There was no way that I could eat anything, so for me it was back to the coffee and cigarettes. I stayed with the instructors in their office, who wanted to know how it was all going. I was feeling a little more confidence, especially so after they told me that the simulator session had not been quite as bad as I had made it seem in my imagination, so that when the officers returned from lunch I was revved up and ready to get this thing finished.

Immediately I went back into the room I sensed something different about the Commander. He was quite bright eyed and alert, much more so than he had been in the morning, and rather than letting the Engineer drive the exam, he seemed to have decided to continue the questioning himself.

We carried on then from where we had left off before lunch, only now with the Commander posing the questions. He had a quick-fire style, and routinely asked the next question before I had completely answered the previous one. I noticed that if I started answering the question confidently he would very quickly say "Right, right, let's move on!", and formulate a new question. The speed of progress increased greatly, and within a couple of hours my head was pounding. He had an irritating way of pressing a subject if he sensed that it was a weak area for me, asking deeper and harder questions until I admitted that I knew no more, until suddenly stopping, looking at me and exclaiming "That's about as far as we get with THAT subject then!"

I was still struggling to understand his complete change of character from that before lunch before the reason hit me like a sledge-hammer. The guy had been drinking over lunch! I could see it in his eyes which by now had become bloodshot. I felt he was becoming more abrasive too, starting to get quite animated when I stumbled over questions. I was getting more nervous by the minute too as I felt myself tripping over the increasingly difficult questions.

I knew it was all over when we started talking about main engines. We had already talked about the reactor and stuff, and were now on steam systems and the operation of the main turbines. I had memorised all of the temperature limits for the varying turbine stages, and was reciting them to the Commander when he stopped me with the now familiar "Right, right, move on. And why do we have these 'warm through' limits Chief?"

"They are there to prevent the turbines hogging and sagging Sir" I replied.

"I beg your pardon".

"If the turbines are not rotated in that heat they tend to sag Sir—it can cause the turbine blades to touch the stators if they are then turned".

The Commander looked at me, red faced and drew in a deep breath.

"MEO, did you say this Chief Petty Officer was mechanically biased" he asked through gritted teeth.

"Er, yes Sir, Chief Bridgman is a very experience mechanical technician". He was right; I knew what I was talking about with steam turbines.

"THEN WHY DOES HE NOT KNOW WHAT MAIN ENGINE TEMPERATURE LIMITS ARE FOR THEN!!!!" he shouted, banging his fists on the table for emphasis. The three of us jumped with shock.

I was totally confused and frankly frightened by now. We had been through these same questions a couple of weeks ago without any difficulty, and yet apparently I was now wrong.

"The temperature limits are there to MAINTAIN THE SPACING BETWEEN THE TURBINE ROTORS AND STATORS! You should KNOW that!!" He continued, again tapping the table with each word.

I looked at the Engineer with what he must have seen as desperation. Wasn't that what I had just said? He took the hint and said:

"Shall we take a short break there Sir?"

"Yes, yes, wait outside Chief Bridgman"

"Sir" I rose thankfully and left the room, surprised to find that it was now five-thirty in the afternoon!

I gratefully lit up a cigarette, and had noticed that the officers had not come out of the room after me. Going close to the door I could hear heated conversation from within, clearly a deep discussion taking place about me. The discussion continued for a good while before the room went silent. I moved away from the door.

The Deputy Engineer came to get me—he wouldn't look me in the face so I had a good idea of what was coming. I went in and sat down on the same seat after being invited to by the Commander.

"OK Chief Bridgman, I am going to end the Fleet Board at this point, and I am afraid that you have not passed on this occasion. I want you to know though that you put on a good show and that you are not too far away from being ready for Charge Chief. I have spoken with your MEO who is going to direct you in those specific areas I believe you need to look at more deeply. Come back in 6 months and have another go right?"

"Yes Sir" I hadn't heard anything after 'not passed'.

"Thank you Gentlemen. MEO I will speak with you tomorrow" The Commander rose and left the room.

The Deputy left next, commiserating with me and shaking my hand. The MEO stayed though and obviously wanted to talk to me. I wanted to go home.

"Sorry Steve, you were pretty close today, but there were just a few too many little things"

"What was that about Sir, with the main engines? We did the same stuff on the dummy and it was fine then!"

"I'm not sure, but its history. I know you're disappointed right now but it will be easier next time".

"Naw, bollocks to that, there won't be a next time"

"Well we'll see. Just go home and have a good rest. We can worry about that later. Don't be too gutted, you're not the first, and you won't be the last to fail the first time".

"Not feeling better Sir—see you tomorrow"

There was no getting around it—I was totally deflated and utterly disappointed. This had been the culmination of 9 months hard work, no; this was actually the culmination of my entire career! Fine, I would stay a Chief—the pay difference to Charge Chief wasn't much anyway, and why should I put myself through this crap again?

I went to work the next day as normal, and got on with my section duties. Everybody who saw me knew already that I had failed, and to a man they either gave me a "Sorry to hear that" or "You'll crack it next time". It made it all worse for me—I really hadn't realised so many people were interested in what I did, and it just seemed to magnify my disappointment. The Engineer obviously caught my mood and wisely left me alone for a few days before seeking me out. Within some days my mood had lightened slightly, although the humiliation still stung. I was adamant that I would not be taking the exams again, and bluntly told the Boss so. He again told me to think about it, particularly since Commander Jackson would be leaving his post in a few months time, at which time a new Commander would take over. The Boss had heard that the new guy would be a Commander Wright, apparently a much more affable man. The Boss would need a definite decision from me in the next couple of weeks. If I remained adamant that I was not going to have another go, then I would have to be appointed as an MEAOW onboard and a new Charge Chief Trainee brought onboard. That woke me up a bit, and made me realise that if I gave up now there would not be another chance—ever. Eventually I told the Engineer that I would give it another go, but under no circumstances with Commander Jackson. He immediately agreed and told me that I had made the right choice.

I started studying again at the start of the next trip, the intention being that I would re-sit the exam at the end of it, during the next upcoming maintenance period. Life continued for me, and for the boat much as it had done previously—patrolling the Barents Sea for the boat, and more studying for me! I was heartily sick of the books now, and felt like I was going through the motions with the practical stuff I was doing. I managed this time to get a lot of time in the Manoeuvring Room acting as the

Charge Chief on watch, and at least had the feeling that I was trusted by the Engineer and the other Cat A's, who allowed me to run the watch almost the whole time. We also got quite a bit of machinery breakdowns in, which was great practice for me for when I would once again face the simulator assessment as part of the Charge Chief exam. The whole thing was like a giant axe hanging above me. The previous experience had been something of a shock to the system, and secretly I was dreading a repeat performance. I had determined that the next time I would just up and run if we got into another desk banging situation—there was no way I was just going to sit there and take it this time.

Well, all of the well laid plans went into free fall a few weeks later. On completion of the current patrol the intention was that the boat would be undertaking a Docking and Essential Defects (DED) period. As part of the preparation for that, the boat would visit the ranges in Scotland for some pre-maintenance trials, and the new Squadron Engineering Commander would be coming onboard to have a look around the boat. While he was onboard, he would take the opportunity to conduct my Fleetboard for promotion!

It was a clever move on behalf of the Engineer actually. He knew that I hated the simulator, and that if I was going to cock-up, it would be there that it happened. By getting the Commander to take me through a 'live' board, that eventuality would be removed. For me, it was good news that I would be doing the drills on live machinery, as it limited the options for breakdowns that could be set—obviously nothing that could damage the machinery could be thrown at me, but on the other hand this was a real submarine and reactor I would be using, so no pressure there then. Also the whole boat would now be involved, since for emergency actions the whole crew would be required to man their normal emergency stations. This should be interesting.

In due course the Commander joined the boat by helicopter. I was introduced to him shortly afterwards. He seemed very affable, shaking my hand and wishing me luck for the exam. He had clearly been briefed by the Engineer, and knew my story. He encouraged me not to worry about it. Enjoy it, he said! Yeah, right.

The Cat A's selected a Manoeuvring Room team for me, insisting that they were the best onboard—I had no disagreement with that. I gave them a briefing, asking that they make sure they did their best and that they must report ANYTHING out of the ordinary to me immediately. I knew they would.

On the morning of the assessment I closed up in the Manoeuvring Room, nervous as a kitten and probably showing it. The situation was made worse for me by the close confines of the place, made closer still by the presence of the Commander and Engineer in the back corner, and to my surprise 3 junior seaman officers jammed into the back of the space, there to witness the process of a Cat A exam. I was asked if I minded their being present, but what could I say—they were there at the request of the Captain.

The Engineer gave us all a briefing, ending with the message to the panel watchkeepers "not to fuck the Charge Chief up!", which I am sure didn't do much for their confidence, and then we were off.

The drills came thick and fast, although initially they were fairly uncomplicated and easy to deal with. The complexity increased though as we progressed, and before long we were in single main engine drive, with a single turbo-generator supplying our power. This was followed by an exercise fire in the switchboard room, entailing the whole ship adopting emergency stations. As we recovered from these evolutions, suddenly I heard a commotion behind me. I turned and saw 2 of the junior officers squaring up to each-other, shouting and threatening to fight as a result of some argument. I had heard whispers that this might happen at some time during the test, and so was kind of expecting it. This was money for old rope:

"You two! Take that out of here—if you carry on like that I will have the both of you in front of the Executive Officer!" I saw the Commander nodding sagely out of the corner of my eye—excellent, that was the leadership and taking-charge bit in the bag!

Without further ado the reactor suddenly scrammed—as expected, and for the next hour we set about a recovery. By now I could do a reactor fast recovery in my sleep, and the team made the whole process a piece of cake. They were sharp, accurate and really on the ball—I hardly had to make any orders at each stage of the recovery, and each time I did, the response was instant. It all felt slick and very professional, and I could see that both the Engineer and Commander were content with the whole performance. This was the best start I could make. After they had left I made it a point to thank the guys in Manoeuvring and in the machinery spaces and I also phoned the Control Room to thank the forward guys too. It had been a cracking effort from everyone involved and I felt lucky to have been the recipient of it.

The oral part of the exam took place the same afternoon in the gyro compass machinery compartment—more or less the only place we could guarantee little or no interruption. It was immediately obvious that this board would be of a different nature to the previous one. The Commander was instantly involved, asking astute and very concise questions, but in a friendly way so that we were building up a story of how the submarine machinery operated to achieve the operational requirements, rather than just a set of disjointed questions—I was immediately made comfortable with his un-confrontational style, and although I probably didn't know any more than I did on the first attempt, I felt that this man was more willing to accept that I could not know everything. The exam in all took about 4 hours—he clearly took my previous efforts into consideration—and then I was told to take the horrendous wait outside. As before, the wait was interminable, especially with everybody walking past me in the passageway "How's it going Steve?", "You passed then or what?"

Eventually I was called back in, and walked in like the condemned man, searching their faces for a clue. The buggers stayed straight faced until I had re-taken my seat.

"Congratulations Chief, you have passed" said the Commander as he shook my hand. There followed a quick speech about this being the start, not the end of being a Charge Chief and the usual gubbins about responsibility, professionalism and stuff. I nodded at him like an idiot, but just wanted to go and celebrate.

The Engineer repeated the Commander's congratulations and added that I deserved it. He laughingly told me not to get too carried away—I would have my first watch as a Charge Chief in a few hours!

I didn't take too long for the word to spread around the boat—my big stupid grin would have been something of a giveaway! I spent the remainder of the day accepting congratulations from everybody, even the Captain stopped for a moment to wish me well in my new rank. It felt like a huge weight lifting from my shoulders, and the thought that I would never have to study for another promotion exam was a particularly nice one—crap of course—the studying NEVER finished, but just for now, it was a great thought.

Pretty soon I was taking my first watch as a Charge Chief. It was standard practice for the least experienced Charge Chief kept watches with the most experienced officer, and vice versa, so I found myself on watch with the Engineer. It was quite intimidating at first, but he taught me a lot about controlling machinery, and people. In addition to my watchkeeping duties, I now found myself in charge of all of the mechanical machinery stretching from the reactor compartment to the propulsor, and all the people in the Primary and Main Propulsion sections (2 Chiefs, 4 Petty Officers, 3 Leading Hands and about 6 or 7 Stokers). Part of the responsibility would now entail me writing annual appraisals on the Junior Rates, and assisting the Section Officers in carrying out appraisals of the Senior Rates, and the entire machinery maintenance and defect repair processes would be down to me! It was a lot to think about, but the section Chiefs were all experienced guys who I could rely on to get the work done correctly and on time, so I had no real worries there.

I now had to settle down into the job, and the ideal starting place was the Docking and Essential Defects repair period just coming up. For the next few weeks the boat would be in dry dock in Devonport having the bottom scraped and checked, and having quite a heavy maintenance package that I would now be responsible for tracking to completion—I would even be attending daily dockyard morning briefings and making them aware of any concerns the ship's company had over the work. It would be a stiff introduction to my new duties!

Just for a change I had underestimated the scope of the task! All my previous dealings with the dockyard personnel had been simply to assist them to find a piece of equipment, or to assist in a test that they might be carrying out onboard. Now though, it was a totally different kettle of fish. On the very first daily meeting I attended I was harangued as the boat's representative for not having somebody available for some test or other—difficult since I wasn't even aware that the test would be happening! As I was to find, this became a regular occurrence—take it all out on the ship's company. The dockyard guys had jobs to worry about, and so of course never wanted to 'look bad' in front of their bosses and so everything was our fault. From our side for some stupid reason, we stayed in duties rather than adopting the dockyard shift system, which meant that the duty men were being called by their dockyard counterparts to witness closing inspections and tests from the start of their duty period at 08:00 right until the finish 24 hours later, and subsequently were getting mightily pissed off at being called every couple of hours all night by the dockyard night shift. It was the same for the duty Cat A, either an officer or a Charge Chief, who had to sign off every single inspection or test. Of course he could only be in one place at a time, and it was not unusual to see the harassed man wandering round being chased by 3 or 4 'Dockies', eager to get the poor man to sign his bit of paper so that he could knock-off and get a cup of tea. The DED lasted a long couple of months which for me was probably the busiest I had ever been on a submarine. All the work got done though, and despite an incredibly steep learning curve (another one!) it would stand me in good stead for future docking periods, and for the major refit which was now looming on the horizon a few years hence.

Chapter 19

Life in the Fast Lane

It was straight back to sea after the DED, starting off with an extended Work-Up of the boat orchestrated by the dreaded Commander Sea and Shore Training (CSST) Staff, or 'Green Machines' as they were nicknamed due to the green foul weather gear they always wore. These guys were fellow submariners, specially selected for their training ability, who came onboard boats working up to put the crew through their paces.

For me this would be my first experience of a work-up as a fully qualified Charge Chief, and although I had acted as Attack Party Leader onboard for some of our own drills, this would be a whole new ball game. These people did not take prisoners, and were usually scathing in their criticism of somebody cocking up—be it the Captain or the lowest sailor onboard.

As soon as they came onboard up in Scotland the fun and games began. Even as their boat approached the submarine the drills started—with a simulated 'man-overboard' from their boat. Our casing party then had to fetch the man (dummy), bring him onboard and then the 'Doc' had to deal with him. OK so far.

As soon as that 'serial' had finished, the CSST staff, or 'Staff' as they were always to be addressed, started filtering back into the machinery spaces, so that we knew something was coming. Within a short while an exercise fire in the lower level of the engine room was announced, and off I leapt into action. Leaping down the ladders to the lower level, I was trying in my haste to put on my breathing gear, switch on the radio, carry my bags of equipment and shout orders all at the same time! By the time I got to the scene of the fire and approached the CSST man running the show there I was a tangled mess!

"What the fuck are you doing Charge? Are you the Attack Party Leader?" asked the Warrant Officer

"Yes Staff I'm Attack Party Leader"

"How are you supposed to take charge of the attack party when you arrive in that state?" he said, looking at my tangled hoses, system diagrams hanging out of my bag, radio lead wrapped around my neck and breathing mask half on and half off.

"Right. How long have you been Attack Party Leader Charge?"

"This is my first trip as a qualified Charge Chief Staff"

"OK that makes sense. Listen, you need to remember that in a real fire it is going to be full of smoke in the compartment, and the likelihood is that you will need to feel your way to the scene along the emergency breathing system pipe work, wearing your mask, so you need to have control of the hose. It's best to loop it around your shoulder and unreel as you go. As for the bag, get rid of everything in it apart from the system maps (there was a torch, set of spanners, spare radio battery and all sorts of other stuff in there), and put those in your pocket! When you reach the scene stand far enough back to let the fire-fighters through—you're in their way at the moment—and then clip the aerial extension from your radio to a piece of bare metal, otherwise it won't work. You are better off in the machinery spaces to use the machinery broadcast to send messages. The radios don't work very well down here anyway. Got it?"

"Yes Staff"

We stumbled our way through this exercise, the CSST staff stopping us frequently to offer criticism or advice. As always, the learning curve for me was pretty intense, and it seemed that for each exercise there was going to be my own personal trainer on hand to initially guide, but then to harass me as the scenarios became more complicated.

In fairness though, the advice they gave me on approaching and dealing with the varying types of incidents that could arise was priceless. Straightaway from the next fire exercise onwards the new routine of leaving the bag behind, sorting out my breathing hose properly and using the machinery intercom system paid dividends. I could move more freely, set myself up to actually control the situation much more easily, and subsequently communicate with Damage Control Headquarters accurately. As a consequence I was gaining confidence in the role and becoming much more effective as an Attack Leader.

After the first few days of the work up, where the CSST staff spent most of their time training us and reminding us of what we should be doing in certain situations, the mood changed. They now became much more driving and demanding, and rather than coach us on our actions, their attitude became one of criticism and antagonism—all part of the programme of course, and designed to induce stress within us. It worked.

For the next few days the boat took on a 'war' footing, as we hunted imaginary foes and dealt with the exercise damage inflected in the submarine by enemy action. It was exhausting work, for as well as the almost continuous exercises we were also carrying out our normal day jobs, in our shift system. It tended to be the case that there was peace and quiet between the hours of about midnight to five-thirty or six o'clock in the morning, so if you were lucky in the shift system to be on an 'all-night-in', or off watch overnight then you got a decent few hours sleep. If on the other hand had the 'middle' watch from 2300-0300, or the 'morning' watch from 0300-0700, it meant that there would be no sleep for you on that day. It was just a case of the luck of the draw, and for me meant that I effectively had no sleep for about 3 days. I had been tired before, but this was something on a completely different level. The stress and physical effort of being Attack Party Leader meant that rather than just being tired, I was physically exhausted as well. Every time I sat down anywhere I would instantly fall asleep, head lolling about and body slumped listlessly, only to be rudely awoken again a few minutes later by another 'shout'. It was relentless, and the CSST staff gave no quarter in their drive to make the boat ready for action.

The final day of the work-up was a full on, whole day action stations with us leaping from one emergency to another, and with the condition of the boat slowly deteriorating as the 'damage' intensified. It would not be wrong to say that we were driven to the edge by the continuous action, and the whole thing ended with the boat carrying out a real 'emergency surface' by blowing all of the ballast tanks, causing the boat to leap to the surface like a cork! It was a hell of a ride to the surface and I am sure that the whole thing jumped out of the water for a second! At the time though we were just relieved to have the whole thing over—all I could see in front of me was my bed. I had forgotten what the bloody thing looked like!

With the work-up over and the green machines waved goodbye (and good riddance!) we were off on another patrol. It was to be slightly unusual for this and a couple of subsequent patrols as we were going to be attached to NATO to be used for intelligence gathering from the on-going and escalating Serbian crisis. Once again this really was a job for the much smaller and more manoeuvrable diesel-electric boats, but since we had none left they were going to use us. Before we set off towards Kosovo we embarked a couple of Special Forces soldiers, both fluent in Serbo-Croat, and also experts at artillery spotting and calling in air strikes. Their job would be to monitor the radio transmissions that the boat captured using our ESM mast, interpret the communications and pass on any vital information to their commanders. Our job, it transpired, would be to get close in to land, and then use our periscopes and masts to get the information to the specialists. Sounded straightforward enough—we were pretty sure that the Serbs and Croats had no major navy, and in particular had no submarine force, so it should be pretty much unopposed.

As it turned out it was going to be a LOT more complicated. When they had briefed us that they wanted to go 'close in' to land, what they really meant was that they actually wanted us to get inside the harbour, raise the masts and then listen to the bad guys from there! I think they had watched too many old war films myself—with the old boats you could sneak into a harbour, plonk yourself on the sea bed, and the slowly rise to the surface to do the sneaky bit. It was a bit more difficult with a 5000 tonne displacement boat, about the same size as a modern frigate—and this was patiently explained to the communications guys. The best we could do was get in as close as the Captain dared to the shore, sailing up and down outside the selected harbour, masts raised and collecting data. Of course the equipment we now carried was way in advance of any previous listening gear and was quite capable of collecting anything the guys might want to hear.

After arriving in our operational areas we waited out at sea during daylight hours, and as soon as it got dark we headed in towards land. The Captain and Navigation Officer were visibly stressed as we approached the shore, relying on maps goodness how old and probably not updated with any vessels that may have been sunk during the current conflict. For this first attempt a closing the boat was at Action Stations, with us all closed up and expectant. We had been briefed that there might even be mines around some of the harbours we were likely to be visiting, and they were a truly scary prospect. We were comforted by the knowledge that if we did hit one we were not likely to know much about it, but the thought still put a chill up our spines. The sonar guys reckoned that they would be able to see them on their set well before they became a hazard to us, but we were not really convinced.

In the Engine Room we watched the depth gauges closely as the command took the boat further inshore. We were clearly rising, following the contours of the seabed, and we wondered to ourselves just how shallow we were going to get! Eventually though we sneaked up to periscope depth, stuck up our 'sneaky' mast, and started patrolling outside of one of the main harbours—the communication guys listening to the Serbian military radio bands and furiously noting down points of interest. They were happy as sand-boys doing their thing, but the rest of us, particularly the Control Room team were still a bit jumpy this close to land and potential conflict. We stayed there all night cruising back and forth, and then before dawn turned seaward and headed for deeper water. During the day, far out to sea, the communications specialists sent all of the intelligence back to the UK, and then got their heads down in readiness for the next night's adventures.

This routine continued for the next few days and nights, and the novelty fairly rapidly wore off for those of us not directly involved. After a couple of nights we were no longer required to remain at Action Stations for the entire event, which meant for us 'back-afties' life returned to pretty much normal—on-watch, sleep, eat, watch a movie! It was quite odd knowing we were in a known conflict area, yet here we were cruising just off the coast gathering intelligence at the front end of the boat, and yet doing our normal 'kicking the tyres' and 'checking the oil' at the rear end!

After we had been doing this for a few nights there was a bit of excitement. The boat was called to Action Stations at 'stupid o'clock' as a contact was identified on the radar, moving towards the boat at tremendous speed. We knew that the Serbian navy did have some fast patrol boats that would be intent on attacking us if they knew we were here, but this thing seemed too small to be one of them. As the contact streaked nearer, the Control Room boys desperately tried to identify it through the periscopes, but the boat was running without lights. Finally the Captain took the decision to pull all the masts and scopes into the boat and to head towards open water—we could all hear the powerful engines of the craft as it swept by, entering the harbour without slowing at all. As we crept away, relieved not to be the focus of the speeding boat, the command tried to decide what the boat had been doing flying around like that in the middle of the night without navigation lights. The night's work was ruined for us though, as it was too near to daylight to creep back in. Signals were sent off during the day describing our encounter, and the Boss was pretty annoyed when we received a reply from the Admiralty telling us that it was probably a 'Tobacco Boat', and oops, sorry for not warning you about them earlier! Apparently since the conflict had started, 40ft long speedboats had been coming across from Italy with contraband for sale to the people—speeding through the night laden with all sorts of goodies that the Serbian-Croats could not lay their hands on anymore. That was fine (well, not really, but what could we do about it?), but of course they posed a real danger for any vessels in their way because you simply could not see them coming. It was even more dangerous for a submarine sneaking around with its masts up close to land, and these things would prove to be a constant source of irritation for the Control Room team—they usually came along towards the weekend—I suppose the owners had work to do in the week?

The routine of sneaking in at night then retiring out to sea during the daytime continued day by day for a couple of weeks without a break, and the strain started to show itself on the sailors after a while. At the start of the operation they welcomed us into the Control Room to see what was happening, but as the weariness crept in they began to get a little tetchy. Pretty soon the guys on their way on watch back aft were made to stay well clear of some 'blackout' curtains the sailors had rigged over the navigational chart table, then we were told to keep the volume down on the TV, followed by the constant moans of the forward guys coming in the mess for a quick cup of tea during their watches. We of course had absolutely no sympathy for them—the tables were usually turned when we had a major machinery defect to deal with—we would be the ones rushed off our feet and tired out, while the crumple zone commandos lounged around laughing at our misfortune.

Still, what goes around comes around, and a couple of weeks into the operation we suffered a major defect that was both dangerous and potentially a show stopper. In steam systems there are always small leaks that you have to attend to, and usually they could be tightened for fixed without too much disruption to the operation of the boat. On this occasion though a steam leak was discovered on the bottom flange of one of the two main steam stop valves—8 inch valves that were the main isolations allowing steam to pass from the steam generator to the main steam range, main engines and turbo-generators. This was a dangerous situation as the valves are located at the front of the Manoeuvring Room flat, meaning that if the valves failed completely the Manoeuvring Room would be 'steam drenched' and all those watch keeping there scolded to death. This was such a worrying situation that one of the automatic reactor shut-down parameters included a scenario where just that happened! So we were protected in that respect at least. We needed to get it fixed pronto!

The Engineer briefed the Captain who agreed to stay out at sea for the repair process, missing one night's intelligence gathering close inshore. The sailors were happy for once as they would get a chance to have a decent rest while we toiled back aft, so almost everybody was happy with the defect—well, everybody except for me and the repair team who would have to get up close and personal with a red hot, leaking super tightened steam valve which we would need a sledge hammer to loosen, in a very confined space! Can't please everybody I suppose.

The repair process required that the starboard steam generator be boiled dry, and for the starboard steam range to be drained and de-pressurised to allow the repair team to open up the valve without steam escaping. This in itself was quite a detailed operation, known as 'Single SG Operations'. Since I was still the new boy Charge Chief, I would be the one following the operating procedure to get us into the required plant state, and this was where things were so different from the simulator. In real life, the process of transferring all the steam load onto a single steam generator, and thus throwing off balance the water flow through the reactor core, took several hours to complete safely, yet if we had to do it in the simulator it was done in a matter of minutes! This for me was the exciting thing about being a technician—controlling a live nuclear reactor and steam plant in real time. It showed the professionalism of all the people involved, without the need for silly voices and non-existent problems.

For me personally it was a nerve-racking but rewarding experience. First we had to put all of the reactor output to the 'good' port side machinery, which involved a very defined sequence of valve closure and re-routing of steam and water services. This is always a tense time as there is always a time lag between closing the valve and the required reaction being visible in the Manoeuvring Room—initially giving the impression that a certain valve or other was leaking! There followed a main engine to gearbox clutch operation, again something that had to be down in controlled manner to prevent damage to the turbine that was being disconnected from the gearbox. The electrical part of the programme was then to unload the starboard turbo-generator in a sequence of circuit breaker movements to put the entire electrical load onto the port generator and then to shut down the starboard turbo-generator. All went well to this point. Now that everything was to port, we needed to empty the starboard steam generator of the steam and water remaining inside it so that the repair team would not get burnt when the defective valve cover was removed, which involved 'blowing down' the generator, that is releasing the pressure inside it to sea. Of course since we were underwater, the pressure of water the on the outside of the boat could be substantial, depending on the depth we were operating, so via the Officer of the Watch I asked the Captain if the boat could come to periscope depth to reduce the outside pressure before blowing the boiler. At periscope depth the sea water pressure outside the boat would still be about 2 Bar, so it was vital that we stopped blowing the boiler at about 3 Bar, otherwise the sea pressure would be higher than the boiler pressure, and sea water would come flooding in through the boiler pipe work and into the boiler, which would be disastrous!

Before we started this part of the operation I very carefully briefed the MEAOW what the plan was going to be, and how far I wanted the boiler blown down. During this bit the Engineer kept very close to me, carefully ensuring I was doing everything right, and I felt quite grateful for his presence. Down in the Diesel Room, where the blowing down valves were located, the MEAOW had no accurate indication of boiler pressure, although he did have a boiler level meter. We would have to tell him when to stop blowing down from the Manoeuvring Room, but that would be difficult as the noise in the Diesel Room when we blew down, I knew from experience, was incredible. Still, he had his earphones on and so should hear us ok.

We hadn't conducted a real blow down at sea as long as I had been onboard, and so we were fairly unsure how long it was going to take to get the boiler empty. Finally, everything was ready and I gave the order to start blowing. For a few minutes nothing seemed to be happening, but I knew that the MEAOW had just cracked open the valves, and was letting the flow through them progress very slowly to start with, just to ensure that the pipe work leading overboard was properly warmed through. When he was satisfied that everything was warm, he opened the blow valves to their full extent.

With the blow down valves fully open we instantly got a feel of the potential energy stored inside one of the steam generators. The entire boat started to vibrate and even jump around a bit as the pressurised hot water and steam was released to sea, and the Control Room reported that the boat had started moving sideways under the force of the pressure release! The noise was remarkable throughout the boat, and I was instantly concerned that the MEAOW would not be able to hear the order to stop blowing, and so had another guy standing by to run down to the Diesel Room if necessary. The water level in the boiler started dropping straight away, while the pressure seemed to hang up as the blow down continued—it seemed to be taking a long time for the boiler to empty, and the next thing we worried about was whether the indication was accurate—the boiler emptying was quite an aggressive process and we were concerned that turbulence in the boiler might affect the sensors, particularly when the MEAOW reported that he had lost boiler water level indication in the Diesel Room.

After a few minutes, the boiler level and pressure both suddenly dropped dramatically, with the drop in pressure particularly, indicating that all of the water was now out of the boiler, and that it was now just steam being blown overboard. I picked up the microphone as the pressure dropped through 10 Bar, then 9, 8, 7 6 "Stop blowing down!" I ordered. No response.

"Diesel, Manoeuvring, STOP BLOWING DOWN!" I repeated. No response. Boiler pressure 5 Bar.

I frantically motioned for the messenger to rush down to the Diesel Room and to tell the MEAOW to stop blowing down. He seemed to take a dog's age to get down there, but finally we felt the vibration stopping, and the deafening noise lessening as the MEAOW closed the valves.

"Manoeuvring, Diesel, Starboard boiler blow down valves shut. Stopped blowing down. Sorry, couldn't hear you before" reported the MEAOW.

I looked at the depth gauge and the boiler pressure gauges, we were at 20 metres depth giving and outside sea pressure of 2 Bar, and the boiler pressure was reading at 2.5 Bar. The pressure differential had been sufficient to stop sea water coming into the boiler—well it must have been because we were not wearing the boiler, which is what would have happened had sea water managed to get in! We all heaved a sigh of relief, and I was more than happy to pass the watch over to another Charge Chief while I went to prepare to get the defective valve fixed—it would take a couple of hours in any place for the valve to cool down enough to be worked on.

The repair team was going to be led by 'Tiny' Large, one of the MEAOWs and the Chief of the Primary Section. He was large in name and stature, and a 2 lb hammer looked like a lollipop in his great big mitts! Right away it was apparent that he would not be able to personally get into the small spaces around the valve to fix it, and so he set about controlling the process from about 2 feet away, blocking the view and entry of everybody except the person chosen at that time to do the work.

First of all the huge lumps of silicone lagging had to be taken off the valve body, so that they could get to the parts that needed to be dismantled. It was a horrible task to cut the stuff away as it was hot, dusty and prickling if it got on to loose skin—which it inevitably did in the limited space around the work area! In addition to the discomfort it was important that the fitting of the lagging was remembered for when it would be put back on later—a reverse of the pain and grief, but important to keep the overall temperature of the boat down for everybody. Finally, with much cursing and yelping with pain as still hot metal was touched by fingers, the lagging was off and the guys could attack the defect itself.

We all took turns in inspecting the underside of the valve, and it was instantly clear from the grooves and discolouration of the bottom joint that the steam leak had been for this site. The lad quickly set about undoing the big bolts holding the bottom flange in place—again no easy task in the confined space under and to outboard of the valve body, Tiny shouting encouragement from the sidelines as one of the bent-double technicians held a large sawn-off spanner over each nut in turn as another tried to smack it with a short handled 14 lb sledge hammer to loosen it. Sweat soaked us all just watching the painful process, and it soon became apparent that we simply could not get enough leverage to loosen the bolts which had last been tightened using a hydraulic spanner in the dockyard years ago.

Finally, in frustration and sheer anger, Tiny ordered the knackered technicians out, and then preceded to wedge and manoeuvre himself somehow into the small space, picked up the spanner and sledge hammer, and commenced knocking tens bells of crap out of each nut in turn, veins popping at his temple and fore-arms, forcing them almost through pure venom to loosen. We all stood around looking on in amazement as one by one the nuts reluctantly released their grip until finally they were all removed, allowing the bottom flange to drop clanging on to the deck, and exposing the damaged spiral wound gasket seal inside the valve.

The heat and pressure of the escaping steam had carved a neat channel through the crushed steel of the gasket, and after carefully checking that the mating surfaces of the valve body and flange, the guys replaced the leaking seal with a new one, and commenced putting the bottom of the valve securely back in place—another wrestling match in a confined space. It was vital that that bottom flange was tightened evenly so that the new gasket wasn't 'pinched', and so poor Tiny had to go round in circles tightening each nut a little in turn, before moving on to the next and repeating the process. As the nuts became tighter this of course became more difficult, and we could see him straining like crazy to gain good purchase on each one. Finally after what seemed like ages we passed in a piece of cut-off scaffolding bar to him so that he could get the final tighten down done. At the end he declared that the flange was as tight as he could make it, and we literally had to drag him bodily from the small area he had wedged himself into. He was totally wasted and sat there shaking with fatigue as drinks were passed to him. As soon as he was out one of the Petty Officer Stokers set about replacing most of the valve lagging, just leaving off the bottom section so that we could ensure the valve didn't leak again later on. We were now ready to test the valve and get back on station.

The biggest cause of valves leaking was 'water hammer'. This was where, during warm up, water was either allowed to settle, or was not allowed to drain away so that when full steam pressure was applied, the water became a heavy blunt weapon that smashed its way through the steam range and through the system valves. It was something we were always guarding against, and was easily avoided by taking a nice long time to warm up the steam system when we started up. Some of the younger officers had a tendency to want to 'crack-on' and get the steam pressure up as soon as possible (mostly to please the Engineer), and it was a constant struggle to persuade them that it really was better in the long run to take things nice and slow!

In this instance the side of the system that was still operating was already up to temperature and pressure, and so to heat up and pressure test the repair all we would have to do was to crack open a connecting valve, and slowly bleed the live steam into this part of the steam system. While that was happening and the pressure was slowly rising we could watch the bottom of the valve, and just make sure there was no leakage. As the heat and pressure increased the area of the new seal bubbled and popped as the sealing agent bedded in, but there was no new leakage from the bottom of the valve. It seemed like a good repair, but because the valve was so vital we decided to 'soak' it for a couple of hours before declaring the job done to the command.

After the hours had passed without any leakage from the bottom of the valve we could carry on and get the machinery back to normal. With perfect hindsight we perhaps should have replaced the valve lagging a tad earlier, as now that the system pressure and more importantly heat was back to normal, we had serious problems getting near enough to the thing to replace the remaining pads around the valve bottom. The guys persevered though, and attached the pads using seizing wire and no small amount of cursing!

We had been at this job for almost an entire day now, and the sailors, having had a nice rest were now chomping at the bit to get back to the operating area. The Officer of the Watch in the Control Room was by now ringing the Engineer Officer of the Watch every half an hour asking for updates and estimates of when we would be finished—much to the annoyance of everyone working so hard! They had seen some of the lads going forward for a well deserved sleep and were assuming that the repair was done. In reality though, it was going to take us another couple of hours to get the machinery systems back to normal. As was always the case, the sailors failed to understand the complexity of the repair we had just carried out—it was one that was well beyond the capability of the tools and equipment we carried onboard, and what we should have done was to return to port to have it carried out by the dockyard. What we had done was to carry out a major repair, at sea, in an operational zone, in less than one day. The operations staff should have been slapping us on the back and giving us hardy congratulations for a job well done, but as usual it was "took your bloody time didn't you?"

Following the repair we had a chance to get our heads down while the sailors took the boat back towards the shore for another bout of intelligence gathering. The drama was soon forgotten as we got back once more into our schedule of nights inshore listening to the radio 'chatter', followed by the days far out to sea regrouping and getting ready for the next visit.

The only other bit of excitement I recall from that particular trip involved an unplanned detection of a small diesel electric submarine during one foray into close proximity to the harbour entrance. I happened to be passing through the Control Room going off watch, when I noticed how tense everybody was and decided to hang around to see what was happening. Of course it was always fairly tense in there anyway when we were this close to the opposition, but this was tenseness on another level. I managed to corner one of the guys who told me that sonar had detected a diesel electric submarine on the surface not too far away from us out to sea. One of the very few foes that scares a nuclear submarine crew is a diesel electric boat—they are literally dead silent underwater, and notoriously difficult to defect. In comparison, we felt like a large clockwork toy even when we were in the 'dead quiet' state, and felt that a really quiet diesel boat would have no trouble finding us. This was not usually an issue for us when we were out in the huge oceans and seas, but in restricted water it could make us feel very nervous indeed. It was also not a problem while the diesel boat was travelling on the surface—she would not be able to detect anything over the noise of her own engines—but if she dived it would be a different story!

The first mystery though was of another order. Who was this boat and what the hell was he doing in the same bit of water as we were now occupying? The officers were frantically shifting through their copies of 'Jane's Fighting Ships' trying to determine if the Serbo-Croats or Kosovons (if that's what they were called!) might have had any left over Yugoslavian navy diesel boats—if the Yugoslavian Navy had had any submarines in the first place. If they did have, did their presence here mean that they suspected that a foreign boat—i.e. us!—was on their turf as it were? This could all get very messy indeed, and there was a lot of worried looks passing between the grown-ups. Our super-duper sonar system was supposed to identify to the command what type of boat it was, but it was pretty clear that nobody had a clue.

The decision about what to do next was made for us by the other boat—they dived! That pretty much put us in a position of vulnerability, and the decision was taken straight away to get the hell out of there. We turned out to sea and moved our tail—our big advantage over the diesel boat was that we were much quicker than they under water, and we used that advantage to good effect! We lost another night listening, but there really was no alternative. I don't think the other boat was ever identified, but it seemed that it didn't hang around because after a couple of days we began going back in as normal, and never seemed to encounter it again.

The routine continued for another couple of weeks, and then all of a sudden we were heading out to sea for the final time—it was the end of the operation. The 'sneaky-beaky' boys left us by helicopter a couple of days later, and certainly at the back end of the boat we had no idea whether they had gathered any important intelligence over the weeks, which of course was fine by us—we just moved the thing around!

While the operational part of the trip was now complete, we would not be heading back to Plymouth just yet! This trip had in fact been the last operational trip of the submarine's first commission—we were heading for the boat's first refit. She had now been in effectively continuous operation for about 12 years and was starting to show her age a bit. This was probably mostly in evidence with the reactor itself, which after this long in operation was now in need of being refuelled. The refit itself was a 2 and a half year process during which most of the current ship's company would be sent away—some to rejoin on completion and others not, where the entire boat would be broken down to bare metal and effectively rebuilt. I already knew that I would be one of the people staying onboard through the refit, and had been allocated a role in some of the pre-refit testing we would be undertaking before returning to Plymouth.

The pre-refit testing programme started after a short visit to Faslane in Scotland where we picked up a load of Plymouth Dockyard test engineers.

They would come to sea with us for the trip back down to Plymouth, while on the way they would, with our help, put all of the boat's systems through their paces—the idea being to be able to compare the performance of the boat before and then after the refit.

As soon as we were out of harbour the testing started. The dockyard guys wanted us to set up the machinery in various configurations and then set about taking banks of readings and data as we then ran the different set-ups as they required. Right from the start there was a difference in what they and we wanted, and that would continue to be a theme throughout the entire refit process. While there was absolutely no doubt that the dockyard engineers knew the machinery inside and out, they had absolutely no operational awareness, and would request the strangest set-ups seemingly from nowhere, with no consideration as to what the boat might be doing at the time. They would want us to shift to single main engine drive just as the boat was traversing through some restricted navigation area, or was in close proximity to surface traffic, which would mean that we temporarily lost propulsion! While their dedication was admirable, we found that we had to be wary of their test programme while we were at sea, and once we had got into the idea that the responsibility for the boat still very much rested with us, it was fine. Another thing that wound a few people up was the attitude of the dockies while they were in the mess. Normally mess life was nicely structured and organised, particularly at mealtimes when those about to go on watch would eat first, followed by everybody else in turn. The dockies didn't tend to subscribe to that system though, and would come in, plonk themselves down and then expect to have a nice relaxed lunch or dinner, taking their time and having a nice chat. We explained to them nicely that there simply wasn't time to do that, and if they wanted to sit around and take it easy they could come back after the meal, and after some time they started to get the idea, but that was after a few backs had been put up. I think the problem was that we had been a close-knit team for quite a while now, and we simply didn't like outsiders encroaching into our little world. It wasn't the fault of the dockies—they were just doing their jobs too I guess.

The trip back to Plymouth was one of mixed emotions for many of us. The tests and trials kept many of us busy, but there was still time to reflect of what had been and what was still to come. For me personally this was the final trip after being on the same boat more or less continuously for the previous almost 10 years. With the exception of the various courses I had attended over the years, I had been pretty much on every trip the boat had been involved in, and so in a strange way I was going to miss the routine of preparing for sailing, going out and then returning to port. Also there was the consideration that the current crew would be breaking up—it had been one of the best crews I could recall so it would be sad to see everybody going their separate ways. The other unknown was the refit itself—nobody onboard at that time had ever been involved in one, so we were not sure what we would be doing. Most thought it would be a 'loaf' for those remaining with the boat, although nobody had any real reason for thinking so! I wasn't so sure myself, and suspected (rightly as it would transpire) that as with everything we seemed to be involved in, there would be no such thing as a free lunch!

As usual with these things, there always seems to be more work programmed than time to complete it in, and as we got ever near to Plymouth the pace of the testing increased, so that it seemed we were whipping through them one straight after another. The final testing phase of the run down was a full power trial, first submerged and then surfaced. They were always great fun, and there was nothing better for us back-afties that running the propulsion machinery at full tilt—the entire boat was shake rattle and roll, and it was a nice reminder to everybody onboard that we still had the power onboard! It was an apt way for us to end the first commission, and we sailed into Plymouth with our long de-commissioning pennant flying proudly from the short flagstaff erected on the top of the fin. The Tireless had earned a rest after 12 years of almost continuous service, and would emerge from refit a much more capable submarine for the future.

Chapter 20

A Change is as Good as a Rest—Apparently!

The refit was billed as a rest for that crew remaining onboard, at least for the first 2 years of the 3 year refit period. It would be a chance for me to achieve a bit of home life stability for the first time since my apprenticeship almost 10 years before. As soon as the boat was officially taken out of commission most of the ship's company disappeared, leaving only the majority of the engineering department onboard to assist the dockyard in getting the boat into dry dock and then tearing it to pieces!

The boat was taken into 5 basin almost straight away to carry out pre-refit preparations. The remaining ship's company set about putting all of the loose equipment, ranging from anchor chains to tool kits remaining onboard into a large 'lock-up' on the shore side which had been allocated to us for the purpose. It had been intended that this process would be properly controlled with everything catalogued, tallied and carefully stored away for easy retrieval later, but as always the process turned into a 'pot-mess' as the dockyard pressured us into getting everything off double quick—everything ended up in a pile in the store to be 'sorted out later'. It never was of course, and we had nightmares at the end of the refit putting it all back in place. This would become typical of our relationship with the dockyard throughout the refit—we wanted to slow everything down (as they saw it) in order to ensure life would be easier later, but they were only interested in achieving what they were supposed to each shift (as we saw it). Everything became last minute rush jobs—new deadlines appearing from nowhere each morning at the 'Daily Planning' meetings attended by dockyard and navy representatives. This was just the start of the refit and it wasn't long before we were managing to piss each other off, and on a couple of occasions this resulted in fierce arguments and even a bit of pushing and shoving between Matelots and Dockies onboard the boat! The more easy-going Dockies laughed it off, and assured the less hot-headed of us that this was a normal process, and that things would calm down as the refit progressed. It was certainly clear that we had to get used to being in a different environment than we were used to!

Within a very short time the boat was safely in dry dock in the Submarine Refit Complex (SRC). From the moment the last inch of water was pumped out of the dock the dockyard mateys swarmed onboard in droves and just started ripping the boat apart. In the case of the forward end of the boat, this was literally the case as all of the partition bulkheads were smashed down and carted out piece by piece, finally leaving the forward end of the submarine completely barren of any bulkheads, partitions, messes, galleys or heads, or indeed anything that was not welded on to the bare metal hull of the boat. In the space of a few short weeks the front of the boat had been stripped bare, and a huge access hole had been cut in the side of the boat for the removal of machinery later on. Those of us remaining onboard had seen the boat go from a smart seagoing submarine to a hulk in no time—it was really quite unsettling! We had to rush onboard at one stage and take down all of the boat's trophies, emblems and shields before the dockies ditched them!

It had been something of a similar process at the rear end of the boat too. It all started with a complete de-lag of each machinery space, leaving every piece of pipe work, big or small, unusually exposed and shiny. The Engineer was naturally outraged at the mess this left behind, and more particularly by the lack of concern for cleanliness shown by the dockies. Following the delagging, lengths of pipe work started being disconnected and then removed from the boat until finally there remained just the big pieces of machinery in the spaces—which by the way became very spacious with all of the pipe work removed.

This entire process took weeks stretching eventually into a number of months, and our job throughout was really just to maintain a watchkeeping pattern over the still operating nuclear reactor, and to try to keep an eye on the health and safety of the people onboard—a difficult job as the dockies seemed not to give a toss on that score, leaving piles of oil soaked rags lying around, or lumps of wood left for people to trip over, or Welders happily cutting away chunks of metal above open fuel tanks! We brought these things to the attention of the supervisors but were generally roundly ignored for our pains.

While all this was going on the remaining ship's company had moved into a dedicated navy personnel refit office and accommodation building ashore. As a Charge Chief I now had my own desk and computer to play cards on, and the building also contained Senior and Junior Rates Messes, sleeping quarters and galley for the duty personnel. In no time we had set up the mess with beer and a TV, and it would become our home from home for the next 2 and a half years. As it turned out, I wouldn't see much of the sleeping quarters as when I was the 'Duty Cat A'—about 1 day out of every 6—I would rarely have the chance to get any sleep. The dockyard still worked their 3 shift system which meant that the duty guys would receive phone calls to attend some tank closing inspection or to witness some test or other around the clock.

For the first 9 months or so of the refit life was very nice. I effectively worked a 9 to 5 job, apart from the duty days of course, and it was very enjoyable to be home for more than a few weeks at a time. It even got to the stage where I was actually commuting to work each day, and I even took the opportunity to get a pass so that I could part my car in the dockyard car park, something I had never bothered with before. On the home front we started living like normal people, going out for meals and having weekend breaks and normal stuff like ordinary families do. It was something I could, and was, getting used to, and it seemed that the promised rest we would have during the refit was coming true—I certainly felt refreshed in any case.

All of that came to a grinding halt about a year into it all, at the start of the reactor defuel and refuel process. As the Mechanical Charge Chief I would be required to monitor the entire process, and once the new fuel was installed in the reactor there would be a whole bank of tests and trials required to ensure it was all operating correctly, followed by the first reactor start-up, power trials and goodness knows what else.

In an ideal world I would be capable of being split into 3 people, so that I could have been present during each shift of the defuel/refuel process, but of course I couldn't. At the start of the operation it had been decreed that a Cat A had to be present at all times, but after a few days of the officers and Charge Chiefs going into shifts and becoming mightily annoyed at having to do so, it was finally conceded that the Cat B's (Chiefs) could also be included, meaning that we could skip back to duties instead of shifts. For me personally though it made little difference because as the responsible Charge Chief I had to spend a lot of time on scene in any case. From that point on, whether I was duty or not, I tended to spend very long days at work. My refit rest period was well and truly over!

As you might imagine the nuclear reactor refuelling process was quite a complicated affair. In reality the navy guys had no input into the process other than getting in the way of the dockyard specialised refuelling team. We were required to monitor radiation at certain points around the boat, including in the Reactor Compartment during the whole time that anybody was working down there, which was practically 24 hours a day. In addition we were supposed to 'monitor' the progress of the entire operation, which was quite difficult since most of the time the dockyard did their own thing according to their own procedures, and not usually bothering to inform us of what was going on. I had at least had the opportunity to read the procedures before hand and knew that they were well practised systems so I wasn't too concerned. These people were professionals, and certainly didn't need the likes of me telling them what to do so I stayed pretty much in the distance, just watching and learning.

The entire defueling part started quite slowly really. For a start they didn't want to even think about touching the reactor core until the system had settled down for a good number of months. This would ensure that as much as possible of any dangerous radiation had had a good chance to naturally decay before they started working close up and personal with the thing. A good 9 months to a year into the refit the actual defuel process started with some pretty nasty chemicals being injected into the water circulating around the reactor core and systems. Their job was to act as a kind of bleach inside the reactor to get as much of the dangerously irradiated internal components as possible into the circulating water before the core was drained—again to reduce as much as possible the exposure of the guys working there. After that it was 'simply' a matter of lifting the top off of the reactor pressure vessel and removing the spent fuel rods, putting them into special containers for transport for recycling, and then replacing them with nice shiny new fuel rods. This was definitely a process that we had no input into whatsoever, and it was all done behind very securely closed doors by highly qualified (and hopefully highly paid!) nuclear technical types specially trained for that task, and that task alone. They were very welcome to the job as far as we were concerned and we had no difficulty with the instruction to stay well out of the way!

We rejoined the process once the reactor pressure vessel had been screwed back down nice and tightly. It was quite strange being around the newly refuelled reactor since as the control rods had yet to be raised for the first time; it was effectively benign and required no extra precautions against radiation at that stage. There then followed a series of flushes of the newly installed fuel bundle using very clean water, to ensure that no minute particles of anything had gotten inside the system which could become irradiated later had sneaked in, taking several weeks to complete—all the time with scientists taking samples from here and there, analysing it, taking notes and comparing against graphs. All must have been well though as we seemed to keep on going at some pace.

Finally, and following the installation of some pretty serious monitoring and recording equipment, it was time to start the reactor for the first time. This was a very tense process with some serious Tefal-heads taking over the control of the reactor for the process. Once all was ready the control rods started being withdraw slowly in a pattern carefully designed for even fuel burn-up and minimum radiation and all sorts of other painstakingly calculated parameters. There was silence and intense concentration on meters, dials and gauges as millimetre by millimetre the rods started moving. Records were made, and clipboards were brought to the fore as everything progressed just as it should. It was kind of one of those 'A bus has crashed, nobody injured and no damage caused' moments—everybody was tense, but everything went exactly as, well, it was supposed to! There was some serious planning involved in the whole thing, and nuclear reactors are not the sort of thing where you want excitement really I suppose. Anyway it was a case of "Its all yours now Chaps—do look after it won't you?" and off in to the sunset went the reactor refuelling team leaving us with a nice new one to play with. For us it meant that from now on, there would be somebody watching the reactor for the remainder of the submarine's 2nd commission—the next 12 years or so!

While this had been going on there was also activity around the rest of the boat as newly refurbished machinery and equipment started making its way back onboard. With every piece of gear that came back, there would be an associated installation inspection, followed by some kind of commissioning trial, test or procedure, all of which somebody from the navy side had to witness. At first this was no problem for us as the gear was returning at quite a slow rate, but as time progressed things became more hectic. Later on in the refit it was not unusual to see one of the Chiefs or Petty Officers with a trail of 5 or 6 dockies chasing behind him, wanting him to go and sign off this or that test, until it got to the point of us declaring that if a test was not programmed in the morning meeting, we would not witness it. This caused uproar with the dockies, but as always they had a way around it and simply started forging the signatures of some of the navy guys! This we discovered by accident when one of the Chiefs saw his own signature on a form, and realised he had been away on leave on that particular day! There was no apology from the dockyard who insisted they had a schedule to keep, so we countered by giving the inspectors stamps to use—it seemed to solve that problem (who knows?).

Life in refit wasn't all work though and we had a few decent nights out and sports activities while we were there. With the reduced numbers of people onboard the boat there was not too much work for the mess officials to do, and I was cajoled into taking the post of Mess President for a while. I agreed reluctantly since I kind of suspected it might end in tears, and sure enough, a couple of months later it did. We had organised a bowling night in HMS Drake's Senior Rates Mess skittle alley one evening, and before going up to the place had decided to have a couple of pints in our own mess. On reaching the skittle alley though we found that the place, which was supposed to be ready for us, was still in a shambles! As Mess President it was felt that I should make some complaint to the organisers, and so I made my way to their office to do just that—feeling brave after a couple of pints I suppose. Anyway on getting to the office I spoke to the lady there who told me in no uncertain terms that we had booked the place from 6 pm, not 5 pm which was the time we had arrived. She was as adamant as I was, and we had a bit of a set-to about it, which ended with me perhaps more forcefully than I would have wished, asking here to *please* open the bar in the skittle alley. She was not a very happy bunny though, and was not slow in telling me so either.

We had a very nice evening, but the next morning sitting at my desk and nursing a slight hangover I received a phone call which went something like this:

"Hello, SRC, Charge Chief Bridgman speaking".

"Bridgman. Are you the Mess President from the refitting submarine?"

"Yes, that's right. Who's asking?"

"This is Warrant Officer Graham—Mess President HMS Drake. I have been told about what happened last evening and I can tell you I am VERY pissed off. You do NOT verbally abuse my staff sonny boy, and I can tell you that I am going to be phoning your Commanding Officer and stating a complaint about your behaviour! I would rather just smack you in the teeth personally, since the lady in question happens to be my wife, but unfortunately I am not fucking allowed to!!"

"Sir, look, do I at least get to put my side of the story?"

"No you fucking do not!! I have witnesses here who tell me you verbally abused the lady, and I believe them a fucking sight more than I believe you! We are trying to provide a service here and I do not expect senior rates to come along here and upset my staff. I will be making sure that you for one will not be doing THAT again!"

"Sir, I promise I never meant any disrespect to the lady, I was just surprised that the place was closed, that's all"

"So, you felt that you had to take it out on somebody did you? I tell you, it's lucky for you I was away yesterday or it would have been a different story I can tell you. I suggest young man that you had better write a letter of apology to the lady, which had better be on my desk by 10 am this morning. Clear?"

"Clear. Sorry."

"Don't tell me, save it for the letter. Dickhead!"

I shakily put the phone down. My hangover was suddenly much worse. I didn't remember being *that* horrible, and as I *did* recall, she gave back pretty much what she got! Anyway I was left with no choice in this instance and set about writing a nice apology letter, explaining that I really wasn't normally like that and apologising profusely for any offense et cetera. I put the letter in an envelope and set off towards HMS Drake to deliver it, cleverly (I thought) buying some flowers and chocolates (from Mess funds of course!) from the NAAFI on the way. On reaching the lady's office (there was no way I was looking for the Mess President—he sounded a bit too annoyed for my liking) I was hit by a wave of embarrassment and knocked on the door like a nervous schoolboy, expecting a bollocking and serious derision. I was preparing to eat a rather large slice of humble pie, but instead I was surprised to hear a cheery "Come in" from the other side of the door.

I entered and went straight into my 'I'm Sorry' speech I had been rehearsing all the way up from the dockyard. The lady sat and listened to my sob story with a slightly amused expression, and when I had finished said:

"Oh don't worry—it happens all the time—you guys have a couple of drinks and get all mouthy. No harm done. Did you have a good night then?"

"Er, yes—thanks. Anyway these are for you, and sorry again. I really didn't mean any offense"

I got out of there double quick while the going was good and rushed back to my desk. There were no further phone calls from the Drake Mess President, and I wasn't called in to explain myself to the Commanding Officer so presumably honour had been satisfied. I hurriedly (and to everyone else) unexpectedly then resigned as Mess President, sighting workload as my excuse for having reluctantly to give the post up, and from then on for the remainder of my naval career kept well clear of any in-Mess social responsibility. Fingers well and truly burned!

On the sporting front I had taken the opportunity of being in harbour for a while to try and improve my general fitness and health. Submarine life is not exactly conducive to good health, and over the years I had started to get less fit than I liked to be. Initially I started running again, kind of reverting to what I did most as a younger bloke, but my knees didn't seem to like that too much, and so I started using the gym in HMS Drake on a regular basis instead. The running and cycling machines had improved a great deal in the intervening years and I enjoyed using them. The problem for me though was the 'muscle-bosuns' who used the same gym, huffing and puffing away, and then checking themselves in the mirrors every 5 minutes! It was quite pathetic really and put me off the place. Instead I reverted to cycling and bought myself a nice new mountain bike, and then managed to knacker myself out daily riding it to work and back—I soon got fit though! As well as that I started playing 5-A-Side football, which I hadn't done for years, and which I enjoyed very much until some bastard made a two-footed tackle on me. I was convinced my right leg was broken, and at the time I was in agony—but still wanting to get up and smack the git who did it! I was limping for days afterwards and decided that 39 was a good age to retire from such stupid pastimes.

Back at work the submarine was coming together nicely now, and we were getting to the stage where we were going to have to start operating the machinery and systems in more complicated combinations. Our refurbished diesel generators had been installed by now, and we would need to test them to ensure us a power supply back-up for testing other equipment. Diesel running was normally controlled from the Manoeuvring Room, and it was decreed that for us to run them we would have to once again re-qualify in the simulator in HMS Drake. Initially we were told that each Cat A would have to fully re-qualify, but after much complaint they finally agreed that we could re-qualify in teams, which for me was a great relief—there was no way I wanted to go through the whole rigmarole of doing the Charge Chief's board again, even though it would be no picnic as it stood!

We hadn't been near the simulator for well over 18 months by now, and it showed during the first few training sessions in there. We had lost all of our teamwork skills, and were straight away struggling with even the most basic drills. This was to be expected though, and after a few days of solid work, the procedures started to come together again. In all we had a series of half a dozen simulator sessions each, followed by an assessed set of drills. We all managed to scrape through, but the staff took a lot of pleasure in reminding us that this was the first of many more assessments we would be taking as the situation onboard became more and more complicated. We would need to do sessions for starting the reactor under power, running the engines and turbo-generators and then a full-blown 'standard' simulator re-qualification for each team—nice to have something to look forward to!

As the boat started getting to look like a proper submarine again, ship's company from other departments started rejoining too. Within a short time there were Stores Accountants, Sailors and even a couple of Weapons Chiefs back onboard and starting to take stock of their areas of concern. The equipment stored away at the start of the refit now needed to start being brought back onboard, and it was of little surprise to find that it all needed sorting out, cleaning, oiling, painting and being put into the correct storage locations onboard, a job made more complicated by the haphazard way it was put away in the first place. The new guys onboard were disgusted at the way in which their equipment was stored, but of course it was easy for them to preach when they had not been part of the team putting the boat in refit. Truth was that we really had not had a chance to sort it out in refit—they thought we had been loafing for 2 years, when in fact it had been bloody hard work!

A couple of months before the programmed end of refit and the start of the second commission I was sent away for a week to undergo first aid training in HMS Raleigh. It was a very good course, except for a large gruesome poster of a guy in the act of breaking his leg as completed the triple-jump, which I had to sit facing for 5 days! I came away from the course knowing about 200% more first aid than I did when I started it, which was lucky really since I had to put it into practise about 2 weeks later.

The submarine was by now more or less back in one piece, and there was a huge programme of testing taking place pretty much everywhere around the boat, with test rigs and gauges plugged seemingly into every piece of machinery and system. I was in the process of taking over the Cat A duty in the Manoeuvring Room when suddenly there was a load bang in the Engine Room instantly followed by somebody screaming in pain.

As I and a Chief rushed out and into the Engine Room a man in white overalls came into view lying on the deck, writhing in agony and holding his hands over his stomach. About 8 young junior Stokers, who were on a tour of the boat from HMS Raleigh, were standing back in shock looking at the guy.

I knelt over him while Dickey, the Chief, went for the nearest first aid bag hanging just inside the door:

"OK mate, you're ok, let me see the damage" I said to the man, who continued to cover his stomach with his hands and to scream loudly. The juniors stared with wide eyes, and somebody shut off the air hissing out of an open valve somewhere behind us. There were no other dockies to be seen—they had all scarpered.

Dickey landed beside me with the first aid bag and extracted a field dressing which he started to tear open:

"I told the shut down Senior Rate to phone for an ambulance" he shouted above the sound of the screaming man.

"OK mate, calm down, you're ok, you're ok. We here to help you" I tried to calm the writhing and screaming man, but with little effect. The juniors were looking well spooked by now. At least I knew that he didn't have any problems breathing.

I grabbed him by the ears and turned his head to me:

"Fucking SHUT UP!!" I shouted loudly into his face "You are NOT going to die. We've got you, you're ok" It must have shocked him into silence "Let me see what's happened to you, ok?" He slowly allowed me to move his hands away from his stomach. As the front of his overalls came into view I could see that there was a large hole in the front of them, and as I pull them open there was a similar sized hole just above his belly-button where something had hit him in the stomach with incredible force. Remarkably there was very little blood, but I could clearly see the contents of his stomach oozing from the hole. I managed to keep a straight face, took the field dressing from Dickey and stuck it firmly over the gaping wound. I asked Dickey to hold it tightly in place.

"It's just a scratch mate, you're going to need to go to hospital, but you'll be fine" I told the frightened man

"Jesus, it hurts" he replied, sucking in air noisily.

"Just hold tight ok, we've got an ambulance on the way".

He was lying on his side, and we decided that it would be better if he was sitting up, just in case there was any internal bleeding which might affect his lungs. He wasn't keen on the idea, but we kind of insisted. I got a couple of the juniors to sit behind him to prop him up while we waited for the ambulance.

"What's your name mate?" I asked "Can't keep calling you mate can I"

"Graham. Can you tell my wife that I love her—her numbers in my phone" he gasped

"I'm Steve and this is Dickey. You can tell her yourself when you get to the hospital."

"God it's so painful. I think I'm dying" he stammered, tears appearing in his eyes

"Listen Graham, I know its' painful, but just hang in there ok. You're not going to die"

After what seemed a lifetime there was suddenly commotion at the Engine Room hatch. A pair of green legs appeared and started down the ladder—the ambulance had arrived! The legs started down, then stopped, went up a couple of steps and then down again, and stopped—jammed in the hatch opening because of all the equipment the idiot was carrying! He had to go back up, take off the heart monitors, first aid backpack, splints and goodness knows what else, climb down the ladder and then have someone pass them down to him. This he did as everyone stood around staring at him with bemused expressions. At the foot of the ladder he turned, saw the casualty, started walking briskly towards us, tripped on the hoses lining the deck and fell helmeted head first into the lap of the poor injured man, making him do an involuntary 'crunchie' type sit-up in pain!

The second ambulance man made his way down and we retreated while they tended expertly to Graham—stabilising him and then strapping him into a stretcher so that he could be removed. Once securely on the stretcher we called a dockyard crane to lower his hook into the boat for his extraction, and in minutes he was off the boat and on the way to hospital. I checked all of the young juniors were ok, which while shaken, they were and went back to the Manoeuvring Room to complete the handover. My Boss phoned a few minutes later to check that I and Dickey were fine, and to thank us for taking charge of the situation.

Some weeks later we had a visit from Graham over in the Submarine refit Complex. He came to thank us personally for looking after him. It turned out that he had been doing a high pressure air test, and had mistakenly attached the test equipment the wrong way round, putting 3500 psi of high pressure air in the wrong direction on to a filter, which had then basically disintegrated. The hole in his stomach had actually contained most of the filter basket, which had entered his stomach and been blown all the way round to his side under the force. Remarkably it had hit nothing vital in its travels, and following the operation to remove it he had made a full recovery. He kept the piece of filter basket on a plinth as a souvenir of the accident and asked us if we wanted it. We politely declined, but were glad that he was ok.

With all of the machinery and systems now reinstalled in the boat, we started a whole series of 'harbour checks'. This involved the first power run up of the refuelled nuclear reactor, which would then, piece by piece begin to supply the power necessary to run each and every piece of machinery, first individually, and then in all of the combinations necessary for the boat to become operational. While all these tests, taking several weeks progressed, the dockies would be fixing or adjusting other machinery, so that they could be tested again and finally 'signed off' by the navy as being fully ready. For the most part we were required to either start or then watchkeep on each machinery and then groups of machinery, or to stand by and monitor the dockyard's progress. We also took the opportunity of making a start on cleaning the boat up. Although she would be finally handed back to us newly painted inside and out, the dockyard were not as concerned as we were with the final state of the submarine, and a lot of work was going to be required on our part to get the boat up to the cleanliness standard we knew would be required for the start of the second commission. The culmination of the 'harbour checks' was a controlled static dive in 5 basin, where the boat was taken underwater for the first time in 2 years to check for leaks. There were none, and the boat had dived and surfaced without the slightest problem.

With the harbour checks programme now completed, we now had to complete a whole series of 'Post Refit Sea-Trials'. The boat was still out of commission and still officially in refit, and although we were now moved out of 5 basin and berthed along the submarine jetty opposite HMS Defiance, we were not permitted to fly the Ensign and Jack. Instead, we used to run the Devonport Dockyard plc flag to indicate we were the refitting boat, much to the annoyance of the flag officer in his office overlooking us I expect.

Sea Trials, as the name suggests if the part of the refit where all of the newly installed or refurbished machinery and equipment is put to the test. That includes the equipment throughout the boat, not just propulsion machinery and through the trials programme every machine and system goes through the wringer. For the navy guys its hard work, but at least it gives us plenty of opportunity to get to know and use the gear. We had all had to pass the various simulators to get back out to sea, including the Sailors at the pointy end of the boat, but of course nothing was the same as the real thing.

The trials took the form of daily trips to sea, carrying the various dockyard teams involved in the various areas of the submarine. The trials tended to start with the watertight integrity aspects of the boat—obviously it needed to be watertight before the other equipment could be used, and we had to carry out a series of deeper and deeper dives, right down to designed deep diving depth in order to prove everything was nice and tight. We hadn't dived the boat for almost 2 and half years, and it was pretty tense onboard as we started getting into seriously deep water. The deepest dive was always scary, but after it's done it makes you more confident of the boat's ability to stay dry on the inside!

The diving trials were followed by machinery tests. Every single piece of propulsion, power generation, air purification, and ship's services machinery was put through its paces individually once again, and then in combinations. We, under the direction of the dockyard carried out full power trials surfaced and dived, double and single main engine combinations, emergency propulsion motor runs, various machinery and reactor system breakdowns and endless batteries of re-runs, adjustments and combinations until finally everyone was satisfied that all the machinery was operating correctly. There were defects of course, but they were mostly minor and were either fixed at sea or listed for deferred repair on return to harbour. From our side the trials all went well and we could now relax while the rest of the boat got the treatment.

As the sea trials continued word started to filter through about what we would be doing on completion of the refit. The World was nearing the start of a new millennium, and the brass had decided that this was the time to send a British submarine on an extended 'showing the flag' type cruise. The boat would be visiting Gibraltar, Israel, passing through the

Suez Canal, visiting Singapore, Hawaii, and America's West Coast and there was even talk of going to Japan. The whisper was that we would be the boat! Nobody would confirm it though, and we were told to just wait and see.

By now the sea trials had extended to the operations and weapons systems onboard, and we spent a few weeks with the continual 'whoosh-bang' of the torpedo tubes being put through their paces. It always surprised me how much of a noisy operation the firing of torpedoes was! When one was fired there was an incredible din inside the boat, first a very load rumble and bang as the ram inside the big piston forcing the torpedo to leave the tube reached the end of its travel, and then the equally load hissing of high pressure air as the reservoirs were drained after firing—always reminded me of a massive articulated lorry slamming its brakes on for some reason. As well as that they had loaded on some dummy torpedoes in harbour so that the weapons boys could practise moving them around in the 'Bomb Shop' using all the sophisticated hydraulic platforms and winches. The dummy torpedoes were exactly the same visually as the real ones—same weight as well, so for all intents and purposes the same precautions and limits had to be used for practise. The movement of torpedoes seems to need an inordinate amount of full-volume shouting, even though the guys are about 3 feet away from each other, and since my rack was in the compartment above the Bomb Shop I got to hear pretty much everything that was going on—at whatever time it happened! I think I could probably still remember the sequence of loading and firing a torpedo since I heard it repeated so many times!

In a similar way the Sailors too were feeling the stain of a full testing programme on the Sonar, Radar and optical systems (periscopes to you and me). I have no idea how the things were calibrated or whatever they have to do with them, but we spent ages steaming back and forward along set routes while the experts and our own crew fiddled with gizmos and gadgets to get the things set up. Along with the 'whoosh-bang' of torpedo tubes we now had the added noise of periscopes and masts being raised and lowered, and the annoying 'ping' of active sonar zapping out from the boat at all hours—how was a man supposed to get a few hours shut-eye with all that going on? When we were on watch back aft we could tell by the increased use of hydraulics and the necessity to continually run the high pressure air compressors what was happening at the front end. It was a busy time for everybody I can tell you.

Chapter 21

New Millennium, New Commission, Same Old Problems

We took a break from the sea trials to welcome in a new Millennium, which everybody managed to do pretty extensively by the look of some of the sore heads afterwards. I had spent the evening with my wife and a few friends on Plymouth Hoe, watching the fireworks colouring the mist and clouds that had unfortunately descended an hour before they were due to be let off! In spite of that it had been a remarkable time—celebrating the start of a new century was going to be a once in a lifetime event, and we certainly made the most of it. Shortly into the New Year we set out on the second and final set of sea trials. This was where all of the defects from the first set had been fixed so that the boat could finally be handed formally back to the navy. By now it was pretty clear that the dockyard wanted rid of us, and we likewise, were keen to get back into the fleet. The trials pretty much followed the same pattern as the previous ones, but not to such a depth. There were fewer dockies onboard too, and the boat was starting to feel 'normal' again. We had by now got used to most of the machinery and systems onboard, and were operating them, we thought, pretty well.

With the sea trials nearing there end, and the boat almost ready to be returned to the fleet for her second commission, our thoughts started to turn to the next phase of returning to fleet service, the dreaded post-refit 'Work-Up'. This was an eight week full blown shakedown and work-up programme run by the Captain Shore and Sea Training (CSST) organisation. We had come across them before of course, but up until now it had always been for a maximum of one week, where the boat would simulate being at war for the entire week. It was always bloody hard work for us, with little sleep and constant stress from machinery drills, action stations or damage control, so the sound of eight weeks of the same sent a shiver through many of us.

Before we were exposed to those joys though, we had the small matter of formally taking the boat back from the dockyard on the official completion of the refit. The formal part of it was a parade (of course) where there was a ceremonial rising of the Ensign to signify the boat being back in service, along with a formal inspection of the boat by the Flag Officer Submarines. The boat was supposed to have been 'deep-cleaned' by the dockyard prior to this inspection, but their efforts were nowhere near good enough for our standards, so for a couple of days prior we were all down the boat scrubbing and polishing everywhere ourselves, from lowest sailor to the Captain, to ensure she was good enough for the Admiral. With the Work-Up looming we knew that the cleanliness level was going to have to be raised by several notches to satisfy the trainers, but for now it would have to suffice. The Admiral seemed happy enough anyway.

On the informal side, there were a number of parties and functions organised by ourselves and the dockyard to celebrate the end of the refit, and the return of the boat to service. The 'best' one was a lunch thing organised by the boat in HMS Drake, and attended by the families of the ship's company. We did the obligatory crew photos and stuff, and it was nice for all the families to get together before the start of what would be for many of us, a return to the routine of being away form our families for 6 months of each year. There were a lot of addresses and telephone numbers exchanged, and not a small amount of Pimms consumed! It was at this gathering that it was finally confirmed that we were the boat that would be doing the 'Millennium Trip' as it had become known, and would be going on the trip directly on completion of our impending Work-Up. Everybody was very excited by the news, and plans were hastily put together for the flying out of wives and girlfriends to various destinations. My wife fancied Singapore and Hawaii, and we undertook to find out about travel and accommodation for a trip for her when we would be there. In the intervening 3 or 4 weeks before the start of the Work-Up, we managed to book flights and hotel for her trip, and I looked forward to seeing her again half away through our World Tour. It was going to be great.

The completion of the refit meant that the boat was now officially 'ours' again. More specifically it belonged to the Second Submarine Squadron (SM2), who wasted no time in ensuring that we knew who and where they were. Over the next few weeks while we were trying to prepare for the Work-Up and then an extended cruise lasting almost 6 months we had an endless stream of Squadron visitors, who invariably wanted to carry out some inspection or other. If it wasn't the Squadron Engineer it would be the Squadron Weapons people or some other bugger. The boat was still a mess in terms of where equipment was located and in its general seaworthiness, so we were much more interested in getting it shipshape that pandering to egos, but we had little choice.

Another aspect that we had to think about was what stores we needed onboard for the upcoming trip. The boat had come out of refit with what might be considered as a 'standard' spares and stores fit, that is, the basic requirement for spare nuts, bolts, washers, gaskets and bits and pieces for routine maintenance and repair work onboard. On the World Cruise support for the boat would be very limited, and we were told to create lists of extra components and equipment we thought we might need for 6 months away from base. Being Engineers, we made lists of pretty much an entire spare submarine propulsion system (just in case), which was rejected in no time! As it was though, we were carrying a huge amount of spares—spares that we would now have to get out of the way during the Work-Up somehow. We would be able to offload a lot of it temporarily in Faslane while we were up there being driven nuts by CSST, but obviously if we could avoid carrying the stuff on and off the boat more than once we would do it. At that stage in the game we had forgotten through the refit how serious the CSST people were, so we naively thought that they wouldn't mind us carrying the extra gear—we would soon find out how wrong we were!

Most of us had taken the extra precaution of exchanging our entire uniform wardrobe for new ones since we knew there would be parades as part of the Work-Up too. Right from the off the trip was going to be a pain since normally I had plenty of room in my personal locker and under bed shelves, but now, like everybody else, everything was full to bursting with extra gear, clothing and even equipment. I couldn't find anything now, and had to dig through everything several times a day to start with to find the simplest thing I needed. I think we probably knew it was not a good way to start a busy Work-Up period, but had persuaded ourselves that everything would be fine.

The days before sailing were the usual whirlwind of last minute preparations, machinery flash-up, a 'fast-cruise' where all of the submarine hatches are shut and we pretend to be at sea for a day—just to ensure everybody knows the normal routines, and hurried goodbyes. As always some of the back-afties effectively sailed 2 days before the rest of the boat due to the reactor start-up and machinery preparation, but at least it gave us a chance to try and get ourselves into some kind of order in the machinery spaces all stuffed with extra spares, tools and equipment. The guys made an incredible effort to get most of it stowed away out of sight in all sorts of nooks and crannies, and by the time the boat sailed down the River Plym and out into Plymouth Sound the after ends were in a good state, and ready for whatever CSST could throw at us.

The trip up to Faslane was not really a happy one. We had spent a bit of time at sea since the refit doing post-refit trials, and thought we knew our way around the boat fairly well. We knew though that we were not as slick as we would need to be to get through the Work-Up, and that thought seemed to permeate into everything we tried to do. Most of our time on the 3 days or so it took us to get to Faslane was taken up either with whole-ship fire and damage control exercises, machinery breakdown exercises or simply cleaning all of the parts of the boat we could get close to. It was a very tiring process since on top of that we were doing our normal watch keeping duties, but we were energised by the knowledge that it was going to get much worse before things got better.

The Work-Up started for us as soon as we got alongside. A team of CSST staff descended on to the boat as soon as the lines were across, and commenced without any ceremony to prowl around the boat, making lists and tutting a lot! We looked from one-another in confusion and wondered what that was all about. On asking them what they were dong we were basically ignored, and so we left them to it. We needed to prepare for the formal parade marking the start of the whole thing the next morning anyway. It was never easy to keep No.1 uniforms in good condition onboard the boat and it was going to take quite a bit of work to get them looking good enough for an inspection by the Training Captain. The CSST staff left the boat a couple of hours later having filled several notebooks with their jottings, leaving us wondering what they had found so much to write about! Whatever it was didn't seem to bode well for our future that was for sure.

The next morning saw us struggling to get dressed in our best rigs for the personnel inspection parade. It would take place in a large hangar on the naval base, which we had to walk through large puddles to get to as the morning rush into the base took place. As we dodged the traffic and splashed our way in, the shoes we had spent hours polishing dulling nicely with the soaking, we were harried by shouting parade staff into unfamiliar squads and formed up into nice neat departmentalised platoons for the inspection. Being a Charge Chief I became second in command of the Mechanical Junior Rates platoon. This meant I had to do a bit of shouting myself, ordering the lads to stand to attention, then to "without intervals, by the right—DRESS!", and other such niceties, before handing over the platoon to one of the Assistant Marine Engineer Officers (AMEOs)—a Lieutenant, for the actual inspection and marching bit which was to follow. I and the Lieutenant carried out an inspection of the lads ourselves first, patting down a collar here or straightening a lanyard there, and to us they all looked pretty good. Obviously the shoes had been trashed by the puddles but there wasn't much we could do about that now.

Soon enough we were all called to attention by the Parade Commander as the Training Captain and his staff arrived, breezing into the Hangar to be met by our Captain. A quick exchange of salutes and off they went, wandering along the lines of sailors, stopping here and there to have a few words with somebody, before moving on to the next platoon. As was usual in these situations the Training Captain did not make any comments about the presentation of the personnel, but his entourage following along did the proper inspection on his behalf. A staff Lieutenant and a couple of Warrant Officers trooped along the lines of sailors closely inspecting each uniform, making notes and in some cases taking names. After the Training Captain had passed through our platoon, one of the Warrant Officers followed. I was fairly confident that our lads should be safe from serious criticism, but my confidence waned as the Warrant Officer wrote furiously in his notebook as he moved from man to man, and taking at least 3 names. As he finished our platoon by standing and looking at me at the back, he whispered:

"The shoes are a mess Charge. Some of the suits look like they were ironed with a brick"

"We had to walk through the puddles Sir" I replied.

"Should have carried the shoes and put them on over here, shouldn't you?"

"Yes Sir, didn't think of that"

"Shouldn't worry, some of your lads will get the chance to do it properly at the kit musters". He moved on.

We had heard through the grapevine about the kit musters. So it was true then. It appeared that the names of the people being written down would be those required to present their entire kit for inspection. That was a major pain the in the arse because normally of course, the only kit we took to sea was overalls and working rig (No.8s). We had only brought our best uniforms with us for this parade, and that had been a right pain in itself. The guys selected for kit muster would need to get all of the normal gear we were supposed to have by hook or by crook, and the extra work required to get the gear up to kit muster standard was extra work they, and we, could do without.

After the parade was 'fallen out' we were told to muster at the end of the Hangar for an address by the Training Captain. We all mingled round the man and received what must have been the standard 'Welcome to the Work-Up' speech. It was one of those ones full of 'You get out of it what you put in', and 'Work hard and it will be easier' type of speeches, and ended with a dire warning that the World Cruise planned for the end of Work-Up was not a done deal, and that another boat could still be sent instead of us if we were not up to scratch. We had expected something similar, but the speech did little to lift our collective gloom. After the Training Captain had left it was the turn of the training staff to have their say. These were the people we would be dealing with on a daily basis, and so we paid considerable attention to what they were telling us. We were told that the parade we had just done was 'Just Satisfactory', and that several crew members would be required to present at kit muster of their full kit the following week—a list of names was read out, luckily mine not included. Following that was an outline of the training planned for the following week, known as 'Harbour Training Week'. The first thing on the agenda would be a whole boat cleanliness inspection on the

Monday, closely followed by a full week of harbour drills for each duty watch, ranging from fires, floods and shipboard emergencies, to repelling intruders and assisting 'civil authorities' in controlling disturbances and so forth. It was going to be a busy time for everybody starting right away, as we would spend the coming weekend cleaning the boat from top to bottom. We wandered back to the boat in a pretty dejected mood.

The weekend prior to harbour training week was a busy one. The training staff had made it quite clear that they were not satisfied with all of the extra gear we were carrying onboard for the World Cruise, and so we set about unloading it all. As we removed the spares, equipment and gear into porta-cabins on the jetty, it exposed more and more areas onboard that needed some serious cleaning. On the Friday, Saturday and Sunday we all donned overalls and set to work once again 'deep cleaning' the submarine. Each day we started at the crack of dawn and worked until past midnight, trying to reach every nook and cranny. The machinery spaces were just a nightmare to clean properly, and while the machinery itself was all looking clean and bright, there were some areas where whatever you tried to do, just always look dirty. Tempers became frayed as the guys became tried and bored with 'mop-flopping', but there was simply no choice than to keep them at it.

Monday came around all too soon and before we knew it we were dressed up to the nines again waiting to report our areas of inspection to the inspecting officer and his team. As the mechanical Charge Chief I would be reporting the Engine Room and was expecting, after all the work that had gone into it, a pretty good response from the inspecting team—we had quite frankly worked our bollocks off, and I really didn't think any group of people could have done a better job. The Engine Room was looking the cleanest and smartest I have ever seen it. There were a couple of nasty little corners, but my goodness, overall it was cracking!

I reported to the Lieutenant Commander in charge of the team as they all flooded past me into the Engine Room.

"Thank you Charge—let's have a look around then shall we?"

We were the last area to be inspected onboard, and had waited a couple of hours for the inspection team to arrive. In the meantime we had heard whispers from the other parts of the boat about how the inspection was going, and it sounded fairly mixed. The nice easy to clean electronics spaces and mess decks all seemed to have passed with flying colours, while reports from a lot of the machinery spaces, both forward and aft, were more bleak. In my case the officer went straight to the nasty little corners, which he obviously knew were a problem to clean, wiping his hand over a dirty pipe here or dipping down into the corner of a bilge there. Having immediately spotted and recorded the horrible areas, he then commenced to look around the better parts. All the time the remainder of his team were poking into every single part of the upper and lower parts of the Engine Room, making notes and opening lockers, pulling out rags and buckets, and leaving everything in the walkways. The Engineer looked at me and raised his eyes in a 'here we go' gesture, mirroring my own thoughts. After about half an hour they were done. I saluted the Lieutenant Commander goodbye and they all disappeared. The report would follow later in the day.

With the cleanliness inspection completed we had little chance to relax, or God forbid, catch up on any sleep. We were now in harbour training week, and about 5 minutes after the completion of the inspection the first fire drill started—a small fire in one of the forward offices, just to keep us on our toes! Most of us were still dressed in our best uniforms and had to go to our Emergency Stations like that. The lads were not pleased at having to put the fluff-leaving fire-fighting (wholly bear) suits on over their uniforms, and took the opportunity to have a good whinge about the universe, CSST, HMS Tireless and the fucking Navy in general! The point was that an emergency could happen at any time I suppose, and not at our convenience, but in this instance we felt it was done just to piss us off, and it worked!

The small drills continued throughout the day while we tried to get ourselves into the swing of this training lark. It was becoming quite obvious that the entire process was going to be very painful unless we, the entire ship's company, had a serious attitude change. It was not easy coming from the refit environment straight back to this full-on operational scenario, but we needed to get used to the idea that this was how it was going to be. We were up to speed with this stuff before refit, so it was just a matter of getting back up to speed. The mind was willing in my case, but my goodness the flesh was weak! After just 3 days of restricted sleep I was absolutely knackered—I suppose the stress was there too. It would become easier of course, with time and experience, but the start of the process was bloody hard! Towards the end of the day the report of the cleanliness inspection was received onboard and read out by the Captain. We had failed, and would be re-inspected at the end of the week. We kind of knew it would happen, just to keep the pressure up, but it was still a blow after all the work. It meant that we would have to carry on working in the evenings and night to get all the little areas cleaned well enough to satisfy the inspectors—in fact we undertook to make the bloody place clean enough to eat your dinner off—which of course is the attitude they wanted us to adopt. We drew up a schedule of one day duty, one day cleaning, one day off to get the work done. The mood changed during that period to one of defiance, the start of the team building that we would need to see us through. CSST became the enemy to be fought—give them nothing to find wrong! If you got it wrong once, learn and don't get it wrong a second time! If you see someone struggling, help them out! Together we could beat these bastards!

The harbour training week progressed slowly and painfully for us all. Each day brought new challenges for us, and apart from the standard fires and so forth, the week was livened up by a bit of riot control and the repelling of 'tree-huggers'. The parts of the activists were usually taken by either the training staff or in some cases the Royal Marines of Commachio Group who looked after the security of the nuclear bombers based in Faslane. We tended to leave the Marines alone because they were double hard, but if we recognised any of the training staff amongst the 'protestors' a few of the lads I am sure made an effort to get close and personal with the rifle butts or batons! It was worth a try at least to even the score a bit!

The kit musters and re-inspection of the boat came around at the end of the week with much better results that the first one. We had suspected that the failures had been part of the plan and that seemed to be born out by the relative ease with which the second inspections were passed. The work we had put in though was genuine, and we could be rightly proud of the state of cleanliness of the boat. The week had also had the effect of gelling the crew together into something starting to approach that resembling a team. For now there was no 'crumple-zone commandoes' or 'spanner wankers' separation between forward and aft of the boat, and we were trying to get through the work-up as a complete crew.

The sea going part of the Work-Up consisted of a number of 'phases', the first of which being the 'Safety Phase'. This was a period at sea of purely emergency and action damage drills and machinery and equipment breakdowns. After flashing up over the weekend we sailed on Monday morning and got straight into it. Even before we had left harbour there had been a 'man-overboard', a steering gear failure and some electrical failures, so we could pretty much be sure that it was going to be another stressful week! In fairness It was necessary for us to be doing this stuff, and for the first couple of days the drills were carried out 'slow-time', that is bit by bit to ensure everybody knew what they were supposed to be doing and what was expected of them. The pace didn't stay slow for long though, and soon enough we were being harassed through ever more complicated scenarios at all times of the day and night. The trainers tended to knock off late in the evening and start with the first 'heave' (the wake-up 'heave' as it was known) early the next morning. The routine seemed to be written for the forward watchkeepers so that they all received a good 4 or 5 hours sleep a night, whereas for the back-afties it meant that one watch would get 'all night in' while the other 2 watches would get 4 hours sleep maximum—we were slowly getting used to being permanently tired. I found myself falling asleep in the Technical Office one morning while I was filling out some log—the phone woke me up when the Officer of the Watch rang to see what was taking me so long!

The 'hydraulic bursts', 'HP air bursts' fires, casualties and action damage continued relentlessly. At the end of each day a report would be published by the CSST team, summarising the day's events, and how the crew had handled each one in turn. Slowly but surely we improved as a team, and attacked each new 'heave' aggressively and professionally enough for them to start to become routine. Our confidence improved along with our skills and our endurance, and soon enough there was not a new drill the staff could throw at us that we could not handle. We would now, without needing to be told, run the drill and then recharge all the breathing equipment, repack the fire fighting suits and gear securely away ready for the next 'heave'. We were so quick now that we had time for a cup of tea between each exercise!

With successful completion of the safety phase the training now moved on to the start of the 'Operational Phase'. This part lasted for several weeks and was where the submarine was put through its paces in the spheres of weapons, intelligence gathering and tactical stuff. It affected the forward end of the boat mostly, but if we at the back end thought it would be a break for us we were going to be disappointed. While the sailors and weapons pukes were put through the mill doing their thing, we had the pleasure of more machinery breakdown drills—in effect the CSST staff used the simulated breakdowns as a method of complicating the operations being conducted by Command. The boat would start a simulated torpedo attack or intelligence run, and as we neared the critical point of the attack one of the CSST staff in the Engine Room would initiate a turbo-generator failure, or an electrical fault, or even a reactor scram. Likewise, the whole ship scenarios continued—a hydraulic burst might be initiated in the Control Room just as the Captain was raising the attack periscope for a final look at a target. The resultant 'hydraulic mist' would then ignite and an emergency would take place right in the middle of the attack. It was more interesting than the straightforward emergency drills anyway!

Even while the engineering department was having its 'quiet' phase, we were never left alone. We were required by CSST to carry out one mechanical and one electrical engineering design project, to be presented to the Training Captain and his staff by the end of the Operational Phase. I was placed in charge of the mechanical project, and I came up, together with a colleague, with the idea of inventing something called a 'hatchway water spray system', to be designed to seal the hatchway to a compartment which might contain a fire, to prevent smoke coming out of the compartment into the rest of the boat.

The usual way to prevent smoke escaping from a compartment on fire was to close the hatch once the fire was discovered. That was fine, but meant that entrance back into the compartment to extinguish the fire involved setting up a fire fighting team around the hatch, spraying a lot of water around and then opening the hatch, usually (in a real fire) resulting in a fire ball coming out and into the compartment above. We thought that if we could design a ring of directional nozzles around the top of the hatch, we could avoid all the water being sprayed around, and the fire ball being ejected from below. We chose the Diesel Room hatch as our test rig—smoke coming from a fire in the Diesel Room would make the Manoeuvring Room very difficult, if not impossible to operate in. Also the Switchboard Room above the Diesel Room was not the place to be spraying loads of water around—the consequences were a complete loss of electrical power onboard, plus probably the electrocution of the fire fighting team. Seemed like a good enough place to start!

We did the project as we might a formal one, with report, work sheets, costings, material specifications and all that good stuff. The nozzles and plumbing we manufactured in the onboard 'workshop', and even had the electricians design a remote switching unit for the spray system which could be operated from a spare switch in the Manoeuvring Room. We had the system plumbed into the main ballast pump to provide the water supply, and that meant that we would have a constant water supply even if we lost the normal electrical supply during any emergency—somehow between the almost constant whole-boat exercises, normal watchkeeping duties and the ever-present machinery defects we managed to create a pretty professional job. The system fitted neatly around the lip of the Diesel Room hatch, was unobtrusive, and did not affect the normal operation of the hatch or the canvas smoke curtain that was normally fitted. All that was needed now was the operational test, and because of the seriousness of activating a high volume water system in close proximity to so much electrical equipment, it was decided that the test would be a once-only affair to be witnessed by the Training Captain and his team. No pressure there then.

On the day of the races, having very carefully reviewed our calculations for volumes of water, areas of coverage, pumping pressure and anything else that sounded technical and which might make us look like we knew what we were doing, we decided that a 'belt and braces' approach was probably the best way, and so set about covering almost the entire Switchboard and diesel Rooms in plastic sheeting in an attempt to ensure that should the aim of the nozzles be wayward, none of the saltwater being sprayed around would reach anything vital to the operation of the boat. After several hours of laying out plastic we were ready for the big test, and patiently awaited the arrival of the Training Captain and staff. We were pretty nervous by the time they arrived, but my nervousness lessened a bit by his clear interest in the system, and his astute questions concerning its operation. I showed him and his team around all of the fitting and the work we had done, and some of them spent some time going through the Project report, drawings and manufacturing work sheets, asking questions and requesting clarification of this or that point. Finally we could put it off not longer, and set about starting the functional test. Everybody stood back from the edge of the Diesel room hatch as we carefully closed the plastic sheeting tightly, stood back ourselves, crossed our fingers and ordered the Manoeuvring Room to flick the switch.

There was a satisfying 'clunk' as the solenoid water isolating valve opened. Instantly there was a rush of water through the nozzles, which quickly formed a layer at the top of the hatch. Not a drop of water was trying to escape over the rim of the hatch, and we could clearly see that there were no spaces through which any smoke could have escaped from the compartment. The CSST staff edged closer for a better look, and all seemed impressed that the system had worked. We got the system switched off so as not to flood the Diesel Room—a lot of water was coming out of the nozzles—and waited for the Training Captain's verdict.

He too was evidently impressed. So much so in fact that myself and my colleague were subsequently presented with something called a 'Herbert Lott' award for this innovation in submarine safety. The design and possible introduction into service was transferred out of our hands via the CSST organisation, but I don't think it was ever taken up. Certainly at the time we were just glad to have been marked with a 'Good' for the Work-Up Project, and happy to not have an extra work to do for the time being.

The culmination of the Work-Up programme was for the boat to be in a simulated 'conflict' scenario for an extended period of time. In our case it was decided that this final phase of our work-up would take place during effectively the start of our World Cruise, that is, on the way to our programmed first stop, Gibraltar. In this way, it was felt that we could make some progress both in the work-up, and to start the long cruise. On the way to Gibraltar we would be harried by up to 3 frigates and aircraft, which would provide the opposition in the 'conflict'. It was going to be a long trip to Gibraltar!

Before setting off, we went back into Faslane for the last time to collect all of the spares and stores we had offloaded at the start of the work-up, several weeks before. We spent a weekend doing that, and it also gave us a chance to say a final goodbye to our loved ones, at least until we met again in far-flung foreign parts. I managed to phone home and had a nice long chat with Anna, expecting to see her again in a few short weeks in Singapore. Even though we had another 10 days or so of pain and hard work before the trip proper started, we could see the end of the tunnel now and were ready to get the whole process finished, and bloody CSST off our boat.

The journey to Gibraltar was pretty bloody, and the simulated war conditions made for an uncomfortable ride. As fully expected the fun and games started as soon as we were past the Faslane breakwater, firstly with land based helicopters hunting us. This meant we had to go ultra-quiet right from the start, switching off all and any equipment that was not vital for either moving or fighting the boat. Straight away we had to start using oxygen candles and CO_2 scrubbers rather than the electrolysers and air purifiers, meaning extra work for everybody, and it would stay that way for over a week. Of course it was not going to be that easy, and as well as avoiding the 'enemy' and fighting the boat when required, we still had the almost continual rounds of emergency drills to contend with. It was incredibly tiring for everybody and sleep was precious, but this time as well as the lack of sleep, there was deterioration in the food quality as power was limited, and the risk of pots and pans clattering around made the Command limit the good intentions of the Chefs. By 3 or 4 days in to the simulated conflict a kind of numb acceptance descended on everybody—a mixture of fatigue, tiredness, hunger, pain from bumps and bruises, and probably just stress overload—that made us all more or less submarine zombies. We automatically reacted to each new attack, action damage, emergency situation or machinery breakdown without thinking, by now going into a response mode so well known we could practically do it dead on our feet—it was uncanny really, and personally I thought that what we were going through really was about as near as we could ever want to get to the real thing. War certainly would be hell.

The last few days of the work-up really were hell. Nobody onboard probably got more than a couple of hours sleep over the whole 3 days—I certainly didn't anyway. As well as the war scenario taking place, we had started to suffer some significant machinery defects onboard too. The training staff didn't mind that though as it helped to raise the hassle level for the engineers even more, and the defects had to be fixed around the action stations continually being announced for some new threat. I and the technicians tried to get around all the defects as we went, but could never seem to clear all of them. There were lots of little steam leaks, oil leaks, air leaks and so on, most of which only took a few minutes to fix, but on top of that 2 larger faults started coming to light, which would certainly cause us problems.

The first was a problem with one of the diesel generators, which would require the removal of a number of cylinder heads. In the normal course of events we would take a few people out of the watchbill and set them to work (we carried a few spare cylinder heads), but in the present scenario we couldn't release anybody, and we needed both diesels, defective or not, for the almost daily reactor scram recoveries—one would pop and bang a bit but should be ok until we reached Gibraltar. Of a more sinister nature was an apparent defect to one of our 2 'HP Make-Up' pumps. These were relatively small positive-displacement pumps that pumped water directly into the nuclear reactor when it was required. When the reactor scrammed, primary water had to be pumped into the reactor and primary circuit. This was because as the temperature inside the reactor dropped on scramming; the water level in the pressuriser also dropped and had been replaced to maintain the correct level. Once the reactor was restarted, the water pumped in on scramming would have to be discharged overboard. In normal cruising conditions the 'Make-Up' pumps were rarely run at all, but during the work-up we had scrammed and re-started the reactor more times than I could remember, and so everything was being run to its limit. One of the pumps did not appear to be working correctly, but because they were sealed units we could not strip it down to take a look inside. We would have to order a new one (high grade stainless steel costing about a quarter of a million quid!), and in the meantime our ability to pump water into the reactor was seriously degraded. As a safety measure it was agreed with CSST that the reactor would not be scrammed for training purposes until the new pump was received onboard, and such was the potential seriousness of the defect that the new pump would be helicopter'd out to us at the earliest opportunity. While the importance of the pump was recognised in the urgency of the proposed response, the significance of the defect and degradation of our ability to pump water into the reactor would come to light in a much more serious way in the coming days. As it panned out we didn't get the pump in any case until we arrived alongside in Gibraltar.

The final day of the work-up found us in the vicinity of the Straits of Gibraltar. For us onboard there was no real difference between the days—our lives tended to be governed by the shift patterns we worked, and it mattered little whether the time on the clocks was AM or PM. We generally got the idea whether it was day or night time by the meals we ate—breakfast indicating a new day for what it mattered. This was a good day though, as it was the last day of torment for us, and meant that one way or another we should get some sleep sometime today, no matter what they threw at us it would all end today—*please!*

As expected we got everything and the kitchen sink thrown at us. The 'heaves' continued all day, defects and 'damage' piling up as we went along. We had to break through 3 frigates to reach our simulated objective and sink a strategic fuel tanker or something, and the entire day was a blur of fires, floods, hydraulic and air bursts, smoke clearance, wearing emergency breathing gear and everything else that could be thought of. We had got to the point in the late afternoon where we simply ran out of resources to continue to fight the boat, both in terms of people and equipment, and that was when the end of the Work-Up was signalled to us all by the Training Captain ordering an emergency surface of the submarine from 80 metres. The emergency blow valves were opened from the Control Room and high pressure air from the emergency bottle groups blasted into the main ballast tanks, while at the same time 'Full Ahead' was run on to the telegraphs and the throttle valves were wound open, increasing the engine revolutions to maximum. The boat instantly headed towards the surface at an incredible speed, the deck under our feet tilting upwards at a 45 degree angle. We held on for dear life as the depth gauge unwound on the way up, and as the boat got to the surface it literally jumped out of the water, to crash heavily down again onto the surface. The boat was now on the surface—it had taken about 30 seconds to get there too! It was the end of the exercise and the Work-Up—we were too tired to celebrate, just yet at least. We wearily stowed all of the emergency gear, ventilated the boat properly to get rid of the lingering smoke and fumes, and set about preparing to enter the harbour in Gibraltar.

Before we got alongside the Training Captain came over the main broadcast to give us a final debrief for the entire Work-Up. The boat had been assessed overall as 'Good'—quite a high mark in the scheme of things and reflecting we thought the hard work we had all put into the boat. He wished us well on the forthcoming World Trip, and jokingly expressed jealousy that he was not coming with us. He was followed by our own Captain, who likewise congratulated us on our success, but cautioned us at the same time to remain vigilant to the ever present risks of submarine work. He told us to now take a decent rest during our few days in Gibraltar, and to be ready for the World Cruise to follow. Now we could really celebrate completing the Work-Up and look forward to several months of visiting some bloody nice places! Singapore, Hawaii, USA, here we come!

I managed to escape the reactor shut down in Gibraltar, and got away to my hotel room a mere couple of hours after getting alongside. It was nice to see the old place again, but in truth I was much more interested in getting something to eat, taking a very long bath, and getting my head on to a pillow, in that order. As a Charge Chief I was lucky enough to get a single room, and after filling myself with a very sizable fish and chips, washed down with a beer or two, I fell into a lovely hot bath for an hour (falling asleep in the water) and then staggered to the bed at about 4 pm in the afternoon. Instantly asleep, the night seemed to pass in seconds and before I knew it, my alarm was ringing at 7 am the next morning. 15 hours of solid sleep in one go! Strangely I felt more rather than less tired—I guess I wasn't used to all that sleep in one go. I was required onboard that day and made my way back to the boat on foot. The walk woke me up.

The mood onboard had lifted markedly from that of the last couple of days of the Work-Up, due in all probability to a decent night's sleep and a good meal for most of the people onboard. For us in the propulsion department there was a long list of defects and maintenance tasks to do, and we set about it with a will, wanting to make sure the boat was in tip-top form for the start of the World Cruise. All of the parts we had ordered had appeared like magic on the jetty, and in no time we had got the defective diesel generator in bits, and were changing the trashed HP Make-Up pump, our 2 main defects. The rest of the defects were pretty much minor in nature, and in this instance there was no need for anybody to enter the Reactor Compartment—if we had done so it would have invalidated our previous valve position checks down there, and we would have had to do the whole thing again before re-starting the reactor, and we really didn't want to do that.

In all we only spent a few days in Gibraltar—just enough to recover from the stresses and strains of the Work-Up, and to get everything in order for the start of the World Cruise. The boat was stuffed with everything we could think of that we might need for the trip since support for us would be sparse, and with last minute phone calls home completed we flashed up and sailed out of Gibraltar early in May 2000, this time steering right into the Mediterranean Sea heading towards Israel and eventually the Suez Canal instead of the more normal left into the Atlantic Ocean. The World Cruise had begun!

Chapter 22

Huston, We Have a Problem

The first part of the World Cruise really was going to be that—a cruise. The intention was for the boat to make her own way firstly for a short visit to Haifa in Israel, and then to pass through the Suez Canal, meeting up with a Task Force on the other side, after which there would be a whole series of exercises with all sorts of Navies—a good old bit of flag waving and 'power projection'. It was going to be fun.

The cruise from Gibraltar to Haifa was planned to take about a week—all nice and relaxed. This was the first bit of 'normal' cruising the boat had done since coming out of refit, and it was good to just be in a watchkeeping cycle, without extra 'heaves' and extra work to do. Our thoughts by now were firmly set on having a great World Cruise, and a couple of days into the trip I had even got a couple of the more junior Stokers involved in making a barbecue from an old oil drum, with the intention later on of having our first casing party some time on the surface before we reached Israel.

On the machinery side everything seemed to be working very well. We were still suffering the standard routine small leaks, adjustments and defects to components, but that was normal. Just like the crew, this was the first time that the machinery had had a chance to settle down into some steady running, without constantly changing propeller revolutions or the power being produced by the reactor, and so it was a chance for us to monitor its performance in the 'steady state'.

Concerns started to arise about the state of reactor after about 4 days at sea at more or less constant revolutions. For most of each day the boat was cruising along at a safe depth of about 80 metres, and would only return to periscope depth once a day for the exchange of communications with the Admiralty. The weather was calm and sunny in that part of the world which meant that the boat remained pretty much level most of the time too.

The Reactor Panel Operators logged the water level in the Pressuriser as a normal routine once every hour, and expected the level to remain the same during steady operation. The level was expected to change with changes in the power level of the reactor, but then should settle down again once steady revolutions were re-established. They were reporting that the Pressuriser level was slowly dropping.

The pressuriser was a major component of the primary water system, and was where a bank of heaters in a sealed pressure vessel created the increased system pressure necessary to prevent the water passing through the reactor core from boiling (increased pressure = increased temperature in a sealed vessel). The pressuriser was connected to the primary circuit via a large bore pipe called a 'Surge Line', and the water pumped through the reactor core then had two functions. Firstly it effectively cooled the core during the nuclear reaction that was happening all the time that the control rods were withdrawn, thus preventing the heat being generated from melting the reactor core itself, and secondly exchanging the heat being removed from the reactor core in the steam generators and thereby producing the steam required to drive the main engine turbines and turbo-generator turbines to drive the boat and generate the electrical energy. In a sealed primary water circuit there was a set amount of water present, the amount of which could only be changed by either adding water ('primary make-up') or by removing water ('primary discharge'). Any other movement of the indicated water level could only be by changes in reactor power affecting the density of the water and hence the level, or by there being leakage from the supposedly sealed system, which quite frankly didn't bear thinking about.

It has to be said that their initial concerns were taken fairly lightly. They were used to seeing the Pressuriser level changing a lot over the past few weeks, and the thought was that maybe they were a bit jumpy still from the work-up. It was good that they were being so vigilant, but at the routine Cat A meeting held at that time it was felt that while we should obviously be wary of something being wrong, nobody should get too caught up in the possibility that there might be a fault with the primary circuit. None of us wanted to believe that there could be anything wrong with the reactor, after all we had just completed refit where every centimetre of the primary circuit had been non-destructively tested, and especially now that we had just started the World Cruise! None of the Cat A's could see any constant drop in the Pressuriser water level, and so we cautiously let the problem ride for now.

The problem didn't go away though just by our wanting it to. The concerns of the Reactor Panel Operators (RPO) continued to be raised, and then, slowly but surely, the rest of us started to think that maybe they were right.

For me personally the crunch came on watch one day when the RPO requested permission to make-up to the reactor as the level was a bit low. I looked back through the logs and realised that we had not carried out any discharge recently, although the normal daily chemistry tests had been done. The chemical testing required a small amount of primary circuit water to be removed, but not enough to result in a visual reduction of the water level in the Pressuriser. I gave the order to restore the water level, but in the back of my mind alarm bells had started ringing. Again looking back through the logs it was apparent that we were making up to the reactor with a much higher frequency that was normally the case. I asked the Engineer Officer for a Cat A meeting to discuss what I now thought really was a problem.

All the Engineer Officers and Charge Chiefs got together again, and the first thing that was decided was that we all now agreed that there might be a problem with the reactor or the primary circuit. With that being the case, we had to decide what our next course of action needed to be. There did exist a set of emergency procedures covering similar incidents, but not one that exactly described the predicament we faced, and so the Engineer asked one officer and one Charge Chief to look into those with a view to extracting the useful bits. The next course of action was to try to find out with certainty if the Pressuriser level was actually dropping, and by what rate, and whether there was any evidence of leakage from the primary circuit itself, or from any of the systems connected to it. The order was given that no primary discharge or sampling was to take place until further notice, and that primary make-up was only to be used once the Pressuriser level had reached a certain low limit. In addition the Engineer would talk to the Captain and ask him to set 'steady revolutions' for a continuous period (ideally 24 hours). In this way we could monitor the actual level in the Pressuriser in completely steady conditions, and with any luck be proved totally wrong! In the meantime we got the lads to start monitoring every 15 minutes, the Pressuriser level indications spread throughout 5 places in the boat—we would take a average of the five readings as we went to eliminated any meter errors that might be present in the calculations. We also got the Health Physics guys to start monitoring radiation levels more closely as we went in case there really was a leak of radio-active water happening somewhere we didn't know about. So far there had been no increase in background radiation levels, and none of the high level alarms had been activated onboard, so again for us that was an indication that there was no leak. Better to be safe than sorry though.

For us in the Primary Mechanical Section there was going to be a lot of work needed. We had decided to instigate something called the 'Primary Leak Search' drill, which involved us isolating various parts of systems connected to the primary circuit, and then visually checking each length of pipe work, valve, connection and equipment for the signs of leakage. This was a time consuming and difficult process, involving getting yourself wedged into some of the harder to access areas onboard. Of course we could only do this outside the Reactor Compartment, as there was no access in there with the reactor running, unless you wanted to be able to light up in the dark later! Any system that could either allow water into the reactor primary circuit, or remove water from it, including the primary sampling sink was isolated. There was a viewing window built into the deck of the Reactor Tunnel, consisting of a total of about 10 inches of layered leaded glass and polythene, protected by a heavy hatch cover. Through this could be seen the top of the Pressuriser inside the Reactor Compartment, and with the use of angled mirrors, the top of the Reactor Pressure Vessel (RPV) and the sides of both Steam Generators

(SGs). What could not be seen was the bilge, and whether any water was accumulating there, although there were remote bilge level alarms fitted which should tell us if there was water down there, although they didn't activate until there was about 50 litres as I recall. 50 litres would be a lot to lose from the primary circuit of a nuclear reactor! At that stage what we were more intent on seeing on the bottom of the viewing window whether there was any condensation from any steam being released in the Reactor Compartment. That would be a positive indication of some kind of leakage down there. Initially everything was normal—no leaks, no alarms, no indications, no nothing!

After a good number of hours steady steaming without make-up or discharge it had become quite apparent that the Pressuriser level was indeed dropping very slowly. A mean reading of all the different level indicators throughout the boat had categorically shown a reduction in the level, even though it was only by a couple of millimetres, representing a couple of litres or so of water. The fact was that there should be no water level drop at all, and so we had a big problem—where could the water be going, how could it be escaping, what were we going to do about it, was it a dangerous situation, and was it likely to get worse?

Another rushed Cat A meeting determined what we were going to do next. The Deputy Engineer was absent—already busy sending off long and complicated signals to the Admiralty describing the situation, and requesting technical advice. We had plenty of manuals and engineering information on board to use as reference material, but none of it described what we were experiencing, or how we should deal with it. We decided that in all probability we had a leak somewhere on the primary circuit, type and severity unknown, and what we really needed to do was to find out where the system was leaking. We decided that we needed to adopt what was known as 'single loop' operations in order to determine which side of the reactor circuit the leak was on.

By now word had started to reach the other departments in the boat that there was a potential World Cruise stopping defect starting to emerge 'back-aft'. Some of the Crumple-Zone Commandoes started appearing on the after escape Platform 'for a smoke'. It was plain from our expressions and demeanour that something was up, but at that stage there was little we could tell them about it because we simply didn't know too much ourselves. We tried to reassure them that the cruise was still on as planned, but deep down, I for one had pretty much already guessed that this was a major defect—although I didn't think there was any danger from it. I thought we might have to go into port, probably Gibraltar to have a defect rectified, but then we would be out again. Yeah right!

The Engineer had been with the Captain for an hour or so before he came back and we set about adopting single loop. First we would isolate the port loop of the reactor primary circuit, then recover and then if necessary do the same with the starboard loop. The idea was that we would, with each loop isolated in turn, be able to measure whether the water level in the Pressuriser was still dropping—thus indicating on which loop the leak might be. It wasn't quite as simple as it sounded though. Adopting single loop operation was a complicated affair, requiring some very careful machinery operation and control. We had only practised it once or twice in my entire time onboard the boat and many of those in the department had never done it.

Before getting to single loop operation, we first had to go through the processes of adopting single main engine drive, followed by single Steam generator operation. These served well to make us concentrate properly on what we were doing, and actually it seemed quite strange to be doing this stuff without somebody standing being us and criticising everything we did! These processes were relatively straightforward, and my role in the thing was to be out in the machinery spaces acting as 'safety number' and making sure the young Stokers and watchkeepers followed the procedure properly, and opened and closed the correct valves, started and stopped the correct machinery, and basically took everything nice and steady—it could get a bit hectic at times.

The actual adoption of single loop involved stopping the Main Circulating Pumps (MCPs) on the affected side, and then closing the Main Isolating Valves (MIVs) on that side. Doing this 'for real' at sea was unheard of and new engineering territory for all of us. Normally if we did an exercise single loop we stopped before we reached this stage because of the potential damage that could be inflicted on the pumps and valves. In the case of the pumps they could not be stopped for more than a certain amount of time due to their cooling systems, which needed water flow to work, while the valve seating surfaces of the MIVs could be damaged by the action of closing and opening them—they were designed to close in less than a second, and so smashed shut with enormous force. If the seats were shattered in closing, what happened was that there was more material within the reactor circuit that could become irradiated, thereby creating more environmental radiation onboard. Nonetheless it was something we had to do to potentially stop the leak. The most tense time was when the pumps on that side were stopped—we had to wait for the reactor core temperature to settle down at the temperatures that the manuals we were using said they would—it seemed to take an age for that to happen, and the Engineer was very close to aborting. We jumped with every alarm going off, whether it was from a bilge alarm or some machinery indication, but pressed on. Once flow through the core had stabilised, we shut the MIVs—the 'bang' of their closing sounding throughout the submarine, thereby isolating the port primary loop. Now we had to wait and monitor the Pressuriser level. It continued to fall. The leak wasn't in the port loop.

The entire process had taken about 6 hours to complete, and now we had to recover the machinery and repeat the process with the starboard loop. By now I had been up for over 24 hours straight, but there was going to be little chance for any rest until we had eliminated the starboard loop as the source of leakage. We had to get this leak isolated—worse case was that an entire primary pipe fractured, leading to a reactor meltdown and a huge environmental disaster, as well as the death certainly of all of us onboard. Sleep could come later.

So we worked on, recovering to double loop operation, followed by double Steam Generator and double main engine drive, only to the do it all again with the starboard loop. Finally the starboard MIVs banged shut and the Pressuriser level monitoring started again. The level continued to creep down, which was potentially very bad news, as it either indicated that the leak was somewhere on the Reactor Pressure Vessel (RPV) or in the Pressuriser system, both of which were places which could not be isolated. We were still at that stage in a disbelieving mode, and when someone came up with the idea that the problem might actually be a hole somewhere rather than a leaking valve, we were more than reluctant to consider it—how could that be on the primary system?

At this stage I was out on my feet, along with quite a number of other guys around the machinery spaces. I wanted to wait to see where we were going from here, but instead was ordered by the Engineer to go and get some sleep. If I was needed they would send somebody to get me, and the other guys could recover the machinery to the normal state in the meantime. I reluctantly agreed and went off to my rack. As soon as my head hit the pillow I was out of it.

Chapter 23

One Volunteer Wanted That Would Be Me Then!

The hand shaking my shoulder was insistent and rough. My eyes opened reluctantly and in some confusion—I glanced at my watch and couldn't quite compute what was happening—I had only been in my rack for a few short hours.

"Steve, the Engineer wants to see you—you awake?" the voice asked.

"Yeah, yeah alright. I'm awake" I could here him moving on to other bunks and repeating the same process.

I flicked on my bedside light, blinding myself but ensuring I didn't fall back asleep. My mind and body ached with fatigue, and it was a huge temptation just to turn over and drift back off, but I couldn't now. I heard complaints and groans around me as the other off-watch Charge Chiefs started climbing out of their racks and donning overalls.

"Fucking 3 o'clock in the morning. Wonder what all this is about?"

"What do you think it's about, Fuckwit?"

I listened in groggy silence as the banter flowed back and forth, soon interrupted by "Keep the noise down" and "There's people sleeping here" from the surrounding racks.

"Shut it front cunts! Like you never wake us up right?" came the surly reply.

With a heavy sigh I threw back the curtain of the bunk and rolled out over the 'roll bar' strategically sited to prevent a person being thrown out of bed in heavy weather, but also to catch the unwary in the nuts as they exited the rack. I threw on my socks, overalls and steaming boots, and after splashing my face with water in the heads, started making my way to the Wardroom with the other 3 Charge Chiefs. The splash of water on our faces hadn't really cleared the fog of the rude awakening, but the sight of the Captain, Engineer, Deputy Engineer, Executive Officer and a couple of other senior officers sitting in serious concentration around the Wardroom table did the trick.

"Come in guys, take a seat. Sorry for the unexpected shake" said the Engineer as we entered and found somewhere to sit. The small compartment was pretty full by now. Incongruously a Steward asked if we wanted a coffee—I quickly accepted.

The Steward was asked to leave and close the door. The Engineer took the lead. :

"OK gentlemen, we have called this meeting in order to clarify what the current situation is back-aft, and to determine where we go from here.

First of all, let me bring everybody up to date with where we are at the moment.

As you know, a few hours ago we had completed isolating the starboard primary loop with a view to identifying if there was a primary coolant leak anywhere in the starboard loop. We had already completed that process for the port loop, with the indication that there was no leak that side. The indications for the starboard loop were the same that is no leaks, although in both cases there could still have been leakage back to the Reactor Pressure Vessel through the Main Isolating Valves. We have since recovered to normal operations of both the primary circuit and the propulsion machinery.

While all this has been going on we have been in touch with the Admiralty, in order to keep them abreast of the situation, and to ask them for any assistance they might offer. We must remember that we are in something of a unique and extremely difficult position here—we potentially have a primary coolant leak on a submarine carried nuclear reactor. Just think about that for a moment, and think of the potential consequences of a Loss of Coolant Accident. In any case, the only assistance and advice we have received to date is for us to 'monitor the leak rate' (to laughter), so we are pretty much on our own for now.

As I mentioned, we have now recovered to normal propulsion operation. The problem now though is that since we recovered to two-loop operation the leak rate has increased (dead silence). We can only surmise that the operations to attempt to identify a leak in either the port or starboard loop have caused whatever defect we have to become worse, and hence cause the leakage rate to increase. Certainly as we all felt throughout the boat, the closing of the Main Isolating Valves is a very violent event, and would certainly physically shock the primary circuit and systems. If the leak has increased due to our actions, then we could potentially surmise again, that the source of the leak is something that can be made worse by conducting engineering evolutions—does that mean there is a valves that is becoming loose, a crack in a pipe that is expanding, a pinhole opening somewhere in the system, a flange that is breaking down? At this point we just do not know. What we do know though is that the leak rate is slowly getting worse".

"Sir, one question. Is there any condensation showing on the Reactor Compartment viewing window?" I asked.

"None has been reported to me, but ring up Manoeuvring and get them to check again now."

I did as asked, and was told that they would get back to me straightaway.

The Engineer continued:

"What we now have to decide is where do we go from here? We have attempted to identify where any potential leak site might be by isolating each primary loop in turn without any result. As you are aware, conducting single loop operations is considered as Emergency Operation, and was not something we did lightly. We have already gone way beyond the kind of machinery operation that would normally be expected of us to undertake, and already we are in the realms of theoretical reactor operation—there is not a great deal written in the operating manuals concerning how to operate the reactor in these emergency situations, and the Admiralty is not exactly rushing in with clear instructions for us. For instance, we cannot clearly ascertain whether there is leakage back through the Main Isolating Valves when they are closed, unless there is a considerable pressure differential each side of them, which unless we know for certain makes it impossible to know if a leak is isolated in the loop. Also, clearly the conducting of machinery evolutions in search of any leak has caused the leak rate to increase, and that in turn makes it dangerous to carry out any further investigations for fear of increasing the rate even further."

The phone rang. It was the Engineer Officer of the Watch, and he requested that I go back-aft to the Reactor Tunnel. I asked permission to leave and was released as the meeting continued in my absence.

As I made my way towards the Reactor Tunnel it was clear from the sombre mood of the crew members I was passing that word had got around that there was some kind of problem going on back aft. A couple of guys asked if I knew anything, but at that moment there was little I could tell them.

As the forward inner heavy hydraulic reactor tunnel airlock door hissed and thumped shut behind me, I looked toward the after end of the reactor tunnel to see 2 Artificer Chiefs gazing intently down at the Reactor Compartment viewing window embedded in the centre of the deck. As I approached them, the first, Smudge, spoke up:

"Steve, we think we can see some condensation around the edges of the window"

"How long ago did you notice it?"

"We can't be sure, but we thought we noticed it a couple of hours ago. We didn't want to say anything though because we can't be sure we are not seeing things".

I looked intensely at the thick glass in the deck. It seemed just the same as normal to me, but as I got down on my knees for a closer look, Smudge and Terry pointed out a couple of areas on the bottom of the window where they thought they saw tiny droplets of condensation. I peered even more closely—nose millimetres from the glass, and it became clear that there were indeed tiny droplets of water on the Reactor Compartment side. They shouldn't be there, and the sight of them sent shivers through me as comprehension of the potential situation we might be facing struck me.

I rang the Wardroom from the Tunnel and asked to speak to the Engineer. I explained our findings to him, and requested permission for the ventilation fans and air coolers inside the Reactor Compartment, normally switched off at sea, to be switched on for a short while, in order to try to encourage more condensation at the viewing window. My thoughts were that if there was steam and hence water in the atmosphere of the Reactor compartment, some cooler air in there might cause some of the water to condense on the window. He agreed and asked me to talk to the Engineer Officer of the Watch to make it happen. Five minutes later we had the machinery running, and went into the Engine Room for a fag and cup of tea while we waited for something to happen.

Fifteen minutes later we returned to the tunnel and lifted up the protective cover of the viewing window. We all peered through the window and this time we did not need to look too hard. There was clear condensation on the bottom of the window. I made for the phone and talked to the Engineer again:

"Sir, its Steve. There is definitely some condensation on the bottom of the viewing window."

"OK Steve, come back to the Wardroom."

I made my way back to the Wardroom, my mind in a whirl. For me, there was simply no doubt that there was some kind of leak in the primary system, the water leaking probably into the bilge, but not yet at a rate high enough to set off the automatic bilge level alarms down there. What I couldn't figure out was why the radiation detection alarms were not going crazy—surely there was enough steam in the atmosphere of the Reactor Compartment to do that?

I walked into intense discussions in the Wardroom, people in small groups theorising what the possible problem was, and what should be done about them. Eventually the Engineer reined it all in:

"OK guys, listen in. The basic fact is that we still do not know for sure there is a leak, and the question is, how do we find out?"

"Actually Sir" I said, "We do know there is a leak, otherwise how would there be condensation on the RC viewing window? What we don't know is where the leak is".

"Fair enough. We need to find out where the water is coming from".

There was silence in the Wardroom for the first time in ages. We were probably all thinking the same thing, but nobody wanted to say it. There was an emergency procedure entitled 'Reactor Compartment Entry at Sea' among the operating manuals onboard, which described how to do exactly what we probably needed to do, but it was one of those ones that was very rarely even looked at, since the probability of ever needing to use it was considered so low. I recalled that we had done an exercise Reactor Compartment Entry during the work-up, but it had really only been in the form of a reactor scram and recovery, and checking that we carried the equipment needed for such an event onboard. I could not recall the last time I had personally read the procedure—probably during my Charge Chief training, and then only in case I was asked some obscure question during the exam.

I think it was the Deputy Engineer who finally said what we were all thinking:

"Well, clearly we need to make a Reactor Compartment Entry to find out where the leak is."

"Yes, I am thinking the same thing" said the Engineer. "I don't think we have any choice".

"I will go down and take a look around" said the Deputy Engineer.

"You are not going down there on your own—it needs to be a team of at least 2 people" responded the Engineer.

"Well, since I am the Primary Charge Chief, I had better go with him" I piped up from the corner. "He doesn't get down there very often, and will get lost on his own!" That got a few wry smiles.

"OK with that John?" said the Engineer to his Deputy.

"Yes of course, thanks Steve".

The decision made, a weight seemed to have been lifted off our shoulders. There was no longer any uncertainty—we knew what we had to do, and now we were keen to get on with it.

The 'Doc' or Petty Officer Sickbay Attendant was called into the Wardroom and warned off about our intentions. To him was given the task of ensuring John and my safety during the process, both in terms of radiation and heat protection. He left a worried looking man, but we trusted him to look after us.

For the next hour or so we discussed what the procedure was going to entail. The 'Reactor Compartment (RC) Entry at Sea' procedure was dragged out and dusted off, and the Manoeuvring Room team was instructed to start getting all the gear listed in the procedure together.

The process itself was going to be fairly straightforward in machinery terms. Before the RC could be entered the reactor would need to be shut down, or scrammed. This was a pretty routine process which should not cause us any difficulty. Once scrammed, the reactor temperature would have to be maintained as high as possible by shutting off as much of the heat take-off as possible, by stopping both turbo-generators and any other machinery that we usually kept running during a scram. 15 minutes after the reactor had scrammed the 'short half-life' radiation emitted while the reactor was operating should have totally dissipated so that we could enter the compartment relatively safe from excess radiation, although the long half-life stuff would still be around. We would then have a short window of opportunity to have a look around the RC to try to find where we might have a leak before we would have to get out of there either because of radiation levels, heat stress or a requirement to re-start the reactor due to falling temperature, whichever came first.

From a personal protection side the job was going to be grim. The RC was normally a sealed compartment at sea and there would be no opportunity to ventilate it before entering. There was also going to be radiation levels beyond what we could normally expect to receive onboard, and the environmental heat down there was going to be intense. All this meant that we were going to need to be wearing a considerable amount of protective equipment—primarily against radiation, since there was not much we were going to be able to do about the heat. John and I sat and read the RC entry procedure, and it started to sink in that we were going to be in for a rough ride!

The list of equipment required for the RC entry read like a shopping list for a reactor accident—loads of protective this and shielding that. For our part we would be required to wear a pair of reactor grade cotton overalls, cotton hat, gloves and over-shoes. On top of this we would have a pair of thick clear plastic protective overalls which included a hood and plastic over-shoes, known as 'boil-in-the-bag' suits for obvious reasons. On our hands would be rubber gloves (or 'Marigolds' as we called them—even though they were not) over the cotton ones, which should melt nicely on to our skin if we inadvertently touched one of the super hot primary pipes, and to top it all off we would be wearing 'Emergency Breathing System' (EBS) facemasks to breathe through in the RC, which would necessitate us dragging 60 foot breathing hoses connected to points in the Reactor Tunnel down with us. Just to ensure that no particulate radiation could sneak into the suits, they would be taped around the ankles, wrists and facemask, completely sealing us inside them. Breathing, movement and communication would be extremely difficult, to say the least. As we sat and read the procedure, the Doc came and saw us, and instructed us to start drinking water—as much as we could force down. He told us that the heat in the RC would be our biggest problem, and that there was a real danger of us becoming dehydrated very quickly in the boil-in—the-bag suits. He explained that in the suits, our bodies would sweat like crazy, but that the sweat would not evaporate and cool us down as would normally be the case. In consequence, our core temperatures would probably rocket up, possibly to dangerous levels. He continued that one way the body would try to cool down was by urinating to release heat, and if we felt the urge to pee in the suit, that we should not resist! With all the water we were going to drink, that seemed very likely to be the case!

As well as the personal protective stuff making our lives hell, we were going to have to carry a whole load of other stuff down with us too. First there was a tool box containing enough stainless steel spanners, wrenches, clamps, knives for cutting away lagging and goodness knows what else—we could hardly move in our suits so to expect us to fix anything was a bit of a stretch, but we would take it anyway. We would also need to take down the Doc's medical measuring equipment—radiation air monitor, wet-bulb temperature and humidity meter, Geiger-counter and some other bits and pieces, as well as a portable video camera with which to film our adventures. It ended up as a big pile of gear to transport around, and our biggest concern was the time it would take to get this stuff into and out of the RC when the time we would have down there was going to be limited in the first place. Still, ours was not to reason why and all that.

The Captain made an announcement to the Ship's Company shortly after, briefly outlining the situation we found ourselves in, and explaining what was about to happen. The asked that those people not directly involved in the operation should try to stay out of the way of those that were, and told everybody that he would speak to them again when we knew anything more about the defect.

Preparations now began in earnest for the reactor scram and RC entry. Once John and I had been down for a look around, we were going to need to be de-contaminated. The Junior Ratings (JR's) bathroom was the area designated as the de-contamination centre by the procedure we were now following, and so the medical staff set about building an enclosed path from the reactor compartment to the JR's bathroom using plastic sheeting and tape—no mean task as the path would lead through the Control Room, down 2 deck ladder and then along the entire length of 2 deck to reach the bathroom. It meant that access to those areas would now be restricted to the remainder of the crew, probably bringing home to them to some extent that this was a serious defect we were attending.

By now I had managed to force down a couple of litres of water, and John a similar amount. It's very difficult to drink that much at about 4 am (unless its beer!), but under the stern gaze of the Doc we did try to keep gulping it down. The pile of equipment in the Tunnel kept on increasing, and it seemed as though it would not stop coming. Eventually we had to tell them to stop—clearly whoever had written the listing in the first place had no idea of the logistics of trying to physically get all the gear into the RC, and also, as we were reminding by the Doc, once the stuff was taken in there it would have to stay there until we reached harbour and it could be safely removed. Once it was through the RC door it had to be considered as contaminated. The only thing we would be bringing out with us was what we were wearing and the video camera (that was coming out contaminated or not—much to the irritation of the Doc).

The tension started to build as we approached the time for the operation to start. We would be given 15 minutes notice of the reactor scram, and then would have to wait a further 15 minutes before we could open the RC plug door and make our way into the RC. We would dress in our protective gear while we waited for the reactor scram, and the other people in the Tunnel with us—the Doc, and 2 MEAOWs to help with the plug door and equipment transfer would also need to wear some protective gear and breathing apparatus while the plug door was open. In the rest of the boat the ventilation was going to be stopped for the duration of the RC entry, just in case there was any airborne contamination present, and would only be re-started once the medical team was absolutely certain there was not. The temperature in the Tunnel was already high enough to make us sweat just in our normal overalls, so we were putting off donning the heavy gear for as long as we possibly could. We could feel the boat 'catching a trim' at 80 metres, tipping slowly forwards and backwards at slow speed as the Ship Control Officer of the Watch pumped water between the ballast tanks to balance the boat. Getting this right would reduce power usage later, and the guys were taking their time to ensure it was perfect before we got going.

Finally the word came through to 'standby for reactor scram in 15 minutes'. We took a last long pull on the water bottles and started dressing. First came off the normal overalls, to be taken forward for use after we had been de-contaminated. On went the cotton reactor overalls, hat, gloves and overshoes. In the breast pocket of the cotton overalls went a couple of the old fashioned pen dosimeters, and one of the new electronic ones each, which were already bleeping annoyingly as we dressed. Over the cotton overalls went the thick plastic ones, instantly causing us to sweat profusely in the still, warm air of the Tunnel, followed by the plastic overshoes and 'Marigolds' over the cotton gloves. The Doc fussed around us making sure everything was tight and zipped up, and then set about tightly taping up our ankles and wrists. This process took about 5 minutes, and at 10 minutes to go the watch keeps in the manoeuvring Room started counting down to the scram. At five minutes to go we started the final part of the dressing process. We plugged in our extended EBS masks, checked the demand valves were operating correctly, and after ensuring that the glass in the masks was spotlessly clean we carefully fitted them to our faces, pulling the tightening tapes very hard to squeeze the seals to our already sweating and red faces—we certainly didn't want any nasties getting to us from that route. The 'Darth Vader' breathing noises were very loud in the confined space. There was some confusion about whether we should wear the cotton cap and plastic suit hood over or under the tightening straps for the facemask (that detail wasn't described in the procedure!), but in the end decided that to prevent possible radiation contamination, the straps should be inside. So, on went the cotton cap, then the hood went over the lot. The Doc then set to work once more with his roll of tape, and securely taped the hood to the edges of the breathing mask—all the way round. We were now in a position such that if for some reason our air supply became entangled or interrupted, we really would struggle to get our masks off to breathe. It was not a comfortable feeling.

With only a couple of minutes now until the reactor scram, we made ourselves comfortable and waited. The heat inside the suit and mask was already building up, and we had yet to set foot inside the RC! Next thing we heard and felt was the 'thump' of the reactor control rods dropping into the core, followed by:

"Reactor Scram, Reactor Scram. Reduce electrical loads throughout the submarine!"

"Reactor Tunnel, Manoeuvring. 15 minutes to Reactor Compartment Entry".

"Tunnel, Roger". Replied the Doc on the machinery broadcast system.

There was little we could do now but wait. The masks made it pretty much impossible to communicate, so we each sat in our own little world as the clock ticked down. Even the live-wire Doc had nothing to do as we waited, apart from fiddling with one or other measuring device or instrument for the thousandth time. I imagined I could already feel the rays of invisible gamma radiation slicing through my body, doing goodness knows what damage to my internal organs. Still, I was here now, so best just to get on with it—I felt a bit like a First World War 'Tommy' waiting to 'go over the top'.

"Reactor Tunnel, Manoeuvring. 5 minutes to Reactor Compartment Entry".

"Tunnel, Roger".

"Reactor Tunnel, Manoeuvring. 2 minutes to Reactor Compartment Entry. Don EBS in the Tunnel. Unlock the Reactor Compartment Plug Door".

The Doc and the 2 MEAOW put on their own EBS masks, carefully checking that they fitted tightly, and were operating correctly. One MEAOW removed and stowed the padlock from the latching arrangement of the huge RC entrance door. This door was always locked at sea.

"Manoeuvring, Tunnel. EBS donned in the Tunnel. Reactor Compartment Plug Door unlocked" wheezed the Doc through his EBS mask into the microphone.

"Roger Tunnel, open the RC Plug Door"

Slowly the 2 Chiefs pulled open the half ton plug door on its huge hinge. Shaped like a massive sink plug—hence the name of the door—the door swung round and locked into place, taking up most of the space in the aft end of the Tunnel. The locking latch clicked loudly as the door locked in position.

The walls of the entrance into the RC were about eight inches thick, and all that now remained between us and the atmosphere of the compartment was the 'Inner Plug Door', an inward opening spherical hatch locked in place by a gearwheel handle arrangement. Normally this hatch was 'cracked' open before being fully opened, to allow the atmosphere between the RC and Tunnel to equalise.

"Manoeuvring, Tunnel. Reactor Compartment Plug Door open".

"Roger. Carry on and crack open the Inner Plug Door".

One of the MEAOW's thumped the door handle upwards until a loud hissing was heard as the 2 atmospheres started to equalise. The Doc moved in and placed one of his radiation sensors close to the door as the hissing continued. To me, our electronic personal radiation sensors seemed to increase their bleep rate.

"Manoeuvring, Tunnel. Inner Plug Door cracked open".

"Roger, when equalised, open Inner Plug Door".

The hissing continued for a further minute or so, and then started to dissipate as the pressure equalised. The Doc seemed relaxed about radiation levels, and so the Deputy Engineer motioned one of the MEAOW's to open the inner door. He pushed the operating handle to its full extent, and then pushed the inner door on its hinge into the Reactor Compartment. Now it was our turn.

"Manoeuvring, Tunnel. Inner Plug Door open, entry team making their way in".

"Roger Tunnel. Inform Manoeuvring of team stay time as soon as possible".

"Tunnel Roger".

Before we could enter, the Doc leaned in to the RC and placed a wet-bulb thermometer just inside the entrance. From this he would determine how long we could safely remain in the RC from a heat exhaustion point of view. We would be taking radiation measurement devices with us that would tell him the radiation exposure limits for us. We could already feel that the heat was going to be the limiting factor.

The Doc stepped out of the way, and I stepped over the coaming and onto the top plates of the Reactor Compartment, pulling my ludicrously long breathing hose with me. The heat was an overwhelming force that seemed to smack into me like a physical thing. Instantly my eyes were stinging and my breathing mask was filled with sweat—I could see it dripping out of the exhaust ports down onto my plastic suit.

I turned back to towards the entrance and started taking the equipment being passed in to me by John. I stacked it on the plates, and then set about descending the ladder to the Reactor Compartment mid-level plates. At the bottom of the ladder I turned once more and accepted the equipment being passed down from above, piling it all at the foot of the ladder. I collected the plug in communications microphone and quickly connected it to the comms panel next to the starboard steam generator.

"Manoeuvring, RC. Entry team at mid-level. Commencing search at this level".

Roger RC. You have been in the RC for two minutes so far".

Two minutes! It already felt like about half an hour. All I seemed to be able to think about was the heat—it was just crippling. I tried to rub my burning eyes, but my gloved hands just bounced off the mask.

John reached the mid level plates, dragging and untangling this breathing hose as he came. He was all business and seemed not to be as affected by the heat as I seemed to be. He motioned that he would take the port side and for me to check around starboard. We started out on our separate paths.

Directly in front of me was the top half of the starboard steam generator, effectively a massive cylinder with a large steam take-off pipe coming out of the top, and disappearing upwards and aft into the Manoeuvring Room and then the Engine Room to supply steam to the main engines and generators. Down here though, all I could see was a wall of insulating lagging. I slowly walked around the boiler looking for any sign of steam or water leakage. There was none.

"RC, Manoeuvring. Your stay time is 15 minutes. Repeat, your stay time is 15 minutes. 4 minutes so far".

"RC Roger". 15 minutes was nowhere near enough.

Moving aft from the starboard boiler, I quickly assessed the top of the 3 starboard main coolant pumps, although again there was little to see as these were covered by stainless steel protective covers. There were no apparent signs of leakage here either. In between the 2 groups of 3 main coolant pumps stood the top of the Pressuriser, again swathed in thick lagging. No leaks or signs of the lagging being burned by steam. Turning towards the forward centre of the compartment I headed towards the 'wedding cake' of the nuclear reactor pressure vessel. I climbed up the 2 layers of insulation forming the wedding cake shape, and peered into the recess on top of the reactor which contained the control rods and operating motors where they passed through the thick top of the pressure vessel. Again there were no signs of anything amiss here. Returning to the rear of the starboard boiler I met up again with John, who shook his head to indicate that he had found nothing either.

"Manoeuvring, RC. RC mid-level clear—moving down to the lower level".

"Roger. 10 minutes gone". Damn!

I looked at John, who appeared fresh as a daisy in his suit. I on the other hand was coming to realise the truth of the name 'boil-in-the-bag' suit, and literally felt as if I was melting. I could feel water collecting in the bottom of my suit and sloshing around as I walked, and had already done the 'pee to keep cool' trick, although I was not convinced it made any difference. Sweat was streaming out of the exhaust vents in my breathing mask, which was lucky as I probably would have drowned had they not been there, and my eyes stung constantly from the sweat in them that I could not wipe away. In addition, and for the first time that I had noticed, our electronic dosimeters were now, rather than bleeping forlornly, emitting a single continuous tone to indicate to us that we really should be somewhere else right now.

From the mid level of the Reactor Compartment there were 3 ladders down to the bottom plates, one to port, one starboard and another near to the rear bulkhead. The small deck plate hatchways to the ladders had been locked closed using cable ties (or 'tie-wraps' as we knew them), as was the normal practice before sailing and on the final pre-departure inspection of the RC, to ensure that they did not fly open in heavy weather and damage something important, or make any noise—after all this was supposed to be the 'silent service'. With perfect hindsight perhaps the guys that did the final inspection could have used fewer tie-wraps, and it took us a couple of minutes to snip off and bag the nylon fixings (nothing was ever left in the lying loose in the RC), open and latch back the small hatches to give us access to the lower level. The breathing hoses were a pain and continually got caught up on valves and small pipes as we moved around the space, boiling in our suits and gasping the breath into our lungs through the long thin hoses. We would have to tie-wrap the hatches back into place as we were leaving—another good few minutes work.

As I started down the aft most ladder, my plastic encased feet slipping precariously on the ladder rungs, I heard the PA system for the final time—I wouldn't be able to hear it on the lower level:

"RC, Manoeuvring. 13 minutes gone, start preparing to evacuate". 13 minutes? It felt like about 30 seconds so far. How times flies when you're having fun!

John moved towards the microphone:

"Manoeuvring, RC. Understand 13 minutes gone; we haven't searched the lower level yet".

"John, your stay time is almost up, you need to start making your way out" came from the Engineer.

"We are here now, and we really need to look around the lower level".

"Your call John—make it as quick as you can". I noticed that my opinion was not required.

I continued to the bottom of the aft ladder, squeezing past the side of the Pressuriser ensuring that my breathing hose was clear as I went. The close proximity of the Pressuriser and ion-exchange column, where any radioactive debris floating around the primary system was caught by internal filters, was making my electronic dosimeter go even more crazy than before, in turn causing me to rush as quickly as possible away from the ladder and around to the port side of the lower level to try and get some shielding and hence protection between me and the column. It was noticeably cooler down in the bottom of the compartment, and I stayed low to the plates to maximise the cooling effect. I needed all the help I could get—I was knackered and could feel my energy level dropping and my breathing rate increasing with the strain.

I glanced back in time to see John reach the bottom of the ladder. His dosimeter screaming, as he moved off towards the starboard side of the lower level and out of my view as I started checking around the plethora of system pipes, valves and equipment located around the port side. Most of the forward end of the space was dominated by the bulk of the bottom end of the Reactor Pressure Vessel and its cladding, but at the forward outboard end of both sides of the lower level were the bottom of the steam generators, and the pipes connecting the steam generators to the primary circuit—this was where we thought that perhaps, if anywhere, there might be some kind of leak, especially around the small steam generator level pipework and pressuriser level connections that infested the area. I carefully and closely inspected each and every pipe and connection I could see, but nowhere was there any evidence of leakage. There was definitely a leak somewhere though as I could see a decent amount of water in the bilge from this low down, when I knew that normally the bilges were practically dry down here.

Untangling my nemesis, the breathing hose once more, I turned back towards the Pressuriser and ion-exchange column at the rear of the compartment, expecting to meet John once more at the foot of the ladder. As I turned the corner towards the ladder though, John motioned me urgently to come to the starboard side, a look of some concern in his eyes. As I slowly manoeuvred myself next to him in the maze of pipes, valves, connections and electrical cabling looms in the starboard aft part of the lower level, being sure not to rest my breathing hose on the red hot pipes, he motioned me to look towards the forward part of the compartment.

What could only be described as a cascade of water was running down the side of the Reactor Pressure Vessel cladding, splashing onto the deckplates underneath the bottom of the starboard boiler, and sloshing down into the bilge. From where I was standing it seemed like an awful lot was being ejected from somewhere on the reactor itself, and for a terrible moment I had a fleeting vision of the leak site rupturing right now in front of us, engulfing us in superheated steam and fission fragments—I had to shake myself to dispel the image.

John motioned me to start filming the gushing water. I had totally forgotten about the video camera, but quickly brought it up to shoot the scene. As I adjusted the focus to get as close in as possible to the site of the leak, I could see quite clearly through the viewfinder a light blue tinge surrounding the water falling on the deckplates.

"Fuck me!" I said into my facemask as I realised that the blue tinge was the radiation emanating from the water itself. This was definitely a 'Star Trek' moment, and looking over the top of the camera the blue haze was clearly visible around the entire leak site. Both of our electronic dosimeters screamed at us to get away—whether it was from the ion-exchange column or the leaking radioactive water, who knows. There was no way we could get any nearer to the leak to find out its exact location underneath all that lagging, but I filmed as much as I could see hoping that once the boffins looked at it they would be able to find it. It was time to get the hell out of here.

I moved back to the foot of the ladder up to the mid level, my mind already trying to play over where the source of the leak might be. I gripped the ladder and started upwards, protecting the invaluable camera as I went. I had to stop twice on the way up as I ran out of puff, but eventually I pulled myself out of the hatchway, falling on to the mid level plates in exhaustion. I noticed that I had stopped sweating by now—not a good sign. I could hear John climbing up behind me, but louder than that was an insistent calling from the loud speakers:

"RC, Manouvring"

"RC, Manouvring"

I struggled up and made for the microphone:

"RC"

"Guys, you need to exit the RC NOW! You have now been down there for 35 minutes. We have been trying to contact you". No wonder I was knackered!

"We were on the lower level and couldn't hear anything" I replied "We are making our exit now—just have to tie-wrap the hatches"

"Negative Steve, leave the hatches as they are—just get out now".

"RC Roger"

John had heard the exchange and made his way past me and up the ladder to the entrance of the RC. His steps were heavy up the ladder and he took one step at a time. I took one last look around, and collecting just the Doc's measuring gear, started up the ladder. As I looked towards the top of the ladder it seemed to become more distant as a wave of dizziness swept over me. I stumbled on the next couple of steps, and had to stop for a moment to catch my breath. Looking up again the top of the ladder didn't seem to be any closer as I took another couple of faltering steps upwards. Looking over the top of the ladder towards the exit I saw a couple of faces staring in at me, and hands gesturing me onwards. I was so tired, and knew that I was in real danger of toppling back down the ladder. Just then one of the faces at the door materialised into a body, and I felt hands dragging me up the final couple of stairs and over the door coaming. I flopped onto the plastic coated Tunnel deck next to John and heard the inner plug door clang shut behind me. I was then manhandled out of the way as the massive plug door was swung back into place and locked shut. In the background I heard the main broadcast:

"Commencing Reactor Start-Up".

They were going to re-start the reactor. I looked at John and shook my head indicating I thought that was a bad idea. He gestured that we needed to pass our information to the Boss, and then shouted to one of the MEAOWs to take the video camera forward as soon as he could. In the meantime, the Doc gave us a good bollocking for staying down there for so long, and informed us that we had to keep our full suits and breathing gear on until we reached the Junior Ratings bathroom for decontamination. We headed that way through the plastic tunnel that had been created for us, transferring the breathing hose connection from one point in the deck head to another as we went. We could see people peering at us through the plastic as we passed. The coolness of the atmosphere outside the RC was a real treat.

We reached the bathroom and were ushered into a cubicle each, fully booted and spurred. The water was on full blast and full heat, and we were scrubbed down fully clothed with some decontaminant soap—goodness knows where the water from this was being collected! Finally we were monitored, and the suits declared free of contamination. We could now remove them. The tape was cut free from our wrists, ankles and facemasks, and dumped into 'radioactive waste' bags. As the mask was finally removed, I could see sweat squirting from the pores in my face in the bathroom mirrors as my body desperately tried to cool itself down. With the mask removed I gulped down a full bottle of water before continuing with the decontamination process. Off came the plastic suit, cotton suit and everything else, also destined for the low-level waste bags, and in I went again to the shower. At first they kept the water as hot as I could stand and I had another good scrub with some kind of special soap. I was continually monitored again, and after a while informed that I was not contaminated. I switched the shower to cold, and just stood there for a good 10 minutes trying to get my body temperature sorted out. I felt weak, dehydrated, and bone tired and just wanted to go to bed. First though, I would have to go the Wardroom again to make a report on what I had seen down there. I shrugged into my overalls once more and had a quick cigarette in the corridor between gulps on the water bottle. My face looked as though I had been 10 rounds with Mike Tyson from the tightness of the facemask straps and seal, and now that I was able to drink again I couldn't seem to stop sweating. My working overalls were drenched already and I had a screaming headache, probably from the effects of the dehydration. My eyes still stung and burned, and looking in the mirror I saw that they were red-rimmed and bloodshot. All in all, it was fair to say that I felt like shit.

I walked into a quiet and tense Wardroom. The tape from the video camera was being shown on the TV, and my "Fuck Me!" outburst, which I hadn't realised had been picked up by the camera, got a few derisory laughs. The picture was pretty much self-explanatory, and everybody's attention was fixed on it, the seriousness of the problem we now faced clear enough for all to see. As the picture veered away from the leak site, the picture clicked off. There was silence in the Wardroom for a few moments. Finally, it was the Captain who spoke.

"Well gentlemen, I am not an Engineer, but even to my eye that looks serious. Is it?"

"Sir" replied the Engineer, now back from the Manoeuvring Room, "It's difficult for us to determine exactly where the water is coming from, but the fact is that there should not be *any* leakage from that area of the primary circuit".

"What about the danger posed by the leak" asked the Captain

"Again it's very difficult to quantify, since there has never been anything like this that any of us has come across before. We simply do not know the origin of the leak. Myself and John have assessed the film, and there simply is nothing underneath the lagging in that area that could leak, apart from if there was a crack in either the RPV or one of the major primary circuit pipes in the area, which given that these are seriously hefty pieces of engineering would seem very unlikely".

"Well, the fact is that there is definitely a major leak there, so, I ask again, what is the worst case here?"

"Absolute worst case would be a loss of coolant accident if, assuming there is a crack in one of the primary loops, the crack were to propagate around the entire circumference of the pipe and cause it to fail completely".

"That would happen in that case?"

"If the reactor was operating at normal temperature and pressure, a full bore primary circuit failure could result in us losing all of its coolant almost instantly, and whatever water is left boiling instantly into steam. Due to the lack of cooling the reactor core could melt, and there would be a massive pressure increase in the Reactor Compartment, possibly high enough to overcome the reactor primary containment system, and even the submarine's pressure hull. That in turn would probably sink the boat, and could lead to the release of radiation in this area of the Mediterranean. I must stress though that we do not know that there is a crack or how bad it is".

Silence returned to the Wardroom as the Engineer's words sank in. We all kind of knew that the scenario he had just spelled out could be the case, but hearing it out loud kind of made it more real.

"What does the Admiralty have to say" asked the Captain

"Not much really Sir. They keep telling us to measure the leak rate and to monitor, but are not really offering us any new advice. I think this is all happening too fast for them to react with anything useful—by the time we have sent them the latest update, things have moved on again. I think we are going to have to make our own decisions on this one".

"Right, first things first. What is the current state of the reactor and systems Engineer?"

"We have started the process of reactor scram recovery Sir. We will have double main engine drive in about 20 minutes".

"Are we totally happy with flashing up the reactor when we know there is a leak on it?"

"Given the unknown nature of the defect Sir, I think it is something we have to do so that we can get to a safe harbour as soon as possible".

"But can we be sure that the leak will not increase or get worse by starting and running the reactor".

"No Sir we can't be sure, but we have little choice as I see it".

The Captain now looked around the Wardroom at the rest of us:

"What about you guys, what's your opinion?"

"Re-starting the reactor to get us back into harbour more quickly would have to be a calculated risk. Problem is that if the crack, if that's what it is, did cause the pipe to completely split; we would have a major nuclear accident on our hands. I don't think we can risk it". This from the Deputy Engineer.

Charge Chief Andy Crawley, my electrical counterpart spoke up next. "For me Sir, the risk of a reactor accident, no matter how remote, supersedes everything else. We have to shut down the reactor".

When my turn came, there was no doubt in my mind. "Having been down there and seen the leak Sir, I am certain that we should not operate the reactor with that defect. The leak rate has increased over the last few days which indicates to me that the crack might be growing. I simply do not think that we can responsibly re-start the reactor with a known defect".

"I agree" said the Captain. "Engineer, stop the reactor scram recovery. We need to think about our way forward from here, and how we can make the reactor as safe as possible until we can get to the nearest safe harbour and some help".

"Very good Sir. I would like to talk to my team separately and present you with the engineering plan for the next phase if I may Sir".

"Yes, of course. We will all meet again here in 1 hour".

The meeting broke up. Instantly the Engineer phoned the Manoeuvring Room and ordered the Engineer Officer of the Watch (EOOW) to halt the reactor scram recovery. The EOOW reminded the Engineer that we had been running the submarine on battery power now for over 2 hours, and that there was only a limited amount of time left on the batteries. We needed to surface and run the diesel generators, and then recharge the main batteries. This information was passed to the Captain, who immediately agreed that the boat could be surfaced so that the diesels could be run for power. As the engineers got around a table in the wardroom to discuss the way ahead, we could hear preparations for surfacing being made around us, and the boat had already started taking on an upward angle as we headed to periscope depth.

I was still feeling the effects of the reactor compartment entry—sweating, thirsty and extremely tired, but got myself ready to try to think of what we now had to do. Basically having decided that we would not run the reactor, we were left with very limited propulsion options. With the reactor shut down we would have no steam to drive the main engines, but just as importantly, or even more importantly, we would also have no steam to drive the turbo-generators. This meant that we now had a very small amount of electrical power that we could use. Normally the entire boat's electrical supply originated from the turbo-generators, with the main battery supplying power through the motor-generators (which changed the dc power from the batteries into ac power we could use) when the turbo-generators had to be shut down for short periods, as is the case during a reactor scram. The battery obviously had a limited output capacity when it was being used on full load to supply the ship's essential services and propulsion through the big dc machine of the emergency propulsion motor, and for extended periods the diesel generators could be used either at periscope depth or on the surface to re-charge the main battery. So, while the battery could be re-charged, we were always going to be limited by the amount of power that could be extracted from the motor-generators, which wasn't much.

A further more serious problem was with the reliability of the diesel generators and emergency propulsion motor. The diesels were 12 cylinder dc motor machines, while the emergency propulsion motor was a dc motor about the size of a small car attached by a manually clutched chain drive to the main gearbox. In normal operation I hadn't in nearly 10 years onboard seen the emergency propulsion motor run for more than a maximum of probably 2 hours, while the maximum running period for the diesel generators had been about 12 hours during a number of reactor start-ups in harbour. It was now clear that we would have to sail to Gibraltar several hundred miles away, on the surface, and using this machinery combination. The diesel generators and the emergency propulsion motor were all solidly mounted on their bedplates, and there was a danger that they would simply smash themselves to bits as they ran continuously. Nobody was particularly keen on the prospect, but it was clearly apparent that we had no alternative and would have to make the best of it.

By now I was pretty much out on my feet and really needed to get some sleep. The Boss must have thought so too, as once again like a small child I was sent off to bed for some rest. I was still feeling a bit ill from the effects of the whole experience, and was asleep as soon as I got to my bed. The last thing I heard was the order to surface the submarine—we would be going up slowly since we did not have the power to run the LP blower, a machine that was usually used to get the boat to full buoyancy—this time we would bobble up like a cork using just the high pressure air to fill the ballast tanks. I knew nothing about it though. I was dead to the world in my rack, and would remain so for the next 15 hours! I don't think I ever slept so deeply, either before or after, and when I woke up again, my entire world had changed beyond recognition.

The first thing I noticed on waking was the heat. Submarines are warm places at the best of times, but normally there was a nice cool breeze from the 'punka-louva' air vent sited just above my head. I was lying in a pool of sweat today though, and instead of the usual strong blow through the vent there was something of a luke-warm puff. Clearly the reduced power available was already affecting the boat.

I got up and went for a wash—a bird-bath actually since the showers were now out of bounds to conserve water now that we would not be able to use the evaporators. The boat felt quiet and dark, and was rolling gently in the surface swell. There was little sensation of movement through the water, and I guessed that we were barely making headway using the emergency propulsion motor. I made my way along the darkened 2 deck passage, now cleared of the plastic tunnel I had used to get to the decontamination centre earlier, to the Mess for a cup of tea before going back aft. As I entered a surprisingly full Mess—a lot of the forward staff would have little to do with the boat on the surface—the conversation stopped. I opened the tea cupboard and grabbed by personal mug, and started making myself a cup of tea.

"Steve, you alright mate?" asked a voice from one of the benches

"Yeah, I'm fine—just a bit knackered that's all" I replied.

"We just wanted to say that was a fucking good job you and the Deputy did yesterday."

Then to my astonishment, the whole mess started applauding me. I really didn't know where to put myself as this was totally unexpected. I nodded and quickly made my tea, and red-faced hurriedly took a seat. I was quite touched really, but obviously the environment was too macho to let that show!

There had not been much information flow downwards about the situation and a lot of the guys did not have a clue about what was going on. A lot of rumours had spread as a result, ranging from us going straight back to the UK, a Task Force being sent out to escort us back to Gibraltar, the reactor in danger of 'melting', to the submarine being scuttled in the Atlantic! I told them as much as I knew at least, and asked them to pass on the information to the Junior Rates too, so that they would also be in the picture. There were a lot of questions about whether the diesels and emergency propulsion motor were strong enough to get us to Gibraltar, which frankly, I could not answer myself. I needed to get back aft to take a look—the machinery had been running for almost a whole day now, and it would be interesting to see how it was fairing.

Chapter 24

The Long Run Home

The boat was already feeling quite warm with the lack of air-conditioning, but as I moved to the machinery spaces the temperature increased sharply. Some of the fans were still operating, but they were just blowing warm air around. The main engines and supporting machinery was still cooling down and giving off an awful lot of heat, which could not be dissipated, and with the boat being on the surface the warm May Sun was shining on to the casing adding to the overall heat load. It was quite uncomfortable, and the guys sitting in the Manoeuvring Room and out in the machinery spaces looked tired, hot and irritated.

Entering the Manoeuvring Room I could see that things had moved on a pace while I had slept. Most of the control panels were now dark and silent since the majority of the machinery had been shut down. I could see that the main lubricating oil pumps were just about the only things still running in the Engine Room, being used to cool the engines down slowly and uniformly. The steam ranges were already well de-pressurised, and it was the draining of the steam in the pipes into the Engine and Diesel Rooms that was racking up the atmospheric temperature. The reactor was shut down, and was still slowly being de-pressurised and cooled down, although there was still some way to go for it to be fully de-pressurised, and therefore as far as I was concerned, safe. The primary make-up pumps were being run almost constantly to maintain the level in the Pressuriser as the plant cooled down and contracted, and I gave thanks that we had found and fixed the defective pump before leaving Gibraltar. We could not produce any fresh water and there was concern that we would not have enough to put into the reactor, but there was little we could do about that now. I could hear the diesels thumping away in the Diesel Room beneath my feet, and I knew that it was this constant loud banging that was causing the irritation amongst the men on watch—I had only been there for 10 minutes and already it was getting through!

The electrical panel was the focus of all attention now, and showed that the diesel generators were supplying all the electrical load of the boat via the motor-generators, and were also supplying the dc electrical supply for the emergency propulsion motor. They were just about coping with doing that without draining the main battery, which remained our ultimate power back-up. The diesels were operating at maximum load though, and were subsequently taking quite a hammering, even though the emergency propulsion motor was being operated at just enough power to keep the boat moving, and everything considered as being 'unessential' onboard had been turned off. A new programme was just being sorted out to review the remaining electrical power requirements in order that they could be reduced to the real absolute minimum. This then might allow the diesels to be offloaded a bit, which in turn would reduce the stress on them slightly. There was already a lot of resistance against further cuts in power, and it was going to take some tough action to reduce the load any further. Still, that was not my problem.

My problem was the mechanical state of the diesels and emergency propulsion motor. They had now been running for about a day, and I was anxious to see how they were coping. First I went to the Diesel Room, and nodding a greeting to the watchkeeper, proceeded to take a close look at the machines. First I took a look at the log board used by the watchkeepers, which showed the hourly readings taken since the diesels had started running the previous day. All of the data looked routine for both engines, and there was no evidence of anything amiss from that source. Next I slowly walked around each engine in turn, looking for anything out of the ordinary. Both engines looked pretty good, but already there was evidence of small oil leaks starting to sprout up in different areas of each engine as the vibrations from the solid mountings slowly worked the components loose. Little trails of oil showed the origin of the leaks, and I left instructions that I was to be kept informed as the leaks grew in severity. There were a number of seriously vibrating small bore pipes on both engines which would eventually fracture if not restrained—not usually a problem during the short time period running the diesels were normally submitted to, but with this prolonged running, a potential for serious fuel leaks.

Leaving the noise of the Diesel Room I made my way to the Engine Room to take a look at the emergency propulsion motor. The Engine Room was dark and eerie and unnaturally quiet—normally at sea there would be noise and movement, but now all was still. It was like walking into a furnace though with the air conditioning turned off and few ventilation fans running, and as I made my way to the aft end of the port main gearbox, once again I found myself sweating profusely.

The emergency propulsion motor was running at quite a high speed, which was then reduced through a chain drive directly connected to the output from the gearbox. The chain was in a cover so that I could not inspect it, but looking around the motor all seemed well enough. It was very hot of course, and I was a bit concerned that the heat would cause the grease in the motor bearings to melt, so I asked the Stokers there to rig up some flexible ventilation trunking to the motor—that should keep them cool enough.

Having checked all was well with the diesels and propulsion, I now had a chance to catch up on the process of shutting down the reactor. It was going fairly well considering that we had never done it at sea before, but I shared the real concern that we would not have enough water onboard to make up to the reactor as it cooled. It would take another 24 hours before the reactor was fully cooled down, and so the Engineers asked the Captain to stop all non-essential use of water onboard the boat. Now water could only be used for drinking and cooking. We would see what was left after the reactor was cold before deciding what else it could be used for. This was not a popular move—the sailors liked to shampoo their hair at least twice a day, so they got a bit grumpy after that.

Since I had slept the boat had turned around and was now heading back towards Gibraltar. The Admiralty had been kept informed of our situation, and were fully aware now of the seriousness of our plight. In basic terms we were effectively crippled. We could not dive and were travelling at maybe 2 or 3 knots on the surface, giving us very restricted manoeuvrability. Luckily we were in the Mediterranean in May, which meant that the weather was pretty good for us, but the sailors were very keen to keep an eye on the weather charts for the coming days. A bad storm and heavy weather would make our situation quite dire, but so far the Sun was shining and the seas slight. We were informed that the

Admiralty were despatching a frigate and a tug to assist us in returning to Gibraltar, but they were still several days away.

Life onboard was by now pretty grim. Lack of power meant that any and all forms of comfort were now out of the question. Lighting was down to a minimum throughout the boat, and it was by now very hot everywhere onboard. There was water to drink, but it too was luke-warm, but nobody, even the guys working in the sweat-box of the Engine and diesels Rooms could take a shower, or even wash. Power was seriously limited to the Galley machinery as well, so only basic food could now be served. We had soup and rolls mostly, or every kind of stew—it was a case of chuck everything in the pan and give it a stir. Those guys not on watch had a choice of catching up on lost sleep, if they could stand the sodden sleeping bag, or getting some serious novel reading done, if they could find a bright enough light source!

Over the next couple of days and nights we continued westward at this snail's pace, slowing getting used to our new environment. The reactor was by now fully shut down, and at a much lower pressure and temperature, meaning that while it continued to leak, it was at a much lower rate. We had used a great deal of water during the shut down, and still needed to conserve our very limited supplies for the days remaining to get to port, or for a bit of help to arrive. We back-afties had now arranged ourselves into a new shift system using less people, which had released me to have a free rein to keep a close eye on the diesels and the emergency propulsion motor, all of which were holding up surprisingly well. The boat itself was starting to get a bit rank with the lack of availability of water, but because the sea was so calm the Captain had allowed those who wished to, to have a seawater 'bucket shower' on the casing, just to freshen up a bit.

At about this time we had a visit from a couple of Spanish frigates. They were passing by I suppose, and thought they would investigate why a British nuclear submarine was on the surface barely moving along. In any case they hailed us and asked if we had a problem, to which of course we replied that no, we were fine thank you. Apparently they didn't believe us, and decided to see if the submarine could manoeuvre properly by playing 'chicken' with us—steering directly for the conning tower, speeding up and then veering away at the last moment! Of course we couldn't manoeuvre out of their way and had to sit there watching the frigates steaming full speed at us until the Captain got on the radio, and in no uncertain terms told the Spaniards to go play somewhere else. They somewhat reluctantly withdrew, clearly suspecting that something was amiss with us—we wondered what report they sent to their own Admiralty about us.

That same day we had the first of two fires onboard, started as a result of the continuous diesel running. The exhaust pipe for the diesels passed out of the pressure hull above the Manoeuvring Room, and then passed along the casing, up through the conning tower and then out at the top of the fin, through a telescopic diesel exhaust mast. Inside the fin the pipe was coated in some kind of lagging material which was normally quite damp due to the boat usually being underwater, or just surfaced before running the diesels. Since we had now been surfaced for several days the lagging had completely dried out, and now the heat from the diesel exhaust was causing it to smoulder quite badly. As a result the fin was filling with smoke, and a fire-fighting team needed to enter the fin (quite a feat in itself) and spray water onto the lagging. We would now need to repeat the process every few hours until we reached Gibraltar, but now that we knew about it, just one bloke with a hose could do the job.

My Bloody Efforts

The second fire occurred in the Diesel Generator Room itself, and was started by an injector fuel line cracking due to the continuous and heavy vibration of the engine. As the fuel line fractured, a spray of diesel fuel must have flashed off on any one of the hot parts of the engine, and a flash fire resulted. Luckily the man on watch in the Diesel Room kept his wits about him and immediately pulled the emergency shut down lever for the engine, which as well as stopping the engine, cut the fuel supply to the leaking fuel pipe. He then calmly picked up a foam fire extinguisher and sprayed the little bit of fuel that was still burning on top of the engine. By the time the 'hands to emergency stations' broadcast had been made and the first aid fire-fighting team, including me as Attack Party Leader arrived, the fire was extinguished and all that remained was a bit of smoke and blackened paint. The boy done good!

The emergency shut down of the diesel engine with the fuel leak had caused a chain reaction though, that took a bit of time to sort out. The shut down had been so quick that the Electrical Panel Operator did not have time to take the electrical load off the machine, and so the other diesel suddenly found itself trying to generate enough power to supply the entire electrical load of the submarine. Of course it was not able to do that, and the protection devices fitted to the circuit breakers became overloaded and simply offloaded the second diesel engine as well, putting the entire load in turn on to the main battery. The boat was instantly reduced to emergency lighting only and the emergency propulsion motor tripped off, stopping the submarine in the water. As the load fell off the second diesel engine, it then speeded up dramatically and was in turn tripped off by its own over speed protection device. The submarine was now dark and still, dead in the water and totally silent, lit by eerie emergency lighting. It was literally the darkest point in the entire affair, and we wondered if things could get any worse for us!

The undamaged diesel was quickly re-started and brought on line to at least give the boat a little bit of headway without totally draining the main battery. Before the trip we had berated the diesels Petty Officer for carrying so many spares for the things, and were constantly moaning at him for taking up all of the nooks and crannies onboard with bits of diesel engine. Now though, his forethought was celebrated as he quickly dug out and fitted a new set of diesel injector fuel pipes. A couple of hours later the second diesel was brought back into service and loaded up. We were now back to what had become the 'normal' configuration, and were glad to be so. It was remarkable that the machines had run this long already with very few problems, and although the oil leaks seemed to be getting worse there had been no major mechanical failure with either the diesels or the emergency propulsion motor.

The next day the frigate that had been dispatched from Gibraltar to meet us hove into view on the horizon. She was a Type 22 that had had steamed hard to reach us (although 'steamed' is the wrong word as she was powered by gas turbines!), and was a fine sight ploughing through the water towards us at high speed, ensigns flying from her masts. I happened to be up in the fin when she arrived, and was impressed by her neat turn to put her alongside, as few hundred feet away. A lot of her ship's company were on deck to take a look at us, and a good few gave us a friendly wave as she passed slowly by. It lifted all of our spirits to see her and to know that whatever happened from now on, we were not alone.

Soon there was a barrage of questions from our new escort, mostly along the lines of 'is everybody ok?' We were able to reassure them that all was pretty much fine onboard, with the exception of the discomfort of high ambient temperatures, cold food, few lights and even fewer forms of entertainment. The frigate offered at first to take us in tow to get us moving a bit faster, and when that was turned down, to take some of the crew from the boat onboard and to pass over some hot food and things, which we of course flatly refused. There was simply no way that we would take any assistance from skimmers, and so their kind offers were politely declined. We would have to be just about on the bottom to accept any help—imagine the bragging rights if we had taken anything! A few of the lads looked longingly after the frigate as she moved off to a safe distance, and she spent the next 4 days off our port quarter, her crew sunbathing and doing their fitness routines on the flight deck.

The next day a great big tug came into view. She too had been sent out from Gibraltar by the Admiralty, and was enormous. She too offered to take us in tow, but once again the Captain was having none of it while we could propel ourselves. It was silly really, as we would have got back to Gibraltar much quicker, but on the other hand I could understand his reluctance to give over control of the boat to some stranger. We had been through a lot by now, and wanted to finish the job ourselves. Also, it would not be too good from a PR point of view if the boat had to be towed into Gibraltar, so we continued to plod on ourselves, the tug taking up position on our starboard quarter, opposite our security guard.

The final three days at sea before reaching Gibraltar went by without much incident. The machinery remarkably continued working without any further drama, even though the diesels were by now leaking oil at quite a high rate. We had by now also gotten used to the conditions onboard and were pretty much spending our time planning for the arrival in Gibraltar and subsequent actions. We all agreed that a nice cold pint was very high on the agenda, but unfortunately that would in all probability have to wait until we could make sure the reactor was totally safe. We would be alongside on shore power at the very least, and so the air conditioning could come back on—that in itself would be a huge relief.

Chapter 25

Phew, That was Close!

Our arrival in Gibraltar was made to look as normal as possible, but in reality was simply a 'cold move'. In the Straits of Gibraltar we were met by two smaller tugs, which without any fanfare tied themselves to the boat and in effect became our engines and rudder. So as not to cause a stir, the frigate and ocean-going tug peeled away and made their own way into harbour before us, and then we were unceremoniously dragged in, and tied up at the further most berth on the South Mole. As soon as our lines were attached to the shore, the two small tugs disappeared, and all of a sudden we were safe alongside, connecting up shore electrical cables. The only difference from a normal coming alongside was an armed police presence on the jetty, and quite a large welcoming party of naval brass.

The electrical shore supply was connected in double-quick time, and without further ado the air conditioning plants were started. With the full lighting and cooler air the boat seemed to come alive once more, and with a stable electrical supply onboard we could at last stop the diesel generators. They had been running almost continuously for over 6 days by now, and the silence with them stopped was initially oppressive and strange. Remarkably we still had a lot of diesel fuel left over—enough certainly for several more days running, and we wondered if, by carrying so much diesel fuel onboard, the original design had been for this type of running of the engines in an emergency.

The top brass came onboard and disappeared into the Wardroom for what we were sure was going to be a pretty intense meeting with the Captain and senior officers, who would no doubt have to justify their actions. We at technician level though just wanted to get back in the Reactor Compartment, with the aim of getting a closer look at the leaking pipe, and perhaps even stopping the leakage at the now reduced pressure and temperature of the primary loop. We would also need to pump out the bilge down there, which would require some sort of primary effluent discharge tank—by now there must be quite a bit of water there. The fact was that the primary circuit at this very moment was still leaking. That meant that there would continue to be a potential airborne radiation hazard in the Reactor Compartment, and we would require pumping water into the reactor core all the time, which in turn meant that there would also be radio-active water being drained into the bilge. That water would have to be disposed off as nuclear waste, albeit low level waste, but none the less a problem. If we could get down there and stop the leak, then all of those problems could be controlled until it was decided what kind and degree of repair was necessary.

All that could wait though for a day, and soon after hitting the wall most of us were packed off to a nice hotel for the night. I was lucky enough to get my own room, and after phoning home to the intense surprise of my wife, I had a bath and went straight to bed. I told my wife that the expected trip to Hawaii and the like was now almost certainly not going to happen, but couldn't really explain the reason why. I suggested it might be a good idea for her to cancel her flights—I knew that the problem onboard was not going to have a good ending. Of course she was very disappointed, but at that time was more interested in ensuring that I was not hurt in any way. I managed to reassure her that I was fine, and promised that we would have an alternative holiday in the summer. At that time I had no idea when I would next be home, but at least we could talk on the phone.

The next day onboard we had a meeting in the Wardroom to decide on where we would go from here. We were informed that a team of Rolls Royce specialists would be coming out to Gibraltar the next day to assess the defect, and that we needed to prepare for their arrival by clearing the leak site of lagging and cladding. This would entail another Reactor Compartment entry in protective gear and breathing apparatus, but at least this time the temperature would be much more bearable. The Doc would come down there with us too, and if the atmosphere down there was within radiation limits, we would be able to dispense with the heavy protection gear.

Dressing in the gear once more brought back memories from the first entry a few short days back. This was a much more comfortable exercise though, and once the Reactor Compartment plug door was opened it was a straight run down to the lower level and around to the starboard side of the reactor, almost directly under the starboard steam generator. At the new lower pressure in the reactor, the water was still leaking form the defect site, but now at a trickle rather than the previous cascade. There was quite a bit of damage around the leak site caused by the blast of water across the lagging, but that was pretty much expected. The Doc placed his instruments around the compartment, but indicated we should keep our breathing gear on until he had definitive measurements for airborne contamination.

I and one of the Primary Section Chiefs started to cut away the lagging surrounding the surge line. The lagging was of a sectional type, with shaped blocks forming the sections around the different parts of the pipe work. The blocks were held on with large metal bands which had to be snipped off in turn, allowing each section of lagging to be removed. All of the lagging was soaked with primary water, and we were careful not to get too wet. Eventually we exposed the tee piece pipe work where the leak was clearly visible, and for the first time got a clear look at the crack in the pipe. It was about an inch long, and followed the circumferential weld which connected two pipes together. There was definitely potential for the crack to propagate further around the weld, and we could consider ourselves pretty lucky that it had not. If that pipe had sheared totally in service we would all have been dead, and the 'Tireless' incident would have been World news for many years to come—a kind of seaborne Chernobyl probably!

The crack was located in the junction between two quite large diameter pipes, and it was clearly going to be difficult to seal the leak with any of the makeshift equipment we carried onboard. All we had really was banding that maybe we could transform into some kind of leak stopping system, but on first viewing I could see nothing that we could secure it to, to prevent the band simply slipping down the pipe and once again exposing the leak site. The location was also awkward to get to, and involved anybody working there dangling almost upside down in order to reach the area at full arms' reach. It was very tiring work, and even after simply removing the lagging my spindly arms ached severely. We made our way out of the compartment once more, but at least this time there was no major decontamination required. The radiation levels had dropped significantly, and also we would continue to wear breathing gear until the leak had been stopped, we could now do away with the heavy plastic 'boil-in-the-bag' suits.

The next day I was invited along with the other Charge Chiefs to a meeting with the Rolls Royce team that had just arrived from the UK. They had seen the video produced at sea and the photos we had taken the previous day of the crack itself, and were dead keen to get cracking on finding a way to stop the leak. It all started pretty well, with ideas coming thick and fast from several team members on how the leak should be approached. As each one was presented I was asked if they might work, since I had been down there and seen the actual physical geometry of the crack. Many of the ideas would not work because the team couldn't fix in their minds the layout and difficulty of access to the crack, and I had to keep explaining the problems with each suggested fix. The Rolls Royce guys became more and more frustrated as I and the others pooh-poohed each suggested remedy, and as time passed the ideas became more outlandish and complicated until finally, they threw their toys out of the pram, upped sticks and cleared off to their hotel, telling us that they would be back with a leak stopping device at some undetermined later date.

To my mind they had simply over complicated the temporary fix needed to stop the primary water from falling out of the reactor. To me all that was needed was some kind of clamp that would force a pad of some kind against the crack, thereby sealing the leak until a more robust system could be brought into play by the engineering wizards. I was a qualified engineering technician, and so I set about creating a new design of clamp which I would put in place myself. How difficult could it be for goodness sake?

All that afternoon I beavered away on the after Escape Platform trying to create some piece of equipment I could use, cutting, filing and machining various bits of metal, trying to formulate a design as I went along. My thoughts were that I needed a kind of device that I could fit in between the 2 pipes forming the vee, and then expand it somehow so that it would jam in the space between the pipes, forcing one padded end against the leaking crack and sealing it off. It sounded nice and easy in theory, but each time I tried to expand the device using a 'jackscrew' type of affair the material of the clamp simply crumpled and bent out of shape under the force. In the end I gave up.

The next day, after a sleepless night worrying about the leak, I started afresh. I had noticed the previous day a barbecue stored in the after ends of the boat, which I had asked one of the Stokers to manufacture before all the drama started, in preparation for the happier days to come. The legs of the beast had been manufactured from quite heavy gauge angle iron, and were exactly the kind of material I needed for the leak-stopper I envisaged. I set about chopping bits off the legs, much to the disgust of the Stoker who had made it! With the strong angle iron I was able to create a new stronger clamp, fixed by a bolt at one end and with a jackscrew at the other which could be used to expand that end once the whole thing was between the 2 pipes in question—somewhat like the kind of car jack that fits against the side of a car and is then wound open to raise the car. With the basic structure set I needed to think of some way of ensuring the padded end which would sit against the crack was a snug fit. For this I added a bended end to that side of the clamp, using a piece of pipe the same diameter as the leaking one in the Reactor Compartment on which to create the same shape. Then to the inside of the bended end piece I glued a thick piece of rubber mat which would form the seal on the crack—I hoped.

Well, the proof of the pudding was in the eating, and I now had to take the device down to the leak and fit it. Before doing that I showed it to the Boss and to some of the Rolls Royce guys, who had a good laugh at the rather agricultural construction of the part. They wished me half-hearted good luck in trying to fit it, which of course made me even more determined to succeed!

Reaching the leaking pipe down in the Reactor Compartment, dressed once again in the now familiar breathing equipment and plastic gloves, I had a momentary loss in confidence as I was reminded of the inaccessibility of the leak point and surrounding area. The part I had manufactured looked rough and basic surrounded by the shiny stainless steel and sterility of the Reactor Compartment, and for a moment I felt ridiculous lying there trying to fix a nuclear reactor with a few bits of angle iron and some nuts and bolts! The laughing faces of the Rolls Royce Technicians spurred me on though—there was no way now that I could walk out of the compartment with the reactor still leaking!

The access to the leak was extremely limited. I had to do all of the work at the extreme of my reach, and often one handed as I clung on to the pipes below to prevent myself tumbling to the bilge below. The leak stopping device was extremely fiddly too, and needed two hands to operate properly—I would set it up in between the 2 pipes forming the vee near the leak, only to find that as I attempted to screw out the clamp I would dislodge the entire device from the pipe, thereby having to reset the whole thing again. After a few hours repeating the process over and aver again, and with my arm muscles burning with fatigue, I decided it was time for a fag break and a cup of tea.

The Doc didn't want me to take the leak stopper out to the Reactor Compartment now that it had been in contact with the leaking primary water, but in this instance I overruled him. I needed to make a few modifications to the design, and this far in there was no single way that I was going to stop. Before leaving the Reactor Compartment I had carefully measured the gap between the pipes so that I could set the clamp just slightly smaller to prevent me having to wind it a long way, and hence dislodge it each time I tried to open it. In addition I added a second end piece to the other side of the clamp which I hoped would stop it from sliding around the pipe each time I applied pressure to the jackscrew, as had been the case up until now.

The Doc tried to advise me that I should wait until the next day to fit the thing again, but stubbornly I wanted to get it done the same day. I should have listened. As it was I returned once more to the Reactor Compartment and spent the next 4 hours trying unsuccessfully to attach the clamp to the leak site. My arms shook and wobbled with tiredness as I tried time again to get the thing to sit on the pipe properly, and then to screw open accurately against the crack in the pipe. Each time though, the entire clamp would walk back along the pipe and off the crack, requiring the entire process to be repeated. Eventually, exhausted and dejected, I gave up once more and called it a day.

Once more I was unable to sleep, my mind going over the plan and trying to work out a different form of attack. Finally, at 'stupid o'clock' I had a eureka moment—I needed to hold the device in place before I started to wind the clamp, and I could do that by using some of the steel bands we had previously removed from the lagging pads! Obvious really, but in my stubbornness I had not been thinking clearly. I would try it in the morning.

The next day started again, this time using a couple of steel bands to attach the bottom of the clamp to the pipe before trying to wind the jackscrew. This time it all worked a treat, and at last the clamp remained solidly in place as I wound up the top half of the clamp against the leaking crack. The rubberised end piece located nicely against the crack, and almost instantly there was a reduction in the leak rate. As I wound the jackscrew more and more tightly, the leak reduced to a trickle, and then finally stopped completely. I was overjoyed with my own success, while wearily keeping an eye on the site of the leak, not quite believing the clamp had really done the trick.

I wasted no time in reporting that the leak had been stopped using a bit of old barbecue frame and a few nuts and bolts, to the initial disbelief of the Engineer and particularly the Rolls Royce guys. The Engineer decided that we should leave the clamp for 24 hours 'just to be sure' before officially declaring the leak stopped to the Admiralty. In the meantime the Rolls Royce guys would continue to brainstorm a 'more robust' leak stopper in case my device failed in operation. They seemed pretty sure it would.

For the next 24 hours I tried to get on with something useful, but couldn't help the occasional visit to the Reactor Compartment to check on the temporary repair. It remained completely tight though, and not another drop of primary water was to pass it from that day until it was finally removed with the defective piece of pipe some 5 months later.

The next day there were congratulations all around as it was formally announced that the leak had been stopped—not by Rolls Royce but by the Ship's Company. Rolls Royce was gracious about it in the end and finally congratulated me on the innovative creation of the leak stopper. The also accepted that the device would be sufficient for them to work around. There was now no danger of airborne radiation activity in the Reactor Compartment so that everybody could dispense with the heavy and uncomfortable breathing gear and plastic suits for working down there. It was a great relief to everybody.

With the reactor finally made safe attention turned towards longer term plans. For the Ship's Company the situation was a strange one. Normally in harbour the crew would be put in hotels, but clearly that was only usually for relatively short periods. In our case, after a couple of weeks in hotels and just coming into work each day we were informed that a Royal Fleet Auxiliary ship would be coming out to Gibraltar in the coming week, which would become our home until it was decided what was going to happen to the boat. We were not best pleased, but it wasn't as if we had any choice in the matter. Better news was that all of the ship's company would get home for a bit of leave in rotation, which in my case happened after being in Gibraltar for about 6 weeks. It was only a week at home but very worth it.

On returning to Gibraltar we found out the plan for the future of HMS Tireless—she would be repaired by Rolls Royce in Gibraltar! That seemed incredible to us, but plans were well in hand by then, and so again it was a case of us having to just get on with it. We would be playing quite a supporting role for the repair, and for me there was a great deal of preparation in terms of the set up of systems and equipment for the repair.

By the time I left the boat in January of 2001 the repair was well in hand, and was at the stage where a huge piece of primary pipe work had been cut out of the primary circuit, and a new one (minus crack) welded back in its place, all while the submarine remained tied up to the South Mole wall. Remarkable really. After a short leave spell in the UK I joined HMS Defiance in Plymouth as the Deputy Quality Manager, and didn't see the Tireless again until about a year later, by which time she was fully operational again.

Postscript

After I left the boat the primary repair continued until about February of 2001, and was then followed by a comprehensive programme of testing, first of the primary circuit and supporting systems and then the entire machinery of the boat, after which there was another full programme of sea-trials and Work-Up for the crew, by then consisting of about 50% of the guys who had sailed the boat into Gibraltar nearly a year previously. Gibraltar finally got rid of the boat around April when she returned to fleet service, embarking on a long series of patrols. The Gibraltarians were apparently not sorry to see her leave.

In the summer of 2001 I was undertaking a whole series of non-destructive testing courses in the North of England as part of the preparation for my new quality post. I was walking to one such course from the hotel one day when my mobile phone started ringing. It was my wife, and the conversation went something like:

"Steve, we received a strange letter this morning".

"What was strange about it?"

"Well, it's from somewhere called the Chancellery of Buckingham Palace."

"What?"

"Yes, and it says quote, 'The Queen has graciously awarded your membership to the British Empire' What does that mean?"

Silence

"Steve, did you hear me?"

"Yes, I heard you. I think it means I am getting a medal off the Queen!"

Silence

"Bloody hell! You better go out and buy a nice new outfit—we're going to Buckingham Palace!"

"OK bye then. I'll phone you later"

And that was how I found out I had been awarded the MBE.

Myself, my wife Anna, and my brothers Andrew and John (who had flown over especially from the United States) went to the Palace on 15th October 2001, where I was presented the medal by Prince Charles. It was a great day out, and one I shall remember for the rest of my days.

John, Me, Anna and Andy at Buckingham Palace October 2001

That year I was not promoted to Warrant Officer Marine Engineering Artificer, and so decided to call the end to my naval career. I left the Royal navy in July of 2002, and almost immediately immigrated with my Maltese wife to the island of Malta, where I now work in the aircraft industry, still in the area of quality assurance.

About the Author

In May 2000 the British nuclear 'hunter-killer' submarine HMS Tireless limped into Gibraltar harbor using emergency propulsion and with her nuclear reactor shut down. Several days earlier, while traversing the Straits of Sicily the crew had discovered a crack in one of the nuclear reactor pipes, requiring them to shut down and de-pressurise the reactor in order to prevent a potential reactor accident, an operation never before conducted on a British submarine at sea.

The previous six days had been a desperate time for the crew of the submarine. Initial indications of a problem with the nuclear reactor had very quickly escalated into a full scale potential nuclear reactor accident at sea, requiring immediate and decisive action by the crew to make the reactor safe, to identify the defect and attempt to repair the reactor, and then to surface the submarine and to sail her safely back to the nearest safe harbor using emergency propulsion machinery designed for very limited use. The lack of power onboard had resulted in the crew having to sacrifice lighting, air-conditioning, bathing facilities and even hot food until their return to harbor, and to suffer in the excessively hot interior of the boat. Throughout, there remained the fear of exposure to deadly radiation and the uncertainty that the reactor might still be one step away from a major accident.

For one man onboard in particular, the strains of the last few days had formed something of a natural culmination of a 25 year naval engineering career which seemed almost fated for this moment. Charge Chief Stephen Bridgman, the senior nuclear propulsion technician onboard, had needed all of his engineering knowledge and experience gained in a long and varied career in the identification and eventual repair of the leaking reactor.

It had indeed been a remarkable career, starting as a 16 year old Stoker on the final 'proper' British aircraft carrier HMS Ark Royal in 1977, through the Falklands War, being selected for Technician training and submarine service, submarine training, submarine patrols in the supposed 'post cold-war' period, the Kosovo conflict from beneath the water, progression through the ranks, submarine refitting and refueling and through to the nuclear reactor accident onboard HMS Tireless. Lack of educational qualifications would ensure that promotion would be a slow and painful process, and it took marriage at age 21 for Stephen to eventually realize that it was time to grow up and take control of his future. Finally knuckling down and achieving some educational qualifications in 1981, he caught the studying bug and through hard work managed to get selected for training as a Naval Engineering technician, a three year apprenticeship leading to promotion to Petty Officer. Selection for submarine service followed, and Stephen rose to the challenge of working in the confined and tense environment onboard Britain's nuclear submarine fleet, rising to the rank of Chief Petty Officer within two years. Gaining valuable seagoing experience during long and challenging patrols, he was selected to become a Senior Technician with responsibility for the nuclear propulsion machinery in 1994, and was forced in remarkably trying circumstances to display all of that knowledge and experience in responding to a very near nuclear reactor accident onboard HMS Tireless in 2000, actions for which in 2001 he was awarded Membership of the British Empire (MBE) by Her Majesty Queen Elizabeth II.

During this stressful military career, the tense moments were often balanced by a home life far removed from the close-knit submarine environment, and strangely ordinary. Stephen was married to his wife of 30 years Anna at the age of 21, and together, they build a family life around the frequent requirements to move between naval bases in the UK.

Stephen and Anna moved lock, stock and barrel to the beautiful island of Malta at the culmination of naval service in 2001.

Printed in Great Britain
by Amazon